Destination Europe

or return

MANCHESTER
UNIVERSITY PRESS

To my sons Vilhelm and Edvard,
that they may live in a Europe and a
world of peace, liberty and tolerance

Destination Europe

The political and economic
growth of a continent

Kjell M. Torbiörn

Manchester University Press

Manchester and New York

distributed exclusively in the USA by Palgrave

Published by Manchester University Press
Oxford Road, Manchester M13 9NR, UK
and Room 400, 175 Fifth Avenue, New York, NY 10010, USA
www.manchesteruniversitypress.co.uk

Distributed exclusively in the USA by
Palgrave, 175 Fifth Avenue, New York,
NY 10010, USA

Distributed exclusively in Canada by
UBC Press, University of British Columbia, 2029 West Mall,
Vancouver, BC, Canada V6T 1Z2

British Library Cataloguing-in-Publication Data
A catalogue record for this book is available from the British Library

Library of Congress Cataloging-in-Publication Data applied for

ISBN 0 7190 6572 0 *hardback*
    0 7190 6573 9 *paperback*

First published 2003

11 10 09 08 07 06 05 04 03   10 9 8 7 6 5 4 3 2 1

Typeset in Sabon with Univers
by Koinonia, Manchester
Printed in Great Britain
by CPI, Bath

Contents

For the mystery of human life is not only in living, but in knowing why one lives. Without a clear idea of what to live for man will not consent to live and will rather destroy himself than remain on the earth, though he were surrounded by loaves of bread. (Fyodor Dostoyevski, *The Brothers Karamazov*, Book Five, 'The Great Inquisitor', 1879)

Foreword

In this book I attempt to describe, interpret and interrelate the major political and economic developments in Europe since the end of World War II to the present, and to look ahead to see how the continent may evolve in the future. 'Europe' is understood to be not only the European Union but the whole of the continent, from Iceland and Ireland in the west to Russia in the east, from Norway in the north to Turkey in the south. 'Developments' sometimes are dealt with so broadly as to touch on the *'Zeitgeist'* of the different periods covered, and which future generations will no doubt understand better than we do.

It is my hope that this book will fill what I perceive as a definite lacuna in the current literature on Europe, and that it will give the reader – whether a student of modern Europe or one interested in European affairs in general – a deeper understanding of the continent and its current challenges, as well as a more solid foundation to assess the factors likely to affect its future.

There is no more important task than to ensure that peace, democracy, respect for human rights and the rule of law survive and flourish in a part of the world that has known so much of their opposites, nearly destroying itself and the rest of humanity in the process. These values must be defended anew by each generation, and this can only occur through an understanding of both past and present. If this book can contribute toward this goal, my work will not have been in vain.

An explanation is owed about the title, *Destination Europe*. It alludes to Andrew Shonfield's classic *Europe: Journey to an Unknown Destination*, published in 1973. A fair distance has been covered since, but it would be presumptuous to claim that the destination has come any nearer. History, as is known, has a penchant for never ending, and that of Europe is no exception.

Acknowledgements

I am deeply grateful to several friends for their constructive comments on various drafts of this book. Martin Westlake, a renowned writer on political and especially European Union affairs, encouraged me from the start and suggested vital improvements to the book's structure and central chapters. Geza Mezei, a Council of Europe colleague and Hungarian scholar specialising in European post-World War II history, offered invaluable advice on the chapters dealing with this period. James Bridge, a political affairs adviser; and David Adamson, an academic and formerly of the US State Department, shared with me their unique knowledge in their various fields of expertise. Ambassador Janos Perényi, also of Hungary and a scholar on central and east European affairs; Stanley Hunt MBE; and Peter Sich, a Council of Europe colleague and an expert on the Caucasus region, also gave valuable advice.

Marie-José Schutz of the Council of Europe Library was of invaluable assistance in tracking down various literary sources throughout my work, and I thank her warmly for her support and enthusiasm, as well as her colleagues. Sylvie Baudoin of the Council's Vedovato Library also helped me greatly in drawing upon that library's growing body of literature on Europe. Hazel Bastier and Marianne Haddock were always available to type the manuscript in their precious free time. The staff of Manchester University Press believed in the project from the start and supported me throughout.

This book could not have been written without the experience I have gained of European affairs during my many years in the Council of Europe – an organisation whose goals and ideals never cease to inspire me. In this context I wish to thank its former Secretary General, Daniel Tarschys, for the encouragement he gave me in embarking on the project when I showed him a first outline in 1999. All the views expressed in this book are, however, my own and should in no way be attributed to any particular organisation or the people mentioned above.

Abbreviations

ABM	Anti-Ballistic Missile
ACP	African, Caribbean and Pacific
BMD	Ballistic Missile Defence
CAP	Common Agricultural Policy
CCT	Common Customs Tariff
CET	Common External Tariff
CFE	Conventional Forces in Europe
CFSP	Common Foreign and Security Policy
COR	Committee of the Regions
COREPER	Committee of Permanent Representatives
CSCE	Conference on Security and Co-operation in Europe
EAPC	Euro-Atlantic Partnership Council
EC	European Community
ECB	European Central Bank
ECSC	European Coal and Steel Community
ECU	European Currency Unit
EDC	European Defence Community
EEA	European Economic Area
EEC	European Economic Community
EFTA	European Free Trade Association
EMU	Economic and Monetary Union
EPC	European Political Community
ERM	Exchange Rate Mechanism
ESCB	European System of Central Banks
ESDP	European Security and Defence Policy
EU	European Union
FPÖ	Freiheitliche Partei Österreichs
GATT	General Agreement on Tariffs and Trade
ICC	International Criminal Court
IGC	Intergovernmental Conference
ITO	International Trade Organisation
LMU	Latin Monetary Union
MAD	Mutual Assured Destruction

MAP	Membership Action Plan
MBFR	Mutual and Balanced Force Reduction
MCA	Monetary Compensation Amount
NATO	North Atlantic Treaty Organisation
NRF	NATO Reponse Force
OECD	Organisation for Economic Co-operation and Development
OEEC	Organisation for European Economic Co-operation
OPEC	Organisation of Petroleum Exporting Countries
OSCE	Organisation for Security and Co-operation in Europe
ÖVP	Österreichische VolksPartei
PfP	Partnership for Peace
SALT	Strategic Arms Limitation Treaty (or Talks)
SEA	Single European Act
SPÖ	Sozialdemokratische Partei Österreichs
START	Strategic Arms Reduction Treaty (or Talks)
UN	United Nations
WEU	Western European Union
WMD	weapons of mass destruction
WTO	World Trade Organisation

1

1945: Europe's 'zero hour'

History teaches us that men and nations behave wisely once they have exhausted all other alternatives. (Abba Eban, Israeli diplomat)[1]

Summary

At the end of World War II, Germany – formerly the dominant power in continental Europe – found itself under the occupation of the victorious powers: the United States, the Soviet Union, the United Kingdom and France.

Although tensions would soon arise between the two emerging super-powers – the United States and the Soviet Union – and lead to the division of Europe into two hostile blocs, the new situation also offered a unique opportunity for reconciliation and budding co-operation especially between Germany and France, whose rivalry had underlain both world wars.

The Marshall Plan launched by the United States in 1948 kick-started economic recovery and co-operation in Western Europe, permitting democracy and a market economy to take hold. In Central and Eastern Europe, however, the Soviet political grip hardened and communist regimes posing as 'people's democracies' were installed, emphasising state owner-ship of the means of production and central planning of the economy.

Europe's two halves grew increasingly apart and a 'Cold War' ensued. The establishment of NATO under US leadership in 1949 confirmed this division and extended it to the security field.

A new departure

The fact that serious European co-operation, even integration, started shortly after World War II was not self-evident or an automatic result of what had preceded. If things had gone slightly differently, it might not have taken place at all.

On the other hand, it could hardly have happened before. European powers largely dominated the world in the eras of colonialism and, later, imperialism and competed fiercely with one another in what they saw as a 'zero-sum game' in the world at large and within Europe itself. Enemy images, and national histories, had been formed in centuries of warfare. Wealth was so scarce that the thought of sharing it with a rival, or trying to increase it through open trade, was virtually impossible.

Not that these struggles diminished the resourcefulness of European powers or, seen from the outside, of Europe as a whole. The historian Paul Kennedy in his classic *The Rise and Fall of the Great Powers*[2] makes the case that Europe rose to world domination precisely through its divisions. No power was able to dominate any other – in part also due to Europe's inhibiting geography with criss-crossing rivers and mountains – and so each had to work hard on improving its machinery and strategies for diplomacy and war. The result was an outburst of European energy towards the rest of the world, that is to say, that energy which was not expended in such continent-wide catastrophes as the Thirty Years' War of 1618–48. This outburst led to the domination of much of the rest of the world through competition among the European powers.

Wars were, on the whole, considered as somewhat of a game, for autocratic rulers to engage in more or less at will – *Dieu et mon droit*. There was no aerial bombing, or nuclear weapons promising mutually assured destruction. Only with the arrival of the sub-machine gun – the great killer in World War I – the aeroplane, the big guns capable of distant shelling, such as that of Paris by German guns in 1870, gas warfare and the like, did rulers (and populations) begin to realise that wars were not just a few battles to be fought glamorously on horseback or in infantry attacks, with sons and fiancés back in glory afterwards. Wars had become something far more terrible and all-encompassing than in the past, costly in terms of lives lost and destroyed, affecting the future of generations and whole countries.

The Thirty Years' War, causing the devastation of wide swaths of central Europe, had given rise to serious reflection and a certain prudence against upsetting the European balance of power. The Napoleonic Wars had a similar, though even more profound effect, and led to over fifty years of relative peace in Europe following the 1815 Congress of Vienna (if the Crimean War is excluded, which did not put overall European peace in jeopardy).

However, the tensions, alliances and counter-alliances were still there, and Germany's creation under Prussian domination in the 1860s (in part a reaction to the Napoleonic Wars) did not help matters, for the

newcomer filled the Northern European power vacuum on the
but threatened the established powers on the other – as demo
France in its defeat against Prussia in the 1870–71 war. 1
Kingdom was still the dominant European and world power, with an
impressive war fleet and an empire upon which 'the sun never set'.
However, Germany had begun to threaten that power, and soon German
aspirations in Europe and beyond were fundamentally to upset the
power balance until then so delicately upheld among the major European powers. A series of blunders and character faults among leaders
and rulers – paramount among them the foolhardy bellicosity of the
German Kaiser Wilhelm II – was all that was needed to provoke war in
1914. It was a European, and worldwide, conflict that was effectively to
last for thirty years, albeit with a hiatus from 1919 to 1939.

The inter-war period, with its heavy war reparations exacted especially on Germany, was characterised by a retreat from the much more
benign climate for trade, investment abroad and freedom of travel that
had characterised a pre-World War I era of 'Victorian capitalism' and
stable currencies based on gold. This pre-war period had been dominated
by the United Kingdom, Russia, Austria-Hungary and Germany, with
the latter as the economic centre and locomotive of continental Europe
in particular. Suspicion among the major powers was in the air and
protectionism and mercantilism won out over open trade, eventually
leading to a return to rearmament and the pre-war system of alliances
and counter-alliances.[3]

This is certainly not to belittle the importance of personalities in the
historical events of the first half of the twentieth century. However, and
this is the crucial point, true European co-operation and integration
could scarcely have begun without the completely new reality created by
the fundamental overcoming of the heritage of World War I – without,
in fact, a French–German reconciliation starting from scratch. The outcome of World War II created such a 'zero hour'.[4]

Germany lay prostrate in defeat, occupied by the four victorious
powers of the United States, the United Kingdom, France and the Soviet
Union. Europe was no longer the power centre of the world. That had
moved elsewhere, across the Atlantic, to the United States, which stood
supreme in terms of economic might, military force and political
influence. Only gradually, over the years 1945 to the early 1950s, would
this 'monopolar world' become 'bipolar' with the rise, at least in military
and nuclear terms, of the other superpower, the Soviet Union.

This evolving bipolar world was nuclear, as from 1945 through the
United States, and from 1949 through the Soviet Union (and later on

through the United Kingdom, France, the People's Republic of China and others). This meant that, with Europe as the evolving main battle-ground between the opposing economic, national, political and ideological interests of the United States and the Soviet Union, European countries would have to provide stability – as opposed to the kind of instability that had started two world wars. The only way to do that was to start to work together.

In this they were, of course, helped by the outside occupying powers – the United States in Western Europe and the Soviet Union in Central and Eastern Europe – who were themselves keen on maintaining stability in Europe, since any confrontation would rapidly risk becoming nuclear.

West Germany's[5] orientation towards the West – Western Europe in particular, but also North America – was facilitated by the fact that it was hermetically sealed off from its former neighbouring countries and markets in the East. An 'Iron Curtain' had been lowered in the heart of Europe, as Winston Churchill put it in May 1945.[6] If West Germany wanted to survive economically and politically, it would therefore have to seek reconciliation with the West and particularly with France, which, thanks to de Gaulle's skilful policies, had gained major-power status as an occupying power of Germany and a permanent seat on the newly formed United Nations' Security Council. Such reconciliation was all the more easy since demands by France for war reparations from Germany had been substantially tempered by the other Western war allies – the United States and the United Kingdom – who were determined not to repeat the mistakes of the Versailles Treaty of 1919, in which enormous (though eventually reduced and abandoned) war reparations by Germany had added to German resentment vis-à-vis France and the UK and had facilitated Hitler's rise to power.

Help from the United States

The major questions that had to be addressed immediately after the war – and which had formed the core of the negotiations between the leaders of the United States, the United Kingdom and the Soviet Union at Yalta in February 1945 – were firstly the future of Germany and secondly the dimensions of the 'sphere of influence' of guaranteed friendly countries that the Soviet Union could reasonably demand in order to protect itself against any German aggression in the future. The Soviet Union was still considered by many in the West as a country evolving toward democracy and so it was reasonable to believe that it would permit free and fair elections in the countries under discussion, such as Poland, the future of which had taken up most of the time at Yalta.[7]

The talks among the victorious powers continued in Potsdam near Berlin in the summer of 1945. At first the United States joined the Soviet Union in requesting stern punitive measures for Germany for its role in the war, a demand that would have been all the easier to realise considering that Germany now, unlike after World War I, had no government but was ruled by military governors in the several 'occupation zones' trying to work together in an Allied Control Council. The United Kingdom, however, was less keen on heavy war reparations, not least out of fear of an eventual Soviet takeover of the whole of Germany.

Work of the Allied Control Council, now joined by France under de Gaulle, soon became bogged down as France, which wanted a virtual break-up of Germany as a country as a safety measure, started vetoing all important decisions. Furthermore, Russia, insisting on major reparations, stopped supplying food to the starving populations in the western military zones as had been agreed at Potsdam, whereupon the US in April 1946 abandoned its commitment to sending war reparations from its zone to the Soviet Union. Instead it began sending food to Germany and other countries such as France. More generally, the US now joined the UK in beginning to fear Soviet intentions and was urged by its ally to maintain a military presence in Europe instead of withdrawing its troops as it had after World War I and as it had announced at Potsdam it would do this time, too.[8] Meanwhile, Germany's food situation continued to worsen, with no solution in sight.

The problems of Western Europe were so great that it is doubtful whether reconciliation between West Germany and France, and between West European countries in general, could have succeeded without the remedy eventually suggested: the Marshall Plan, announced by the US Secretary of State, George Marshall in June 1947 and enacted by Congress in April 1948 as the European Co-operation Act and, at the operational level, the European Recovery Programme.[9]

The functioning of the Marshall Plan was straightforward. The flow of dollars from the United States enabled receiving countries to import goods and machinery. Each government was to use its own currency to place the equivalent of the dollar amounts it received in a special fund. Virtually all the funds transferred into this account were placed at the disposal of the government, provided they were used for reconstruction and economic development. A small part could be used to cover administrative costs and/or technical assistance.[10] The assistance was both material – going to agriculture, basic industries, transportation and the like – and conceptual, such as in engineering and management advice. It was distributed through the Organisation for European Economic Co-operation (OEEC), in which all the recipient countries participated.[11]

Close to US$13 billion were channelled to seventeen European countries from 1948 to 1952. All European countries had been invited to participate, including the Soviet Union, but the latter had declined and pressured the Central and East European countries under its influence to do the same, no doubt out of fear of 'capitalist contagion' and of losing political control over its client states.[12] The UK, France, Italy and West Germany were the most important recipients, together accounting for some 65 per cent of the total. But also countries that had managed to avoid the war, such as Sweden and Ireland, participated.

The Marshall Plan was a major success, so much so that its name has been invoked many times since, such as when massive aid has been sought in support of developing countries or a Central and Eastern Europe country liberated from communism. One reason for the success of the Marshall Plan in post-war Europe was the enormous demand in basic and labour-intensive sectors of the economy at the time. This led to considerable 'multiplier effects' on the economy as a whole – the recon-struction of railroads, roads, entire cities. Furthermore, populations in the recipient countries were not only eager to go to work and build up a normal existence after all the war years, but also equipped with suffi-cient education and experience of the market economy to 'make the Marshall Plan stick'.

There was a huge demand for all kinds of goods. This, together with relatively low labour costs in comparison with the emerging new trading partners, the United States and Canada, raised the national product of most of the recipient countries, and in particular West Germany, to the pre-1939 level already by the early 1950s. (In West Germany the increase from 1947 to 1950 was over 300 per cent.[13])

Another factor explaining the success of the Marshall Plan was the near-total absence of competition from areas of the world outside North America. If today Western Europe fears for the maintenance of its manu-facturing in the face of competition from emerging economies that were formerly developing countries, as well as from Central and Eastern Europe (both with hard working populations and lower labour costs) then the situation in the post-war years was entirely different, even if Japan is included, which had yet to emerge as a major economic power.

The United States provided economic stability, permitting both intra-European and transatlantic trade to grow on a sound footing. The US dollar was the undisputed world reserve currency, offering a rock-steady reference value for emerging intra-European trade. The United States had also taken the initiative in creating the so called Bretton Woods Institutions of the World Bank (providing funds for long-term investment around the world, particularly in infrastructure) and the International Monetary Fund (for short-term assistance to countries in currency-exchange-rate difficulties).

Finally, the Americans insisted on more open trade: at European level through the OEEC as a condition for Marshall Plan money and at world level through the General Agreement on Tariffs and Trade (GATT), concluded in 1947. The International Trade Organisation (ITO) was to have formed – together with the Bretton Woods Institutions in the economic field and the United Nations (with its Security Council) in the political and security domain – the 'triad' for a New World Order. However, in the end the ITO was not ratified by the US Senate and so had to be turned into a simple 'agreement', the GATT, which nevertheless achieved a great deal on behalf of freer world trade until it became, in 1995, the World Trade Organisation (WTO).

A Europe divided in two

Although the division of Europe into two halves assisted West European co-operation and involved the United States (and Canada) firmly in European affairs, it also delivered large parts of Central and Eastern Europe to Soviet hegemony, hindering economic development not only in the countries concerned but in Europe as a whole. In the years that followed, the Soviet political grip hardened and communist coups d'état or takeovers multiplied in countries like Poland, Czechoslovakia, Hungary, Bulgaria and Romania, leading to intense international tension and fear of a new world war. Stalin, the Soviet leader, increasingly failed to distinguish between 'friendly' and 'puppet' governments in the Soviet sphere of influence.

Especially after the communist coup d'état in Prague in February 1948, tension rose to new heights. There was intense fear in Western Europe that the Soviet Union, working through the so-called Cominform established in September 1947, would stage similar events in other countries, notably France and Italy. Efforts to form a German state out of the British, US and French occupation zones accelerated. This led, in June 1948, to a currency reform in the three Western zones (and in the Western sectors in Berlin) and to the so-called Frankfurter Decisions, defining the political steps towards the establishment of a West German state. The Soviet blockade of the Western sectors of Berlin the same month – and the Western resolve not to abandon them – in turn hastened talks in Washington in August 1948 for what a year later would become NATO.[14]

The eastern part of the continent – after the countries there had been forced to refuse participation in the Marshall Plan – went its own way economically, cut off from the rest of the world. Diplomatic, trade and even traffic links with Western Europe were severed. A new economic system based on state ownership of the means of production was introduced by force, and economics became the 'servant' of the political aims of the ruling communist parties.

A Soviet economic reply to the Marshall Plan, the Council for Mutual Economic Assistance (more widely known as Comecon) was established in 1949, building not on material assistance but on a plan for trade where each country would specialise in certain types of products, or even part-components for given products, in a 'socialist division of labour'.[15] This system was meant to favour the Soviet Union economically, and to bind Central and Eastern Europe closer to it as a buffer against a Germany that only a few years earlier had invaded the Soviet Union, and caused the death of some 20 million of its citizens. In the end, because of the inefficiency of Soviet communism in general, and the Comecon system in particular, the latter benefited neither Central nor Eastern Europe, nor the Soviet Union itself. This is a matter, however, to which we shall return later.

A new type of human being, a communist one, was to be formed, reflecting the widespread belief at the time that humans could indeed be moulded and reformed. All behaviour was due to the environment, none to innate factors. The new human being would be unselfish and work for the common weal. Thus would society evolve toward an unparalleled state of prosperity and happiness.

The belief in communism – as harboured by the European elites who had taken over following the thorough purges of the traditional ruling classes, and even more among many intellectuals in Western Europe and, to a lesser extent in the United States – was aided by the fact that this was the golden era of industrialism and large projects. Individual creativity was considered far less important for economic development than the planning and mobilisation of capital and people joining together in the realisation of large enterprises, such as steelworks, dams or construction plants.

The acquisition by the Soviet Union of a nuclear weapons capacity, whether by its own effort or assisted by espionage in the United States, seemed to confirm the strength of the communist system in general and the Soviet Union in particular. The huge scale of Soviet and East

European projects; the belief in massive resources and in the malleability of humans; and the vastness of the Soviet Union's land mass awed the West and led many there to despair of the future of capitalism and democracy. In this, the post-war years resembled the 1930s, when the United Kingdom had stood virtually alone in Europe in defence of those principles against fascist Italy and Germany and the communist Soviet Union. The crucial difference between the two periods was of course the United States – the strength of its economy and military and its increasing commitment to Western Europe. The post-World War II era thus continued, from the inter-war period, to be one of ideological division and confrontation – no longer mainly between fascism and communism, but between communism on the one hand, and capitalism and democracy on the other.

The United States' creation of the North Atlantic Treaty Organisation (NATO) in 1949 together with eleven West European countries merely confirmed the American commitment to the old continent as manifested through the Marshall Plan. Based on the Washington agreement, NATO committed the participating countries to consider 'an attack on one of them as an attack against them all'. It supplemented agreements among in particular France and the United Kingdom (the Dunkirk Treaty of 1947), but also Belgium, Luxembourg and the Netherlands (the 1948 Brussels Treaty, eventually leading, in 1955, to the creation of the Western European Union), by giving them a transatlantic dimension, and hence greater credibility vis-à-vis a Soviet Union increasingly considered as being hostile to Western Europe, after having been a doughty ally in defeating the Axis powers.[16]

However, in what was known at the time as 'double containment', NATO had the added aim to allay the fear of the Brussels Treaty parties of a revanchist Germany, encouraging countries like France and the United Kingdom to start co-operating with that country and eventually, in 1955, allowing it to become a NATO member. (The radical importance for Europe as a whole of bringing Germany into formal co-operation with France and the United Kingdom – of in fact turning those potentially quarrelsome rivals into a trio playing the same tune – would not be apparent for some time.)

In conclusion, the end of the 1940s saw a Europe as fundamentally reshaped as in the 1840–80 period. The United States was firmly in charge of the western half, the Soviet Union of the eastern half. Even Germany, indeed Berlin itself, were equally divided up. Western Europe was well on the way to recover economically, if not emotionally, from the ravages of war. There was embryonic co-operation, and an overcoming of enmity, among Western European countries under American prodding. Central and Eastern Europe were facing a more uncertain future under complete Soviet domination and a forced economic interdependence in the East based on state communism and Soviet economic and political interests.

It was a historically unique situation, which was to prove particularly propitious to economic, and later political, co-operation and integration among a number of major European powers, prominent among them France, Germany and Italy.

Today all these circumstances have been overturned. Germany is re-united (minus the eastern part of the country, ceded to Poland after the war, and that part of the former East Prussia which is now the Kalinin-grad region of Russia). Europe is no longer divided but increasingly united within an enlarging European Union. The Soviet Union no longer exists, with a resurrected Russia and many other equally reinstalled countries succeeding it. Comecon is gone. The Warsaw Pact, the Soviet Union's riposte to NATO, has been dissolved, with NATO itself enlarging rapidly into Central and Eastern Europe and Russia being a close partner to it. One question that will occupy us in later chapters will be whether there is any risk that Europe may slide back to a geopolitical situation similar to that prevailing before the two world wars, or whether European co-operation and integration – notably through the European Union but also at a transatlantic security level through NATO – have made such a regression impossible.

Notes

1 Speech in London on 16 December 1970; as reported in *The Times* the following day.
2 Kennedy, P. (1987).
3 See e.g. Keynes (1920, Ch. 2).
4 However, Grosser (1980, pp. 3–4) does not consider 1945 as Europe's 'zero hour' or 'year zero', as he calls it, but only as a gradual transition from arms to politics. In US–Soviet relations he rather sees 'year zero' as either 1941 (when the US entered the anti-Hitler alliance) or 1949 (the establishment of NATO). Nor did 1945 mark a break, he says, in European colonial ambitions or in de Gaulle's political struggle against his American ally and for a greater role for France in Europe and the world.
5 The Federal Republic of Germany as from 1949.
6 Quoted in McCullough (1992, p. 383), in a cable by Churchill to President Truman, and (p. 489) in a speech in March 1946 at Westminster College in Fulton, Ohio.

7 The Moscow-based British diplomat Clark Kerr in a colourful cable to London expressed the optimistic sentiments at the time concerning Soviet intentions. He wrote: 'The Soviet Union is now in a state of high buoyancy and utterly confident of her strength. The manifestations of this confidence are often rough and boisterous. The Soviet Union tends to disport herself like a wet retriever puppy in somebody else's drawing room, shaking herself and swishing her tail in adolescent disregard for all except herself. We must expect her thus to rampage until she feels that she is secure from any unpleasant surprises in neighbouring countries, and then we may, I think, foresee that she will emerge from her puppydom and settle down to the serious and respectable business of collaboration with her major allies' (Ross, 1984, p. 198).

8 Instrumental in raising US suspicions of Soviet intentions was the famous 'long telegram' sent by George Kennan, the scholarly US chargé d'affaires in Moscow, to the State Department in early 1946. The Kremlin, Kennan wrote, had a neurotic view of the world, stemming from an atavistic sense of insecurity. The Soviet regime was 'committed fanatically' to the notion that no peaceful co-existence was possible with the US and that 'it is desirable and necessary that the internal harmony of our society be disrupted, our traditional way of life destroyed, the international authority of our state broken'. Marxism, Kennan continued, was just a 'fig leaf' for the ambitions of the country's leaders, who were 'only the last of a long session of cruel and wasteful Russian rulers who have relentlessly forced their country on to ever new heights of military power in order to guarantee external security for their internally weak regime' (McCullough, 1992, pp. 490–1).

9 The Marshall Plan was in fact the result of a year-long effort on the part of a group of visionary men in the US State Department, in particular Dean Acheson and Clark Clifford. President Truman declined to have it named after himself, arguing: 'Anything that is sent up the Senate and House with my name on it will quiver and die'. For a detailed account of the genesis of the Marshall Plan, see Jones (1955). The main purpose of the Marshall Plan was to assist economic development and thereby political stability in Germany, but it was also meant to do the same in especially France and Italy, where the communist parties were strong and seen as subservient to the Soviet Union.

10 For a comprehensive account of the functioning of the Marshall Plan, see e.g. Gimbel (1968).

11 As from 1960, the OEEC was transformed into the OECD (Organisation for Economic Co-operation and Development) and made, with extended membership such as Japan, into a world policy-formulating institution in the economic field.

12 This was in fact what the United States had hoped for, not least to enable the Marshall Plan to pass through Congress. Especially contemptible to Stalin were conditions such as having the Plan form part of a multilateral co-operation programme, including the German occupation zones in it; and

obliging recipient countries to account for their use of funds. Molotov called the Marshall Plan 'nothing but a vicious American scheme for using dollars to buy its way' into the affairs of Europe. After meeting in Paris with the French and British Foreign Ministers in late June 1947 to discuss the European response to the Marshall proposal, Molotov left in anger on 2 July 1947, refusing Soviet participation. This cleared the way for the Plan's realisation in accordance with US intentions. See e.g. Bohlen (1973, p. 264).

13 As given in von Csernatony (1973, pp. 159–60).

14 The government functions of the three Western occupation zones in April 1949 were transferred from the military governors of each zone to an Allied High Commission with its seat in Petersberg near Bonn. The Commission – with the American John Jay McCloy as the driving force – oversaw the creation of the Federal Republic of Germany and was dissolved, its mission accomplished, in 1955.

15 The Council for Mutual Economic Assistance (Comecon) was buried without fanfare in 1991, at the time of the dissolution of the Soviet Union. It never achieved much except trying to fix prices in trade between socialist countries on a bilateral basis, co-ordinating national economic plans and organising economic, scientific and technical co-operation. Still, as Bideleux (1996, p. 174) notes, 'by 1984 its member states purportedly accounted for one-third of the world's industrial production and, with 455 million inhabitants (385 million within European states), 10 per cent of its population'.

16 However, the Dunkirk Treaty was primarily directed against the possibility of German aggression. In its preamble it stated that it was designed to prevent the eventuality 'that Germany should again become a danger to peace'. The Brussels Treaty, by contrast, already held out the possibility of a democratic Germany (and Spain) joining it. See e. g. Ellwood(1992, p. 102).

2

Europe's 1950s:
reconstruction and reconciliation;
confrontation and oppression

If ... the European Defence Community should not become effective; if France and Germany remain apart ... That would compel an agonising reappraisal of basic United States policy. (John Foster Dulles)[1]

Summary

Reconstruction in Western Europe, completed by the early 1950s, led to unbounded optimism about future economic growth and to a strong desire for closer integration. Following the creation of the Council of Europe in 1949 among ten West European countries, six went further in 1951 by founding the European Coal and Steel Community (ECSC). After attempts to set up a European Defence Community and a European Political Community failed in 1954, negotiations between the 'Six' (belonging to the overall successful ECSC) in 1957 led to the creation of the European Economic Community (EEC).

However, West European integration projects and Central and Eastern European adaptation to Soviet communism were overshadowed (and intensified) by pronounced East–West tensions, as expressed in the 1950–53 Korean War, the formal division of Germany into two states with a divided Berlin deep in East German territory, and the Soviet Union's rise to nuclear power status together with the United States. Ideology took over from (dormant) nationalism as the prominent geo-political force, even though tensions were reduced in the mid-1950s following Stalin's death. There was an agreement on Austrian independence and neutrality in 1955, and 'de-Stalinisation' began in the Soviet Union under Khrushchev.

Neither the Hungarian uprising against Soviet rule nor the Suez crisis the same year could tempt the Soviet Union and the United States into open confrontation or the abandonment of a slowly achieved, bipolar stability, which guaranteed them both a dominant influence over events in their respective 'spheres of interest'. Major Western European countries such as West Germany, France and the United Kingdom also saw certain advantages in the situation.

Europe between the superpowers

By the early 1950s, post-war reconstruction in Western Europe was virtually complete. In the Soviet-controlled part it would take much longer due to the poor economic performance of the centrally planned economies, but also due to their being cut off from Marshall aid and deprived of their traditional trading partners on the other side of the Iron Curtain.

Regions such as the Ruhr area in West Germany, which lost much of their industrial machinery as war reparations, found themselves with a head start over the UK and France, thanks to Marshall Aid allowing them to rebuild with the latest equipment. The port of Rotterdam, for example, heavily bombed during the war, owed its new prominence as a gateway to Europe to the fact that it could expand on adjacent waste land and invest in the latest cargo-handling facilities. The Soviet Union, which exacted more war reparations on its occupation zone in Germany (as from 1949 the German Democratic Republic) and Austria than the Western victorious powers, by contrast found itself in possession of older industrial plant.

Reconciliation in Western Europe – as opposed to the sub-surface hostility and suspicion that prevailed in Central and Eastern Europe between the 'Soviet satellites' and the Soviet Union itself – was greatly helped by the success of reconstruction. Similarly, reconciliation between former enemies, especially France and West Germany, made possible further reconstruction and economic development.[2] Italy and West Germany had become democratic and were eager to join a European family of democracies – in Germany's case even more so to counteract a perceived Soviet threat and to compensate for the virtually complete loss of markets in the East (including East Germany). A 'virtuous circle' had begun. Conversely, the geopolitical forces that propelled Western European countries to varying degrees of political co-operation or even integration also turned Europe into a focal point for US–Soviet super-power rivalry.

From August 1949 the US–Soviet confrontation became dramatically more worrisome for Europe when the Soviet Union's nuclear capability was revealed and the Chinese civil war ended in victory for the communist side two months later. Tension rose to new heights in June 1950 when North Korea invaded South Korea, leading to US military intervention under United Nations (UN) authority and to an even more confrontational US stance vis-à-vis the Soviet Union.[3] Any military conflict between the two blocs had the potential to escalate to a nuclear conflict, with Europe likely to serve as the nuclear battlefield. 'Better dead than red?' or 'Better red than dead?' was the agonising potential choice for Europeans. The fear promoted the quest for political and economic integration in Western Europe.

The post-war era was focused on ideology rather than nationalism – almost the very opposite of today – and it was one of great fear for the survival of European (and world) civilisation, even though the full, long-term health effects of nuclear weapons were largely unknown and nuclear tests were conducted with disregard for the risks to soldiers and civilians alike. Nationalism was not dead, but dormant, as Western Europe grouped together to escape communism and Soviet domination, and as the latter suppressed nationalism in Central and Eastern Europe in the name of a 'new age of mankind'.

European colonial powers at this time also began to grow tired of their overseas possessions. The United Kingdom granted India independence in 1947, and the following decades would see the near dismantling of European imperialism. The reasons were not only a growing realisation that it was 'immoral' to refuse independence to peoples far from Europe's shores, and of the sheer economic and political costs of maintaining colonies, but also an increasing national consciousness among colonised peoples whose nationhood often preceded those of European nations, leading, for instance, to French defeat in Indo-China in 1954.

There was also the shift in the world economy away from raw materials as a source of wealth for industrialised countries, and towards an emphasis on 'value-added' – finished products of greater and greater sophistication. In other words, the brain was becoming a more important lever of the world economy than the arm (and eventually the hand), a process that has accelerated ever since.[4] Especially in a world of freer and freer world trade in raw materials under GATT, the 'mother countries' no longer had to hold on to colonies at ever greater cost. To grasp this fact the European colonial powers only had to look at West Germany, which had no colonies but which surged ahead past much of the rest of Europe during the 1950s; or at Portugal, which refused to see the writing on the wall and paid for its stubborn clinging to Angola and Mozambique well into the 1970s with a painfully slow rate of economic growth.

If we add all the factors together, it is not surprising that the 1950s became *the* decade of integrative will in Western Europe: ideology replacing nationalism, relentless political and military pressure from the East, optimism about a joint economic future fuelled by annual growth rates that today seem unreachable, the still vivid memories of the war – and fears of a coming one.

Co-operation: how far?

Europe would not, however, be Europe if all these things were felt with the same intensity everywhere. The European Movement was able to unite some 750 prominent Europeans around its call for the nations of Europe to create a political and economic European Union – a 'United States of Europe'. But by the time this led to an international treaty in 1949 it had been watered down considerably by the governments concerned. The Congress of Europe held at The Hague in May 1948 was a grand rally of 'Europeans' attended by leading statesmen, including Winston Churchill, who in a famous speech in Zurich in 1946 had even called (uncharacteristically for a Briton) for a 'United States of Europe'. However, Churchill had taken the lead in this movement in part to ensure that it would lead not to unbridled supranationalism, but rather to a structure where countries, including the United Kingdom, would maintain their individual identity.[5]

The Congress adopted a resolution that called for the giving up of some national sovereignty prior to the accomplishment of economic and political union in Europe. Subsequently a proposal was put forward, with the support of the Belgian and French governments, calling for a 'United Europe' and the creation of a European parliamentary assembly in which resolutions would be passed by majority vote. This was, of course, contrary to the unanimity rule, which was then characteristic of international organisations.

A Committee of Ministers of a Council of Europe was to prepare and implement these resolutions. Needless to say, the United Kingdom was opposed to this form of supranationalism and in the end the British view largely prevailed. The Committee of Ministers, which is the executive organ of the Council of Europe, alone has the power of decision and generally decisions are taken on the unanimity principle. The Consultative Assembly (today called the Parliamentary Assembly) is a forum for debate, pressure and influence on the European public, and not a legislature.

In short, the British and Scandinavian 'functionalists' – who believed that European union, in so far as it was desirable, was to be attained by intergovernmental co-operation and be essentially restricted to economic integration – triumphed over the 'federalists', who sought unity by the more radical method of creating European institutions to which national governments would surrender some of their sovereignty.[6]

The statute of the Council of Europe is telling of this development. Its Article I states:

> The aim of the Council of Europe is to achieve a greater unity between its members for the purpose of safeguarding and realising the ideals and principles which are their common heritage and facilitate their economic and social progress.
>
>   This aim shall be pursued through the organs of the Council by discussions of questions of common concern and by agreements and common action in economic, social, cultural, scientific, legal and administrative matters and the maintenance and further realisation of human rights and fundamental freedoms.

The European Movement's 'United Europe' had become the Council of Europe's 'greater unity', highlighting the continent's continuing uncertainty about where it wanted to go. Countries like the United Kingdom and Sweden were among those hesitating most, feeling perhaps that if God had really wanted them to be part of Europe He would not have made the English Channel or the Baltic. But others were also ambivalent to different degrees. France, for instance, wanted European unification provided it could itself play the leading role in it, especially vis-à-vis Germany.

Neither France nor smaller countries on Europe's periphery, such as Norway and Denmark, wanted to abandon national identity altogether – a natural reaction considering their recent occupation by Germany. That latter country – like Italy – was ready to move decisively in the federalist–integrationist–supranational direction, not least for reasons of guilt on account of the war.

In the smaller countries of Belgium, the Netherlands and Luxembourg, there was a genuine will across the political spectrum in favour of the same process. These countries were too small to be able satisfactorily to develop their economies on their own. They had been occupied by Germany and sought protection from it by embracing it and their neighbours. They had no ambition to lead, only to co-manage. In addition, they were already, since 1948, working together within the Benelux customs union (with antecedents from the inter-war period), which functioned much in the way the European Economic Community would do later.[7]

Integration through coal and steel?

It is not surprising that the next step in the economic and political unification of Western Europe would be taken without the British and the Scandinavians. In 1951 the European Coal and Steel Community (ECSC) was established by the 'Six' (Belgium, the Netherlands, Luxembourg, France, West Germany and Italy).[8] The direct precipitating factor was the renaissance of the West German economy. The rebuilding efforts of the German people and the aid made available by the United States both contributed to the 'economic miracle' or *Wirtschaftswunder* that was about to unfold. It was generally admitted that the German economy would have to be allowed to regain a stature in the world commensurate with its size and strength, and that Allied control of coal and steel could not go on forever. [9]

Concerns remained however, about how the German steel, iron and coal sectors (the basic materials of a war effort in those days) could be allowed to regain their previous powerful position without therefore endangering future peace on the continent.

One suggestion came in the form of a French plan, conceived by Jean Monnet and presented by Robert Schuman in May 1950. The Schuman Plan was highly political in character. It attempted to end the historic rivalry of France and Germany by making a war between them not only inconceivable but physically impossible in practical terms. In this way, a 'European federation', considered indispensable to peace, would ultimately come about. The means would not be the nationalisation – or indeed the internationalisation – of coal, iron and steel production, but rather the creation, through the elimination of quotas, customs duties and so forth, of a 'common market' in these products. Every participant in this common market would have the same access to the products of these industries wherever they might be made. Discrimination on grounds of nationality would not be tolerated.

The Schuman Plan had a number of appealing characteristics. Firstly, it could help solve the Saar problem. The return of the Saar (north of French Lorraine) to West Germany was likely to be more acceptable to the French if West Germany became a full partner in such a coal and steel community. It also appealed to the Germans since membership of such a community would help it re-attain international respectability, and thereby speed up the ending of occupation and avoid the imposition of various measures to impede German economic expansion, such as those that had been in force after World War I.

The Plan was also supported by the federalists, who were as

disappointed with the OEEC as they were with the Council of Europe. The OEEC observed the unanimity rule and did not foresee any powers to be delegated to an independent commission or commissariat. If this was frustrating, so were the prospects for the OEEC as such, for by 1952 the four-year period of the Marshall Plan would end. The UK and other countries wanted the OEEC budget to be cut thereafter, with some of its work handed over to NATO. (In the end, the OEEC would live on with the same limited powers as at its creation, becoming, in 1960, the Organisation for Economic Co-operation and Development and equipped with a more global economic role.)

The ECSC's proposed structure was also very much in line with federalist, supranationalist thinking. It was to have as its supreme organ a High Authority – a name that would be difficult for Europeans to accept today – endowed with direct political powers to be exercised, in periods of crisis for either steel or coal (due to, say, overproduction), independently of a Council of Ministers, i.e. the representatives of the governments of the Six. A Common Assembly consisting of delegations from national parliaments was thrown in almost as an afterthought, reflecting the weak power of parliaments vis-à-vis executives at the time. Finally, a Court of Justice was to ensure compliance with the ECSC Treaty.

If the Schuman Plan was welcomed by the Six, it was rejected by the British. The British Prime Minister, Clement Attlee, for instance, told the House of Commons: 'We on this side are not prepared to accept the principle that the most vital economic forces of this country should be handed over to an authority that is utterly undemocratic and is responsible to nobody'.[10] However, the Six went ahead, and in April 1951 the corresponding Treaty of Paris was signed. The ECSC came into being, and the Community took its first step along the road to economic integration. With the British absent and the Germans leaving the leading role to France, the ECSC developed its institutions in line with French bureaucratic thinking, a legacy felt to the present day.

Integration through defence?

The next event in European co-operation concerned the military and security field, again with Germany at the centre of attention. When the Korean war erupted in 1950, the United States proposed the rearmament of West Germany. France was against, just as it had objected to West Germany becoming a member of NATO. Through its Prime Minister, Pleven, it instead suggested that, rather than there being a German army, a European army should be established, to which each participating country, including West Germany, could contribute.

The United Kingdom, while not opposed to the project, said it would not be party to it. However, the Six were positive and started negotiations in 1951 for a European Defence Community (EDC). It would include a Joint Defence Commission and a Council of Ministers. A Parliamentary Assembly and a Court of Justice would also be established, similar to those within the ECSC. Rapid progress was made and the EDC Treaty was signed in May 1952.

The ambitions of the Six did not stop there. If military capabilities were pooled, then this would leave little room for independent foreign policies. Political integration would be a necessary further step, since the proposed European Army would have to stand under effective political control.

The Benelux countries in particular felt that progress in the military field, to be viable, had to have its counterpart in that of political integration. The governments of the Six therefore asked the ECSC Assembly to propose ways of establishing a European Political Authority. In 1953, an outline for a European Political Community (EPC) was presented. It proposed that, following a transition period, the institutions of the ECSC and the proposed EDC be merged within a new framework. One European Executive would be answerable before a European Parliament (to consist of a Peoples' Chamber elected by direct universal suffrage and a Senate appointed by national parliaments). Finally, one Council of Ministers and one European Court would replace the corresponding bodies created under the ECSC and EDC treaties.

The European Movement seemed close to its goal. The Six had already successfully started limited economic integration in the sectors of coal and steel. They had signed a treaty to merge their defences and were set to create a political community. Moreover, the draft treaty called for economic integration to progress still further, through the establishment of a common market based on the free movement of goods and factors of production.

To understand how all this was politically possible and close to being realised, we have to understand the Zeitgeist of that era. The memories of the fratricidal European war were still vivid. There was a strong belief in 'big is beautiful', quite unlike today's economic reality, where the limitations of huge projects and of centralised control have become more apparent and given rise to opposite trends towards smaller economic units, decentralisation and 'subsidiarity'. Keynesian thinking was still in vogue, with its belief in state intervention in economic life to counter heartless market forces, not least through deficit spending to counter any recession, and 'social engineering' that was capable of creating a more perfect society. Faith in central planning was gaining ground, in France, for example, through extensive state planning and *dirigisme*, but especially in the Soviet Union where Stalin created what seemed like an economic juggernaut based on heavy industry. (This was long before any but a few had any doubts about the economic impossibility of state communism.) And the fear was not far below the surface that an economically reawakened Germany might try to exact revenge for its loss of the war.

The French plan for an EDC, a European Defence Community, was, however, stopped by the French themselves. The parliaments of the other five countries in line for membership approved the EDC Treaty, but a succession of French governments did not muster the courage to ask the National Assembly to ratify it. Efforts were made by the government under Mendès-France to modify the treaty in order to make it more palatable to the National Assembly, but the other five refused to go along. The treaty as it stood was in the end presented to the French Assembly which, by refusing to consider it, killed both it and the EPC. Among the reasons were the fear of rearming Germany; the loss of French sovereign control of its military forces; doubts about the workability of an integrated army; unease that the strongest European military power, the United Kingdom, remained outside; and a belief that the end of the Korean War and the death of Stalin (in early 1953) would make the case for an EDC less urgent.

The failure of the EDC was followed by a British initiative in part aimed at dealing with the problem of rearming West Germany in a way that the French could accept. Several agreements were concluded in 1954 between the United States, the United Kingdom, Canada and the Six. As part of these agreements, the Brussels Treaty Organisation was modified and extended. West Germany and Italy were accepted as members and a new intergovernmental organisation – the Western European Union (WEU) – was created. The agreements foresaw the termination of the occupation of West Germany and that country's admission to NATO. As a counterbalance to the West German army, the United Kingdom agreed to station forces in the country. The basic aim of the agreements was to establish a European framework in which Germany could be rearmed and join NATO, while having the British ease French apprehensions about a possible German military predominance. When Germany was admitted as a member of the WEU in October 1954 and of NATO in May 1955, the Soviet response the same month was the establishment of the Warsaw Pact. With the French decision at about this time to create an independent nuclear *force de frappe*, the 'German question' seemed, if not solved, then at least stabilised.

Whether the European Defence Community would have worked is unclear. The problems to overcome would have been formidable. What would have been the common language, necessary in combat? Would German soldiers have accepted, let alone understood, French commands? Would it have been possible to integrate national military structures and traditions to create an efficient, effective and united fighting force, or would that force have suffered the same fate in battle as, say, the combined Russian and Austrian armies against Napoleon at Austerlitz in 1805, where utter confusion, rivalry and vanity led to total defeat? Finally, how much would British rejection and American coolness to the idea have affected its viability over time? NATO was already in existence, and the United States was determined to have an important say over West European security affairs. An EDC, especially one without the United States' most important ally, the United Kingdom, risked creating a 'decoupling' of the old world from the new – an unattractive possibility given the growing US–Soviet rivalry with Europe as its main focus.

Integration through trade? The birth of the EEC

1954 had been a poor year for European unity. The supranationalist cause had suffered a serious setback and the establishment of the WEU – a purely intergovernmental as opposed to supranational organisation – now held centre stage. However, the European Movement already by 1955 came up with new ideas to bring unification forward.

The initiative came from the Benelux countries. They called for a general common market and for particular action in the fields of energy and transport. The Benelux approach was that political unity would not come easily. It remained the final objective, but it could only come about over time. The more immediate objective should be economic integration. As the countries worked closely together in the economic field, political integration would follow naturally. The Benelux initiative called for the creation of a European Economic Community. In other words, a change from EDC to EEC.

The Six met at Messina in Italy in June 1955 and gave the project their approval. Work aiming to establish a general common market and an atomic energy pool was to commence. The United Kingdom, a member of the WEU and associated with the ECSC, would be invited to participate in the work in preparing the EEC. However, as work progressed, differences between the Six and the United Kingdom became evident. The latter wanted a free trade arrangement, while the Six were intent on forming a customs union. Furthermore, the UK felt that little extra bureaucracy was needed to put the new arrangement into effect. Perhaps the OEEC would be enough. This view was, however, bound to meet with the resistance of the federalists, who emphasised the creation of supranational institutions capable of achieving more than just economic integration. Eventually, the UK representatives withdrew from the discussions, in November 1955.

Meanwhile, the Six advanced, although not without problems. The French, for example, wanted a long transition period for tariff reductions. They also called for escape clauses, the harmonisation of social charges and high tariffs around the union, while others, such as the Benelux states, wanted low ones. The French wanted to see an atomic energy community established, a field where they were predominant, but they were less enthusiastic about a general common market. Finally, in March 1957, the EEC Treaty and the Euratom Treaty were signed in Rome. They entered into force on 1 January 1958.

The inclusion in the EEC Treaty of topics such as social policy and agricultural policy is indicative of the many compromises between the Six, and especially between France and the Federal Republic of Germany. France feared that Germany would benefit most from the more open markets of the proposed customs union and wanted compensation in other fields. Thus France insisted on special protection for agriculture, which had historically been sheltered from competition from abroad and from which one in five French workers still earned their livelihood. Furthermore, France wanted an atomic energy community, which could in due course give France a leading role in the EEC in energy production. Finally, France sought especially close relations with the Six for France's overseas possessions.

Some of today's major problems of the European Union were born out of the Rome Treaty compromises. The Common Agricultural Policy (CAP), originally meant to compensate France for feared German industrial domination, gave rise to the bloated, inefficient and endlessly complicated CAP of today, still swallowing about half of the European Union's expenditure. The Customs Union, foreseeing a common external tariff between member states, would give rise to a lasting temptation to practise protectionism and thus delay structural adaptation of the economies of member states. But more about this later.

The institutions foreseen for the EEC (and for Euratom) were, in brief:

- An appointed Commission, which would take over the role that the High Authority had under the ECSC. It would be the main policy initiator, with some decision-making authority. It would have a number of responsibilities for policy implementation. However, it would be granted less extensive power than the High Authority when it came to imposing decisions on member states. The member states had become aware of the dangerous animal they had created in the High Authority and were not willing to take the risk of losing too much national sovereignty. In a way, the Commission reflects the hybrid nature of what eventually became today's the European Union, with a supranational element working in parallel with an intergovernmental one.[11]
- A Council of Ministers, with more powers than its ECSC counterpart. It would be the main decision-making body. Sometimes its decisions would have to be unanimous, while at other times majority and qualified majority votes would be allowed.
- An Assembly would maintain advisory and certain supervisory powers. In a first stage it would be composed of delegates from national parliaments. However, in due course it would be elected 'by direct universal suffrage in accordance with a uniform procedure in all member states'.
- Finally, a Court of Justice would ensure compliance with the treaty.

These institutional arrangements were rather more intergovernmental in character than the integrationists would have liked. Thus, the Council of Ministers was considered to have been given too much power, at the expense of the Commission and the Assembly. At the same time, the Council was seen as being weakened by the fact that most key decisions would have to be made unanimously.

However, federalists agreed that the system could pave the way for later supranationalism, especially if, as expected, majority voting was introduced in the Council after the Community became more established. Furthermore, the Assembly might soon be elected by direct suffrage, and its powers correspondingly increased. Finally, if the Community became a success, member states would become less preoccupied with their national prerogatives and would be more willing to yield powers to the EEC.

The East–West split deepens

What of the part of Europe behind the Iron Curtain? With the death of Stalin in March 1953 and the end of the Korean War in July of that same year (indeed obtained through Soviet mediation), world tension had been reduced. In June 1953 new Soviet leaders Malenkov and Bulganin suggested German unification along the principles of the 1945 Potsdam Agreement, including the abandonment of a plan to force socialism on to East Germany. When the initiative was not heeded by the Western powers, the effect was to fortify the 'Two German States Theory' formulated in 1949. An uprising against the regime by East Berlin workers in June 1953 was, however, suppressed forcefully by the Soviet Union and the East German government. Only with the visit to Moscow by German Chancellor Adenauer in September 1955 could Soviet–West German relations become more normal.[12]

Tensions were further reduced in 1955, first with the signing of the Austrian State Treaty, establishing that country's sovereignty, neutrality and the withdrawal of foreign troops from its soil, and subsequently through the departure of Soviet troops from a base in Finland (Porkala) and from Chinese Manchuria. Furthermore, a thaw in Soviet relations with Yugoslavia took place the same year and, in February 1956, Khrushchev's criticism of Stalin at the Twentieth Congress of the Soviet Communist Party led to further 'de-Stalinisation' of the Soviet Union and lessened tension with the West.

However, the desire of the Soviet Union to pursue political control in its *cordon sanitaire* vis-à-vis Germany continued undiminished, as did its intention to hold firm to the economic tenets of state communism. Its crushing of the East Berlin uprising in 1953, the Polish unrest in 1956 and the Hungarian revolt the same year made this determination clear enough. At the same time, the crushing of the Hungarian revolution deeply discredited the communist ideology in Western Europe. Instead of being considered the 'centre of a new religion', the Soviet Union came to be perceived as just another imperialist power. The shock created by 'Budapest' contributed to the decline of the (once mighty) communist parties in the western half of the continent.

The refusal of the West – the United States and its NATO allies in Western Europe – to enter into open conflict with the Soviet Union signified that a certain acceptance of the post-World War II status quo had set in. Western Europe was content with its rapid economic progress and the measure of economic, political and military integration that had been achieved. It felt less vulnerable, especially under the US nuclear umbrella. The United States for its part probably welcomed the fact that Western Europe was uniting economically, perhaps even politically, while leaving military co-operation in the relatively ineffectual hands of the Western European Union.

The United States was determined to remain involved in European affairs this time around – after all it had done to contribute to the Allied victory in the World War II – that is, not to repeat the security withdrawal it had undertaken after World War I. This had, in its view, left Europe a victim of balance-of-power politics among unstable, shifting alliances. A lively debate within the US administration pitted those who actively sought the demise of the Soviet Union in the Wilsonian tradition of a US universal mission on behalf of democracy, against those more *Realpolitik*-oriented, who wanted a more passive 'containment' of Soviet power. In the end, the latter view won out, and the US settled into a long wait for Soviet strength to ebb, holding on to Western Europe while not risking war over the parts under Soviet sway.

War had become a particularly perilous prospect since 1953, when the Soviet Union had exploded its first hydrogen bomb and was readying an intercontinental system for weapons delivery. US territory could now be reached, especially as from 1957, when the Soviet launch of the first satellite, Sputnik, produced a veritable shock in the Western camp. A nuclear exchange would all of a sudden almost certainly result in MAD, or Mutual Assured Destruction.

This meant a rather rigid alliance system for both sides, but one which – unlike the situation before and between the world wars – was generally stable and left little room for the lesser powers to break out on their own and risk a generalised conflict. It was, after all, a situation that suited both the US and the Soviet Union rather well, with the latter not realising that it had overextended itself militarily and politically in a way that would in due course lead to its disintegration.[13]

The Soviet Union's hegemony in Central and Eastern Europe went unchallenged in reality if not in the rhetoric of the Cold War, thus providing it with both a buffer zone against Germany (indeed, directly including one part of that country and indirectly another part which had been ceded to Poland) and a territory in which to apply central planning and hence further economic dependency on Moscow.

France felt satisfied with its predominant position in West European affairs through the Western European Union, the ECSC and the EEC, and it was not too unhappy about the division of Germany. France had, so it seemed, managed to rein in Germany by embracing it.[14]

Maybe even the Federal Republic of Germany preferred a divided Germany – with its largest part firmly anchored in the West – to the kind of neutral, disarmed but united Germany suggested by the Soviet Union in the early 1950s. A new Germany including the eastern part would have given added weight to the nascent Social Democratic Party and a stronger communist role in German politics – and would perhaps even have carried the risk of a coup d'état along the lines of that in Czechoslovakia in 1948.[15] The declaration of the day of the East Berlin uprising – 17 June – as a national day of the Federal Republic, and the 1949 *Grundgesetz*, which spoke about the country as being the true continuation of Germany as a country, were in a way pointers to the future, while the country concentrated on being a new, 'good' European country committed to democracy and co-operation with its western neighbours and allies.[16]

Finally, the United Kingdom had managed to bind Germany firmly in a defence context that could both withstand pressure from the Soviet Union and counteract any risk of too dominant a military role for France's sensibilities. The 'umbilical cord' with the United States was intact, both in the United Kingdom's 'special relationship' with it and in the US commitment to overall European security through NATO. European federalism had been held at bay, at least in the military and political field. If the Six had been foolish enough to embark on the ECSC and EEC projects, so be it, and God speed to them! The UK would decolonise what had to be decolonised, keep what could be kept and create a Commonwealth to keep the old Empire together, but in a more morally and politically acceptable way. The UK believed that it would show the Six what could and should be done economically with the rest of free Europe.

Already at the close of the 1950s the British could witness, not without a certain *Schadenfreude*, the first setback for the European Coal and Steel Community, which it had refused to join. The High Authority – the ECSC's supranational body that would take over if there was a 'manifest crisis' in the coal or steel sector – was not given that authority by the ECSC's Council of Ministers in 1958–59, when cheap oil imports and a fall in energy consumption led to over-capacity in coal production.[17] Coal and steel policies over the years remained largely in the hands of ECSC member states and continue to do so up to this day, despite the decline in importance of these industries.

However, few people doubted that the ECSC crisis was anything but a minor incident on the road to a more and more united Six, showing the way to and eventually including others, and that economic integration would soon lead to its political counterpart. The ingredients that would later wither away were all there: the memories of the war; rapid, seemingly painless economic growth; pressure from the East; and a bipolar world with Europe in the middle.

Notes

1 In a speech to the NATO Council in Paris, 14 December 1953.

2 The dowry brought by France to Germany following World War II was the nuclear weapon, which gave Germany added security but also reminded it of its vulnerability and France's dominant military position. Germany in compensation contributed strength to what was eventually to become the European Union via the strong Deutschmark. Germany was able to look to France for political muscle, while France counted on Germany to provide the economic dynamism and funding it lacked.

3 The policy foundation for the more assertive US policy was the famous NSC 68 report of the National Security Council. It was largely drafted by Paul Nitze, who would later become chief US negotiator in the Strategic Arms Limitations Talks (SALT). The report laid out options for fighting international communism and called for larger US military expenditure. It argued that conventional US rearmament and strategic superiority were indispensable to maintain the United States' preponderant position in the international system and to prevent the Soviet Union seizing the industrial heartland of Europe and gaining the upper hand in the developing world. The US rearmament programme would in due course contribute to the rise of the so-called military–industrial complex. See e.g. Leffler (1992, Ch. 8).

4 Peter Drucker (1993), a leading exponent of the 'Knowledge Revolution', sees the Industrial Revolution as having lasted from around 1750 until around 1880, with knowledge being applied to tools, processes and products. The 'Productivity Revolution', ending at about the time of the end of the World War II, concentrated on the work process as such, as manifested, for instance, in 'Taylorism'. The 'Management Revolution', in the midst of which we now find ourselves, is, according to Drucker, based on the notion that everything revolves around knowledge, where 'knowledge is being applied to knowledge', i.e. by enhancing, combining and using the knowledge of oneself and others in the joint management of projects.

5 Churchill's speech has been wrongly interpreted as a British commitment to forming an integral part of such a 'United States of Europe'. Churchill in fact always considered the United Kingdom as being 'with' and not 'of' Europe and rather saw his country as forming part of 'three overlapping circles': UK–USA, UK–Commonwealth and UK–Europe (the Labour Party largely shared this view of things). Churchill in his Zurich speech made this clear when he said: 'In all this urgent work, France and Germany must take the lead. Great Britain, the British Commonwealth of Nations, mighty America, and I trust the Soviet Union – for then all indeed is well – must be friends and sponsors of the new Europe and must champion its right to live and shine. Therefore I say to you: Let Europe arise!' (Brugmans, 1965, p. 266).

6 For a discussion of the 'federalists' or 'integrationists' versus the 'functional approach', see e.g. Urwin (1991, Chs 2 and 3).

7 The Benelux union is an intergovernmental institution that, interestingly

enough, continues to prosper parallel to the European Union (EU) in matters concerning Belgium, the Netherlands and Luxembourg. It started as a monetary agreement in 1943, evolved into a customs union in 1944, and into an economic union in 1993. The 'Benelux effect' has no doubt had an impact on EU integration and is an example of what smaller countries in Europe can achieve together. See e.g. Busschaert (1998).

8 The European Coal and Steel Community Treaty had a duration of fifty years. The ECSC was consequently dissolved in 2002. Its provisions now sort under the general EU legislation and its functions under various Directorates General of the European Commission.

9 This was then the very opposite development to that foreseen in the so-called 'Morgenthau Plan' floated within the US administration in early 1945, foreseeing the dismemberment of Germany and the country's conversion into 'a country primarily agricultural and pastoral in its character'. The proposal was soon buried as it became clear that European peace and development could not be secured without re-industrialisation and that there was still a political vacuum in its midst. Various further plans were presented and subsequently abandoned prior to the finally adopted Schuman Plan (May 1950). One was for Four-Power (the US, the Soviet Union, France and the United Kingdom) international control of the Ruhr, abandoned after British objections. Another was for a Ruhr Authority under West European control, with a weak position for Germany. Only the Schuman Plan could pave the way for Germany's eventual integration into the new Western Europe and hence for the German 'economic miracle'. For a detailed account see Gillingham (1991). The perhaps best account of the *Wirtschaftswunder* is provided by its architect Ludwig Erhard, who vowed, and managed, to put 'a refrigerator in every household'. By coincidence or not, when he resigned as Chancellor in 1966, Germany's economic boom also came to a halt. See e.g. Erhard (1963).

10 Quoted in Swann (1995, p. 8).

11 Many of the problems of today's European Union result directly from Jean Monnet's more or less single-handed imposition of an elitist, technocratic ECSC High Authority, with the Commission as its only slightly weakened offspring. Although European integration as we know it may not have been feasible without such a set-up, the question now is whether it is viable in today's radically changed context.

12 From this time until the 1970s, the Federal Republic insisted on representing Germany alone, that is, to the exclusion of the German Democratic Republic, through the so-called 'Hallstein doctrine'. The latter signified that only countries that did not have diplomatic relations with East Germany (excepting the Soviet Union) could have similar relations with West Germany.

13 See e.g. Kissinger (1994, Ch. 18).

14 Charles de Gaulle's thinking on Europe evolved remarkably from his wartime exile to his presidency under the Fifth Republic. During and immediately

after the war, he worked toward a dismemberment of Germany and the 'association of the Rhineland with a Western bloc' and a 'Federation between France, Belgium, Luxembourg and Holland, which Great Britain might join also'. France would 'assume a leading role for the benefit of everybody' in such a federation. By 1958, when the Federal Republic of Germany was a well-established European actor, he saw the EEC as a vehicle for French leadership over Germany and Western Europe, provided the United Kingdom could be kept out, lest it be able to carry out its '"Trojan Horse" mission of transforming the Common Market into an "Atlantic Community"' (Gladwyn, 1969, pp. 32 and 63).

15 German Chancellor Konrad Adenauer was firmly Western-oriented, keen on German membership of the Council of Europe, NATO, the European Coal and Steel Community and the EEC. See e.g. Ash (1993, Ch. 1).

16 Even the name the 'Federal Republic of Germany' indicated this, just as the name the 'German Democratic Republic' showed an admittance by that country that it was only German, not Germany.

17 The High Authority, a brainchild of Jean Monnet and chaired by him until 1955, consisted of nine international civil servants and could, by the requested majority, take decisions binding on the six governments concerned in the interest of some abstract 'European General Will' – detached from the popular or political will expressed by governments or parliaments. It was a major reason why the UK felt unable to join both the ECSC and the EEC, with Prime Minister Harold Macmillan declaring that his country 'could never allow any supranational authority to close down our pits and steelworks'. De Gaulle, too, was against the ECSC (established when he was out of power), calling it an 'unfortunate project which could injure Europe' and an 'imbroglio of pools' (Gladwyn, 1969, p. 29).

3

1960–75: the new Europe takes shape

The present situation of Europe is abnormal, or absurd. But it is a clear-cut one
and everybody knows where the demarcation line is and nobody is very much
afraid of what could happen. If something happens on the other side of the Iron
Curtain – and we have the experience of a year ago – nothing happens on this
side. So a clear partition of Europe is considered, rightly or wrongly, to be less
dangerous than any other arrangement. (Raymond Aron)[1]

Summary

Following the second Berlin crisis, which had led to the construction of
the wall in August 1961, and the US–Soviet 'nuclear brinkmanship' over
Cuba in October 1962, where the Berlin issue formed an important role,
the two superpowers took various steps to diffuse tensions while continuing their ideological struggle with undiminished intensity. The new
European Economic Community (EEC) made major progress toward free
trade and a common external customs barrier among its members (Belgium,
France, Germany, Italy, Luxembourg and the Netherlands), even though
its Common Agricultural Policy also led to clashes among them.

The United Kingdom, which had not wanted to join the EEC in the
1950s and instead had created a non-political, purely free-trade European Free Trade Association in 1960, now realised that its interests
might instead lie in EEC membership. Following essentially French objections, the UK was twice refused entry in 1961 and 1967 and could only
join in 1973 (with Denmark and Ireland) after the departure of President
de Gaulle of France. The nine-member EEC from this moment on became
the main vehicle for West European economic and political integration,
forming the 'rich men's' club' of (essentially Northern) European countries.

Even a first plan for an EEC Monetary Union was conceived in 1970
in order to counter international currency instability largely occasioned
by US financial strains owing to its Vietnam involvement. Plans for a
single currency never went further, however, due to too great an

economic divergence between EEC members and to the economic effects of the 1973 oil crisis.

The beginnings of 'big power détente' over Europe permitted a country such as Hungary to engage in limited market-oriented reforms and in 1968 led Czechoslovakia toward an open break, soon suppressed, with the Soviet Union. Furthermore, West Germany, under Willy Brandt, could start a cautious *Ostpolitik* of contacts with the Soviet Union, Eastern Europe (especially Czechoslvakia and Poland) and – last but not least – East Germany. The 1975 Helsinki Final Act seemed to confirm the Soviet hold over Central and Eastern Europe in 'peaceful co-existence' with the West, although, in reality, it marked the beginning of the end of that Soviet domination and of the Soviet Union itself.

An emerging prosperity

The Six of the EEC, like the rest of Western Europe, were to enjoy growth rates of 4–7 per cent per year throughout the 1960s and up until the first oil crisis of 1973–74. Rapid restructuring of the economy took place as internal EEC tariffs and quotas gradually disappeared. People left the countryside in large numbers (largely a result of the Common Agricultural Policy's encouragement of larger, more viable farms), but plentiful work could be found in the cities, where wages were higher.

Competition from abroad was essentially restricted to North America, where US direct investment in particular would lead the French politician and journalist Jean-Jacques Servan Schreiber to write admiringly, even despairingly, in his 1968 bestseller *The American Challenge* about the risk of Europe becoming a mere economic and political appendage to the United States. Despite the attention this book received, it did not lead to any political action to try to counter the phenomenon, for it was a 'win–win' situation for both sides, bringing capital, jobs and increasing transatlantic trade. The US–Soviet bilateral world seemed to have a US–Western Europe economic counterpart, and increasingly a US–EEC one as North American firms began to prefer the territory of the Six to that of the United Kingdom. Central and eastern Europe and the Soviet Union for their part appeared headed for their own, separate economic system, with central planning and state-owned means of production.

Political pressure from the East continued unabated. Encouraged by its sudden, at least apparent atomic weapons parity with the US, the Soviet Union under Khrushchev increasingly engaged in brinkmanship 'atomic diplomacy'. An ultimatum to the US, the UK and France in November 1958 to leave their sectors in Berlin ultimately led to the

August 1961 Berlin crisis and to the building of the Berlin Wall. It was followed by the even more dangerous Cuban missile crisis in October 1962.

On the cultural scene, pop music through stars like The Beatles, The Rolling Stones and Bob Dylan provided a certain emotional affinity between North America and Europe, while the few records that managed to slip past customs controls in Central and Eastern Europe began to spread a subversive message of individual freedom, joy and material wealth.

Meanwhile, the recently formed EEC continued its work. The Council of Ministers – reassured after the ECSC High Authority crisis of 1958–59 that it, and not a supranational body, retained ultimate authority – began to give the Commission greater leeway. Although it wanted to go further along the road to economic integration, it realised that this could carry political risk at home, for instance vis-à-vis the still strong communist parties. It was convenient to have the Commission to do the handiwork and present the governments with, say, a draft directive which, after negotiation with the other member countries, could be agreed to as a sacrifice in the name of Europe, and for which the Commission could if need be provide a suitable scapegoat.

The Commission – appointed not elected, and with a growing army of devoted 'Eurocrats' in its charge – did this, and nobody had any major reason to complain. The undergrowth in the EEC's economic forest was cleared away, permitting trade to grow and, for the first time, significant intra-EEC foreign direct investment. Weaker companies, previously sheltered by protectionism, disappeared, and those that took their place prospered. National governments could hide behind the Commission in explaining to their respective parliaments why a given policy was being, and had to be, pursued in the overall EEC interest, while the national parliaments hardly cared, recognising they could not do the job individually. Finally, the general public did not complain, for every year they earned more and esteem for government and international institutions was still strong.

When the first clash came, in 1965, it was, significantly enough, with the French government, which found that 'vital' French agricultural budgetary interests had not been taken into sufficient consideration by the Commission and other member states. After France left its seat in the Council of Ministers for over six months, thereby paralysing it, the so called 'Luxembourg compromise' was reached in early 1966, signifying that unanimity would henceforth be required when 'very important interests' of a member state were at stake – in fact, a step 'back' from supranationalism to intergovernmentalism.[2]

To the British, watching all this from across the Channel, the Luxembourg compromise made the EEC method seem less threatening. After trying in vain to reach an acceptable free-trade area agreement with the Six in 1957–58 (having failed *inter alia* due to the UKs Commonwealth Preference System), London formed a free-trade area among the 'other seven' in Western Europe – Austria, Denmark, Norway, Portugal, Sweden and Switzerland and the UK itself. The differences with the EEC were stark: no political ambitions, only free trade among the members; no common customs barrier vis-à-vis third countries; a limited staff with no executive missions or competencies; and the exclusion of agriculture.[3]

However, hardly was the ink dry on the 1960 Stockholm Convention creating the European Free Trade Association (EFTA), when the United Kingdom began to reconsider. A number of uncomfortable truths were becoming evident. The United Kingdom was no longer a world power, neither politically (demonstrated by the Suez crisis), nor economically. The United States and the Soviet Union increasingly engaged in direct consultations to the exclusion of the middle-sized European powers, underlining the trend toward bipolarism. The Empire was giving way to the Commonwealth, but these countries were still developing and could not provide the same economic and technological boost as the mature economies in Western Europe. The Six meanwhile sped ahead, growing more quickly than the UK, and the EEC was gaining increasing prominence as the economic and political spokesperson of Europe. More and more US foreign direct investment bypassed the United Kingdom, up until then the preferred location, in favour of the Six. At once the English Channel seemed both narrower and too wide to the pragmatic British. 'If you can't beat them, join them', the thinking seemed to go.

However, 'they' included France, and France was governed, since 1958, by Charles de Gaulle. He was adamantly opposed to UK membership, for reasons both personal and national. He bore a grudge to the British for having treated him with what he perceived as disdain during the war, when he had been the leader of the 'Free French'. He feared that the United Kingdom would rival and try to thwart his desire to place France at the centre of the European stage. He believed the UK would unsettle the developing Franco–German alliance that in 1963 had led to a Friendship Treaty between the two countries. He was afraid of a British Trojan horse with the United States inside, adding to the threat depicted by Jean-Jacques Servan Schreiber. Neither did he wish to see NATO – whose integrated military command France left in 1966 – as the only defence option for Western Europe, when French interests might require the development of an independent European defence identity with a strong French role.

Two UK applications were made – in 1961 and in 1967 – and both were rejected by France. It took de Gaulle's resignation in 1969 (and his death in 1970) and Pompidou's election as his successor to achieve a change of heart in France. By now, Paris saw things differently: the UK might serve as a useful counterweight to an increasingly strong and self-confident Germany; it would lend support to the French opposition to pressures within the Community for increased supranationalism; and France would probably gain economically by virtue of having better access to UK markets and as a result of the UK's being a net contributor to the Community budget.

In December 1969 accession negotiations were opened with the UK – as well as with three other EFTA-members whose economic and political fate were closely tied up with that country: Ireland, Denmark and Norway (Sweden did not apply for membership, ostensibly for reasons of neutrality but in reality probably as much for those of economic and political sovereignty).

Meanwhile, behind the Iron Curtain the Soviet grip over its satellites had if anything hardened after the 1961 Berlin and 1962 Cuban crises. State communism was relentlessly pursued, and Soviet leader Nikita Khrushchev could boast that the Soviet Union would overtake the United States by the end of the decade, an altogether plausible bet in the eyes of many, especially since the country had put an astronaut, Yuri Gagarin, in orbit in 1961 – before the Americans.

These achievements in space, however, displayed as much the many weaknesses of the Soviet economic system as it did its few strengths. Although unable to enhance wealth for the large majority of its citizens – those outside the *nomenklatura* – it could, nevertheless, mobilise resources for giant, specific projects, such as steelworks, chemical plants and space. They were good for statistics – the number of tons of steel produced – but not for the well-being of citizens, and they were on the whole based on yesterday's technology.

In 1963 the Soviet Union was for the first time in peacetime compelled to import grain from the West to cover its needs. This tangibly illustrated the limits of Soviet economic policy. (Russia had been major wheat exporter to Europe throughout the nineteenth century and early twentieth century until the Bolshevik revolution.) This effectively marked the end to Soviet efforts pursued until the 1950s to achieve economic autarchy. It also became more difficult for the Soviet Union to forbid its satellite countries in Central and Eastern Europe to make contacts with the West, when it itself did so. The new openness also showed up in the security field. Negotiations for an agreement with the United States to limit strategic nuclear weapons was started in 1964 (leading, in 1972, to the signature and ratification of the SALT I Treaty).[4] It was preceded by the Partial Nuclear Test Ban in 1963 forbidding atmospheric nuclear tests (though not under water).

The Soviet economy, and those bound up with it in Central and Eastern Europe, fell helplessly behind those other market economies, including the Six of the EEC and the EFTA countries. However, this was not evident to many in the West, due to Soviet propaganda and the paucity of information spreading past the Iron Curtain about the true conditions. Paradoxically, the first major rebellion against Soviet rule in the 1960s, the Prague Spring of 1968, was to coincide with the first youth revolution against state and authority in the West. The '1968' events in France, Germany, the United States and elsewhere were largely in reaction to the US involvement in Vietnam, and they showed the frailty of many a European government as they soon took the form of a rebellion against state authority as such.

To the youth of the early 2000s – perhaps intimidated by a lack of job prospects and caught up in a major shift of world economic activity away from the developed to the developing world – their parents' revolt some thirty-five years before may seem a bit strange. The youth of the 1960s lived in economies growing by 5–6 per cent a year on average, and they were sure of having well-paid jobs, especially if they had any education. They could 'afford' to rebel without risking their golden future. However, their concern – if perceived as misguided and ill-informed by some of their contemporaries – was genuine. Many were angry with multinational corporations and their alleged role in developing countries (this was before the same multinationals, with subsidiaries in the same developing countries, began to move jobs away from the industrialised world). In Europe, fear of military conflict with the East created a strong pacifist sentiment, accentuated by aversion to the United States' role in Vietnam.

East and West: the calm after the storm

Following the Cuban crisis in 1962 came the beginnings of détente. Both the United States and the Soviet Union realised they had come within hours of a nuclear showdown. The Nuclear Test-Ban Treaty of August 1963 – forbidding tests in the atmosphere, in outer space and under water – marked the start of a long process of diminishing tension that would include the reduction of strategic nuclear weapons (and later conventional ones) and, eventually, startling events such as the 1989 fall of the Berlin Wall, the dissolution of the Soviet Union in 1991 and, in 2002, Russia's close partnership with NATO.

A certain stability established itself in Europe in the latter half of the 1960s, as the United States became increasingly engulfed in the war in Vietnam. Both the United States and the Soviet Union were interested in preserving the status quo. As President Nixon began his disengagement from Vietnam in the early 1970s and 'played the China card' by visiting Mao-Tse-Tung in 1972, he revealed not only a desire to play that country out against the Soviet Union, but also a realisation that the 'Communist threat' was far from monolithic, and that nationalism was also a force to be reckoned with (even though few at the time would have predicted that it would ultimately become a main driving force in world affairs).

If détente had a price for the United States – withdrawal from Vietnam – it also meant complications for the Soviet Union. Growing emancipation in Central and Eastern Europe – as exemplified by the Prague Spring in 1968 and Polish unrest in 1970 –was one, and greater exposure to the Western media, especially television, was another. Walter Ulbricht, the leader of the German Democratic Republic at this time, used to say that the enemy of the people was on the rooftops in the form of television antennae.

The Soviet Union felt that it had to gain Western, including American, recognition of its post-World War II borders, even if the price to be paid – as in the 1975 Helsinki Final Act (of the Conference on Security and Co-operation in Europe) – meant the pro forma guarantee of human rights and the free flow of information. However, formal recognition of borders or regimes matters little in comparison with the yearnings of people. The human rights provisions were to eat like a cancer on the body of the Soviet Empire, leading to its dissolution within twenty years, and along with it the solemnly guaranteed borders.

In the meantime, West Germany began to show impatience with its 'economic giant, political dwarf' status (over time economic power and political power tend to equalise). It wanted to strengthen contacts with the sixteen million German citizens living under the communist yoke in the German Democratic Republic, or East Germany. Lucrative business beckoned on the other side of the Iron Curtain, if only the latter could be made more porous (over time it is difficult to stop trade between contiguous regions, however stringent the political separation).

As the German Chancellor Willy Brandt embarked on his *Ostpolitik* in 1969 – in contacts first with the Soviet Union and, after securing its acquiescence, with countries like Poland, Czechoslovakia and especially

East Germany – it was for the above reasons that he was ready to pursue it, in spite of grave misgivings held by France and other countries. Yet the policy worked, both commercially and among domestic political opinion. Separated families could establish contact and even see each other. Dissidents were brought to West Germany against government payment. Détente was given a first, tangible expression.

At this time, the question could be asked: who was and would be strongest, the Six of EFTA led by the United Kingdom, or the Six of the EEC led by France and the Federal Republic of Germany?

The decisive factor was West Germany. With West Germany in the EEC – at the heart of Western Europe – the EEC had to win out. Economic Europe had to form around an 'oval' stretching from the Rhine Estuary in the Netherlands to south of the Rhine sources in northern Italy, and West Germany was that oval's indispensable heartland. Furthermore, West Germany had been led, at the insistence of the other EEC five, and in particular France, to join a Customs Union, instead of a free trade area, which would have been more in line with the General Agreement on Tariffs and Trade, formed in 1947.[5]

To the Customs Union was added a powerful executive machinery – the Council of Ministers and the Commission – built very much on French bureaucratic tradition and with large financial resources at its disposal, especially through the Common Agricultural Policy obligations. Finally, because of a special French–West German relationship bequeathed from World War II and its aftermath, the EEC was given a push in the political direction, essentially to rein in West Germany within a wider European fold.

Here, then, is the post-war European crossroads: between, on the one hand, a non-political, non-bureaucratic EFTA-type of economic co-operation surging ahead of GATT in trade liberalisation but clearly conforming to it; and on the other hand, an EEC-type arrangement - economic but with political aims, ahead of GATT among its members yet otherwise protectionist in an increasing number of fields such as agriculture and steel, and with executive power (with both bureaucratic and centralising tendencies).

For the United Kingdom the die was cast. Precisely because the EEC was protectionist – not necessarily vis-à-vis GATT but because it obliged all its members to observe the same tariffs for given types of goods (often in the direction of the more protectionist members) – the United Kingdom could not afford to stay out. With the UK in, how could Ireland and Denmark stay out and still hope to garnish British breakfast tables with their food? For Ireland, its outlying location made the UK an even more vital trading partner. For the Danes, who voted 'yes' to entry into the EEC in 1973 by a 60–40 margin, it was bad enough to face the EEC-wall at Flensburg. Another one at Harwich could spell serious economic trouble, forcing them to look exclusively north at peripheral Scandinavia.

The Norwegians, however, said 'no' in the 1972 referendum by a 53 per cent to 47 per cent margin, for a number of reasons. These included a fear of losing fishing rights to a budding EEC Common Fisheries Policy promising the right to all EEC members to fish anywhere in the EEC area; anxiety on the part of farmers to lose out in the competition with continental agriculture; newly discovered oil fields holding out the prospect of new prosperity; and suspicion vis-à-vis the Brussels bureaucracy.

Sweden had not even applied for membership, instead seeking associate membership in order to preserve existing trade benefits with the three new entrants and not be left completely in the cold. (A bid in 1971 to persuade the Danes to remain outside the EEC by forming a Nordic Economic Union had failed, mainly due to Finnish and Danish misgivings.)[6] With Finland prevented by its eastern neighbour from contemplating anything but the most limited contacts with the EEC; with Spain and Portugal still under dictatorship (obsolete and on their last legs, but still standing); and with Central and Eastern Europe still sealed off, the Nine were not to increase the membership of their club for another seven years.

Integration through a single currency?

Meanwhile, the international currency situation had begun to stir, causing the EEC to react. The Vietnam War had lead to an overheating of the US economy, with growing budget deficits and inflation as the main consequences. The US balance of payments steadily deteriorated, exacerbated by large-scale investments by US companies abroad. In 1971 President Nixon, threatened with a run on Fort Knox by dollar bearers around the world, was forced to take the dollar off the gold standard.

European currencies, and business people, suddenly found themselves without a reference point, with competitive devaluations and general trade uncertainty as unwelcome results. Even with tariffs this would have been a problem; but with no tariffs between EEC-members since 1968, the internal market was under acute threat. In addition, the Common Agricultural Policy, which had by this time grown to absorb about half of the EEC budget, was being calculated in a theoretical EEC European Currency Unit (ECU), meaning that farmers in countries whose currencies appreciated (with respect to others) lost out and vice versa.[7]

The EEC Council of Ministers had sensed the approaching storm already in 1970, creating the so called Werner Committee. In June of that year, the Werner Committee presented its ideas for a European Monetary Union which, although soon abandoned, were uncannily similar to those of the Economic and Monetary Union today (EMU). The Werner Plan proposed a economic and monetary union by 1980. Community currencies would be freely convertible against one another, with their parities fixed. In due course they would be replaced by a Community currency. A single monetary and credit policy would apply to the whole Community and a common monetary policy would be followed vis-à-vis the rest of the world. National policies would be harmonised and capital markets integrated. The chief aspects of budgetary policies would be agreed at Community level. The Werner Plan recognised that, for this to happen, significant institutional changes would have to come about. A central decision-making body would supervise national budgets and currency parities. A Community central banking system was to determine monetary conditions for the Community as a whole.

The path towards economic and monetary union set out in the Werner Plan proposed action on both exchange rates and the co-ordination of economic policies, within an Exchange Rate Mechanism (ERM). When one Community currency was exchanged for another, only a relatively narrow band of fluctuation around previously established 'central parities' would be allowed – narrower than that between Community currencies and the dollar. This was the famous 'snake in the tunnel' scheme. The 'snake' was the narrower band of fluctuation permitted for intra-Community exchanges, while the 'tunnel' was the wider band allowed in respect of exchanges against the dollar. All this presupposed major harmonisation of national economic policies.

The dollar crisis of 1971, leading towards the end of that year to an 8 per cent devaluation against gold, had caused confusion and disagreement among EEC members – especially between Germany, which wanted a 'joint float' of European currencies, and France, which favoured curbing inflows from the dollar to EEC currencies that were threatened by revaluation. Another problem was making the 'snake' behave, whether inside or outside the 'tunnel'. In June 1972 the United Kingdom – which together with Ireland and Denmark had joined the ERM in anticipation of membership – allowed the pound to float out of the 'snake' and the 'tunnel', and Denmark and Ireland followed suit. By early 1973 Italy was out, followed by France in 1974, leaving Germany, the Benelux countries and Denmark as the only remaining members of the system.

At the Paris Summit in December 1974, the EMU scheme was effectively abandoned. The heads of state and government noted the difficulties which in 1973 and 1974 had combined to frustrate the Werner Plan. They reiterated their desire to achieve an EMU but did not give any deadline. The 1972 Paris Summit declaration that the EMU would be reached by 1980 was not repeated. A 'mini-snake' continued to exist between Germany and a few other countries closely aligned with it economically, but that was of course a far cry from the Community-wide ambition at the outset.

One reason for the collapse of the EMU attempt in the 1970s was that the EEC member states did not take seriously enough the need to co-ordinate their policies. Without a convergence of economic performance on matters such as price levels, exchange rates would have to be adjusted. Many people blamed the oil crisis. However, the first oil price increase did not take place until October 1973, that is, about three years after the launching of the Werner Plan, and its impact was not felt until some time thereafter. By then the EMU was already essentially abandoned. As the oil crisis soon added to inflation and budget deficits, any thought of reviving the EMU became illusory. Finally, the EMU was launched at an unfortunate moment. The international monetary system was highly unsettled, not least by the dollar leaving the gold standard. Lack of confidence in the dollar caused great strain on the 'snake' and the 'tunnel' arrangement.

Leaving Europe for a moment, and turning to Asia, we find that Japan by the 1970s had surreptitiously joined the long-static club of indus-trialised countries. With labour costs still considerably lower than those in Western countries, and with efficient protectionist barriers still around its no-longer-so-'infant' industries, Japan was by this time beginning to be a serious competitor. However, the general feeling in the West was that Japan could at best copy, and possibly produce, certain products more cheaply at the lower end of the technology range, but not take the lead at the top, where true wealth was created. In addition, Japanese investments were still mainly in neighbouring regions, essentially there to extract raw materials for Japanese industry and to escape stiff environmental legislation at home. In spite of increasing trade surpluses with Western Europe and North America, Japan was therefore still not seen as a major competitor, but rather as assisting in the economic development of South-East Asia. In addition, it was still faithfully following the US lead in the foreign policy arena.

Meanwhile, by the mid–1970s the student revolt was dying down. With the Vietnam war coming to a close and the 1973 oil crisis showing the West's vulnerability in the area of a critical raw material, there was nothing tangible to protest against, and the economic future of the young seemed less secure, making many more politically cautious.

The oil crisis did not cause the countries of the EEC and EFTA to call into question the social foundations that had begun to be laid in the 1960s, for instance through the Council of Europe's European Social Charter of 1961. Budget deficits soared, as did inflation, but with accumulated public debts still relatively limited this was not yet a source of major concern. Many people began to have doubts, however, about the virtues of Keynesian recipes to fight economic downturns through deficit spending and a bigger role for the state in the economy, and instead argued for 'structural reform' to increase competition and give freer rein to 'market forces'.

The EEC of the Six had become the EEC of the Nine, and had adapted rather well to its new size. The UK did not turn out to be such a 'wrecker' of the EEC as in particular the French had feared. The British revolt against its excess contribution to the EEC was a few years into the future. True, the cosy Paris–Bonn relationship, with Rome as a benevolent bystander, had become a *ménage à trois*. However, Paris could also flirt with London if there was a quarrel with Bonn, for instance over the allocation of CAP money, and Bonn with London if Paris started calling into question the transatlantic security link or adherence to GATT principles. In brief, a breath of fresh air entered the at times rather tense French–German marriage, and economic Europe had begun to overlap more with the Europe of security and defence. Free trade agreements with the, by now, reduced EFTA (Denmark and the United Kingdom had left for the EEC, although Iceland had joined) brought further impetus to West European economic co-operation and allayed British and Danish fears that their links with EFTA countries would be impaired. The 'yes' in the British referendum of 1975 on continued membership in the EEC, by a margin of 67 per cent to 33 per cent, confirmed that country's basic satisfaction with the gains made through the 1973 adhesion, and calmed fears in Europe and the rest of the world of a disruption of the new status quo.

The 'rich men's club' aspect of the EEC had been reinforced by the move from Six to Nine, if the still comparatively poor Ireland is excluded. The EEC had also become a decidedly Northern European institution, a fact which started to reflect itself in the type of agricultural commodities supported by the Common Agricultural Policy. Italy, and the split 'North–

South Europe' personality of France, did not fully appreciate this northern bias, but at this period there were no serious candidates for accession in the South – with Spain, Portugal and Greece being not only too economically underdeveloped but dictatorships as well (until the mid 1970s).

Finally, the pressure from the East was still there as an impetus to further EEC integration. The Soviet Union and the Central and East European countries within its orbit were responding to the Helsinki Final Act – and the thirty-five-nation Conference on Security and Co-operation in Europe set up through it – with a clamp-down on dissident groups established to monitor its human rights provisions such as the Charter 77 in Czechoslovakia. In the absence of anything beyond verbal commiseration from the West, these dissident groups seemed no match for the state apparatuses. The 'Brezhnev Doctrine', as brought to bear in Czechoslovakia in 1968 and seemingly sanctioned through the Helsinki Final Act, made the Soviet Empire look unassailable.[8] The fact that this was a chimera would only become clear some fifteen years later: that indeed the inertia *brought on* by apparent Soviet victories at Helsinki – and the 'cancerous', long-term effect of dissident groups encouraged by the West – were combining slowly to erode that empire.[9]

Notes

1 French philosopher and sociologist, 1905–83; quoted in Kennan (1972, p. 253).

2 The 'Luxembourg compromise' was the conclusion of a rift over whether the income from agricultural levies and customs duties should, as had been the case up to then, be considered as belonging to the member states for subsequent distribution to the EEC budget, or as directly forming part of the Community's 'own resources'. France insisted on the status quo, while the other member states were more positive regarding the reform proposed by the Commission. The compromise was phrased in such a way as to permit all parties to 'save face'. Thus, when 'very important interests' were involved, the Council of Ministers would 'endeavour, within a reasonable time, to reach solutions which can be adopted by all'. The Six member states noted that there was a 'divergence of views on what should be done in the event of a failure to reach complete agreement' but that it should not 'prevent the Community's work being resumed'. See e.g. Nicoll and Salmon (1990, pp. 25–7).

3 The British in 1958 had suggested a European Industrial Free Trade Area, which was meant to include the EEC and perhaps in due course render it unnecessary. The proposal was promptly vetoed by de Gaulle.

4 SALT I (Strategic Arms Limitation Treaty) was signed and ratified by the Soviet Union and the United States in 1972 . It consisted of both the ABM (Anti-Ballistic Missile) Treaty, which limited nuclear defence capabilities,

and an Interim Agreement limiting offensive strategic nuclear arms. The
Interim Agreement, as the name implies, was not a treaty but an agreement.
President Carter's signature was authorised by the US Congress in 1972. See
Talbott (1979, pp. 21–3).

5 Germany's choice in the mid–1950s of the EEC over a wider free-trade
agreement (such as the British-proposed European Industrial Free Trade
Area) was, in the words of Denman (1996, p. 103) 'largely political. Ludwig
Erhard, West Germany's Economics Minister, strongly opposed a common
market on economic grounds. He preferred a free trade area in which
German industry would flourish. It was Konrad Adenauer who persuaded
Erhard to acquiesce in the arrangements for a common market. Adenauer's
main aim was to achieve a reconciliation between West Germany and its
west European neighbours; France was crucial to this. Adenauer, just as
with the European Coal and Steel Community and the European Defence
Community, was determined to continue his west-oriented policy of embedding the Federal Republic in Western Europe. Very similar reasoning would
apply nearly forty years later in the lead-up to the Maastricht Treaty.'

6 Preceding Denmark's and Norway's application for EEC membership, these
countries had, together with Sweden and Finland, tried to form a Nordic
customs union, NORDEK. It never saw the light of day, however, as the
parties could not agree on a common external tariff, Denmark and Norway
were already eyeing the EEC, and the Finns were worried about the Soviet
reaction. Nordic co-operation between Iceland, Norway, Denmark, Sweden
and Finland had already for some time been pursued within the Nordic
Council, while at no time aiming at supranationality. As af Malmborg (1994,
p. 391) points out: 'Nordic co-operation was established in full respect of
national sovereignty … [It] therefore often became 'shapeless' … even though
in many concrete cases it was both more efficient and intimate than that at
European level, and even though the rest of the world became accustomed to
considering *Norden* [the Nordic countries] as a political and cultural entity
… This difference largely explains why *Norden* has never assumed any permanent shape, while the European Community/Union has survived its various
crises and has been able both to deepen and to widen geographically.'
(Translation from the Swedish original.)

7 The problem with artificially set, or 'green', currencies within the CAP
would become acute with the collapse of the Bretton Woods system in the
early 1970s and the resulting widely fluctuating currencies among EEC
members. The Monetary Compensation Amounts (MCAs) set in place to
correct for this would continue to bedevil the EU up until the introduction of
the euro in 1999, when the problem ceased to exist at least among the eleven
(and in 2002 twelve) countries participating in the EMU.

8 The Brezhnev Doctrine signified the duty, as during the Soviet invasion of
Czechoslovakia in 1968, of all countries in the 'socialist camp' to come to
the rescue of socialism if it was under threat in any one socialist country. It

would eventually, under Gorbachev, give way, as the joke went, to the 'Sinatra Doctrine' ('I did it my way'), permitting socialist countries to choose their own political and economic system.

9 Hurlburt (1995, p. 5) sees the Soviet goals for the Helsinki Final Act as having been: 'Western acceptance of the division of Europe, and specifically of Germany, and development of freer economic, trade and aid linkages'. Less concrete goals included 'drawing Europe closer to Russia and further from the United States, and some nostalgia for the 19th century Concert of Europe and Russia's decisive voice in European architecture'. However, these ambitions were frustrated by the corrosive effect that the links with the West created by Helsinki had on the rigid command economies of the East and their growing dependence on Western credits. This in turn limited the room for action of communist decision-makers. Finally, Helsinki brought the issue of human rights to the countries of Central and Eastern Europe and created new momentum for civil resistance.

4

1976–89: recovery and hubris; effervescence in the East

Some of you may ask, when and how will the Cold War end? I think I can answer that simply. The Communist world has great resources, and it looks strong. But there is a fatal flaw in their society. Theirs is a godless system, a system of slavery. There is no freedom in it, no consent. (President Truman)[1]

Summary

West European economic recovery after the 1973 oil crisis came quickly, although at the price of high inflation and sizeable government budget deficits. The US withdrawal from Vietnam in 1975 did not lead to the feared 'domino effect' of communist takeovers in the region, but instead exposed rifts among communist powers. In Western Europe, too, communism became more diversified with the rise of more reformist 'euro-communist' movements in Italy and elsewhere.

The nine-member EEC became the 'Twelve' as it accepted three new Mediterranean members: Greece in 1981 and Portugal and Spain in 1986. It thereby became more of a political, and less of a purely economic, institution, since all the three new members were considerably poorer than the existing Nine and also members of NATO (showing the US interest in a politically stronger EEC). However, inner EEC solidarity became more difficult with a more heterogeneous membership in terms of economic performance and policy orientations – weakening in the process the traditional common understanding between France and Germany. Monetary co-operation was revived through the European Monetary System, but the latter led an anaemic existence in the coming years, due to still highly divergent EEC economies.

Economic underdevelopment in Central and Eastern Europe and in the Soviet Union itself due to increasingly ill-adapted central planning led to unrest in Poland in 1981, followed by a clampdown by domestic forces. This did not, however, subdue the popular desire for change there and in neighbouring countries. A last Soviet effort to maintain its hold over Central and Eastern Europe (and perhaps even gain one in Western Europe) through the stationing of intermediate ballistic missiles there in the early 1980s was met by similar deployment by NATO in 1985, leading to the scrapping of such weapons on both sides in 1987. A final Soviet attempt to save the essentials of communism failed as the contradictory forces released proved superior even to its new, reformist leader Mikhail Gorbachev.

The EEC, in an effort to overcome the 'euro-pessimism' of the early 1980s, in 1987 embarked on its '1992 Internal Market project' to eliminate remaining trade and investment barriers by that date. The prospect of the deadline released great energy among EEC reformers, shared by business and the general public, especially since everybody could feel that reformist change was under way also in Central and Eastern Europe. The '1992 project' coincided with a major new effort further to liberalise world trade through the so-called Uruguay Round. A sense of new purpose in the West combined with despair in the East to produce the events leading up to the fall of the Wall of Berlin in November 1989, and to the collapse of the Soviet hold over Central and Eastern Europe.

EEC enlargement

The fears of the West – essentially North America, Western Europe and Japan – of an economic collapse in the wake of the 1973 oil crisis did not materialise. The price hikes of the OPEC (Organisation of Petroleum Exporting Countries) oil cartel – termed 'the moral equivalent of war' by the then US Secretary of State Henry Kissinger – were more a healthy reminder to the industrialised countries that they could not go on wasting energy in the way they had been up until then. The truth of the adage 'a barrel of oil saved is a barrel of oil produced' began to sink in, leading to companies and individuals starting to economise on an asset previously taken as both cheap and inexhaustible – in the form of less energy-consuming machinery and vehicles and better insulated plants and houses. Not only did this give rise to new economic activity, but by the end of the 1970s it had brought down the price of oil to almost pre–1973 levels, a development aided by the increasing exploration of, and production from, new oil finds, such as in the North Sea.

Arab countries, the main partners in OPEC, almost immediately began to 'recycle' their petro-dollars into the West's banking system, leading to easier credit and lower interest rates. OPEC countries were also eager to buy from the West everything from new weaponry' to defend against neighbours, to communications satellites and industrial installations.

The latter were seen as particularly important by countries like Iran and Iraq, which wanted to ensure an economic future after the depletion of their oil resources. (And as far as the arms bought were concerned they would soon, at least in the case of these two countries, be used to devastating effect in a war between them that was to last throughout most of the 1980s.)

As European countries recovered they did not, however, draw all the lessons they might have from the oil crises; for while they had, overall, followed Keynesian policies of higher budget deficits to overcome the recession of 1974–75, they did not reduce them to any noticeable extent as their economies picked up. They thereby laid the foundation for the accumulated national debt that today renders any return to Keynesian economics more difficult. The inflation that followed led employees – who had suffered real losses in income during the oil crises and were eager to recoup them – to even higher wage demands. Employers gave in, not least because labour was still relatively scarce (with unemployment in the OECD area standing at only about 5 per cent in the mid–1970s).

After its peace agreement with the Democratic Republic of Vietnam, or North Vietnam, the United States had, by 1975, withdrawn its troops from South Vietnam. The feared 'domino effect' – that is, the belief that if one country became communist, its neighbours and eventually the rest of the world would suffer the same fate – did not materialise. The United States, and the world in general, began to understand that the struggle in the world was not principally between ideologies, but between nations and ethnic groups; and that the 'ideological period' in world history – which had started in earnest in the 1930s with fascism and national socialism pitted against communism and which had continued during the Cold War – was perhaps more an interlude and an exception than the beginning of a new era.

When hostilities flared up in 1979 between the now united Vietnam and the People's Republic of China, the rest of the world was amazed to see two communist brethren nations fight, even though students of the region's history knew that this conflict was centuries old. A new understanding of what drives history was emerging: less abstract ideas than passions, less ideology than religion, less the domination of the world than the fate of one's own nation or ethnic group or, ultimately, oneself and one's family or village. Two decades later Europe would see the same in the former Yugoslavia.

Meanwhile, in Western Europe communism was undergoing change in the form of 'euro-communism'. A new generation of communists had come of age that was less doctrinaire, more reformist, more conciliatory and especially less Stalinist after the Soviet Union itself had undergone 'de-Stalinisation'. Even though communist parties were not yet deemed trustworthy enough to form or even participate in most governments – an attempt in Italy in 1978 at a *compromiso storico* between them and the Christian Democrats failed and led directly to Prime Minister Aldo Moro's murder at the hands of terrorists – 'euro-communism' helped to further defuse Cold War tensions.

At about this time came the breakthrough of the microchip in computers (preceded by the transistor a few years earlier), an innovation which within a few years would have as much economic, social and cultural impact on the world as Gutenberg's printing press. Prior to the chip, computers and technology in general had been electromechanical, with punch cards and valves reacting to pressure, temperature and the like. With the first transistors, radios and electronic calculators, a revolution was set in motion which today has brought us the laptop computer, CD-ROM and internet. We are still only at the beginning of this transformation.

Meanwhile, on Europe's southern fringe important events were under way. Greece's dictatorship, having existed since 1967, foundered under both the weight of international isolation and the political and economic stagnancy of its policies. Portugal discovered what other European countries had realised long before, namely, that colonies make the mother country poorer, not richer, in an era of advanced industrialisation and depressed raw material prices – especially if one is a small nation and has to send one's sons across the oceans to fight highly motivated insurgents, as in Mozambique and Angola. Portugal was impoverished by its colonial struggle; retarded in its development due to its concentration on overseas, even more underdeveloped, territories; and internationally isolated by Europe and the rest of the Western world. The overthrow of the Caetano dictatorship (succeeding that of Salazar) in 1974 and the establishment of democracy the following year seemed long-overdue events.

Spain had little left in the way of colonies, but it had turned inward under Franco, trying to heal the wounds after the 1936–39 civil war. It was, like Portugal, underdeveloped and considered an international 'pariah', especially by Western Europe. When democracy was re-introduced in Spain in 1976 (following Franco's death the year before), this also seemed an event as belated as it was welcome.

Greece immediately cast about to join the EEC, following its 1962 Association Agreement, which had been virtually suspended during the dictatorship years. There were several reasons for Greek interest in the EEC: it would, it was hoped, reinforce the newly re-established democracy;

it would help Greece economically, in particular through the expected largesse of the Common Agricultural Policy (about 30 per cent of the Greek workforce was in farming) and regional aid; it would shield Greece against its eastern neighbour Turkey, with which it had uneasy relations; and it could assist in a badly needed modernisation of the Greek economy through competition with other EEC members.

However, if Greece were admitted this would mean a fundamental change in the nature of the EEC. The EEC had essentially been composed of rich, developed and geographically contiguous economies of the North-Western European type. Now a comparatively underdeveloped country would join, separated from the nearest EEC member, Italy, by a sea (the Adriatic) and from the others by the entire Balkans. Yet how could anyone deny that it was a Western country, indeed a wellspring – together with ancient Rome – of Western civilisation? Had not the West fought for Greece's liberation from the Ottoman Empire? Had not western allies done so in World War II to free it from Nazi occupation? And had not the Truman doctrine of containment of Soviet communism been drawn at the country's northern border in the 1946–49 civil war?

Was it at this time that the European Economic Community became fully political as well as economic in character? Possibly, for the concerns about EEC finances and the state of the Greek economy felt by several EEC members (especially in Northern Europe) as well as the Commission (which indeed suggested a pre-accession transition of unspecified duration) were soon overshadowed by political considerations of the same kind as those harboured by the Greeks themselves: fear for the future of the newly reconquered Greek democracy; and a wish (strongly supported by the United States) to consolidate Greece's West European and NATO bonds. In brief, the EEC's Council of Ministers overruled the objections raised by the Commission, and membership negotiations were opened in 1976.

Concern for the future of democracy and political stability was paramount also in the consideration of Portuguese and Spanish requests for membership presented the same year (even though there was no requirement in the Rome EEC Treaty that a member would have to be a liberal democracy). The United States weighed in with defence arguments, for Portugal had been a NATO member since the organisation's foundation in 1949 and Spain, although it was not to join NATO's integrated military command until the mid 1980s, was host to important Alliance bases. Binding the Iberian peninsula more strongly to Western Europe politically and economically would also tie it more closely to NATO and hence help Western European defence in the event of a Soviet attack – by offering a larger territory on which, possibly, to retreat and additional ports and supply bases for a counter-offensive.

On the other hand, the economic reservations against having Spain as an EEC member were less strong than in the case of Greece, for Franco had allowed a continuous and 'technocratic' modernisation of the country in his later years. Portugal was also at this time arguably more developed than Greece, so much so that it had been able to join EFTA already in 1960.

Yet the Spain–EEC preferential trade agreement of 1970, like the Portugal–EEC one in 1973 (forming part of a deal between the EEC and EFTA) proved trickier than in the case of Greece. EEC governments, burdened by large budget deficits since the 1973–74 oil crisis, began to feel the pinch in their financial calculations from soaring EEC expenditure, in particular for the CAP. Perhaps Greece could be absorbed, but could Portugal and Spain as well?

The 'southern' European countries – Italy and France – were torn. On the one hand the three newcomers would correct the, in their eyes, excessive northern bias which the EEC had suffered since the 1973 enlargement through Denmark, Ireland and the United Kingdom, especially when it came to CAP support for temperate zone commodities like beef, dairy products and cereals. With the new candidates inside, it would be possible to exert political pressure more effectively for similar support to be given also on behalf of such products as wine, olive oil and fruit.[2] However, with Greece, Portugal and Spain as members, Italy and France would by the same token lose their privileged 'Community preference' position as producers of wine and other Mediterranean products.

The negotiations proved hard and lengthy, and they were further complicated by the prospect of labour migrating to northern members (the free movement of labour being one of the 'four freedoms' under the EEC) and by that of Iberian fishing vessels operating in northern waters under the emerging 'Blue Europe' principle of sharing fish resources communally.

When Greece finally joined the EEC in 1981, and Portugal and Spain followed in 1986, it looked as if the EEC had more or less come of age. Some 340 million people inhabited the Twelve's territory and would presumably give rise to more trade, investment and prosperity. The EEC included all the larger and more influential countries in western Europe. It had become the world's principal commercial power – indeed one political area in the sense that it spoke with one voice under the Common External Tariff Policy in fora like the GATT or in trade negotiations with the USA. It accounted for a fifth of world exports and imports.

However, the EEC's original *raison d'être* – the Franco–German axis which had guided developments in the 1960s and 1970s – had become even less prominent than following the British entry. Even though the larger countries were given preponderance in EEC decisions, they could not always prevail when a 'vital interest' of a small country was invoked, or when small countries banded together, sometimes even gaining the support of a larger one. Nor could any *ménage à trois* among the French, the Germans and the British – which had by now often become a *ménage à cinq* with Italy and Spain asserting themselves more strongly – be taken for granted.

Reaching decisions had become trickier with twelve around the table instead of nine (which had in turn been more difficult than with six). A much wider range of national and political interests had to be reconciled, underscored by the growing heterogeneity of members. However, with money always available to smooth over differences – the EEC could since the early 1970s rely on an annual budgetary mechanism, sometimes referred to as 'own resources', instead of national contributions *à la* United Nations – the institution could often advance by offering financial compensation to recalcitrant partners.

Thus, at about this time, if not earlier, began a process whereby decisions became less 'pure', less uniform and more political. The 'common market' had eliminated all tariffs and many non-tariff barriers to trade, leading to greater competition among countries, regions and companies, and to a situation where some of them were losing out. It seemed only natural that they should in some way be compensated through various forms of EEC financial support. This contributed, however, to the development of a mentality of assistance-seeking rather than relying on one's own national resources – not only on the part of the poorer countries but also on the part of 'special interests' who felt their position threatened, whether it be sugar beet growers, cattle raisers or shipyard owners. Today, as the EU is trying to rein in its expenditure in a much harsher economic climate, these sentiments come out all the stronger in the streets and in the meeting rooms.

Turning momentarily from Europe to the world in general, the Carter presidency in the United States from 1976 to 1980 had a strong ideological component – not so much anti-communist or anti-Soviet as emphasising human rights and democracy. Coming on the heels of the 1975 Helsinki Act, this message had a strong appeal in Central and Eastern Europe, and even in the Soviet Union. In the 1980s, the combination of human rights/democracy and nationalist sentiments were proving more potent a potion than the Molotov cocktails that had been thrown in Budapest in 1956.

East–West: a new cold war?

The economic and social backwardness of the Soviet Union and its dependent countries as a result of the inherent shortcomings of communism was becoming apparent amongst both their youth and their elite. Why, they increasingly asked themselves, did economic conditions not improve, when those in the West seemed to do so constantly? Why could one not speak freely, criticise one's government or read what one wished? Why did the Soviet Union keep Central and Eastern Europe under semi-colonial rule when it criticised Western powers for colonialism or, after decolonisation, neocolonialism?

The Soviet invasion of Afghanistan in December 1979 was to be the last expression of the Brezhnev doctrine – i.e. that Soviet domination had to be maintained at all costs wherever it had been established – and it marked the beginning of the end of the Soviet Empire and the Soviet Union itself. Certain Western commentators saw the invasion as a sign of the Soviet Union's desire to push southwards, to the oil of the Middle East and to the warm seas, just as they warned of a Soviet naval build-up in South-East Asia and the Indian Ocean. Politically such an interpretation served the interests of political hawks in the West who sought larger defence budgets, not least in the Reagan administration. However, there are indications from the crucial discussions in the Kremlin in the autumn of 1979 that the Soviet Politburo was very much divided on whether to invade or not, and that there was little strategic reasoning behind the final decision to go ahead. It was a process perhaps not too dissimilar from the one by which the United States had sunk into the Vietnam morass some twenty years earlier.

The Afghanistan adventure – which was to take the lives of some 15,000 Russian soldiers and would end in February 1989 with the withdrawal of the last Soviet troops – was indeed the Vietnam of the Soviet Union. The terrain was different – no jungles – but there were inhospitable mountains for the rebels to hide in and ambush from, and the insurgents, though internally divided, were fighting for their Muslim faith and their country's liberation from the 'infidels'.

The West, in particular the United States, supplied weapons (especially highly effective anti-aircraft missiles) and financed bases in neighbouring Pakistan – just as the Soviet Union and China had supported North Vietnam a decade earlier.[3] In brief, the Russians, like the Americans in Vietnam, gravely underestimated the force of nationalism, and exaggerated the importance of ideology. The corrosion of morale was not confined to the Soviet armed forces. It spread to the Soviet people with every body bag sent home. The boycott of the Moscow Olympics in 1980 by many countries brought home the message of the country's international isolation even more clearly.

When a young electrician at a Gdansk (Poland) shipyard, Lech Walesa, helped form an independent trade union, *Solidarnosc*, he would set in motion events that would ultimately lead to the liberation of the whole of Central and Eastern Europe. *Solidarnosc*'s demands were first for better pay in the face of food and other shortages, but soon included demands for true national independence and an end to communism.

This development was seen as highly worrying by the Soviet Union leadership, for at stake was the main corridor for the defence of East Germany and a principal buffer against any threat from the West. In addition, unless suppressed it could provide the impetus for a general popular uprising in the satellite countries. However, the Soviet leadership, marked by the Afghanistan experience, showed less inclination to have Warsaw Pact troops intervene in Poland in 'socialist solidarity' than they had done in earlier decades in Hungary and Czechoslovakia. New archival evidence even indicates that Moscow might have been ready to 'lose' Poland in recognition of Russia's growing weaknesses and dependency on good relations with the West under 'détente'.[4]

The clampdown by General Jaruzelski in December 1981 – he would later, somewhat disingenuously, claim it was the only way to save Poland from a Soviet intervention – did not solve anything. The imposition of martial law only enhanced the inertia in Poland and elsewhere in the region, adding fear to the general discontent of the population. (However, it may have facilitated the eventual peaceful break-up of the Soviet Empire by giving it a few years' extra time to realise the extent of its weaknesses and need of reform.[5])

The situation in the Soviet Union was becoming precarious. Economically weakened by communism, it added to its economic woes not only by continuing to engage its armed forces in Afghanistan but more generally by overspending on its military. Whole secret cities were built in the Urals and Siberia for military purposes alone. Nuclear weapons were produced en masse, as were rockets to deliver them, as well as tanks and ships.

To its south, the Soviet Union faced religious fundamentalism in Iran, which could well spread to the Soviet republics in central Asia. In the west, there was a broadly prosperous Western Europe. To the south-east there was an equally wealthy Japan, with which the Soviet Union had a territorial dispute over the Kurile Islands (taken by the Soviet Union in the last days of World War II). Next to Japan was China, which was overcoming the wounds of the Cultural Revolution in the 1970s and which was now developing both economically and militarily. Finally, the Soviet Union seemed headed for a costly arms race, especially in missiles, with the United States, as President Carter abandoned efforts to have the US Senate ratify the SALT II (Strategic Arms Limitations Treaty), which built on the earlier SALT I.[6]

In this situation the Soviet leadership presumably decided to play what was to be its last card: the effort to achieve the political subjugation of Western Europe and its 'decoupling' from the United States and Canada. The means to this end was the stationing on a large scale, as from the early 1980s, of intermediate-range (as opposed to intercontinental) ballistic missiles (termed SS–20s) deep in Soviet territory, capable of hitting Western Europe (but not North America), and the deployment of a new powerful nuclear bomber aircraft, referred to in the West as the 'Backfire'.

The Soviet leadership was counting on the fear of the West Europeans of having a nuclear confrontation confined to Europe alone, and on the growth in size and influence of the already strong anti-nuclear peace movements, often calling for unilateral nuclear disarmament. Pressure on the West European governments would mount, so the Soviet leaders thought, to have the Americans reduce their short-range, tactical 'battlefield' nuclear weapons (and possibly their conventional forces as well), and thereby to soften West European resolve in the political field. This would limit the security risk to the Soviets opened up by the *Solidarnosc* movement in the 'strategic corridor' of Poland, and generally widen Soviet policy options in its relations with Western Europe and the West as a whole. It would also counter the threat to Soviet territory posed by British and French medium-range nuclear weapons, which were less significant than the US ones but nevertheless awesome.

It is not certain that Soviet aims were ultimately military, especially when considering the country's stake in the Helsinki Act's provisions on the inviolability of borders, its weak geopolitical position, the dubious loyalty of its Warsaw Pact partners if it ever came to war, and the questionable quality of its own troops and conventional arms. It is equally likely that military muscle was being flexed for the sake of political gains.

The United States reacted swiftly to the Soviet move by offering to fill the gap in its NATO partners' European nuclear deterrent, through the construction and deployment of medium-range missiles aimed at the Soviet Union heartland (i.e. supplementing the short-range, Europe-based battlefield missiles and the US-based intercontinental ones). The question was only whether the Europeans would accept the offer.

For five years, from 1979 to 1984, the outcome was uncertain, as the Soviet Union mixed threats, promises and channelled considerable money to numerous peace movements in Western Europe that opposed the US response. However, it had underestimated both the US resolve not to abandon its NATO commitments and the alliance's capacity to react. France's President, François Mitterrand, even went to the German Bundestag in 1983, fervently pleading with it to accept the US offer, an act which is generally recognised to have contributed to swinging the balance at a crucial moment.[7]

In the end, by 1985, over 100 medium-range missiles of the ballistic Pershing type and over 400 terrain-hugging cruise missiles had been deployed in the several NATO countries that accepted stationing – sometimes, as in Germany, over considerable domestic opposition. (A US offer of neutron-bomb missiles, which have the characteristic of killing people through radiation while leaving buildings relatively undamaged, was rejected on ethical grounds, but also because they were perceived by many as lowering the 'nuclear threshold'.)

At the same time, NATO offered the Soviet Union negotiations for a return to the *status quo ante*, i.e. the dismantling of *all* intermediate-range missiles in Europe – Pershings, cruise and SS–20s – that is, a return to the situation before Soviet missiles were installed. This so-called 'two-track' decision by NATO held up a stick and a carrot, satisfying both 'hawks' and 'doves' in the West and struck a cord with European populations (including parts of the peace movement) as being reasonable. In due course, by 1987, the two-track strategy was to prove successful, in that both sides agreed on the complete dismantling of their medium-range missiles under verified conditions – a process that would be completed over the next few years and that would also be accompanied by agreements on the reduction of conventional forces in Europe and of strategic missiles.

What might have happened had the Soviet design been successful? It could indeed have led to at least a degree of North American 'decoupling' from Western Europe. Why, the Americans might have argued, should we defend NATO partners who so easily succumb to pressure? Do they really want to defend themselves? Isolationist feelings were not pronounced in the United States at this time, not least because the Pacific Rim with South-East Asia at its centre was still economically insignificant in comparison with Western Europe. But they might nevertheless have taken hold.

There would probably, at least initially, have been a mobilisation of defence efforts among the West Europeans, in particular efforts to revive a Western European Union that over the years had become lethargic.

However, it is also likely that there would have been splits within the WEU, with the British especially, but also with other more Atlanticist-oriented countries such as West Germany, Denmark, Norway and the Netherlands trying to avoid having any strengthening of the Western European Union take place to the detriment of NATO. For France it could have been the opportunity for a stronger Western European defence, which was more independent of North America and under more of a French leadership. However, was France ready for this, especially if it meant the United Kingdom and Germany drifting out into the Atlantic? And did France really wish to see the US disengage from Europe? Presumably not, since President Mitterrand went to Bonn to plead the opposite course.

Thus the Soviet strategy, had it worked, could have led to serious disputes within NATO, the WEU and within the European Community, which latter would have been called upon to take up more of a political and security role to match that of the WEU in defence. Soviet control over Central and Eastern Europe could have continued beyond 1989.

But the Soviet Union had run out of means. As Pershing and cruise missiles were being deployed, Western Europe, and the Atlantic Alliance seemed to have overcome their divisions. Economically the Soviet Empire had long ago stopped growing, losing ground to all the neighbouring regions as well as popular support at home. Fewer and fewer intellectuals in Western Europe and elsewhere were seduced by the Soviet system.

In addition, in 1980 Ronald Reagan had been elected President of the United States on a platform built on the need to fight the 'evil empire' (the term was not used until some time later) through vastly increased military spending, including a plan – later abandoned (but revived in 2002 under President George W. Bush) – to counter the Soviet nuclear threat through a Star Wars system of interception of incoming enemy missiles. It was clear that the Soviet Union, in spite of its own efforts to build a 'Star Wars' defence, could not match the US defence build-up, which was itself made possible largely through government borrowing, thus exacerbating the decline of the Soviets.

Upon the death of the Dalai Lama, the high priests of Lhasa start a search for his successor – a boy with a birthmark behind his right ear and living in a house by a fork in a river below a cherry tree with an owl's nest. In a similar way the Soviet establishment must have searched for the right man to succeed the ailing Chernenko. (Chernenko, a conservative, had succeeded the more, but not sufficiently, reform-minded Andropov in 1984.) Find us a man, the Politburo and the military might well have said upon Chernenko's death in 1985, who can reform the

Soviet Union and still preserve it; someone who can make the centrally planned economy grow and develop while maintaining state ownership; someone who can start a democratic dialogue in society without jeopardising the leading role of the communist party (and the Politburo itself).

Mikhail Gorbachev, already a member of the Politburo, was about the only person, it was thought, who might be able to do all this. But even for him, this was ultimately to prove to be one miracle too many.

The call for reform was as likely to have come from the military as from the Communist Party. After all, the party formed an elite in Soviet society and had an intrinsic interest in preserving its own privileges. Nor would it be particularly prone to noticing the system's shortcomings from its ivory tower. The military, on the other hand, saw how the quality of its equipment had declined due to the drop in overall quality in production, the latter largely owing to dwindling overall investment, resources and sagging morale among workers. And we have already referred to the perceived threats from the rising powers all around the Soviet Union. The only way to defend the country, the military must have argued, lay in civilian reform.[8]

Overcoming euro-pessimism: the 1992 Internal Market project

The Soviet Union was not, however, the only power searching for new solutions. To the West, the European Economic Community of the Ten (through Greece's adhesion in 1981) at the beginning of the decade was hit by 'euro-pessimism' which in turn, it was argued, was caused by the severe 'euro-sclerosis' afflicting its economy. The 1979 oil crisis (with prices rising from some $12 to over $40) had dealt Western Europe a second blow, especially since the region had barely recovered from the crisis of the mid-1970s. Yet the United States under the stewardship of Ronald Reagan continued to grow much faster and attract more investment than the EEC area, while Japan's rise seemed unstoppable. What was the EEC doing wrong?

There were three main reasons for the EEC's relative decline. Firstly, most of the rigidities that had crept in as a result of the building of the welfare state in the 1960s and early 1970s – and which had been 'papered over' through deficit spending in the years after the 1973 oil crisis – were still there, and they had to compete not only with the laissez-faire US economy under Reagan, but also against the virtually impenetrable protectionist walls of Japan and of other rising economies in South-East Asia, such as Hong Kong, Taiwan and South Korea. These latter countries now started to flood Western Europe with their exports.

Secondly, trade among the EEC countries (as with the EFTA countries, with which a wide-ranging co-operation agreement had been concluded in 1984 following the free-trade agreement of 1972) had not grown as quickly as expected, and had failed to turn the EEC area into the world economic powerhouse it had been expected to become following a quarter-century of integration. Although intra-EC tariffs had disappeared by the late 1960s, non-tariff obstacles – red tape, safety regulations, technical specifications and the like – turned out to be much more difficult to eradicate, and indeed had a tendency to appear after the introduction of (some would say in reaction to) free trade. The EC's supposedly 'common market' had not been fully realised and was often fragmented, rendering it the more vulnerable to increasingly fierce overseas competition. Cartels had formed both within countries and among them, restricting competition and driving up prices.

In addition, many EEC countries stood by their pet industries, which were often in government hands or under government control. Indeed, the struggle against such practices had been rendered more difficult through the adhesion of comparatively less developed Greece, Portugal and Spain.

In brief, the EEC was perceived as having lost much of its momentum, not least because the far-flung plans to pursue a common foreign policy had been thrown to the winds following the failure to forge a common energy policy after the 1973 and 1979 oil crises. The EEC was also increasingly bedevilled by internal conflicts over that most mundane of issues: money. Poorer EEC members were expecting more, received more and, understandably enough, came to regard this state of affairs as the natural one – especially when it came to agriculture and regional support. Richer members, on the other hand, were net contributors to the EEC budget, and while some, such as Germany, did not yet object, others, in particular the United Kingdom, began to complain that their contributions were excessive.

The main reason for the 'problem of the UK budget' as it came to be known, was that British farmers were (and still are) far fewer than in most other EC countries. The country had, ever since the nineteenth century, relied largely on imports from the rest of the world, especially the Empire and then the Commonwealth. Since the bulk of Common Agricultural Policy funds was being paid according to the volume of agricultural production, and to some extent (in the case of structural aid) by the number of farmers, the UK received less.

In addition, imports from non-EEC countries were subjected to levies that were earmarked, not for the UK, but for the EEC. In spite of a 'correction mechanism' introduced already in the 1970s to compensate the UK, its excess payment in 1979 still amounted to well over £1 billion. Only several years later – and after much anti-British sentiment in other EC countries and much anti-EC rhetoric in the UK – could a compromise be found (namely, paying the UK more regional aid money) which satisfied all parties. However, it highlighted one EEC weakness: how one bureaucratic procedure (the CAP) led to unforeseen consequences, which had to be corrected through further bureaucratic corrections.

European Community summits in the early to mid–1980s – held at the level of heads of government, and, in the case of France, heads of state *and* government – in this situation started to call for the 'completion of the EEC's Internal Market'.[9] The EC Commission – at the origin of this initiative through its new and dynamic President Jacques Delors (since 1984) and Commissioner Lord Cockfield – followed up this call with a White Paper entitled *Completing the Internal Market*, which was presented at an EC summit in Milan in June 1985. It led to the Single European Act (SEA), adopted in 1986, which entered into force in 1987.

The Single European Act is a complicated treaty (although less so than its successor, the 1992 Maastricht Treaty on European Union). The most important parts are not those by which the competencies of, and interplay among, the EC's organs were being modified.[10] Rather, it was this one article, 8.A, which was incorporated so as to amend the founding EEC Rome Treaty: 'The Community shall adopt measures with the aim of progressively establishing the internal market over a period expiring on 31 December 1992 ... The internal market shall comprise an area without internal frontiers, in which the free movement of goods, persons, services and capital is ensured in accordance with the provisions of this [the EEC] Treaty'.

For the realisation of the SEA, the EC's member states came to rely mainly on the Commission's White Paper, and the project became known popularly as the '1992 project'. The White Paper sought to give new impetus to a basic treaty objective which had advanced far too hesitantly and, indeed, in some respects, had steered off course. It specified three sorts of barriers that needed to be removed if a true common market were to be realised: physical, technical and fiscal. In the Single European Act these were covered by four main 'pillars'. The first pillar was the guarantee of free movement of goods, persons, services and capital between the member states. The second pillar dealt with the approximation, or harmonisation, of legal provisions in the member states which directly affected the establishment or functioning of the common market. It included the elimination of non-tariff, non-quantitative barriers.

Competition policy formed the third pillar. It aimed to eliminate cartels, monopolies, state subsidies considered excessive or as negatively affecting EC trade, and mergers having the same effect. The fourth pillar was the Common Customs Tariff (CCT) or the Common External Tariff (CET). Since the EC was a customs union, it had to have all member states observe the same conditions for imports from non-EC countries.

The '1992 project' may not have led to all that had been hoped for at the time, but it energised a number of audiences near and far: company managers, for example. Those within the EC thought they had to jockey themselves into stronger positions for the 'post-1992' period through mergers of all kinds, in order to withstand the supposedly fiercer competition that would result. Those outside the EC area – EFTA countries, North America, Japan and the 'emerging economies' – thought they had at all costs to be inside lest they be excluded from a suddenly closed 'Fortress Europe'. Thus, '1992' had a cathartic effect.

The 'Fortress Europe' fear was of course unfounded, not only given the EC's obligation to respect GATT principles but also because of the presence of many multinationals in an increasingly interdependent world economy. Yet the anxiety was widespread, sometimes leading to ill thought-out and overly expensive mergers, takeovers or green-field ventures.

Another effect was in a region seemingly not involved, namely the Central and Eastern European countries under Soviet domination. As these countries were already far behind in economic development as a result of communism, the reaction among intellectuals and government officials was one of near panic. The '1992 project' formed a major impetus to political, and later economic, reform in several of the countries concerned – including, of course, the Baltic countries and hence influenced the eventual break-up of the Soviet Union itself.

The '1992 project' was a psychological masterpiece and almost everybody in Europe became infatuated with it.[11] Suddenly there was a concrete deadline, within which concrete goals had to be reached. National bureaucrats worked hard with their EC counterparts to shape some 300 measures – usually in the form of directives – to enable the Internal Market to be completed. A 'new approach' was even adopted as regards harmonisation, whereby countries could choose different standards and specifications and yet have to accept products from other EC members, provided the latter met certain essential requirements. This sped up the work of removing non-tariff barriers considerably.

The enthusiasm over '1992' is somewhat difficult to explain, for '1992' was (and still is, for it has yet to be fully realised) a business project aiming to open national markets to competition from other EC countries. Workers employed in less efficient companies, which up until then might have been sheltered by more or less visible intra-EC trade barriers, would now risk falling by the wayside, leading, at least temporarily, to more unemployment. Furthermore, there were hardly any social provisions in the European Single Act, a politically embarrassing fact that was eventually to be remedied in the Maastricht Treaty (1993). In sum, '1992' was a rather cold-hearted project, with precious little in it in the way of federalism and supranationalism. This latter fact probably explains why even an initially sceptical United Kingdom under a Tory government went along with it so enthusiastically.[12]

This was also the golden era of the 'yuppies', Europe-style. With stock markets and property prices booming as a result of the general optimism, everybody wanted a piece of the pie. Ronald Reagan's laissez-faire policy in the United States, with Margaret Thatcher adopting similar policies in the United Kingdom, left no doubt that capitalism was the answer and communism was ready to be thrown, as President Reagan put it, on the 'trash heap of history'.

Unemployment in Western Europe stopped rising and even declined a little, though few noticed that jobs in the private sector showed only modest net gains as it started to 'downsize' personnel, or that the public sector was the one that really grew. Even fewer noticed that little was done domestically in the EC, or EFTA, countries to tackle what the OECD was already labelling as 'structural adjustment', that is, a fundamental liberalisation of national economic life making it more internationally competitive.

Furthermore, few noticed that the world economy was starting to change fundamentally, away from the Atlantic seaboard – eastern North America and Western Europe – towards a host of emerging economies in South-East Asia and Latin America, which were dynamic, with little or no social welfare, and with drastically lower labour costs.

In 1986 the world community began a new round of trade liberalisation talks under the auspices of the GATT and known as the Uruguay Round. As a result primarily of US prodding, the Round took on not only hitherto 'taboo' issues such as agriculture and textiles (so far heavily protected in most of Western Europe), but also attempted liberalisation in new areas like services, intellectual property, telecommunications and maritime transport. Liberalisation was coupled with the breakthrough of the high-capacity personal computer; satellite link-ups permitting larger and larger volumes of data to be transmitted anywhere at ever lower cost; and more and more economical means of transport. Together these developments had eventually to spell trouble for a high-wage, high-tax, high-welfare region such as Western Europe. But few saw it coming.

Western Europe marched on, with the European Community in the lead, heading for that great day of 1 January 1993 when the Internal Market would be 'completed'. Governments in EFTA countries like Norway, Sweden, Finland and Austria were becoming fidgety, frightened of being left out in the cold on the wrong side of the lowered portcullis of a 'Fortress Europe'. However, with the Soviet Union still intact, the room for manoeuvre of at least Finland and Austria was limited. Over the next few years these countries would try to be within the 'Fortress' as far as trading regulations were concerned, while they would attempt to stay outside it in matters affecting national sovereignty, foreign security policies, the EC budget and agriculture.

For EC members, however, foreign policy co-operation was again attempted. The EC had to show that the label 'economic giant, political dwarf' was unmerited. Thus, the 1986 Single European Act formally recognised European political co-operation as one of the twin pillars of European unity, together with the European Communities (EEC, ECSE and Euratom). It declared that the high contracting parties would endeavour jointly to formulate and implement a European foreign policy, with the European Council providing regular guidance.

This seemed entirely credible. Pressure, though weaker than before, still came from the Soviet Union in the East, and that country still had troops in Afghanistan, not to speak of Poland, the German Democratic Republic and several other countries in the region. The Yugoslav tragedy still lay some three years ahead, and few of those who looked at that country could imagine that ethnic hostility, dormant since World War II, could again rent asunder what forty years of economic and political integration under Tito and his successors had achieved. Indeed, for the European Community itself it seemed unthinkable that political integration would not follow naturally from the '1992 project' of a completed Internal Market.

Another natural concomitant to the '1992' Internal Market seemed to be a single currency, or at least close currency co-ordination within the European Monetary System (EMS), set up in 1979. Indeed, a depreciation of the currency of EC country A vis-à-vis EC country B of, say 10 per cent, would have the effect of a 10 per cent tariff for B and a 10 per cent export subsidy for A. There was a widespread fear that less scrupulous member states might resort to 'competitive devaluations'.

It is useful here to look briefly at monetary co-operation within the EC. As the preceding chapter described, the first EMU attempt in the early 1970s collapsed rapidly because of insufficient commitment to convergence.

In 1977 the then President of the EC Commission, Roy Jenkins, again took up the idea. However, the European Council would only agree to a less grandiose scheme. Conceived principally by German Chancellor Helmut Schmidt and French President Valéry Giscard d'Estaing in 1978, the aim was not a common currency or even immutable exchange rates, but instead a zone of relative monetary stability in Europe.

There were several reasons for both the ambition and its being modest in scope. The system of floating exchange rates that had replaced the fixed rates of Bretton Woods made trade both with the United States and within Europe less predictable. Business leaders complained that they could not give companies a full European dimension because the value of imports and exports could not be forecast with any certainty. In addition, when the dollar weakened, capital was moved to European currencies, overwhelmingly into the Deutschmark rather than other less reliable currencies, causing further imbalances.

The European Monetary System of 1979 was based on the European Currency Unit (ECU). The ECU served not only as a denominator of currency transactions (like its more rudimentary predecessors the Unit of Account of the 1960s and the European Unit of Account) but also as the central feature of the EMS. It was a 'cocktail' of the national currencies of the participating countries, with the Deutschmark making up about a third of the value, the French franc about a fifth and a small currency like the Danish krona about 3 per cent. The different currencies would not be allowed to fluctuate more than ±2.25 per cent against each other and against the ECU (±6 per cent in the case of Italy), and if they came close to that floor or ceiling, national central banks would prop up a weakened currency by buying it up, or weaken a currency that was too strong by selling it.

The EMS suffered difficulties similar to the Exchange Rate Mechanism. The United Kingdom did not join, and neither did Greece nor the new EC members (as from 1986) Portugal and Spain. Between 1979 and 1987 the EMS collapsed no less than eleven times (the collapses were euphemistically termed 'realignments'), either through revaluations of the stronger currencies (mainly the Deutschmark and the Dutch guilder) or devaluations of the weaker ones (mainly the Italian lira, but sometimes also the French franc and the Irish punt). One reason were the different rates of inflation in the participating countries, largely reflecting different standards of economic performance and the lack of what under Maastricht would be called 'convergence' of national economies. In sum, speculators had a field day during this period, whilst central banks became poorer and governments more humbled.

With the '1992' Internal Market in place, EC member states agreed, this state of affairs could not continue. In consequence, the 1986 Single European Act, though not containing any blueprint for a single currency project (this would come in 1992 with the Maastricht Treaty), nevertheless added an Article 102A, under a section headed 'Co-operation in Economic and Monetary Policy (Economic and Monetary Union)', calling for measures to ensure the convergence of economic and monetary policy.

Collapse in the East

The Soviet Empire continued to crumble. Gorbachev, after becoming the leader of the Soviet Union in 1985, set in motion changes that at first seemed to satisfy all domestic camps. Central planning was modestly reduced, while certain forms of private initiative – shops, services, private plots of farmers on collective farms – were tolerated and even encouraged. It was becoming easier to breathe both in the Soviet Union and in the countries of Central and Eastern Europe dominated by it. Citizens were able to question the political system privately and even in the media. Gorbachev was openly searching for ways to withdraw from the Afghanistan imbroglio, meeting the wishes of both a bleeding Soviet military and the families of soldiers.

But the process was impossible to stop, like a river following its course towards the sea – a flow of spiritual, intellectual, national and material frustration seeking satisfaction at long last. In October 1989 Gorbachev went to East Berlin to attend the fortieth anniversary of the German Democratic Republic. The East German leader, Erich Honecker, had hoped that Gorbachev would rein in the people, and the reformist members of the East German Politburo. Instead, Gorbachev effectively undermined Honecker by telling the leadership to change while there was still time, and by engaging in spontaneous street conversations with demonstrators calling for reform.[13]

Beamed by West German television that same night into East Germany, these exchanges helped sealed the fate of communism and Soviet control over events in that country, and in Central and Eastern Europe as a whole. If the leader of the Soviet Union had spoken of the need for democracy, human rights and economic reform, then how could a Honecker – and after him a Krenz or a Modrow – resist?

In the summer of 1989 Gorbachev went to speak before a European assembly. He chose not the twelve-nation European Community's European Parliament, but rather the Parliamentary Assembly of the Council of Europe, which had been in existence since 1949 and which had pursued a more prudent, intergovernmental, agenda than the European Community, seeking only 'greater unity' among sovereign member countries. (In other words, 'intergovernmentalism' and 'interparliamentarianism' instead of 'supranationalism'.)

The Council of Europe turned out to be the 'hidden card' of Western Europe in accelerating the liberation of Central and Eastern Europe. Countries joining would not feel threatened in their new-found sovereignty, since 'supranationalism' (except via conventions) was beyond the Council of Europe's remit. Quite to the contrary, their flags would be hoisted alongside those of all other Council of Europe members, signifying the official recognition of their statehood by as many countries and a place in the 'European family'. In addition, the Council of Europe's emphasis on democracy, human rights and the rule of law held out the promise that those values would be more secure – being internationally supported and shared – against any communist backlash. Thus started a long period of expansion for the Council of Europe (from twenty-three member states in 1989 to forty-five in 2003), with the accession of Russia, Ukraine and a host of other countries, large and small.

Gorbachev's speech before a packed hemicycle in Council of Europe's *Palais de l'Europe* in July 1989 was truly memorable, marking a startling departure from an old era to a new:

> Now that the twentieth century is entering a concluding phase and both the post-war period and the cold war are becoming a thing of the past, the Europeans have a truly unique chance – to play a role in building a new world, one that would be worthy of their past, of their economic and spiritual potential ... As far as the 'common European home' is concerned, we regard as a realistic prospect – though not a close one – the emergence of a vast economic space from the Atlantic to the Urals, where eastern and western parts would be strongly interlocked ... Europeans can meet the challenges of the coming century only by pooling their efforts. We are convinced that what they need is one Europe – peaceful and democratic, a Europe that maintains all its diversity and common humanistic ideas, a prosperous Europe that extends its hand to the rest of the world. A Europe that confidently advances into the future.'[14]

Gorbachev oversaw the liberation of Central and Eastern Europe from an unworkable system and – eventually though unwittingly and to his own discomfiture – the dissolution of the country he had been appointed to lead. With such words from him as the leader of the Soviet Union, how could the process be halted?

In the summer of 1989 an unusual number of East Germans 'inexplicably' chose to holiday in Hungary, rather than, say, on the Baltic, at home or in Poland. Large numbers went on to Prague and beleaguered the West German embassy there, seeking visas. Others tried to enter West Germany from Hungary, and were unexpectedly helped by Hungarian border guards who simply cut open the barbed wire along the border. The river broke all dams along its path. Street demonstrations in more and more East German cities followed in the early autumn of that year. The Berlin Wall started to look ridiculous. The East German Politburo hesitated between a clampdown which could have led to civil war and demonstrations which could only lead to the country's disappearance and unification with West Germany.

By October 1989 the pressure was becoming irresistible. A simple misunderstanding of orders led East German border guards to hesitate when, on 9 November 1989, the first East Berliners defied the guns and crossed to the West. As a crane, surrounded by ecstatic crowds on both sides of the Brandenburger Tor, opened a first breach in that monstrosity which had stood since 1961, the Berlin Wall, the whole world watched in disbelief, fascination and tears of joy. The river had reached the sea. Freedom had won. The market economy had triumphed. Western resolve, coupled with offers of co-operation since the Cold War and over the many Berlin crises that had followed, had finally paid off. All those people who had spent most or all of their lives under the Damoclean sword of East–West confrontation, from the Cuban missile crisis onwards, would have a new world to consider as from that night. A world of black and white would soon be one of a more confusing appearance, much more difficult to comprehend, and to master, not least for Europe.

However, in this night of jubilation, 9 November 1989, the Berlin crowd sang: '*So ein Tag, so wunderschön wie heute, So ein Tag, der dürfte nie vergehen!*' ('A wonderful day like today. Such a day should never end!').

Notes

1 Radio address to the American people, 15 January 1953; quoted in Leffler (1992, p. 495).
2 The principle here, as in so much other Community financing, is that of the so-called 'Brussels lunch': 'Since we all share the bill, I shall have lobster!'.
3 The United States would regret its support some twenty years later, when Osama bin Laden, who fought in the war against the Soviets, would be the leader behind the Al Qaeda terrorist attacks against the United States on 11 September 2001. The Mujahiddin resistance against the Soviet occupation of Afghanistan contributed significantly to the radicalisation of this movement in the 1990s and their increasingly hostile attitude to the United States and its allies.

4 For archival support in favour of the thesis that the Soviet Union tried at all costs to avoid intervening militarily in Poland in 1980–81, see Mastny (1998).

5 See Westlake (2000).

6 SALT II was in due course to be superseded by the START I (Strategic Arms Reduction Talks) Treaty, which entered into force in 1994. A START II Treaty was concluded, committing both sides to cutting the number of long-range missiles from 6,000 to around 3,000 on each side by 2007 and banning multiple-warhead land-based missiles. It was ratified by the US Senate, but not by the Russian Duma and therefore did not enter into force. A planned START III Treaty would eliminate another 1,000 warheads on each side by the year 2007. Both START II and START III were made redundant following the signing of the even more far-reaching Treaty of Moscow by President George W. Bush of the United States and President Putin of Russia in 2002. This startling development reflects the speed with which the improvement between the United States and Russia in the early 2000s took place.

7 President Mitterrand's sudden transformation from a comparatively anti-Atlanticist French socialist to an ardent advocate of the stationing of nuclear weapons in the Federal Republic of Germany can be explained by a French fear for France's own security should Germany turn 'neutralist' and US forces be withdrawn from Europe. A stronger Soviet Union would also be in a better position to sow discord between France and its principal ally Germany. See e.g. Alting von Geusau (1992, pp. 95–8).

8 Brown (2000, pp. 6–7), on the other hand, sees Gorbachev as more a fluke of history than a candidate of design either of the Communist Party or the military. He portrays Gorbachev as skilfully concealing his reformist tendencies while moving up the ranks, and even as changing his opinions, in the course of his reign, from those of a 'Communist reformer to [those of] a socialist of an essentially West European social-democratic type' and a 'systemic reformer'. Wherever the truth may lie, Gorbachev's importance in saving world peace and permitting the peaceful dissolution of the Soviet Union will no doubt be duly recognised by posterity.

9 The term 'the EC', or the European Community, instead of the European Communities (The European Economic Community, the European Coal and Steel Community and Euratom), began to gain hold in the 1980s, especially as the use of a plural for European unification seemed counterproductive for that purpose and was confusing to many people. As from the Treaty on European Union in the early 1990s, the European Union, or the EU, became the commonly used label when talking about the institution as a whole, even though the various Communities continued to exist and to be named as such in expert language.

10 These included the official status being given to the European Council; qualified majority within the Council of Ministers replacing the unanimity

rule in internal market legislation; and the rebaptising of the organisation as such to the European Communities (incorporating the European Coal and Steel Community, the European Economic Community and Euratom).

11 The infatuation with the '1992 project' extended into the world of pop music. The well-known British pop group The Kinks in 1990 had a hit with a song called 'Down All the Days till 1992'. It included passages such as these:

The future waits for me and you
Down all the days till 1992.

Here is hope for all the people
And generations yet to come
And the future's bright tomorrow
Illuminated by the morning sun.

Here's for all the working people
And the ordinary man
For assembly workers in the factories
For farmers toiling on the land.

Down all the days till 1992
All nations will unite as one
A new horizon clears the view.

(Quote reproduced by permission of the composer and lyricist, Ray Davies.)

12 By 2002, a decade after the '1992 project' was launched, much had been done to realise the Internal Market, but much also remained to be done. Some countries – such as Greece, Italy and France – lagged behind in implementing certain of the close to 300 directives constituting the Internal Market. Prices of cars were still much too different in different countries due to various national taxes. Money transfers between EU countries were more expensive than those inside each. Public procurement still favoured domestic companies. Important service sectors, such as electricity, gas and the mail system were being liberalised only slowly.

13 Fowkes (1997, p. ix) sums up Gorbachev's quandary in these words: 'For whatever reason, he decided to consult the Soviet population, which involved allowing the people to speak freely. This included the non-Russians. His reforms, moderate though they were, allowed the accumulated grievances and resentments to break through; national elites or segments of them either articulated national demands or were swept aside by more radical forces. The accelerating process of economic collapse after 1989 led more and more people to see their salvation outside the Soviet system. Bits of the 'exploding Soviet galaxy' began to fly off in all directions. They did not, in the sequel, fly very far, but far enough certainly to make it impossible for Gorbachev to realise his dream of a remodelled Soviet Union.' A 'Tocqueville effect', referred to in the opening quote in Chapter 5, may also have been at play, as 'non-negotiable' demands were progressively abandoned. Thus, the demands for 'continuation of Communist Party supremacy' turned into multi-party

elections; the 'immutability of the Berlin Wall' into the latter's demise; the 'permanent reality of the two German States' into a united Germany; and the 'eternal bonds of the Warsaw Pact' into its dissolution. To the surprise and relief of the world, the Soviet citizenry and the elites and populations of the countries in Central and Eastern Europe, the Red Army packed up and went home.

14 *Official Report of the 41st Ordinary Session of the Parliamentary Assembly of the Council of Europe*, Eighth Sitting, 6 July 1989, pp. 197–205.

5

1989–92: Yalta farewell; how new a world?

Only consummate statecraft can enable a king to save his throne, when after a long spell of oppressive rule he sets to improving the lot of his subjects. Patiently endured so long as to seem beyond redress, a grievance comes to appear intolerable once the possibility of removing it crosses men's minds. For the mere fact that certain abuses have been remedied draws attention to the others and they now appear more galling. People may suffer less, but their sensibility is exacerbated. (Alexis de Tocqueville)[1]

Summary

The fall of the Berlin Wall in November 1989 led, in rapid succession over the next two years, to German unification, Baltic state independence, the dissolution of the Soviet Union and its replacement by Russia and other successor countries, the fall of communist regimes all over Central and Eastern Europe, and the dissolution of the Warsaw Pact. Capitalism, liberalised world trade and new electronics technology seemed to have carried the day.

The West offered massive financial assistance to Central and Eastern Europe, including Russia, and also gave advice on how to go from a planned to a market economy ranging from 'shock therapy' to more gradual reform. Western international organisations – including the EU, the Council of Europe and NATO – followed suit with various co-operation and association agreements. The hope of the countries concerned for a new Marshall Plan was not met, but a new European Bank for Reconstruction and Development was meant to fulfil a similar function.

The European Union in 1993 concluded a European Economic Area (EEA) agreement with various EFTA countries, tying them closer to it in the areas of trade and investment. The EU also agreed, in 1992, on the ambitious Maastricht Treaty on European Union, foreseeing, especially, an Economic and Monetary Union (a single currency) by the end of the decade and a common foreign and security policy.

The disintegration of Yugoslavia beginning in 1990, and the several wars it led to, posed serious challenges to the EU and NATO, apart from signifying a tragedy for the people of the region. A further challenge to the EU came with an unexpected Danish referendum 'no' to the Maastricht Treaty in 1992 and a surprisingly narrow 'oui' in a French referendum soon after. Even as the 1992 Internal Market was entering into force, a new sense of uncertainty settled over the continent.

Exit communism

In a political cartoon of the fall of 1989,[2] Hitler and Stalin are seen bidding one another, and the world, farewell, on a stage where the curtain is coming down and in whose background can be seen a city in ruins and flames. It is hard to imagine a better illustration of the world these two men left behind, an era which was to come to a close only on the night the Berlin Wall came down.

The fall of the Berlin Wall, so heavy in symbolism, came to represent a series of monumental events that were to follow: the disappearance of East Germany and its incorporation into the Federal Republic of Germany on 3 October 1990; the declaration of independence of the Baltic states of Estonia, Latvia and Lithuania in the summer of 1991; the dissolution of the Soviet Union in November 1991 and the country's transformation into thirteen successor republics soon after, the biggest being Russia; the fall of dictatorships across Central and Eastern Europe, most of them disappearing peacefully but some violently such as the Ceausescu regime in Romania in December 1989; and the dissolution of the Warsaw Pact in April 1991.

These events were of historic importance, and the historian can only marvel at their taking place with so little bloodshed. The Soviet Empire was a 'tired' and overstretched empire – politically, militarily, socially, culturally and above all economically, collapsing under its own weight and inertia, not unlike the Roman Empire in the fourth century AD or the Ottoman Empire in the late nineteenth century. People, including the majority of Russians, failed to see the point of it any longer, especially since it seemed to impoverish them only further.

However, the peaceful demise of the Soviet Union was also due to the constantly peaceful posture of the West – that is, democratic Western Europe and the Atlantic Alliance as a whole – during this period, At no point during the events of 1989 to 1991 did the Soviet Union have reason to feel threatened, militarily or politically. On the contrary, the West went out of its way to reassure the Soviets that it wanted to help –

before, during and after the events.

The importance of the existence of what might be called the 'international organisation network' was fully shown during these momentous times. The Conference on Security and Co-operation in Europe, the European Union, the Council of Europe, the World Bank, the International Monetary Fund, the OECD, the United Nations Economic Commission for Europe and the several arms limitations negotiations under way: all in their various ways made contact, issued declarations, voted financial and expert assistance and tried to include rather than exclude.

At no point did NATO take on a threatening posture to try somehow to exploit the weakness of the power which had lain behind its creation. Indeed, why should it, when it had all along been a purely defensive organisation? And how could it, when it was composed of democracies, with peoples who asked for nothing more than an end to the Cold War?

If communist ideology was in agony, nationalism was reawakening, showing that it had only been forced into a decades-long slumber – nearly 40 years for the countries of Central Europe and over seventy years for the nationalities of the Soviet Union. If such relatively abstract notions of forming a new communist human being, a new society and a new world of proletarian brotherhood had ignited passions in the 1920s, now a flag free of any sickle and hammer had the same effect.

Communism as an ideology and an economic doctrine seemed to have reached its nadir. Communist parties previously in power in Central and Eastern Europe were swept away in elections in the early 1990s, and have only been able to make a come-back by shedding most of their communist ideology and remaining as the often only viable and well organised opposition to the new parties in power. Sometimes reformed communist parties have come back to power and continued on the reform path to a more market-oriented economy. Outside Europe, communism survived only in a handful of places such as the Democratic People's Republic of Korea (or North Korea) and Cuba (in somewhat diluted form), and then only through heavy repression of domestic opinion and with the aid of that other ideology, the personality cult.

Has communism disappeared forever? On the one hand, mankind will have learnt from hard-earned experience, at least for some time to come, that the teachings of Marx, especially as distorted by a Lenin or a Stalin, do not produce the desired results when tried in reality, and that they in fact run the overwhelming risk of producing personal oppression and material impoverishment. On the other hand, one has to account for the galvanisation of the minds of much of the world in the first half of the twentieth century, among them the Russian revolutionaries and large parts of the intelligentsia of Western Europe and in much of the then developing world (even though in this latter case it was often more a camouflage for a quest for national liberation). Whatever part of the human psyche, at least in some people, was impassioned by the call of communism could, logically, become impassioned again. That part is the quest for equality – not just of opportunity but also in rewards; and revolt against privileges, nationalism, religion or superstition.[3]

However, a revival of communism in the near or medium term future seems unlikely, not only in Russia but also in China, which embraces capitalism while holding on to a communist one-party state, largely as a means of holding the country together.

Communism's nemeses: capitalism, trade and technology

In the wake of the fall of the Berlin Wall capitalism enjoyed a new honeymoon, and so did democracy. The economic boom in Western Europe carried on into 1990 and much of 1991, spurred and prolonged by Germany's vast spending on the 'new *Länder*' of the former East Germany. Nobody had any doubt that the countries of Central and Eastern Europe would start growing rapidly once democracy had been firmly installed, privatisation of state-owned companies carried out, and trade with the West and other 'transition' countries resumed ('transition' being the term widely used to describe the transformation from a central planning system to a market-oriented economy).

Principally, two things brought down the Soviet Union and Empire as well as world communism: capitalism and world trade, both using the computer chip. Capitalism's contribution was that the shortcomings of communism could only become apparent to people living under either system through communism's unfavourable comparison with the economic success of capitalism. World trade was helpful because capitalism could then use its tested tools of international division of labour – or specialisation – creating greater overall wealth (although not necessarily equally shared) and ever sharper competition, within as well as among countries. The multinational enterprise – a symbol of both division of labour and international competition – could not have developed without capitalism. Nor could it have done so without the open trade system largely based on the universal rules set up under GATT in 1947.

GATT, it will be remembered, was – until as late as 1995 when its main work was handed over to the new WTO – only an agreement (as the name implies), not an institution. As such, it was essentially a 'tit for tat' set-up: 'You give me "most-favoured-nation" treatment, I'll give it to you; you raise tariffs, I'll do the same'. Since the United States was the dominant actor on the world economic scene then, and has remained so with ups and downs to this day, world trade has developed largely as the US has wished it to develop, i.e. in a largely open and non-discriminatory manner. This has been an ideal environment for the growth of multinationals, first predominantly American, then also West European and eventually from most other parts of the world.

The multinationals not only brought foreign direct investment to the far corners of the earth, but also know-how in all fields, from organisation to technology. As the process accelerated, they not only enhanced world trade but they also made any large-scale retreat into protectionism by individual countries more costly in terms of trade disruption and the loss of foreign investment and know-how.

The microchip, for its part, has enhanced competition, which engenders inventions – the need to transmit information as cheaply and effectively as possible. Its use has above all been in the transmission of information over large distances, permitting companies to expand worldwide in a highly intricate web of co-ordination – internally within the organisation and externally with consumers and suppliers. The same holds for researchers and individual users.

Parallel to co-ordination and thereby control, the chip has permitted decentralisation of decision making. Since a company's centre knows better what its far-away subsidiaries are doing – and subsidiaries know more of what headquarters knows – there is more of a give and take between them, and greater possibility for adaptation of products and services to local preferences. Again, this is something a state-owned, centralised economy cannot muster, apart from the fact that it would not feel any real need to innovate, enjoying as it does a monopolistic position in its market (the nation).

Copying the invention of the chip would not have been enough for, say, the Soviet Union, given the continuous rapid product development in computer technology in the market economies – a development which the centrally planned economies simply could not emulate. Indeed, the Soviet authorities in the late 1980s tried to restrict the sale and use of personal computers to stem the freer flow of information (just as China has sought to restrict access to the internet), even though this hurt economic development. The paradox had come full circle: by trying to halt the advent of the information revolution in order to save central planning and the government's monopoly on opinion, the economic system collapsed, demonstrating in no uncertain terms the need for reform.

The microchip rendered possible the explosion in knowledge and the sharing of data that fuelled world economic growth in the 1980s and up to this day. To a large extent, however, this growth passed the communist countries in Central and Eastern Europe by. Unable to harness the chip's potential under the central planning system, these countries increasingly realised that they had to change. The chip made transmission of information – through computers or satellite television – into Central and Eastern Europe all the more easy to achieve, and all the more difficult to resist.

If communism had thus been rendered possible in the early part of the twentieth century by the communication possibilities opened up by the telegraph, the telephone and the radio, it was undermined by further developments in communications technology – television and the personal computer fuelled by the chip. The chip revolution is not finished. It has in fact only just started, with unknown consequences for mankind as a whole.

To stress the importance of the chip in the downfall of the Soviet Union and Empire as well as communism is not in any way to belittle other factors at play. These include the international political system, the foresight – some would say illusions – and the willingness to reform of Gorbachev, the message of Christian humanism beaming out from the Vatican by the first East European Pope – John Paul II – as from 1978, and the shared wish by reformers and conservatives in the Soviet Union and elsewhere in Central and Eastern Europe to avoid civil war. However, the role of the simple chip merits highlighting for its importance is rarely recognised.

The resumption of history: from ideology to nuts and bolts

The disappearance of the Soviet Union and also its hold over other parts of Central and Eastern Europe left a void, both political and mental, in a world that had become used to a notion of two blocs and two ideologies standing against each other. The American historian Francis Fukuyama, in his book *The End of History and the Last Man* published in the early 1990s, talked about an 'end of history', as the exclusive striving for larger market shares and profits – was seen as taking exclusive hold of mankind.[4]

To others, however, it was more as if the train of world history, having been shunted on to the side track of ideology for the better part of the twentieth century, was now returning to its main line of rising and sinking empires, with international co-operation competing against the spectre of national – and nationalist – confrontation. Now the world would no longer have the luxury of debating such arcane ideas as whether the means of production ought to be state-owned or private. Instead, it would be faced with issues of survival such as climate change, environmental deterioration, AIDS, terrorism and the proliferation of nuclear weapons. No longer would war be principally a matter for the two superpowers, of which one no longer existed and whose main successor, Russia, was in a much weakened state. With that bipolar discipline gone, the question of war or peace would become more decentralised, tribal and national. Now the only things keeping humans from war would be their own survival instinct; the international machinery (in the widest sense) they had set up for keeping peace and co-operation dominant over war and conflict; and possibly the interdependence that would come from trade and cross-country investment.

The liberation of Central and Eastern Europe from communism left the region in a sorry state, but not without hope or potential. If it is regrettable that change did not come earlier – say, in the 1970s, if the Prague Spring had been allowed to spread to the whole region – it is as well that it did not come later than it did, by which time the region would have suffered even greater environmental destruction, even more economic backwardness vis-à-vis the surrounding market economies, even more oppression, despair and humiliation, and even greater destruction of 'civil society' – that myriad of independent associations in all walks of life, including business, that form the backbone of any free and thriving society. As the region set about rebuilding that civil society by re-establishing democracy – or, in a case like Russia's, establishing it for the first time – most people, including those in the West, thought that economic reform and renewal would be as easy.

However, building a functioning market economy on the ruins of a collapsed central planning system is much more difficult than establishing or re-establishing formal democracy, itself a difficult task. The expression 'It is easier to turn an aquarium into a fish soup than to turn a fish soup into an aquarium' made the rounds. Today, well over a decade after reform began, many of the countries in the region have made spectacular progress and show higher growth rates and degrees of privatisation of economic life than many countries in Western Europe. This is little less than miraculous and a tribute both to the peoples of these countries and to the international community which assisted in the process.

The differences in the pace of reform, and in its results, were largely due to the particular policies followed by individual governments and their experiences of the past. Generally, countries that followed the 'shock therapy' method – rapid (and fair) privatisation of state-owned industry and agriculture, a check on inflation through sparse money supply and clear legislation for economic life – fared better. Proximity to prosperous Western Europe, favouring Central Europe and the Baltic states in particular, also played a role, as did the extent of time the countries had been under communism (seventy years for the Soviet Union's successor states, some thirty-five years for the other countries in Central and Eastern Europe).

Finally, the existence or non-existence of democracy before World War II, sometimes referred to as the 'democratic tradition' may also have been significant. Democratic tradition is more than just voting to elect a parliament at national, regional or local level, or making sure that elections are fair. It is about the give and take among the many different constituencies that form the electorate. It is about checks and balances among different authorities, and about free and independent media.

Russia is a case in point. The reforms undertaken in the 1990s were on the whole haphazard or existed only on paper. A 'shock therapy' was tried, but it was more shock than therapy. Corruption was widespread, and the vast financial aid given by the West was poorly used or siphoned to 'safe havens' abroad. Democracy had difficulty penetrating into daily life, since 'civil society' had been so utterly destroyed under communism. When the 'bubble economy' burst in August 1998, world financial stability was shaken and Russia left with a largely unreformed economy and massive foreign debt.[5]

The legacy of the communist era weighed heavily upon Central and Eastern Europe, but the region also had advantages. They included an educated workforce – even though it was not familiar with market economy principles, such as its paramount emphasis on efficiency and ever higher productivity – and, importantly, much lower labour costs than in Western Europe.

The labour cost issue is worth highlighting. Rarely if ever in history did two neighbouring regions display such a disparity of wealth between them. Perhaps Spain and Portugal after the gold discoveries in Latin America in the sixteenth and seventeenth centuries showed the same wealth gap vis-à-vis their European neighbours to the north. However, they were feudal, not market, economies. Normally a prosperous region pulls up its neighbours through increased trade, leading over time to increased prosperity overall. However, the Iron Curtain between Eastern and Western Europe – plus the fundamentally opposite economic paths they chose or were compelled to choose – prevented virtually all trade and other economic contacts for decades.

When the Berlin Wall fell, a Europe eagerly seeking co-operation found, on the one side, massive reconstruction needs and pitifully low wages, and on the other a rebuilt society with an elaborate social welfare system and overall high labour costs (including extra-salary costs to employers). Virtually overnight the obstacles to the two sides growing together economically were gone, threatening the work and conditions of some through industries moving to or buying in the East, and offering others the challenges of the market economy but also more and better paid jobs. The full impact of this development would not be felt for some time.

Most Russians were delighted to rediscover Russia as a country in its own right rather than as only one, albeit the main, component of the Soviet Union (although many Russians in the other successor republics were distressed at suddenly finding themselves outside). The formerly dependent countries in Central and Eastern Europe were jubilant over their newly rediscovered freedom and national independence. The East Germans eagerly awaited integration into the Federal Republic, which occurred on 3 October 1990, and in this they were joined by the large majority of West Germans. (The mutual recriminations between 'Ossies' and 'Wessies' would come only later.)

Western Europe – whether EU or non-EU, NATO or neutral – was elated over the liberation of Central and Eastern Europe and the disappearance of the military threat that the Warsaw Pact and the Soviet Union had represented. An 'implosion' of the Soviet Union, possibly leading to an outward 'explosion' had been averted. Now the task would be to help in any way possible: materially with funds, and also with all kinds of advice, from running a country to running a company.

But there was also a certain apprehension. The first worry had to do with the abrupt change to the status quo of European and world bipolarity to which Western Europe, and the rest of the world (in particular the United States), had become used over nearly half a century. Although international politics is driven by the desire of each power to alter the situation in its favour, there is often general unease when the status quo is fundamentally upset.

Suddenly, NATO had no counterweight. The very reason for its foundation had ceased to exist. Operation 'Desert Storm' – in which an international coalition of twenty-eight countries led by the United States and acting under a UN mandate had liberated Kuwait from Iraqi occupation in early 1991 – had not been a NATO affair, even though virtually all its members contributed. Even the European Union – whose integration had largely come about, and had been made possible by, the pressure from the East – had lost part of its significance as that pressure disappeared. At least it would now be more difficult to pursue integration or even unification, for any such undertaking among states requires not only the prospect of intrinsic rewards but also a better protection against an outside threat. Looming world economic hegemony by the United States or Japan over Europe was invoked by some Europeans as the new menace that would justify further integration (for instance toward a common currency). Some cited distant China as the new world threat, but others saw it as a new marketplace.

Another worry was about what would happen with Germany. During the Cold War it had been divided – the western one, the Federal Republic, necessarily turning West. Now it was becoming united with the second biggest slice, the former East Germany. Would its allegiance still be exclusively westward – to the Atlantic Alliance, to Western Europe, and in particular France? Would France and the United Kingdom again have to worry about a German dominance over *Mitteleuropa* and over a Europe where an essential equilibrium had previously existed, in population if not in economic wealth, between the middle-sized powers of the UK, France and Germany (to which one might add Italy and Spain)? All of a sudden, Germany had over eighty million people, not sixty million as before. Furthermore, would Russia be content with its post-Soviet borders? After all, it had millions of ethnic Russians in the 'near abroad' of successor republics, where they were now a minority. Following the independence of the Baltic states, the Kaliningrad enclave (now cut off from the rest of Russian territory) and Saint Petersburg were Russia's only outlets to the western seas.

Western assistance

Any concerns the West may have had over the new geopolitical realities in Central and Eastern Europe did nothing, however, to diminish its resolve to help. Massive bilateral and multilateral aid poured into the region, including Russia, as from 1991. The aim was simultaneously to preserve the newly established democracies by encouraging economic and other reform, to establish trade links, to invest, and more generally to tie the region more closely to Western Europe and to the international economy in general. Virtually the entire set-up of international institutions – the European Community, the Conference on Security and Co-operation in Europe (CSCE) and its successor, the Organisation for Security and Co-operation in Europe (OSCE), the International Monetary Fund, the World Bank, the United Nations Economic Commission for

Europe, the Council of Europe, the newly created (in 1992) European Bank for Reconstruction and Development and others – enthusiastically threw themselves into the job of helping Central and Eastern Europe to get back on to its feet, creating some overlap and confusion in the process, but also some genuine assistance.[6] (For some institutions it even created a new lease of life as their traditional tasks had started to appear less relevant.)

In 1990 NATO had concluded an epoch-making treaty on conventional forces in Europe with the Soviet Union and other Central and East European countries. The Conventional Forces in Europe (CFE) Treaty bound both NATO and the Warsaw Pact to far-reaching cuts in conventional forces, thus removing a further threat to European peace. With the collapse of the Warsaw Pact many of the stipulations of the CFE Treaty were in fact soon more than met, and the agreement lost some of its relevance as many countries in Central and Eastern Europe became de facto western allies.[7]

The security emphases of individual Western European countries varied. For the Scandinavian countries and Finland – all relatively small – it was particularly important to help the equally small Baltic countries to survive as independent states, and turn the Baltic Sea into an area of prosperity and co-operation. In this they were joined by Germany.

Germany for its part was eager to help turn Central and Eastern Europe into a zone of stability rather than instability. Germany between 1989 and 1995 gave over DM100 billion in assistance to Russia and other countries emerging from the former Soviet Union and another DM50 billion to the other countries of Central and Eastern Europe. German unification itself meant a net transfer of some DM880 billion to the new *Länder* between 1991 and 1997. The support continues to this day. Much aid to Eastern Germany and elsewhere was also channelled through the European Community. Other Western European countries large and small contributed both bilaterally and through the international organisations mentioned above.

However, neither the one-to-one exchange rate between the Deutschmark and the East German Mark (rather than the one-to-two rate favoured by many economists) nor the budgetary transfer that followed had their full intended effect. The nationwide German trade unions immediately demanded pay levels in the East that would rapidly approach those in the West (already by this time among the highest in the world). This had the unintended effect of preventing the new *Länder* from using lower labour costs as a tool for development and drove German and foreign direct investment on to countries like Poland and Czechoslovakia.

If official aid to the transition countries was important, of even greater importance were the direct investment flows beginning in 1990, once it was clear that the process of democratisation and economic reform was going to proceed. Such investment went predominantly to countries closest to Western Europe and to those exhibiting the greatest will to reform.

Although the reforms would have to vary according to the circumstances in each country, a number of areas stood out as particularly important: stable and democratic political institutions; an efficient and accountable public administration, including a fair, authoritative and comprehensive legal and judicial system (which was equally fair to foreign investors); privatisation of state-owned enterprises; restructuring of industry; promotion of small and medium-sized enterprises; a modern tax system including efficient tax collection; and a measure of social protection, not least to gain public approval of continued and often painful economic reform.

Many of the countries in Central and Eastern Europe now began to aspire to becoming members of two clubs: NATO for their external security, not least vis-à-vis Russia; and the European Community for their economic development, both in view of funds (e.g. for agriculture and regional development) and in order not to have to remain outside any emerging 'Fortress Europe'.

NATO reacted quickly. In 1992 it created the North Atlantic Cooperation Council as a forum in which NATO and Central and Eastern European countries could discuss issues of common security. It was soon followed (in 1994) by the Partnership for Peace programme, aiming to involve also non-NATO member states in European peacekeeping. Meanwhile, NATO members reduced and reconfigured their armed forces to achieve better peacekeeping and crisis management. US forces in Germany, for example, were down to 35 per cent of their pre-1989 level by the mid-1990s.

The European Community also took speedy action. Association agreements, so-called Europe Agreements, were ultimately concluded with ten countries in the region, all of which would soon apply to become Community members: Bulgaria, the Czech Republic, Estonia, Hungary, Latvia, Lithuania, Poland, Romania, Slovakia and Slovenia. Between 1989 and 1994 alone, over $12 billion was given in special assistance programmes or through the European Investment Bank. Efforts were also made to facilitate market access for Central and Eastern European exports to the Community, and the Community took it upon itself to co-ordinate assistance from Western donors in general (the 'G-24' group).

However, even though the European Community was quick to expand contacts with Central and Eastern Europe, many of its member states did not yet feel ready to let the institution be enlarged. (Cyprus and Malta were also candidates, bringing the waiting list to twelve.) For one thing, how could agricultural expenditure, which already accounted for over 50 per cent of the EC budget, be kept in check if Central and Eastern European countries joined – most of them with fertile (if still underdeveloped) agricultural land? There was in particular great apprehension about the possible effects on the Common Agricultural Policy of Poland's large agrarian economy.

Moreover, how could regional development aid (through the European Regional Development Fund, the European Investment Bank, the Cohesion Fund and the Common Agricultural Policy) already accounting for over 10 per cent of the budget – be afforded, considering that potential new Central and Eastern European members were poorer than most of the current beneficiary regions in the EU? If there were to be no increase in funds, would previous net beneficiaries, such as southern regions and countries, receive less as central/eastern regions were given more?

How would the EC institutional machinery, already bursting at the seams, be able to accommodate four, five, six or more newcomers? And should not the EC first 'deepen' the integration among its existing members before going on to 'widen' membership to others? More particularly, if 'widening' came before 'deepening', would not Germany (this was a chiefly French concern) risk becoming more attached to *Mitteleuropa* than to Western Europe, and to France in particular? Could, perhaps, time be bought to achieve 'deepening' before the eventually inescapable 'widening' took place through arrangements short of membership and by drawing out the accession procedure into the future?

The EC–EFTA European Economic Area

The European Community was already trying the 'other arrangement' tack, by proposing, in 1989, a European Economic Area (EEA) to the six EFTA countries of Austria, Finland, Iceland, Liechtenstein, Norway, Sweden and Switzerland, to come into effect at the beginning of 1993, that is, in parallel with the completion of the EC's Internal Market (the '1992 project'). The EEA would essentially mean an extension of the '1992 project' to the six EFTA countries, without the latters' participation in other aspects of the EC, such as the Common Agricultural Policy. It also meant that the EFTA–EEA partners, as the incomparably weaker side, would be able to make observations but not to participate in the decision making on an equal footing with EC members. The arrangement suited both sides. The EC was relieved of the complications of expansion, while EFTA countries were freed from the political complications of applying, or indeed being granted, membership.[8]

For a country like Switzerland, such a prospect would indeed have been a nightmare, a fact borne out in 1992 when even EEA membership was rejected in a popular referendum. For others as well – Sweden, Finland and Austria – an important question was whether their constitutionally enshrined or otherwise established neutrality would be compatible with an EC membership which, rightly or wrongly, was assumed also to have far-reaching political ramifications.

However, the EEA agreement came with a price tag for the participant EFTA countries. The less wealthy European Community member states called for, and obtained, financial assistance from them in the form of a financial mechanism, one argument being that these EC industries would suffer in the EEA market as a result of stronger EFTA economies joining. One would have thought that, when in the end Switzerland did not join the EEA, this sum would be reduced. Instead, the remaining countries had to fill in the missing contribution. By the time Austria, Finland and Sweden joined in 1995, 110 million ECU had been paid by the EEA–EFTA countries into the financial mechanism (and the payments continue to this day for the three EEA members Iceland, Liechtenstein and Norway).[9]

As the EEA was given more concrete form – some 1,400 EC texts based on over 10,000 pages of EC legislation – it already began to appear obsolete to the governments of EFTA countries, which in the wake of the disappearance of the Soviet Union and the Warsaw Pact started seriously to consider EC membership (afraid of being overtaken by rapid modernisers such as Hungary, for example). Those interested included all except Iceland and Liechtenstein. In the 1991–92 period these governments were all to present applications to join the EC, although, as will be seen, only Austria, Finland and Sweden eventually joined, while Norway and Switzerland stayed outside.

Was the EEA, which eventually came into effect in January 1994, a lot of work for nothing? On the one hand it must be remembered that it originated at a time when EC membership for countries that were later to join was not yet under consideration, given that the collapse of the Soviet Union had not been foreseen. It did give rise to a divisive referendum in Switzerland, although that country later on incorporated virtually the entire EEA framework into its domestic legislation.

On the other hand, the EEA agreement presumably helped those countries that would ultimately join in 1995 – Austria, Finland and Sweden – familiarise themselves with the workings of what had by this time become the European Union. Finally, Iceland, Norway and Liechtenstein (and to some extent Switzerland) would have an EEA agreement tailored to their particular desire to be 'inside' the EC economically, yet 'outside' it politically.

The Treaty on European Union (Maastricht Treaty)

Europe, and in particular the European Community, had an even more important concern than that of smoothing economic relations with EFTA members. The challenge was, since November 1989, how to respond to the political vacuum left by a vanished Berlin Wall and a weakening Soviet hold over Central and Eastern Europe; and, since November 1991, a Soviet Union that had vanished altogether.[10]

Other factors were at work. Many of those involved in European Community decision making were disappointed with a 1986 Single European Act which in their view did not sufficiently advance the process of integration. The '1992 project' was seen as too down-to-earth and in need of a loftier vision to supplement it, including a sorely missing 'social dimension'. Furthermore, how could an internal market function in the long run without a single currency (indeed as envisioned in the Single European Act)? A common currency would make 'competitive devaluations' impossible and eliminate the unpredictability caused by fluctuating exchange rates.

Moreover, the Internal Market had given new prominence to such phenomena as drug trafficking, cross-border crime, international terrorism and immigration, the latter notably from North Africa but also, it could be expected, from a newly opened up Central and Eastern Europe.

At the December 1989 Strasbourg meeting of the EC's European Council, one month after the Berlin Wall came down, the decision was taken to set up two Intergovernmental Conferences (IGCs) – one on political union and another on economic and monetary union. (The IGC on the EMU was convened against the wishes of the United Kingdom government.) These two IGCs were formally launched in Rome a year later, and were able to present their results after an additional year, in December 1991. Signature by all the Twelve of the new treaty resulting from these Intergovernmental Conferences – called the Treaty on European Union – took place in the Dutch city of Maastricht in February 1992.[11]

A number of terms in the Treaty on European Union, popularly known as the Maastricht Treaty, merit attention. Article 1A of its Common Provisions states: 'By this Treaty, the High Contracting Parties establish among themselves a European Union, hereinafter called "the Union". This Treaty marks a new stage in the process of creating an ever closer union among the peoples of Europe, in which decisions are taken as closely as possible to the citizen.'

'Union' would lead one to believe that a federation had been formed, along the model of, say, the former Soviet Union. However, already the next sentence went some distance (presumably at the insistence of the British and others) toward distancing itself from the previous one in saying that, though a 'new stage' had been entered into, this was only a 'process' of creating 'ever closer' union, that is, something that would never be fully completed, like an asymptotic curve approaching but never reaching 'full' union.

On the other hand, the treaty went on to talk about the 'introduction of a citizenship of the Union' – citizenship being normally a subject of international law, that is, citizenship of a country, state, federation or confederation. Union citizenship does, however, mean something less than, say, having a passport, which *only* indicates citizenship of the European Union (although national passports with an EU cover can today be obtained in all member states). Rather, it gives every national of a member state the right to live and work anywhere in the Community. He or she is further given the right to vote and stand as a candidate in local elections and elections for the European Parliament.

In Article B of the treaty's Common Provisions, the Union set itself the goal of the 'creation of an area without internal frontiers'. This essentially stood for the completion of the 1992 Internal Market ('frontiers' meaning less than 'borders' would have). The 'strengthening of economic and social cohesion' was a call for funds to poorer regions and countries of the Union.

Decisions were to be taken 'as closely as possible to the citizens', reflecting something of a negation of supranationality. This so called 'subsidiarity principle', was included especially, but not exclusively, at British insistence.[12] It stipulated that 'in areas which do not fall within its exclusive competence, the Community shall take action, in accordance with the principle of subsidiarity, only if and insofar as the objectives of the proposed action cannot be sufficiently achieved by the member states and can therefore, by reason of the scale required of the proposed action, be better achieved by the Community.'

The Treaty on European Union is based on a number of 'pillars'. One contained some institutional changes designed to improve the EU's efficiency and democratic appearance. The Council of Ministers was empowered to take a greater range of decisions on the basis of qualified majority votes. The European Parliament was given increased powers and influence in several respects, in particular regarding legislation.

The so called 'co-decision procedure' – subsequently revised under the 1997 Amsterdam Treaty – provided for two readings by the European Parliament and the Council of Ministers. Furthermore, the European Parliament was given a sort of legislative veto power over legislation subject to this procedure. Areas covered by the veto power included the freedom of movement, the freedom of establishment, the Internal Market (including competition), research and development, the environment, trans-European network guidelines, education and training, social policy, public health, culture, consumer protection, development policy, and implementation of the Regional Development Fund.

The term of office of the members of the European Commission was extended from four to five years, so as to align the life span of a Commission with that of a European Parliament. The entire proposed membership of the Commission was subjected to a vote of approval by the European Parliament before it was formally appointed by common accord of national governments.

A Committee of the Regions was established; the Court of Justice was given the power to impose fines on member states failing in their obligations; and the European Parliament was empowered to appoint an ombudsman to receive complaints from citizens 'covering instances of maladministration in the activities of the Community institutions or bodies'.

The Maastricht Treaty also defined the main features of an Economic and Monetary Union (EMU), as well as a timetable for its establishment passing through three different stages. The EMU included the irrevocable fixing of exchange rates, leading to the introduction of a single currency and to the establishment of a European Central Bank (ECB), which was to operate within the framework of a European System of Central Banks (ESCB). The main objectives of the ESCB would be to maintain price stability. It was to define and implement the monetary policy of the Community, conduct foreign exchange operations, hold and manage the official foreign reserves of the member states, and promote the smooth operation of payment systems.

The EMU was to be established in three stages. Stage I, begun in 1990, and stage II, started in 1994, were essentially concerned with promoting economic and monetary co-operation, co-ordination and convergence between the member states. By the end of 1996 (subsequently postponed to 1997) the Council of Ministers, acting by qualified majority was to decide: first, whether a majority of the member states met certain convergence criteria for the adoption of a single currency (involving low rates of inflation, low government deficits, currency stability and low interest rates); and second whether a majority of the member states wished to enter stage III. If a date for the beginning of stage III had not been set by the end of 1997, this third stage would start automatically on 1 January 1999 for those states that had met the convergence criteria. (All this indeed took place on schedule as will be seen in the next chapter, with eleven member states participating in the EMU project at its start in 1999, forming what popularly became known as 'Euroland'.)

In a protocol to the treaty it was recognised that the United Kingdom should 'not be obliged or committed to move to the third stage of economic and monetary union without a separate decision to do so by its government and parliament'. In another protocol the Danish government reserved the right to hold a national referendum before participating in the third stage of EMU, and subsequently Finland, Germany and Sweden declared that their respective parliaments must approve this last step. (Such approval was subsequently achieved in Finland and Germany.)

In another part of the treaty, the Community's commitment to helping developing countries was reaffirmed. New policy areas were introduced, although in a rather tentative manner, in the sense that the Community's responsibilities were carefully restricted to education, public health, consumer protection, trans-European networks and competitiveness of industry. A Cohesion Fund was created to provide financial assistance in the fields of environment and trans-European transport infrastructures, benefiting mainly peripheral and southern EU regions.

The treaty also contained a commitment to the shaping of a common foreign and security policy. While the 1987 Single European Act had stated that member states should 'endeavour jointly to formulate and implement European foreign policy', the Treaty on European Union went much further. Here, the Union and its member states agreed to 'define and implement a common foreign and security policy ... covering all areas of foreign and security policy'. The common policy 'shall include all questions related to the security of the Union, including the eventual framing of a common defence policy, which might in time lead to a common defence'.

The objectives of the Common Foreign and Security Policy (CFSP) were defined in relatively general terms. One was to 'safeguard the common values, fundamental interests and independence of the Union' and another was to 'develop and consolidate democracy and the rule of law, and respect for human rights and fundamental freedoms'.

The Western European Union was considered 'an integral part of the development of the Union' and should 'elaborate and implement decisions and actions of the Union which have defence implications'. In a declaration annexed to the treaty the, at the time, nine EU members belonging to the WEU stated that it 'will be developed as a defence component of the European Union and as the means to strengthen the European pillar of the Atlantic Alliance'.

The CFSP thus put the already well-established European Political Co-operation (EPC) within a broader framework. For the first time foreign policy, although essentially intergovernmental in character, became at least in theory subject to some qualified majority voting. Furthermore, defence made its first formal appearance on the Union agenda, although provisions were couched carefully. Thus there was talk only about the 'eventual' framing of a common defence policy (at the insistence of more Atlanticist members of the Union anxious to maintain the strength of NATO). The term 'common defence' was there, but only as something to which a common defence policy 'might in time lead'. 'Might', 'in time' and 'lead ' are all heavy qualifiers, again there at the insistence of those who did not wish any strengthening of a European security and defence policy to come at the cost of transatlantic ties.

Co-operation in the spheres of justice and home affairs constituted a separate pillar of the treaty. It comprised such things as asylum policy, border crossing, crossings by persons, immigration, the fight against drugs and international fraud, judicial co-operation in civil and criminal matters, co-operation among customs authorities and police co-operation to combat terrorism. In this pillar it was also said that any measures taken in regard to these areas must be in compliance with the Council of Europe's European Convention of Human Rights and Fundamental Freedoms.

The significance of the CFSP and the justice and home affairs pillars lay in the broader contribution they might make to the integration process in Europe. A legal base was given to co-operation in areas that in the past were dealt with purely on a national basis or in loose and informal co-operation between the member states.

The Maastricht Treaty is long, some seventy pages. It has seventeen protocols and thirty-three separate declarations, mostly stating reservations against wordings in the treaty itself. Thus 'social policy' is dealt with in a protocol eventually ratified by all EU member states including the United Kingdom. Another protocol, previously referred to, exempts the United Kingdom from the EMU commitment to move to the third stage of economic and monetary union without a separate decision to do so by its government and parliament. Other protocols or declarations deal with such things as the acquisition of property in Denmark, the protection of animals, co-operation with charitable institutions and the hierarchy of Community acts, but also the statutes of the European Central Bank (ECB) and the European System of Central Banks (ESCB).

Interpreting the Maastricht Treaty

To the layman, the language of the Treaty on European Union is frequently impenetrable and sometimes borders on the incomprehensible. It is a far cry from, say, 'We, the People of the United States' or the United Nations Universal Declaration on Human Rights. One reason is that the treaty built on and revised the earlier treaties, and therefore had to indicate numerous references to the changes undertaken. Another is that it had to specify in great detail all the different modes of consultation and co-decision among the numerous Community bodies, as these vary depending on the issue.

The complexity of the treaty also, however, derives from the host of areas it covers. And these in turn represent not only the reasons just mentioned for drawing up the treaty in the first place, but also the many wishes thrown in by different member states and EU institutions as the negotiations got under way. With so many contributing authors, the result could hardly be expected to read like high prose; in this the Treaty on European Union very much resembles, indeed surpasses, the Single European Act. (There is a joke among bureaucrats that 'a camel is a horse designed by a committee'.)

Of greater importance than any exegetic difficulties was the political significance of the treaty. Generally speaking, it represented a compromise between those who would have liked to go further (such as Germany, Italy and the Benelux countries) and those who felt it had gone too far already (in particular the United Kingdom).

The integrationists could rejoice in numerous competencies passing from the member states to the European level, and a strengthening of the powers of various EU institutions. Thus there would be more qualified majority voting in the decision-taking Council of Ministers (implying a reduction in sovereignty for countries in the minority, but also for those in the majority to the extent that they would have to compromise with others to reach that majority).

Furthermore, the European Council (of heads of government, or head of state in the case of France) was recognised as being the body to define the 'general political guidelines' of the EU. The European Parliament was given greater powers (without, however, receiving full legislative ones like a national parliament), both through the new 'co-decision procedure' and the extension of the so called 'co-operation' and 'assent' procedures to more policy areas. The European Court of Justice was given the right to fine member states found in breach of EC legislation. New policy areas were brought explicitly into the EC framework for the first time, such as culture, consumer protection, environment, research and technological development, industrial competitiveness, and economic and social cohesion. Above all, however, it was the provisions for an Economic and Monetary Union that would provide the greatest impetus toward political integration.

Those suspicious of more integration also scored some successes. For one thing, the 'F-word' – federal – did not appear at the insistence of, in particular, the British. The 'subsidiarity clause' was there, although it would be hard to define when exactly something promises to be better done by a member state than by the EU (especially in the economic field under a single currency). The two pillars of a Common Foreign and Security Policy and Co-operation in the Spheres of Justice and Home Affairs, were kept outside the European Community framework, thus remaining more intergovernmental than *communautaire*, with less of a say for, for instance, the European Commission. Furthermore, there were the virtual 'opt-outs' given to the United Kingdom and Denmark on the EMU and the refusal by one country, the United Kingdom, to participate in the Protocol and Agreement on Social Policy.

The Treaty on European Union was therefore a flexible treaty, placing certain activities in the more supranational EC framework and others in more ad hoc arrangements. In this it followed in the tradition of, say, the Schengen Agreement – at the time a separate agreement between some of the member states and concerned with the free movement of persons. However, flexibility has its price. Nobody at the time of the ECSC or the EEC Treaties would have dreamt of any opt-out possibilities or ad hoc arrangements. Uniformity was the order of the day and was possible due to the relative homogeneity of the member states; to the still relatively peripheral Community activities, which did not yet touch on the essentials of national sovereignty; and to the more favourable economic climate of that time.

First spanner in the works: the Yugoslav crisis

It would not be long before the Treaty on European Union would be put to the test. The disintegration of Yugoslavia, begun in 1990, continued in 1991 with declarations of independence by Croatia and Slovenia, followed by an EC-sponsored conference at The Hague to discuss a political settlement and an offer to consider, within the EC framework, requests for independence presented by any of the emerging republics before the year's end. Such requests did indeed come from Croatia, Slovenia, Bosnia and Macedonia (today the 'former Yugoslav Republic of Macedonia').

Soon, civil wars erupted in Slovenia, Croatia and Bosnia, and Germany recognised Croatia and Slovenia (in December 1991), prematurely according to some other EU countries. In the months following the signing of the Treaty on European Union at Maastricht, fighting subsided in Croatia (parts of which were under Serb military control) and Slovenia – both of which were internationally recognised as independent states. However, fighting flared up in Bosnia and Herzegovina – which had been recognised by the EU member countries in April 1992 – between Serbs who did not want to be citizens in that new country (aided by the Yugoslav army) and non-Serbs (Croatians and Bosnians). The revulsion of the rest of Europe and the world at seeing such large-scale fighting on the continent itself – indeed geographically closer to its centre than EU member Greece – was manifest, especially since the atrocities included massacres, rapes, mass expulsions and imprisonment in camps reminiscent of those seen during the Holocaust.

The situation was further confused by the proclamation, in March 1992, of a Serb Republic of Bosnia and Herzegovina, with a constitution saying it wanted to join Yugoslavia; and by the declaration by the predominantly Croat region in western Herzegovina that it was now an autonomous region (prompting international criticism that Croatia, too, was seeking Bosnia's partition).

Europeans and others could not understand why a country that had been in existence since the end of World War I should have to come apart. Was there a difference between a Serb, a Croat and a Bosnian? Did they not speak much the same language? Europeans, in brief, underestimated the force of nationalism and the legacy of history (even fourteenth-century history such as that invoked by Serbs to claim a right over the largely Albanian-populated province of Kosovo). Europeans also underestimated the forces of disintegration, at a time when Western Europe lived under the impression that the general trend in history was integration, as demonstrated through the European Union.

The question was: what could and would Europe, and more particularly, the EU, do? Send young men to die in a country on Europe's periphery – with internal conflicts that no outside power could fully comprehend, in mountainous terrain that is particularly difficult to conquer? How many body-bags would have to be sent home before public opinion would have had enough? (There would, alas, be many over the years to come, as international forces began to suffer casualties – but no large-scale pressure to disengage became apparent.)

Furthermore, for what cause would soldiers be sent to die or be wounded? For keeping belligerents apart, in which case they might be attacked by either side (as subsequently happened to UN troops)? Or for helping one side against another? But on what moral or statehood grounds, since atrocities were carried out by all and statehood considerations also must take into account the wishes of the population (such as the majority of Serbs in Bosnia-Herzegovina who did not want to live under a Sarajevo government)? And who would pay for the dispatch of the, some argued, 100,000 to 200,000 ground troops that would be necessary, especially if they were dragged into a military adventure from which there was no easy or early retreat?

Moreover, who should send soldiers, if such were to be sent? Germany could hardly do it in view of Hitler's occupation of Yugoslavia during World War II. A contingent from the Western European Union – of which Germany was a member – thereby became more difficult, apart from the fact that the institution did not have a direct military mandate, especially outside its membership area. NATO also experienced difficulties in sending troops for purposes that did not involve the collective defence of a member state, especially since the United States considered that this European conflict was something for the Europeans to solve in the first place. The Conference on Security and Co-operation in Europe (later the Organisation for Security and Co-operation in Europe), apart from lacking any military mandate and being hampered by a unanimity requirement before acting, also included a Russia religiously linked and historically favourable to the Serb cause.

On the other hand, if nothing was done, would there not be a risk of the conflict spreading across the Balkans and involving other parts of the former Yugoslavia and beyond – Serbs in Kosovo against ethnic Albanians, a civil war in the multi-ethnic 'former Yugoslav Republic of Macedonia', perhaps involving Yugoslavia and Greece? Might Turkey intervene to help the Moslems in Bosnia? Might Russia do the same on behalf of the Serbs? Furthermore, might other post-World War I or post-World War II borders in Europe, in particular in its central and eastern parts, be called into question by restive minorities? Could Europe, or the world, stomach daily television images of war and massacre without doing anything?

Divergences on what to do were becoming apparent among EU members. Partly they were due to different historical relations with the different sides to the conflicts, dating back even to the previous century. Partly they also arose out of different economic interests in the region, or because of bickering among EU countries over each other's action or non action.

Second spanner in the works: ratifying Maastricht

The EU could of course argue that the Treaty on European Union had not yet been ratified and that it could therefore not act with the same resolve in the foreign policy field. After ratification by all the Twelve – expected to be easy since all had signed – the provisions in the Common Foreign and Security Policy pillar could be put into effect.

However, would ratification come so easily? Denmark – where ratification was defeated in the *Folketing* by a narrow margin – submitted the Treaty on European Union to a referendum in June 1992, and a knife-edge majority rejected it.[13] This sent shock waves through the EC. How could a small nation like Denmark upset this carefully erected edifice, upon which the EC's very future depended? (The Treaty on European Union would have to be ratified by all EU members to come about at all.) There was shock that normally well-behaved Danes could rise against what their entire political elite – five of the eight parties in the *Folketing*, business circles, industry and most labour organisations – had said was best for them, in a campaign raising the spectre of all the disasters that would occur in the event of a 'no'.

To understand the Danish 'no' – which, it must be remembered, would have been a 'yes' but for a scant 46,000 vote difference – one has to grasp the mentality of this intensely democratic country. Denmark had joined the EEC in 1973 largely to preserve trade links with countries like Germany and the United Kingdom, not believing that its sovereignty would be in danger. Over the years, however, Danish objections began to arise against increased bureaucracy in Brussels; depleted fish stocks allegedly due to the EC's 'Blue Europe' rules of sharing fish resources among all members; and increasing net payments to the EC as a wealthy member. Much of the earlier support for the EU started to fade.

We shall later return to this particular issue, namely that the EU is rightly or wrongly seen as essentially elite-driven – by the Commission and, to some extent, the governing classes in the capitals of member states – and hence unable to comprehend the sentiments of member states' populations. Suffice it to say at this stage that 'eurosceptic' British conservatives burst out in a jubilant 'Wonderful, wonderful Copenhagen' and began to clamour for a similar popular referendum in the United Kingdom.

The German government quickly ruled out the possibility of a referendum, especially since the constitution did not foresee it, and this in spite of a reluctance on the part of many Germans to lose their cherished Deutschmark in favour of an EMU single currency. In most other EU countries referenda were not held and ratification passed parliaments easily, not only because pro-EC sentiment was stronger in these countries but also, presumably, because these countries stood to gain financially as net receivers of EC funds. Only in the United Kingdom did the government have to fight hard and long to achieve ratification, at the price of several derogations, such as the EMU.

France took a different course. President Mitterrand, who in late 1991 had described the EMU as 'one of the most important events of the century', announced on the very day the Danish 'no' was announced that France, too, would have a referendum on the issue. At first the matter seemed a foregone conclusion, especially after a joint session of the National Assembly and the Senate in June 1992 had approved, by a wide majority, the constitutional reforms necessitated by the ratification of the Treaty of European Union (all that was formally required under the constitution).

However, over the summer the French began to reflect, much as the Danes had done a few months earlier. The main opposition party, the RPR (*Rassemblement Pour la République*) became deeply divided, displaying the traditional French ambivalence about, on the one hand, more integration in order to rein in Germany and to permit France to play a dominant role in European affairs and, on the other, less integration to preserve French sovereignty in a Gaullist *Europe des patries*.

The referendum increasingly became one on the Mitterrand presidency and on various scandals that had begun to rock French society. It was suspected that Mitterrand had announced the referendum to regain the domestic initiative and his earlier popularity. Especially after the Prime Minister said that the President would not resign in the event of a '*non*', many French people felt they could express general dissatisfaction with things as they stood – including irritation over US pressure for CAP reform under the Uruguay Round – without causing a constitutional crisis. All these things combined to produce a surprisingly narrow 'yes' margin of 51.05 per cent (with Alsace, home to the Council of Europe and the EU's European Parliament, saving the nationwide result by a 60 per cent vote in favour).

However, it was as if something had snapped with the Danish and French results. The Treaty on European Union might be ratified, but for the first time the people in a key country in the European equation had expressed serious misgivings about the extent and method of EU integration.

The autumn of 1992 came, with many EU citizens wondering whether the Treaty on European Union had been a good thing after all, and with morale sapped among those who were convinced of its merits. The long-awaited date of 1 January 1993 arrived – the day when the Single European Act and the Internal Market would enter into force – but it was just like any other day, with unemployment in the EU of the Twelve at 11 per cent and rising. Where was the promised prosperity?

Notes

1 In *The Old Regime and the Revolution*, 1856.
2 Cartoon 'The Final Curtain', in the *Independent*, 13 September 1990.
3 The 'Internationale' (Engstrom, 2000), that favourite battle cry of the socialist and communist movements of the early decades of the twentieth century, was perhaps the best known expression of this yearning:
   Arise! ye starvelings from your slumbers;
   Arise! ye criminals of want.
   For reason in revolt now thunders,
   And at last ends the age of cant.
   Now away with all your superstitions,
   Servile masses, arise! Arise!
   We'll change forthwith the old conditions,
   And spurn the dust to win the prize.
   Then comrades, come rally
   And the last fight let us face.
   The Internationale
   Unites the human race.
4 Fukuyama (1993).
5 The Russian financial crisis was also a crisis for the so-called 'Washington consensus', formulated in 1989 at the beginning of the transition to a market economy for the countries in Central and Eastern Europe. It was based on neo-liberal policies emphasising fiscal discipline, liberalisation, deregulation and privatisation by countries borrowing from the International Monetary Fund and other financial institutions. The latter were to impose strict conditions that these precepts were respected. The Russian crisis led to doubts that this was always the right course for countries in financial difficulties. Perhaps a more gradual and socially sensitive transition was sometimes better.
6 The European Bank for Reconstruction and Development, with sixty countries and two institutions (the European Union and the European Investment Bank) as members, has been of great assistance to its twenty-seven 'countries

of operations' in Central, Eastern and South-Eastern Europe and the Community of Independent States (CIS) area (the countries of the former Soviet Union, minus Estonia, Latvia and Lithuania) since its creation in 1992. It is the largest single investor in this region and combines lending operations with a mandate to promote democracy.

7 The importance of the Conventional Forces in Europe Treaty can hardly be overstated. Without the mutual confidence it created, not least through extensive verification on both sides, German unification would in all likelihood have been much more difficult to bring about, as would have been the dissolution of the Soviet Union and the Warsaw Pact.

8 Joint bodies – an EEA Ministerial Council, a Joint Parliamentary Committee, a Consultative Committee composed of the social partners, an EFTA Surveillance Authority and an EFTA Court – would oversee the functioning of this 'Twelve and Six Common Market'.

9 As the EU enlarged from fifteen to twenty-five states in 2004, the new members would also enter into its European Economic Area (EEA) agreement with Iceland, Norway and Liechtenstein, all members of the European Free Trade Association (EFTA). They, like Switzerland (an EFTA member but not part of the EEA), were asked by the EU to increase their payments into the funds foreseen for the new members (and presumably some old). There was little the EFTA countries could do other than accept, especially as the EU pressed for greater access to the fishing waters of Iceland and Norway.

10 President Mitterrand of France at first tried to inhibit or at least delay German unification in 1990. The Maastricht Treaty with its 'deepening' of the EU, especially through an Economic and Monetary Union, represented France's all-out effort to tie Germany closer to it and to the EC in general. Further EC integration would, in Mitterrand's words, have to precede 'changing borders' (i.e. unification) and the latter would have to 'take the European balance into account'. Germany under Chancellor Kohl immediately set out to assuage French fears by statements such as 'the German house must be built under a European roof', a policy which it has since steadfastly followed. See e.g. Baun (1996, pp. 41–4).

11 The European Union is an organisation composed of different treaty-based parts, hence the slightly confusing terminology surrounding its appellation. The term 'European Union' describes the general edifice of 'unification' among the member states, and it is also to be used whenever one is referring to the Common Foreign and Security Policy or Co-operation in the Spheres of Justice and Home Affairs. Two of the European Communities – the European Economic Community, and Euratom – continue to exist (although the relevant Treaties are revised in the Treaty on European Union). The European Coal and Steel Community disappeared in 2002 when the relevant treaty reached its fifty-year duration. However, the European Economic Community is renamed the 'European Community'. Therefore, the European Community is part of the European Communities, which themselves are part

of the European Union. In this book, the 'European Union' is normally used throughout to describe the institution generally as from 1992.

12 The 'subsidiarity' caveat was in fact sought by several of the players. As van Keersbergen and Verbeek (1994, p 220) point out: 'Subsidiarity has primarily served to reconcile the conflicting interests of principal actors affected by the consequences of the common market [i.e. the '1992' Internal Market project]: the United Kingdom, Germany and the European Commission. The United Kingdom feared that the completion of the European market would slowly eat away at portions of national sovereignty. The German federal government, as well as the European Commission, had met strong resistance from the German *Länder*, who feared that the completion of the Internal Market, based on negotiations between Bonn and Brussels, would actually lead to a shrinking of their regional competences. The European Commission, of course, was predominantly interested in playing down the impression that the '1992 programme' would lead to ever growing power-wielding by Brussels.'

13 Under the Danish constitution, any change to it, such as would result from the Maastricht Treaty, would require a qualified majority in parliament. Since this majority was narrowly missed, a referendum had to be called. The traditionally democratic Danish government decreed that copies of the draft Maastricht Treaty should be made available at post offices to all those requesting them. Presumably the reading did not convince a sufficient number of citizens. Furthermore, referenda results are frequently bound up in the popularity of the governments that decide to hold them. Denmark in 1992 was no different. The outcome was 50.7 per cent against and 49.3 per cent in favour.

6

Challenges in waiting

Why didst thou promise such a beauteous day,
And make me travel forth without my cloak,
To let base clouds o'ertake me in my way,
Hiding thy bravery in their rotten smoke? (Shakespeare)[1]

Summary

While the Russian economy under its new leader, Boris Yeltsin, began to slide in the early 1990s as a result of an uncertain mix of change and standstill, economic reform in Central European transition countries started to bear fruit in the form of higher growth and adaptation to world markets. Military tensions diminished considerably with the ratification of the US–Russia START I Treaty reducing intercontinental nuclear missiles; the entry into force of the Conventional Forces in Europe (CFE) Treaty limiting troop levels all over Europe; and NATO's Partnership for Peace programme, also including Russia.

The European Union's Exchange Rate Mechanism (ERM) collapsed in 1993 but was revived in a more flexible form, permitting plans for Economic and Monetary Union (EMU) to proceed. The conclusion of the Uruguay Round and the establishment in 1995 of the World Trade Organisation meant a major push for Europe toward globalisation and its being exposed to greater competition from emerging non-European economies. Austria, Finland and Sweden joined the European Union in 1995, increasing its membership to fifteen.

Other institutions, such as the Council of Europe, also included more and more members in Central, Eastern and South-Eastern Europe and began to form – with NATO, the European Union and the Organisation for Security and Co-operation in Europe (OSCE) – a rather complicated European 'security architecture'. All these organisations were faced with immediate challenges, such as successive wars in the former Yugoslavia and in the southern Russian province of Chechnya. The former led to the first 'out-of-area' NATO deployment of troops in Bosnia and Herzegovina, as a result of the 1995 Dayton Agreements.

The post-Maastricht blues: recession and confusion

In 1993 the world – and with it Europe – was in its first major recession since the early 1980s. In 1991 the recession had been delayed by Germany's major transfer of funds to the new *Länder*, leading to export gains for other European countries, especially in the West. However, by early 1993 the recession started to bite, as many Western European governments tried to reduce large public sector deficits and to contain inflation (not least to meet the still relatively distant, but approaching, European Monetary Union (EMU) convergence criteria).

The EU countries most committed to the EMU stuck to one of its key preparatory requirements, namely adherence to a maximum variation between each other's currencies of ±2.25 per cent. For the relatively weaker economies in the group – such as France and Belgium – staying within this band vis-à-vis the Deutschmark meant, however, having to raise interest rates to levels such that their economies suffered even more. In June 1993 the Exchange Rate Mechanism (ERM) collapsed – enriching speculators and impoverishing some central banks. However, it was revived after a ±15 per cent widening of the currency bands had been introduced, reducing the scope for speculators but also taking away some of the seriousness of the ERM. (In the end it did, however, work rather well, as governments successfully stuck to fairly narrow fluctuations.)

Nobody seemed really sure any longer where Europe, or the world, was heading. On the one hand, Iraq's invasion of Kuwait had been repulsed and oil supplies were not in danger. On the other, however, Europeans knew, in their heart of hearts, that although they had fought alongside the Americans and other nations in this action, it would not have come about without US resolve in what was after all a crisis closer to Europe than to North America.

The economic slide in most Central and East European countries had given way to modest growth – with Poland, Hungary and the Czech Republic in the lead. However, even this growth was seen by some in Western Europe as reflecting a beginning industrial exodus from West to East. Would that East – so long neglected, and commiserated with because of its being on the 'wrong' side of the Iron Curtain – now rob the West of its wealth, until some distant future when both could prosper together? Would, in the meantime, immigration from the East add further to unemployment in the West?

Events in Russia in the autumn of 1993 did nothing to soothe such fears. A long-simmering dispute between the reformist President Yeltsin and a conservative parliament came to a head in a 'second October revolution', lasting one day and ending with the (narrow) victory by the Yeltsin forces (supported by the military, the former KGB and the Ministry of the Interior) over angry demonstrators barricaded in an official building and shelled by army tanks.

If the forces of reform appeared to have won the day, the state of the Russian economy gave rise to concern. Gross domestic product (GDP) in 1993 fell by 12 per cent compared to the year before, after an approximate 20 per cent drop in 1992 from the preceding year (although these falls also reflected the fact that the economy was undergoing reform away from a wasteful communist-era production pattern). Problems were everywhere: a budget deficit of 10 per cent of GDP with continuing massive aid to state-owned industries; a monthly inflation rate of 20 per cent; slow privatisation of an agricultural sector whose situation was further aggravated by poor harvests; absent, confusing or conflicting legislation; and growing crime and corruption. All this added to the general feeling of uncertainty over the country's economic future. Foreign investors began to have cold feet, including the International Monetary Fund, which had made aid contingent on economic reform and stabilisation. It was clear that Russia had enormous potential, but when would domestic conditions permit that potential to be realised?

Russia's economic difficulties were upsetting to the rest of Europe. What would have happened if the forces of reaction had managed to oust the Yeltsin government? Would the new independence of the Baltic states have been in danger, together with that of states which many in Russia would now call the 'near abroad', i.e. the other successor republics to the Soviet Union? (The latter soon joined together in a loosely structured Community of Independent States as a result of Russian prodding.) Would Central and East European countries again have risked coming under Russian sway? Would economic reforms have been undone? Would the thousands of new private enterprises that had been formed have been forced into liquidation? Even with Yeltsin winning, would an economically distressed Russia become politically unpredictable?

Clearly the West, including the EU and other European organisations such as the Council of Europe, had a strong interest in trying to assist Russia in every way possible. Even so, a certain shift from financial to other types of assistance was taking place, and a certain weariness could be detected among donors as to the wisdom of continuing to fund a country with such uncertain prospects.

A new defence context

There was no longer any serious military threat from Russia, at least not in the NATO area. Russian aircraft were rusting on abandoned airfields. Warships were being mothballed or scrapped. Morale in the formerly feared Soviet armed forces was low, because of lack of pay and worsening material conditions. The threat now was rather the accidental firing of a missile by a crazed unit in a Siberian silo or due to decay of the equipment, or the theft of a nuclear warhead or stored fission material by some rogue nation in, say, the Middle East. (In 1994 the United States actually paid for the removal of a large stock of bomb-grade plutonium from Russia to the United States.)

The threat of large-scale military conflict suddenly seemed remote. The 1990 Conventional Forces in Europe (CFE) Treaty between the NATO and Warsaw Pact countries – begun already in the 1980s with the Mutual and Balanced Force Reduction (MBFR) talks and painstakingly pursued through the highs and lows of the détente years – became binding in November 1995. It obliged the thirty participating states to much lower force levels than before and to the elimination of 60 per cent of their heavy weapons.

Most countries were already moving to or going beyond these targets – a natural enough process when one considers that there was no longer any genuine East–West conflict. Why, indeed, should a country have large conventional forces when these cost money increasingly needed elsewhere, and when technological improvements added further advantage for the defender rather than the attacker? Put simply, why invest in a tank when it could be easily knocked out by an increasingly 'smart' anti-tank weapon?

In January 1994 NATO invited all the former members of the Warsaw Pact and the successor states of the Soviet Union to join the organisation's Partnership for Peace (PfP) programme – allowing them to develop co-operative military relations with NATO, particularly in the area of joint planning and training for humanitarian and peace-keeping operations. By the end of 1994 Russia and all the other successor states to the Soviet Union except two (Belarus and Tajikistan) had joined the PfP, as had such countries as Finland, Slovenia and Sweden. The Western European Union also began to build up contacts with Central and Eastern Europe.

Finally, at world level, the US–Soviet Union START I Treaty entered into force in 1994 after nuclear weapons in Belarus, Kazakhstan and Ukraine were either destroyed or moved to Russia. Efforts to have the even more far-reaching START II ratified by both Russia and the United States were resumed.[2] The sword of Damocles hanging over Europe (and the world) seemed to have been reduced in size, even if it had not disappeared altogether.

A new trade context: the Uruguay Round and the World Trade Organisation

In December 1993 another event of importance to Europe occurred: the conclusion of seven years of negotiations for a new GATT round to govern future international relations in trade and investment. The signing of the Uruguay Round meant that the world's long march towards more and more open trade relations – started in 1947 with the setting up of the GATT – would continue for years if not decades to come.

World trade issues would henceforth be dealt with by a new WTO, rather than the more or less informal GATT. It would have more powers, particularly in the settling of disputes and in enforcement procedures. Moreover, the Uruguay Round was the first agreement to cover agriculture, textiles, intellectual property rights and certain services (even though some, such as telecommunications, shipping and audio-visual and financial services, were left out for want of an agreement). In this, the treaty went far beyond traditional issues of tariffs, quotas, dumping and countervailing duties, and into the traditionally domestic affairs of participating countries, such as competition laws and investment conditions.

The significance for Europe of the Uruguay Round, and the new World Trade Organisation to be created, was that the long process of an increasing 'division of labour' between the different regions of the world that had started with the GATT in the late 1940s would continue. In the old days that division had been easy for Western Europe. The rich, industrialised countries produced the advanced products and services the world needed. The less developed countries continued to produce at a lower rung of the production ladder, and while they made inroads into some of the domains of richer countries, the latter made up for that by developing new domains. It was assumed that the richer countries would continue to give development assistance to the poorer ones with the aim of lifting them out of poverty. However, it was never imagined that this process might some day challenge the wealth or relative position of the wealthiest countries vis-à-vis the developing world.

The developing countries – at least those that did not become too dependent on foreign aid – saw it differently. In the 1950s and 1960s the emphasis had been on replacing industrial imports by domestic production and on exporting raw materials and agricultural commodities to the rich countries. This was the cardinal aim behind the United Nations Conference on Trade and Development formed in 1964, and behind the much-touted proposals for a New International Economic Order of the early 1970s. (That ambition collapsed, since the forming of cartels among producing nations proved impossible in all but a handful of commodities. Even OPEC rapidly lost ground after its brief heyday in the 1970s.)

Now, however, more and more developing countries began to concentrate on attracting subsidiaries of foreign multinationals and foreign direct investment generally. While developing countries used to fear free trade in advanced products and had been generally reluctant participants in earlier GATT rounds, they now became more and more eager proponents of open trade. (This did not, however, extend to intellectual property products, where many did not feel enthusiastic about paying royalties to, say, a US record company, a Michael Jackson, a Dior or a Chanel, especially if these could be made through 'underground' copycat factories at home.)

By the time of the signing of the Uruguay Round, an impressive number of 'emerging economies' in East and South-East Asia, Latin America and elsewhere had become major competitors with the 'old' industrialised countries. They had the advantage, from a trade competition point of view, of paying their workers much lower wages and providing little or no social protection (thus reducing extra-salary costs to employers). In some countries, child or prison labour was used. Although the workforce pool was large and labour was permanently added through migration from countryside to city, rising salaries in some of the countries had begun to drive out companies to poorer neighbours, finally engaging virtually the entire world in what had become known as the 'global economy'.

Again, this process was accelerated – indeed it could hardly have occurred – without the technological breakthrough symbolised by the microchip, making the transfer and sharing of information several orders of magnitude less expensive as well as instantaneous. Add to this an increased share of services in world commerce, cheaper and more efficient means of transport, and a shift toward higher value per weight unit in trade (giving air cargo a major share in overall transport), and the growing advantage of developing countries vis-à-vis the traditional industrialised countries in the trade arena becomes obvious.

Europe, which began to feel the effects of a number of closures of factories large and small across the whole industrial spectrum, had begun to take a more defensive stance in areas like agriculture, textiles, steel, coal and shipbuilding, while being more open-trade minded in areas like services and intellectual property. If at long last, after particularly bitter agricultural negotiations between the US and the EU, the Uruguay Round could be submitted for signature by the spring of 1994 and set to enter into force by the beginning of 1995, then this was largely because the two most important parties, the US and the EU, had been able to agree. Everybody at least believed that they had obtained a little more and sacrificed a little less than they would have done in the absence of the Round. However, everybody soon realised that the Uruguay Round Treaty, even at the time it was to enter into force, described the past rather than the present or future. A new treaty would be needed unless all matters could henceforth be dealt with on a continuous basis within the new World Trade Organisation.

Parallel to the worldwide framework for trade and investment provided by the Uruguay Round and the World Trade Organisation, a process of trade regionalisation was also under way. To the 'older' European Union and EFTA (and about a dozen other, less far-reaching trade arrangements in different parts of the world), would now have to be added the North American Free Trade Agreement (NAFTA) involving Canada, Mexico and the United States. In addition, a whole series of more extensive regional free-trade agreements were concluded: in Latin America (Mercosur, the Andean Pact, the Central American Common Market, the Caribbean Community and Common Market), in South-East Asia (Asian Free Trade Association) and in the Pacific rim including the United States and Canada (Asia-Pacific Economic Forum, or APEC). The tide was thus firmly in the direction of freer trade, the prime motor being technological change and foreign investment, mainly through multinational companies.

Knocking on the EU's door: the Austrian, Finnish, Norwegian and Swedish candidatures

The Treaty on European Union, commonly known as the Maastricht Treaty, entered into force in November 1993. However, this was only after a second, this time positive, Danish referendum (and considerable concessions to Denmark by the other EU members); a year-long ratification battle in the British Parliament; and an extremely thorough and 'barely passed' examination by the German Federal Constitutional Court (following a citizens complaint that the treaty violated the country's constitution).

In December 1993 the so-called Schengen Agreement on free circulation of people came into force between nine EU member states (all except Denmark, Ireland and the UK), although France continued to have reservations owing to alleged Dutch liberalism with regard to its drugs policy.[3] Furthermore, on 1 January 1994 the previously mentioned European Economic Area came into being, extending the essentials of the '1992 project' of the Twelve to six of the seven EFTA states (all except Switzerland).

Hardly was the ink of that treaty dry, when it appeared that within a short time it would lose much of its significance through the expected EU membership of the four EFTA countries Austria, Finland, Norway and Sweden. (Switzerland had withdrawn its application following the negative referendum on the European Economic Area in December 1992). Iceland had never applied, as it was wary of sharing its main resource, fish, under a common EU fisheries policy.

Why were the governments of the four EFTA candidates for EU membership not content with the European Economic Area? There were two main reasons. Firstly, the disappearance of the Soviet Union had swept away any apprehensions that Finland in particular, but also Sweden and Austria as neutral states, might have harboured about joining a Western political club such as the EU. Secondly, the EEA was essentially about the participating EFTA countries accepting existing and future EU legislation on even less than a 'take it or leave it' basis. If the Internal Market was further deepened through a series of EU decisions, how could the non-EU countries in the EEA say 'no', without the risk of economic loss?

The EU countries for their part, it must be remembered, had suggested the EEA as a 'stop-gap' solution. They wanted to avoid the decision-making indigestion that would follow with an even greater number of members, and they needed time to implement the '1992' Internal Market project. Now that this had been done, and with the four candidate countries knocking on the door for membership, enlargement was inevitable. Perhaps it was even desirable considering that the aspirants were comparatively wealthy. They were even likely to become net contributors to an ever more expensive and cash-strapped European Union.

Even if some of the four candidate countries, such as Austria, could have joined the EU simply through a vote of parliament, a referendum had become a political must, given the historical significance of joining, and following the hotly contested Danish and French referenda on the Treaty on European Union. This was especially so since the candidate countries, once admitted, were expected to ratify the Treaty as part of the deal.

Austria went first. On the one hand, Austria needed the closest possible economic links with Germany. If the country remained outside, these links might suffer. Austria had also become an important hub for economic contacts between Western Europe and the transition countries in Central and Eastern Europe. As an EU member, Austria could strengthen this role.

On the other hand, the country's 1955 State Treaty, which had ended Allied occupation after World War II and restored Austrian sovereignty, obliged it to remain neutral. Was this compatible with the political union held out in the Treaty on European Union? To circumvent this problem the Austrians had their agreement with the EU state that, as an EU member, the country would not station foreign soldiers on its territory, take part in a new war or sign any military pact (even though the question of a later participation in a European defence pact was left open). In June 1994, despite an early strong showing by the 'anti' camp, Austrians voted two to one in favour of joining the EU.

The governments of all the four candidate countries – naturally enough eager to join as they had waged the accession negotiations and called referenda – were counting on a domino effect. The Finns, scheduled to vote in October, were expected to be swayed by the positive Austrian vote in the summer, and do likewise. Sweden was to follow in a vote in November, presumably impressed by a positive Finnish vote, whereupon the even more sceptical Norwegians could be assumed to toe the line a week later.

The calculation nearly worked. In October 1994 the Finns voted 57 per cent to 43 per cent in favour, reflecting a widespread fear of a possible renewed threat in the future from their neighbour to the east, but also their search for more extensive economic links with the EU area following the collapse of the considerable barter trade the Finns had enjoyed with the Soviet Union. Unemployment had risen rapidly over the past few years, and now affected nearly 20 per cent of the workforce. For a small, geographically peripheral and exposed country, it is often important to find protection and support in a continent's political centre – in this case the European Union – especially since NATO membership was not, yet, deemed possible. Opposition came mainly from the Communist Party that had earlier been closely aligned with that of the Soviet Union, and from many subsidised farmers who feared competition from more productive farms in the EU.

Sweden followed the Finnish example in November 1994, through a 52 per cent to 47 per cent vote in favour of joining the EU, thus ending a nearly forty-year-old tradition of shunning Community membership by invoking the latter's incompatibility with Swedish neutrality. The political establishment and business leaders had advocated membership, arguing that the economic crisis that had hit the country in 1991–92 would only deepen as companies would leave and foreign investment dry up if Sweden did not join (adding to the already, by Swedish standards, unheard-of 13 per cent unemployment rate). The Social Democrats, back in power in September 1994 after a three-year absence, were seriously split over the issue, as many rank-and-file members feared an erosion of the Swedish welfare state under a supposedly more capitalistic Brussels regime. The Communist Party was against for the same reason, while environmentalists feared that similar concessions would have to be made in their particular field of interest. Even a number of conservatives were against, fearful that power would move from a democratic Stockholm to a bureaucratic Brussels.

City – in favour off membership – stood against countryside, which was mainly opposed to joining. The north, already peripheral in an oblong Sweden where two-thirds of the population live in the country's southern third, was more against, while the south was more in favour. Even Stockholmers, for now geographically in the centre, were less enthusiastic than the good people of Malmö who were facing a Copenhagen inside the EU across the Öresund straits. Following reports that *snus*, a form of chewing tobacco to which over a million Swedish men (and women) are addicted, would be banned once the country was in the EU, pro-EU sentiments took a deep dive. As it was, however, following EU assurances on this point, the 'yes' prevailed.

Would the Norwegians, who had said '*nei*' in the referendum in 1972, follow? A joke made the rounds that the latest fashion was for nouveaux riches Norwegians to have a Mercedes and a Swedish chauffeur. Long the poor cousin of wealthy Sweden, Norway had now become Western Europe's biggest oil producer (surpassing the United Kingdom), with strong economic growth fuelled by that resource and low unemployment. Why should a country with such wealth join a European Union, with which it was already linked through a European Economic Area agreement, to whose budget it would be a major net contributor, and which promised to take power away from a – for many in the north – already distant Oslo to an even more remote and impenetrable Brussels? The new name that the European Community had given itself, the European Union, evoked negative feelings with many Norwegians, against the historical background of involuntary 'unions', first with Denmark over 500 years ending in 1814 and then with Sweden nearly ending in war in 1905.

More security was scarcely needed than that provided by NATO, of which Norway was a founding member. Farmers were largely against, as they feared losing generous government support in exchange for much tougher competition from EU farmers. Fishermen were also subsidised. Why should they join an EU which pursued a 'Blue Europe' policy of Community sharing of fish resources – especially as they feared it would deplete stocks? Why risk the country's precious sovereignty over its other rich resources: oil, gas and light metals? For these assets as well as for its important shipping industry, the world – rather than just the EU – was Norway's main market. Finally, many women feared EU membership would undermine Norway's cradle-to-grave welfare system.

The Social Democratic government under Gro Harlem Bruntland, who had made the country's joining the EU a central political goal, found little response to its warning of an industrial exodus and economic hardship if the country said 'no'. This it did indeed do, on 20 November 1994, through a 52.4 per cent against joining the EU, to 47.6 per cent in favour.

The striking thing about the debates in all the four candidate countries was that they had centred on the self-interests of the particular nation. A 'what's-in-it-for-us?' attitude had settled in, whether it be farmers worried about EU competition or eager for CAP benefits; regions expecting money from the EU regional development fund or fearing to become even more peripheral from the Brussels horizon than they had been, say, from those of Oslo or Stockholm; or ordinary people worried about a company exodus in the event of non-membership, or of new trade barriers arising between, say, a Sweden within and a Norway without the EU (this was of course unrealistic, since it would risk being in breach of increasingly free trade GATT/WTO rules, apart from being unacceptable to the country inside – reduced trade, for example in Swedish regions bordering Norway, would hurt Swedish as much as Norwegian interests).[4]

A materialistic 'it's-your-money-we-want' attitude had also been prevalent on the part of certain EU countries during the membership negotiations, reflecting a departure from the more idealistic approach of earlier decades. For the poorer EU members it was a question of how much the new entrants would pay into the Cohesion Fund of regional aid mainly benefiting them, or how their agricultural produce would take the place of that which the candidate countries had previously imported, often at a lower price, from outside Europe. EU countries with a colonial past sought the same preferences for that nebulous and ever-growing group of nations gathered under the label of ACP countries

(African, Caribbean and Pacific) already comprising over seventy states.[5] However, there were none of the 'transition periods' that had been so frequent following the accessions of Greece, Portugal and Spain, the reason being that the new candidates had been part of the EEA (apart from being so competitive that no transition periods were needed).

On 1 January 1995 the European Union welcomed Austria, Finland and Sweden as new members – while noting that, for a second time, the Norwegians had refused the offer of entry. The Twelve were now the Fifteen, with a new northern bias as two of the newcomers – Finland and Sweden – were on the EU's polar flank and a third – Austria – was at any rate not Mediterranean. They were also comparatively wealthy, thus contributing to an EU budget beyond which the organisation was statutorily obliged not to go, and which EU member governments were increasingly unwilling to augment as spending was increasingly demanded at home. The EU seemed to have fulfilled a new stage in its geographical expansion, now having as members all those wealthy Western European states that desired membership, while maintaining privileged trade relations with those that did not.

An EU of fifteen; a NATO at peace?

Another achievement was that Europe now seemed to have a pan-European security structure which, though it was political rather than military, included the two transatlantic powers of the United States and Canada, whose presence, it was widely felt, was needed for future peace. The Conference on Security and Co-operation in Europe, the CSCE, had by 1995 been transformed into a formal institution, the Organisation for Security and Co-operation in Europe, or the OSCE. As such it was endowed with a permanent, if small, secretariat and a consultative Parliamentary Assembly branch.

Meanwhile, NATO had its Partnership for Peace programme and was postponing the thorny issue of enlargement into Central and Eastern Europe. The Council of Europe entered a hectic period of enlargement – culminating in February 1996 with the inclusion of Russia, to be followed in the coming years by virtually all remaining European states not yet members.

The ghosts of Stalin and Hitler seemed to be leaving the scene reluctantly, even though they ought perhaps to have been content with having so affected Europe and the world half a century after their deaths. Yet some traces remained. These included the Russian Kaliningrad enclave on the Baltic (the northern part of the former German East

Prussia). It was now cut off from the rest of Russia but remained heavily armed and of continued strategic importance to Russia. There was also the redrawing of other national frontiers in the aftermath of World War II, setting the stage, at least potentially, for future conflicts among and within countries, in addition to those which the post World War I borders might supply.

However, the situation was far from problem-free for any of the organisations or countries involved. The European Union was immediately confronted with the request by numerous Central and East European countries to join, to which should be added those, of longer or shorter standing, of Cyprus (supported by Greece) and Turkey (opposed by Greece). How would EU finances, already strained, be able to cope with some, most or all of these countries as members? How would EU institutions cope, under strain from the already considerable divergences among member states, in what was still, essentially, an intergovernmental framework following, in most cases, the 'one-country-one-vote' principle?

Finally, how would the previously mentioned 'deepening' of EU integration fare, with so many more – and less economically developed – newcomers? (Although this was one reason why at least some EU governments were so eagerly seeking enlargement in the first place.) Even if enlargement could be delayed, how could 'deepening' be achieved in the wake of the highly divisive process of ratifying the Treaty on European Union, which had brought to the surface deep-seated popular scepticism against further integration?

The OSCE was similarly hampered by continued reliance (as under the CSCE) on the unanimity principle before intervening to defuse a conflict. Its efforts, for instance, to contribute to a peaceful solution to the conflict in Chechnya in southern Russia – where separatists had been waging a bitter war of liberation against Russian troops since the autumn of 1994 – were largely fruitless.

NATO also faced many challenges. What role would it have after the disappearance of any threat from the East? On the other hand, many people felt NATO was needed as a sign of continued US–Canadian involvement in European security, and the disappearance of any such major institution would risk upsetting the status quo and leaving a dangerous void. No longer was anyone shouting 'Yankees, go home!' in Europe. On the contrary, most people were anxious that they stay in order to provide the stability that Europe had historically not seemed capable of mustering itself, and to guard against perceived threats from one or the other neighbour. In some NATO countries, such as Germany, the departing troops meant unemployment for thousands of civilians working on closed, or radically downsized, bases.

Meanwhile, on the other side of the Atlantic, voices were heard in favour of even more drastic reductions in military strength in Europe than those foreseen in the various international agreements. Why, many Americans argued, should the United States supply protection for Europe, when there was no longer any Soviet Union or Warsaw Pact to defend it against? Would the Old World never be able to stand on its own feet? For a younger generation of politicians from the western and south-western states, the future lay in Asia and along the Pacific Rim – not in Europe as the now less dominant 'Eastern Establishment' from the county's eastern seaboard had thought.

Although France was eager to create a more independent European defence and security identity and therefore wished a less prominent NATO, it would in that event be left with a Germany – which though a close, democratic and peaceful EU partner – was perhaps nevertheless not to be fully trusted. If France thus was both attracted to and repelled by NATO, the matter appeared for some time to near a solution, at least temporarily, when the country in 1996 said it wanted to rejoin NATO's integrated military command structure (following its departure in 1966 under President de Gaulle). Although continued French hesitations have since prevented formal reintegration, France apparently concluded that its own, and Europe's, interests were after all best served with continued North American involvement in European security.

One reason for the French change in attitude was doubtless the situation in Bosnia and Herzegovina. In spite of repeated joint European Union and United Nations initiatives, and a four-month ceasefire in early 1995, the war in the region continued (with Croatian forces retaking from the Serbs several areas in Krajina and in western Bosnia and Herzegovina). It was only in October 1995 that a US-sponsored cease-fire could be proclaimed to give time for peace talks in Dayton, Ohio.

The so-called Dayton Agreements provided for a Bosnia-Herzegovinian state consisting of two entities: the Muslim-Croatian Federation (approximately 51 per cent of the territory, including the whole of Sarajevo) and the Serb Republic (Republica Srpska) with about 49 per cent. People indicted as war criminals would not be allowed to hold public office in either of the two entities. Bosnia-Herzegovina was to have a constitution and central institutions. Free elections were to be held within a specified period, and all refugees were to be allowed to return to their homes or – if this was not possible – awarded proper compensation. The Agreements provided for the presence of 60,000 NATO troops (including 20,000 from the United States) for one year to supervise the implementation of the Agreements. NATO, whose forces were deployed immediately after the signing of the Dayton Agreements, took over officially from the UN in Bosnia in December 1995.

This type of 'out-of-area' assignment was new to NATO and unforeseen in its 1949 Statute. The rationale – apart from the humanitarian aspect, which had by this time become an important NATO consideration – was that 'out-of-area' conflicts could easily spread to NATO-Europe and should therefore be seen as compatible with the organisation's mandate. (NATO had been involved since 1993 in the UN-mandated economic embargo against Yugoslavia – Serbia and Montenegro – and in the monitoring of a 'no-fly' rule for military aircraft in the civil war in the area.) Even though the joint endeavour operation in Bosnia and Herzegovina – initially involving some 60,000 troops and today far fewer – was costly, this was clearly an area where NATO was assisting European peace.

There remained the thorny issue of NATO enlargement. While it was clear that Russia would not be able to, or want to, go beyond its special co-operation agreement with NATO (within the Partnership for Peace framework) to full membership, numerous Central and East European countries wanted to join as early as possible, precisely to avoid any Russian threat in a more or less distant future. Yet how could they join without having Russia feel frightened or provoked, depending on how one interpreted that country's sentiments?

Furthermore, would NATO members be willing to live up to their commitments under the Washington Treaty of 1949 if, say, a Baltic country or Poland were attacked from the east? Was not NATO going beyond its 'natural' defence perimeter, biting off more than it could chew if it did let some of these countries in? In addition, would NATO perhaps be brought into new territorial quarrels between members of the type it was already facing between Greece and Turkey?

On the other hand, did these candidate countries – democratic and constructive European partners – not have the same right as, say, a Denmark or a Luxembourg to seek collective defence of their freedom and national independence if they were ever threatened by an outside power? Besides, if a new status quo was not sought now, when there was no threat from the East, would that not in itself invite trouble, perhaps tempting an aggressor in the future?

The method applied by NATO members at the time was based on caution. Membership was held out as a prospect for the candidate countries, but the timetable was left vague, in the hope that time would make things clearer. Moscow's reaction to any overture was carefully registered – especially in Washington, which had the largest say. Washington also had to take into account the opinions of various ethnic groups in the US which hailed from Central and Eastern European countries and which clamoured for NATO membership for their several countries of origin. When membership was at last offered to the Czech Republic, Hungary and Poland – with the other candidates left either in various antechambers or out in the cold – the joining date was, however, set early, as will be seen later.

Enlargement of the Council of Europe

The Council of Europe faced a similar dilemma. Founded in 1949 to achieve European political co-operation (rather than integration), it had been largely overshadowed by the EEC–EC and EU in subsequent decades, concentrating mainly on its role as a guardian of democracy, human rights and the rule of law.[6] This role had been easy whilst communism existed. With the new situation in Central and Eastern Europe, however, the political mission of the Council again came to the fore, signifying that certain human rights principles might have to be compromised in the larger interest of political inclusion.

At the same time, how could an organisation, which had staked so much of its reputation on its work on behalf of democracy and human rights, live with certain members in its midst who did not seem fully to meet these requirements? What impact beyond its moral one did an organisation like the Council really possess? If it sacrificed its principles, would its soul survive?

Alternatively, others argued, if it excluded countries rather than include them, would that not prevent a 'critical dialogue' necessary to encourage improvements in human rights and democracy? If exclusion took place, that might risk having adverse consequences for many in the country targeted, and indeed for Europe as a whole, since the country in question might turn away from Europe towards, say, fundamentalist regimes in the Middle East. Did not Europe need an 'agora' – a forum – where differences could be aired and ironed out, where faulty behaviour could be criticised, prejudices overcome and guidelines and general principles agreed on?

The process that followed, especially from 1994 onwards, was largely dictated by geopolitical considerations and the concern for inclusion and dialogue. The first Council of Europe summit, held in October 1993 with the participation of almost all European heads of state or government, gave rise to the so-called Vienna Declaration. It stated that:

'The Council of Europe is the pre-eminent European political institution capable of welcoming, on an equal footing and in permanent structures, the democracies of Europe freed from communist oppression. For that reason the accession of those countries to the Council of Europe is a central factor in the process of European construction based on [the] Organisation's values.' By 2000 the membership of the Council of Europe had grown to forty-one countries, and more were to join.[7]

Meanwhile, a pattern of political and economic development was becoming discernible in the eastern half of the continent. In the foremost group were countries like Poland, the Czech Republic, Estonia, Hungary and Slovakia. They had pursued economic reform with determination. Aided by their proximity to Western European markets, they were growing at 5 per cent per year or more – that is, faster than the majority of Western European countries. Institutions were being reformed and democracy was taking firm root.

In a second group of nations, economic, political and institutional reform was proceeding more slowly, resulting in slower economic growth. Countries like Albania, Bulgaria, Romania and the 'former Yugoslav Republic of Macedonia' – all of which had in addition been seriously affected by the international embargo against Yugoslavia – were in this group, as were Latvia and Lithuania.

A third group of countries – such as Belarus, Ukraine and Russia – seemed to experience the worst of both worlds: the relative, though ossified, stability of communism was no longer, but the fundamentals of a market economy were still missing. The contraction of output which had characterised all the countries in the region following the dismantling of the state economy and the collapse of 'East–East' regional trade seemed never to end. Yet it was generally regarded as a healthy prerequisite for subsequent growth in an emerging private sector. The social, political and legal framework which should have assured foreign investors was slow in the coming. Corruption, mafia-like criminal organisations exacting 'protection money' from foreign or domestic entrepreneurs; confused and often contradictory legislation in areas such as property rights, accounting, taxation and repatriation of profits; all contributed to inhibiting international and locally engendered investment.

Russia had to cope with a festering sore in her southern underbelly: Chechnya. There, a war that had raged on and off since 1994 had taken some 30,000 lives among civilians, Chechen rebels and Russian troops. The effect on the Russian army and public was similar to the case of Afghanistan a decade earlier: a sapping of morale and a sense that the nation was sinking into a quagmire. When a fragile peace was reached in the summer of 1996, the international community – where general sympathy with the rebels' quest for national independence mingled with worries about the wider ramifications for Russia's territorial integrity – drew a sigh of relief, though nobody knew for how long the arms would remain silent.[8]

The general trend in the region was, however, one of continuing integration into the world economy. The fastest growing economies were setting an example for the rest and, by their very growth, provided increased trade with the others. None had any real choice but to continue to move, though sometimes in fits and starts, toward 'more market'. Any other course would mean delay vis-à-vis neighbours and a loss of foreign investment and innovation. Being in the world's 'loop of knowledge' meant opening up, not closing, society to ideas from the outside. Thus the Zeitgeist of the 1990s was fundamentally opposite to that of, say, the 1930s, when most countries in the region had fallen prey to fascist or communist dictatorships, seen as more conducive to economic growth through 'national mobilisation' and state management or outright ownership.

If Western Europe, and the world, were on the whole accommodating in this process, it was in part for moral and in part for more pragmatic reasons. There was a desire to help peoples who had for so long been oppressed and deprived of the kind of prosperity that the rich nations had started to take for granted. Helping them would also assist democracy, and the latter would assist economic growth, trade, and regional peace and stability. A pan-European system of co-operation and long-term peace and stability might even come about, with an as yet undefined co-ordination among NATO, the OSCE, the European Union, the Council of Europe, the Western European Union and the United Nations.

An unsettled Western Europe

While these were the priorities of politicians and institutions, the business world thought primarily in terms of the comparative advantages of the region, in particular its low cost of labour. And this was becoming costly politically to the politicians in Western Europe, who for the reasons stated, wanted to help. When companies started to move production to the East – say, from France or Germany to Poland or to the Czech Republic – unemployment rose in the West, in particular among the unskilled in the labour force.

Only in part could this be offset by increased exports of, for example, machinery for new plants in the East – machinery which as likely as not would now come from, say, South-East Asia. And only over time would increased prosperity among, say, Polish or Czech workers give rise to trade volumes that could benefit wide sectors of West European economies.

The dilemma was how to reach 'from here to there'. Increased unemployment was becoming particularly expensive to Western European states with their elaborate and generous welfare systems. If unemployment benefits were almost as high as the salaries lost, then tax levels would have to be raised for those who still worked, and for the companies that remained. However, higher taxes would mean less disposable income, and hence less domestic demand, while higher taxes for companies would mean higher cost of production, and hence an even greater incentive to move the production to lower-cost parts of the world.

Annual growth already at this time needed to be at least 2.5 per cent only to halt, let alone reverse, an increase in unemployment. Many countries in Western Europe therefore felt compelled to reform and open up their domestic economies for both products and services to international competition (under pressure to do so also from the EU and the WTO in particular), or else risk entering a vicious circle where insufficient growth, and growing unemployment, would sap growth even more. The conviction was taking hold in many Western European countries that major elements of the welfare state, built up over decades, had to be trimmed down. The strikes and social unrest in France in the autumn of 1995 and 1996 were essentially about that – as was the fierce opposition in 1999 by EU farmers against any reform of the CAP under the European Commission's Agenda 2000 proposal (which sought to replace price support measures linked to production levels with direct aid payments decoupled from production and instead related to environmental goals).

Germany – which before its entry into the EMU in 1999 maintained a strong currency that held down inflation but also inhibited exports – was faced with a debate about the *Standort Deutschland*, or the very future of German industry in Germany (as distinct from German industry abroad through multinationals). The German economic machine had become more ossified, conservative and inflexible, causing it to lose out in competitiveness to many other countries, including in the EU. The country's problems were accentuated by the unexpectedly difficult task of lifting the new *Länder* (the former East Germany) up to the levels of prosperity enjoyed by the rest of the country.[9] Reasons for this included, on the one hand, a persistent difference in the work ethic and work efficiency between 'Ossies' and 'Wessies', where the former felt that the latter were not helping enough and the latter thought that they were already doing too much; and salary increases insisted upon by the powerful German trade unions that were so high as to scare away German and foreign investors, who could now just as easily go to Poland, the Czech Republic, Slovakia or further afield.[10]

As Keynesian solutions became an unreachable option due to high indebtedness and the exigencies of the EMU, the political crisis also deepened for other reasons. At the time of 'easy' growth, in the 1950s and 1960s, say, the political Left typically argued in favour of a more generous welfare state, and whenever they came to power they expanded it a little more. All the political Right could do, when in power, was to halt or slow down the process but not reverse it, as this would have cost it the next election. From the oil crises in the 1970s onwards this could only be done through increased government borrowing, leading by the mid 1990s to a situation where even the political Left, when in power, started to have no other option than to reduce the welfare state.

A prime example is Sweden, where the Social Democrats, after three years in opposition, were voted back into power in 1994 on a promise to restore the traditional Swedish welfare state. However, once in power they immediately had to start pursuing the same kind of policies that a right-of-centre type of government would have conducted.

For the ordinary European citizen the situation had become more difficult to understand. Had half a century of building an egalitarian, generous society been in vain? Where was the wealth of yesterday? Where were left and right in politics? The only consolation was perhaps that under a left-of-centre government the cuts might come later and affect fewer areas than under a right-of-centre one. But, if they came later, might not the country's finances suffer even further in the meantime, making eventual cuts even harsher? Was that post-war, unwritten social contract between the governing and the governed – by which the citizens had submitted to the rigours of economic change in exchange for social security and other, normally better paid, jobs – now coming undone? Where were the jobs anyway, and could one be sure any longer about the social protection part of the contract? There was less certainty for everyone, including in public service, to keep their job in the future, as companies scaled down their workforce to regain competitiveness. If 'globalisation', free trade and the economic development of Central and Eastern Europe were at fault, then the jobs of many people still depended on these very phenomena, in the sense that they gave rise to employment in the export sector and in growing multinational companies, as well as in commerce where more could be sold due to lower prices for imported goods.[11]

Such were the thoughts of millions of people in Western Europe. Their anxiety was exacerbated by corruption scandals, especially where public money was concerned, but also in the private sector through insider deals and excessive pay-offs and 'parachute' deals (sometimes kept secret) for executives. The goal was the welfare state. It had come, and now it seemed it was going again. Why? What values were there except money? But money can, in the final analysis, never be happiness itself, only a means thereto. God had been present during centuries of privation, but it seemed He had become more distant, as memories of dictatorships and oppressions started to fade, and recollections of material hardship with them.

Might the European ideal take the place of nationalism, the way it had in continental Europe in the first few years after World War II? But with memories of the war becoming increasingly distant – in spite of the fiftieth anniversary of D-Day, VE-day and the end of the war – that enthusiasm had been hard to rekindle in new generations who had had no direct experience of the horrors of war.

More importantly, as the stages of integration had been passed one after the other, Europe had become more prosaic than visionary. Europe had become a matter of milk quotas, regional aid, EU directives and intermittent squabbles. The Maastricht Treaty had brought home not only the bureaucratic dimension of the European Union – as exemplified in the interminable sentences they contained on the interplay among EU institutions – but also, in the minds of many, that a European super-structure was nearing completion and might indeed mean a loss of one's national identification.

Nationalism had been partly discredited. One variety of nationalism was still *comme il faut,* which found its expression in football matches, whether it was France or England who played, or, at subnational level, Bayern München or Real Madrid. However, that other brand, which maintained that one nation was intrinsically superior to another, or needed to crush another to show that superiority, was fortunately out of fashion. In that respect, happily, most European relations had come a long way from past centuries and the first half of the twentieth century.

There still was a belief in democracy. But democracy, for all its qualities, was still, in the famous words of Churchill, the 'worst form of government excepting all the others'. Especially in times of peace and prosperity, when it was not threatened, democracy could grow 'tired'. Nepotism, favouritism and greed could creep in. Vigilance over its functioning could become more relaxed. Every type of political system carried the seeds of its own destruction, and democracy was, alas, no exception. For democracy to survive, each and every generation must defend it as its most precious legacy, yet paradoxically the generations which most benefited from it saw the least reason to defend it.

The West may have cried victory after the demise of communism in 1991–92, but that did not mean it would remain invulnerable to decay from within. For instance, democracy vitally depended on a free and independent media, but the media could be bought up by powerful economic interests, to such an extent that they all conveyed the same message, thus anaesthetising a public opinion that needed diversity of opinion to preserve its most precious quality, common sense.

The market economy implied competition, which forced everybody to be on their toes and produce quality work in all walks of life, thereby raising overall wealth. Yet even competition in a market economy could, it was now realised, be reduced by mergers and cartels, the only possible salvation being that big conglomerates often collapsed under their own weight, in what the American economist Joseph Schumpeter had called 'creative destruction'. If competition became so harsh that a majority of the population were left outside the economic system, while a minority would have to work so hard to stay on top as to lose their humanism, then the market economy and the democracy that normally accompany it might themselves be in danger.

To many Europeans in the mid-1990s, the United States was in such a danger. On the one hand, they looked in envy at the low American unemployment level – half that of the European Union – and a net gain of some 38 million jobs since 1973, against the EU's zero. On the other hand, Europeans did not want millions of people abandoned by society the way they at least perceived the situation to be in the Harlems and the Wattses of the United States. However, if Europe did not bring down unemployment more and did not grow faster economically, would its weakened public finances not eventually lead to such a situation anyway?

An uncertain world

Such, then, was the overall situation in Western Europe by the mid 1990s, as the ghosts of Hitler and Stalin bid a last farewell, hovering over the bulldozers tearing down the last remnants of the Berlin Wall. A profound feeling of uncertainty about the future reigned. It was a feeling that something was needed beyond materialism – even as material needs became more difficult to satisfy, especially when individuals compared themselves to the very rich and the very famous appearing on the screen and on television.

Central and Eastern Europe were trying to reach the material level of the West. However, even as they did, they too were realising that Western materialism was somehow hollow. People who under communism had nurtured a dream of freedom and prosperity of course welcomed it when it came. Yet past solidarity with equally oppressed neighbours and friends had disappeared, as competition for jobs became increasingly harsh, and as materialism started to replace the more immaterial values which communism had come to engender; there was no longer any guarantee of a job for life nor of a position and status in society.

A new generation was growing up, desperately depending on their parents for material support long into late youth. That it was more moralistic and less spoilt than the previous one – that of the permissive 1960s – was clear, as the menace of AIDS and a largely closed labour market loomed large. No longer was there any room for revolutionary visions of the youth of 1968, as everybody tried somehow to find a slot in the existing system. But then again, not everybody was trying. Many youths with no or little schooling had largely 'opted out' of that system, as hope of finding a job was becoming slimmer with every passing year of inactivity, dwindling along with the capacity and desire to meet the challenges involved.

If the young had perhaps become more moral than their parents under the threat of AIDS, was the visual onslaught of television and video leaving them sufficiently literate to argue in the subtle way that democracy would seem to require in order to prosper? How would dialogue survive in the era of television and Gameboy?

The picture of a confused Europe in the mid-1990s drawn up here is, of course, in many respects an oversimplification. Millions of Europeans tightened their belts and were still happy. Football stadiums were filled with excited crowds, and beaches were filled with summer tourists. Many still had secure jobs, took only a scant interest in politics and perhaps did not know what, say, the Uruguay Round or the WTO stood for.

A country like Switzerland was rumoured to be unhappy and searching for its identity as it celebrated its 700th anniversary in 1991. However, with a low unemployment rate it did not seem too perturbed, even though its male population took to the mountains each year to practise defence against an enemy that no-one could really identify. Luxembourg had equally low unemployment and high growth, and questioned neither its role as a loyal EU member nor its banking secrecy laws, which so irritated many of its EU neighbours. Norway was in a similar situation and prided itself on being a good European without being an EU member. Many a Central and East European country relished its new-found freedom from oppression, with people suddenly able to afford a car and a holiday by the seaside.

Again on the joyful side, there was the major relief from the immediate nuclear threat, as masses of tactical weapons and intermediate-range nuclear missiles were being scrapped on all sides, and as even strategic weaponry was being reduced by most nuclear powers. Europe could 'breathe' for the first time since the early 1950s, a palpable sign of which was that the German 'Easter Marches', which during the intermediate-range missile crisis of the mid-1980s had gathered up to half a million people, now mobilised far fewer, as worthy objects of protest were more difficult to find.

Presumably for the Germans, as for Europeans in general, the vision of war had become less that of a nuclear Armaggedon and more limited in scope – of the former-Yugoslavia type. It had also become messier, as in that region – or for that matter in Somalia, Burundi, Rwanda or Sri-Lanka – it was not quite clear who was fighting whom for what purpose, and hence who was right and who was wrong. There was surely as much violence to deplore as during the Vietnam War, but its complexity was such that, unlike the 1960s, there could be no rallying cry all over Europe to demonstrate on behalf of any one particular side (with the possible exception of the Bosnians during the siege of Sarajevo). Besides, the 'establishment' seemed to have the same views as the young in all these conflicts, making it difficult to present any stand of the young as, simultaneously, a revolt against their parents, as in the Vietnam days.

In conclusion, Europe in the mid-1990s had become more uncertain – about itself and about its role in the world. The old, tired East–West confrontation was gone, and the resulting vacuum posed new challenges for countries and institutions such as NATO and the European Union. New technologies waged a head-on assault on economies, closing many traditional ways of doing things while opening up many new vistas for countries and individuals ready to embrace them. International economic competition intensified, with no country or region able to opt out. It is to Europe's responses to these challenges that we shall now turn.

Notes

1 From Shakespeare's 'Sonnet 34'.
2 The START II Treaty was ratified by the US Senate, but not by the Russian Duma. It was superseded by the 2002 Treaty of Moscow.
3 The Schengen Agreement by 2002 covered fifteen European states: thirteen of the fifteen EU member states (that is all except the United Kingdom and Ireland) and two non-EU countries, Norway and Iceland. The latter have to

respect all Schengen provisions without having any say in their shaping. Sweden, Finland and Denmark insisted that Norway and Iceland be allowed to participate, since all the five Nordic countries abolished mutual passport controls already in 1957.

4 A very complete analysis of the Austrian, Finnish, Swedish and Norwegian referenda is given in Luif (1995, Ch. 13).

5 In 1963 eighteen countries signed the Yaoundé Convention with the European Economic Community to promote development co-operation. The Yaoundé Convention was followed by the signature by seventy countries of the Lomé Convention in 1975. The Lomé Convention has been followed by Lomé II, III and IV, which latter expired in 2000. In the meantime over seventy ACP (African, Caribbean and Pacific) countries enjoy privileged trade and assistance status with the EU and have concluded a new convention, the Cotonou Agreement, which signifies a reorientation of EU development co-operation policies in the direction of a greater emphasis on democratisation and poverty reduction.

6 The Council of Europe in Strasbourg, founded in 1949, is an intergovernmental organisation working for 'greater unity' between its forty-five member states 'for the purpose of safeguarding and realising the ideals and principles which are their common heritage and facilitating their economic and social progress'. The Committee of Ministers (composed of the Ministers of Foreign Affairs or their Permanent Representatives) is the Council's decision-making body. The Parliamentary Assembly is the organisation's deliberative organ, composed of delegations from national parliaments. A Congress of Local and Regional Authorities of Europe is a consultative body representing local and regional authorities. A particularly well-known part of the Council of Europe is the European Court of Human Rights, which bases its judgements on the European Convention on Human Rights and Fundamental Freedoms.

7 Croft, Redmond, Wyn Rees and Webber (1999, Ch. 6) see a 'mix of idealism and instrumentalism' in the attitudes of new and aspiring members to the Council of Europe. Membership is seen by some as a 'return to Europe', following the long separation from it under communism (especially in Central Europe and the Baltic states) – a 'symbolic acceptance of Europeanness'. In addition, 'membership of the Council of Europe satisfies an essential precondition of membership laid down by both the EU and NATO'. The authors conclude that 'the Council of Europe has been challenged in some new fundamental way by the most recent process of [its] enlargement'. While welcoming the organisation's 'proactive' stance on democracy and human rights and its suspension of 'recalcitrant states' such as Belarus, they wonder 'whether such a defence can be sustained in the face of democratic backsliding elsewhere', that is, in geopolitically more strategic countries. This underlines the Council's dual nature, some would say dilemma, as an intergovernmental, i.e. political, organisation and one based on fundamental, i.e. non-political, human values.

8 In the event, hostilities were to break out again in the autumn of 1999. In the war, the Chechnyan capital of Grozny was levelled to the ground, amid massive carnage among the civilian population.

9 Total transfers to the new *Länder* since unification in 1990 until 2002 were estimated at €660 million (DM1.3 billion). (Source: 'Sozialismus.de: Deutsche Subventionsmentalität und Bequemlichkeit', *Neue Zürcher Zeitung*, 1–2 June 2002.)

10 In discussing the growing dissonance between 'East' and 'West' Germans, Knischewski (1996, pp 143–4) says the evolution has gone from the pre-unification state of 'united though divided' (*'Spaltung in der Einheit'*) to the present-day 'divided by unity' (*'Spaltung durch die Einheit'*) due to a psychological 'wall in the heads' (*'Mauer in den Köpfen'*) replacing the Berlin Wall. 'Ossies' call the 'Wessies' *'Besserwessis'* ('know-alls') and the 'Wessies' retort by calling the 'Ossies' *'Jammerossis'* ('whinging Easterners').

11 Sassoon (1997, p 4) summed up the European Left's dilemma in these words:

> Deprived of their pathfinders, the parties of the Left have adopted, more or less overtly, a defensive strategy. Its basic co-ordinates are an acceptance that market forces can be regulated but not eliminated; that such regulation must often be co-ordinated with other countries; that the growth of public spending should be curbed; that the welfare state can be defended but not extended; that privatisation may be unavoidable and, when it eradicates monopolies, desirable; that equality, though still appealing as a goal, may be tempered by the need to preserve incentives and competition; that the power of international financial institutions – and above all, of financial markets – may be contained, if at all, only by international agreement and not by unilateral state policies.

7

The European Union's dilemma: towards a union or not?

From its humble beginnings, [the Roman Empire] has grown so much that it is now suffering under its own size. (Titus Livius)[1]

Summary

In March 1999 the European Commission, the European Union's executive branch, resigned under accusations of fraud, nepotism and mismanagement, leading to intensive soul-searching as to what could be the right form of management for the EU. How could the democratic aspects of the emerging entity be enhanced? How could democracy be improved? How should power be shared among the governments of the member states as represented in the Council of Ministers, the peoples of the Union as represented in the European Parliament, and an appointed but political bureaucracy, the Commission? How open and transparent *could* the EU be, given the many sensitive issues it was now handling, such as foreign policy, security and defence?

Rendering answers to these questions more urgent was the arrival, in January 1999, of the Economic and Monetary Union and the single currency, the euro, among eleven (and soon twelve) EU states. After a strong start, the new currency weakened successively against the US dollar and other currencies in 2000 and 2001 – helping exports but also adding to inflation – before firming again in 2002 and early 2003, though in a more difficult economic climate of slower growth in the euro-zone. It was clear that the EU had now taken a major step towards economic and political integration, begging the question to what extent formal political unification would follow that in the monetary field.

What is meant by a 'union'?

Since the European Union is, at present, the main vehicle for European integration, it seems justified at this point to concentrate on this particular organisation. The European Union's fundamental dilemma – thrown into relief in virtually everything it does, from institutional reform to single currency to common transport policy, to name but a few – is whether it wants to become a true union or not.

The *Oxford English Dictionary* gives a number of meanings for the word 'union'. The most relevant for our purposes are (author's italics):

- 'of persons or countries with reference to *joint action or policy*';
- 'the uniting together of the different sections, parties, or individuals of a nation, people, or other body so as to produce *general agreement or concord*; the condition resulting from this; absence of dissension, discord, or difference in opinion or doctrine; unity';
- 'the action of uniting, or the state or fact of being united, into one *political body*; especially formation or incorporation into a *single state, kingdom, or political entity, usually with one central legislature*';
- 'a number, group, or body of persons or *states joined or associated together for some common purpose or action*; an association, league, or society';
- 'a number of states or provinces united together or incorporated into *one legislative confederacy, a confederation or federation*; especially the United States of America'.

It will not be altogether easy to determine which of these definitions most closely fit the European Union. But the reader will agree that they are all rather far-reaching.

The 1993 Maastricht Treaty on European Union was the first to state that the institution, at least in part of its endeavours, was to be called a Union. However, it did not go so far as to say, for example, that it should be regarded as a new subject of international law, taking the place of the member states (it should not), as happened when the Soviet Union was proclaimed in 1922. Nor did it say that the European Council (of heads of state or government) was to be regarded as the new EU government (it is not); nor that a confederation or even a federation had been formed (it had not), with a commensurate reduction in the sovereignty of member states.

Maastricht left us with a situation where an ambitious word, 'union', had been chosen to denote something rather less, like 'close association'. Was the aim to give Europe and the world the *impression* that something had been obtained which in reality had not? Was it the hope that, once members knew they were in a union, there could be no disunion? A clue from the drafters' intentions could be gleaned from the disclaimers in the preamble, which state that 'The Treaty marks *a new stage in the process* of creating an *ever closer union* among the *peoples* of Europe, in which the *decisions are taken as closely as possible to the citizens'* (author's italics). In other words, the European Union created by the Maastricht Treaty was to be regarded as an ongoing process rather than a finished state.

It can be dangerous to choose words that go beyond the reality they aim to describe; thus frequent quarrels in the European Union may cause the word 'union' to lose its original meaning in the minds of EU citizens – in somewhat the same fashion as the world long ago ceased to regard the United Nations as consisting of 'united nations' (which the world presumably did shortly after its creation). Yet 'united' is something, perhaps the only stronger word remaining, to which the EC–EEC–EU process has not yet had recourse. Perhaps this is because of the discredit the word has suffered in the UN context. Perhaps it is also because its use in, for example, the United Kingdom, the United States and the United Arab Emirates indicates that something much further down the road of political union is required than the EU can hope to achieve at the present time.

The uphill battle for a union

The European Movement at its Congress in The Hague in May 1948 had called for a 'united Europe' in 'economic and political union' – but all it got was a Council of Europe. The European Coal and Steel Community had its High Authority, but the latter was never allowed to come into play, as its prime architect and first President, Jean Monnet, had intended. The European Economic Community was just that – a community of sovereign states, although equipped with a supranational, indeed an 'anational', Commission. The Benelux countries had already pooled parts of their sovereignty within the Benelux union (with Belgium and Luxembourg having also pooled their monetary sovereignty). They and Germany can be said to have joined the ECSC and the EEC in a quest for a United Europe. However, it is doubtful whether France at any stage genuinely contemplated fully giving up its sovereignty, instead seeing the institution as a way to rein in Germany and to play the leading role in Europe.

When the United Kingdom joined it was for pragmatic, essentially economic reasons. The same can be said for the Danes and the Irish. By the time Greece, Portugal and Spain joined in the 1980s – also in a large part for economic reasons – resistance by the British and others to further integration had essentially transformed the European Community into an intergovernmental organisation (with the Commission as a last, and often frustrated, driving force for integration).

The last three members – Austria, Finland and Sweden – faced a partly new situation. Not that the Internal Market posed any major threat to sovereignty, for they had all become accustomed to it through the EEA. However, there was Maastricht. The Treaty on European Union, which the candidate countries had ratified, was part of the body of normative texts of the EU established over the decades, the so-called *acquis communautaire*, and it contained the provisions for economic and monetary union (as indeed did, although in less committal form, the Single European Act).

Economic and Monetary Union (EMU) changed the name of the game. What had been intergovernmentalism flirting with federalism was becoming integration espousing it. At stake was much more than the relatively timid political co-operation foreseen in the Treaties; for once the EMU had been introduced, the EMU would require an increasingly common economic policy. In due, but not so distant, course some sort of body akin to a 'ministry of economics' could be foreseen, needed to settle priorities among EMU participating countries and render possible in the economic field what the European Central Bank was already doing in the monetary field.

As a 'deepening' of the EMU kind is sought going far beyond the Internal Market, the quest for 'widening' the EU in many respects undermines this ambition. This is so not only because a larger number of EU members makes integration more complicated, but because they become increasingly divergent. Yet, in the aftermath of the fall of the Soviet Union and of its regional domination, the need for stability in Central and Eastern Europe is increasingly being felt. Rightly or wrongly the countries concerned, as well as many EU member states, feel that the EU is the answer, since it is the only genuinely integrationist force in today's Europe (NATO being an organisation purely for collective defence and security, although with integrative implications). The EU is perceived as the only organisation able to deliver the results that count most – peace and prosperity. As a form of exclusive club, it has now reached gravitational mass.

At the same time, however, because the threat from the Soviet Union – or from its main successor Russia – is no longer there, the outside circumstances favouring integration are less pronounced in Western Europe, and in the Centre and East there is a paradoxical wish to explore newly found national independence before investing it in the EU, where it could again be reduced or lost.

Meanwhile, World War II has become something young people have to ask their grandparents about for first-hand testimony. This makes further integration out of fear of a European conflict less of a motive. France still seems haunted at the prospect of too strong a Germany, but it is uncertain whether it is out of fear of a long-term threat to France's own security unless harnessed, or whether the apprehension is one of a rival for future leadership in Europe. Other neighbours of Germany may feel similarly, although with every decade of a peaceful and democratic Germany that passes, the fear subsides a little more. This also reduces the motive for integration. Furthermore, the benefits of integration are soon taken for granted and become the norm, leading people to forget the hassles of the past and to feel less appreciative of what has been achieved. Finally, over time additional material gains from further economic integration are becoming harder to reach than in the early decades, as countries begin to realise that structural reform will have to be pursued even more strongly within their own borders. This could also reduce the will to integrate further.

Today, for as long as it may last, no more general war in Europe seems likely. Democracies tend not go to war unless they are attacked or feel under intense threat. With democracies being the rule rather than the exception in today's Europe, there is good reason to hope that overall peace inside the continent will prevail for some time, even though that may not hold for military action by different European countries in regions outside Europe, as the 2003 invasion of Iraq or peacemaking operations in various African countries have shown. No major European power seems bent on imperialist dreams. The large majority of Europe's citizens do not seem to have any higher ambitions than the pursuit of their own prosperity and happiness and that of their families and friends. For once, history appears to be on their side.

A union with less democracy?

How, given all this, do we explain the continuing quest for EU integration? Who wants it? The people? The governments? The parliaments? The EU? But what, then, is the EU? Is integration sought to prepare for an external threat in some future?

Terrorism, especially since the terrorist attacks on 11 September 2001 against the United States, no doubt provides a push for increased integration in the police and security fields, but of a limited nature since – unlike a threatening foreign power – terrorism can scarcely threaten a country's independence or existence.

The question of who is pushing for integration and why becomes all the more intriguing when we consider who is giving up power to whom. It is clear, for instance, that the European Parliament wants to have more power, both within the EU and vis-à-vis the member states. Within the EU it would have to come at the cost of the European Commission and the Council of Ministers. In regard to member states – if we assume a 'zero-sum game' – the European Parliament would have to wrestle it from the national parliaments in particular (and hence from the national governments, which execute the will of parliaments). If, on the other hand, we assume a perfectly functioning subsidiarity, where the European Parliament only deals with truly 'preter-national' European issues, then increased powers for the European Parliament may not have to infringe overly on those of national parliaments. Past experience shows, however, that such a clearly defined subsidiarity will be difficult to find, especially as countries are approaching a 'pre-federal' state through, for instance, the Economic and Monetary Union and the EU's work on a constitution via the Convention on the Future of Europe.

The European Commission, which considers itself, rightly or wrongly, as the 'guardian of the spirit' of the EU, also watches over its sphere of influence between the member states, the Council of Ministers and the European Parliament. However, it is especially squeezed between the latter two – with the Council of Ministers (the governments of the member states) insisting on continued and often increased intergovernmentalism (that is, agreements born and concluded within it, with little or no role for the Commission), and the European Parliament insisting on a greater say as the only EU body with a direct mandate from the people.

The Commission only has such a popular mandate diluted by a factor of three, in the sense that (1) the Commissioners are suggested jointly by the member states' governments (although, under the Amsterdam Treaty, appointed by the European Parliament); (2) each of these governments results from the majority in a national parliament; and (3) the national parliament is elected by the people. Using the same reasoning, the Council of Ministers has a popular mandate diluted by a factor of two. However, the decisions they take are again three steps away from the people, for when fifteen governments agree on a compromise, there is no guarantee whatsoever that this represents the will of the component peoples of the Union. Yet the decision – whether in the form of a directive or a regulation of some other EU instrument – more often than not becomes 'law' for these countries as it joins the by now massive quantity of EU legislation known as the *acquis communautaire*.[2]

The Council of Ministers is, therefore, not willing to give up any power to the Commission, especially as various governments will on any given occasion feel that the Commission is in error or biased against it. (The coalitions of discontented and contented member states vary from issue to issue.) Yet the Council works so closely with the Commission especially at the COREPER (Committee of Permanent Representatives) level, that there often evolves a communality of interests paving the way for agreement (that is, a new directive or regulation).[3]

The result is highly unsatisfactory from the democratic viewpoint. An only indirectly democratic body – the Council of Ministers – reaches a compromise decision on the basis of a proposal from an essentially undemocratic body – the Commission – which is then often asked to implement the decision in question throughout the territory of the EU. Furthermore, the Council of Ministers goes against the Montesquieuian principle of separation of powers between the legislative and the executive (and judiciary), for it is both the executive (the representation of the individual EU governments) and the co-legislature together with the European Parliament in deciding on and giving legal power to directives, regulations, etc. and, more generally, the whole *acquis communautaire*.

The Council of Ministers is equally reluctant to cede power to the European Parliament, for this would reduce ministers' own say over EU policies. In this they are, for the same reason, supported by the national parliaments, for any more power to the Strasbourg–Luxembourg–Brussels body means a commensurate loss for the French *Assemblée Nationale*, the British House of Commons or the Swedish *Riksdag*.

The problem of the lack of democracy in the EU is particularly acute for federal or highly decentralised member states such as Germany, Belgium, the United Kingdom and Spain. The German *Länder*, as represented in the German parliament's *Bundesrat*, have even threatened to veto any reform of EU institutions and EU enlargement, unless there is a clear definition of the meaning of 'subsidiarity' and respect for the rights of the *Länder* to manage their social policy priorities, including subsidies especially in the social sector.[4]

True, the powers of the European Parliament have been continuously expanded ever since the Common Assembly of the European Coal and Steel Community, the EEC and Euratom of the 1950s and 1960s. The Single European Act (1987) improved on the earlier 'consultation procedure' by introducing the 'co-operation procedure' of a more equal, 'triangular' relationship between the European Parliament, the Commission and the Council of Ministers. The Maastricht Treaty (1993) saw the introduction of the 'co-decision' procedure, giving the European Parliament legislative veto power in several policy areas, and referred to a European Parliament–Council of Ministers 'conciliation committee' to reach compromises on difficult issues. The veto areas – fifteen in the Maastricht Treaty of 1992 – were increased to thirty-eight in the Amsterdam Treaty of 1997, including transport, environment, energy, development co-operation and certain aspects of social affairs. The Amsterdam Treaty also refined and simplified the co-decision procedure, granting the European Parliament co-legislative status. Today, therefore, the European Parliament and the Council of Ministers can be considered as equals in the EU's legislative process in those areas where the co-decision procedure applies – with the Commission, however, also retaining considerable power as initiator of the proposals and as executor of the subsequent legislative decisions.[5] This situation is, however, far from the full and exclusive legislative power of parliament that traditionally characterises European democratic systems.[6]

The above situation is unsatisfactory from the democratic viewpoint, and it becomes even more problematic as the EU under the Maastricht Treaty has been given increasing competencies in culture, education, science, research, civil protection and regional policy, to mention but a few. Many regional governments (and local authorities) have tried to respond to this by having offices of their own in Brussels through which they try to influence the national representatives in the Council of Ministers, members of the European Parliament, members of the Committee of the Regions, Commissioners, Commission employees or members of the European Parliament. However, this is not accountable democracy. Perhaps even the European Parliament is not truly accountable. It often seems too vast and too remote to mean much to the citizens of the member states.[7]

As a concession to regions – across the whole confusing range from unitary to federal member states – the Maastricht Treaty on European Union established a Committee of the Regions (COR) for the purpose of providing the Council of Ministers and the Commission with advice on matters of major importance to the regions. However, the 189 members of the COR are appointed by the Council of Ministers on proposals from the member states, not elected to the post by the people of the regions. This is clearly not direct democracy either. Instead, just as the directly elected members of the European Parliament are being trained to try to bend the will of a largely unaccountable, non-democratic Commission and an only indirectly democratic Council of Ministers, so the Committee of the Regions is being conditioned to play along in the same process.[8]

The dilemma of the Commission

In the early hours of 16 March 1999 the twenty-strong European Commission resigned en bloc, in what was perhaps the most sensational event in the history of the European Union. The resignation was in response to a highly critical report by an investigating committee of independent experts created at the behest of the European Parliament a few weeks earlier. The report cited allegations of fraud, nepotism and mismanagement, but its basic charge was that lines of responsibility and, therefore, accountability were unclear. In the wake of the Commission's resignation, EU member states were left with the question of how – indeed whether – a more democratic, accountable and transparent Commission could be built on what had happened.

The core of the debate about democracy within the European Union lies with the European Commission. Many people find it inconceivable that the grown-up, sophisticated democracies that form the European Union should have given so many rights to a statutorily independent and largely unaccountable technocratic body. The answer to this riddle goes back to the 1950s.

The Six of the ECSC set up the High Authority and equipped it with such powers precisely because they wanted it to adjudicate among them in times of crisis (which, as it happened, never occurred, since there were always governments which considered that there was none). Marked by their aversion to such vast supranational powers as they had granted the High Authority, the Six in 1957, at the creation of the EEC, opted for the tamer version of a Commission. It would be an initiator, a maker of proposals, an implementer – but not a ruler in crises.

The Commission formula suited the member states of the EEC in the early years, when the priority was to clear up the whole anachronistic and suffocating underbrush of trade obstacles and other barriers in the economic field.[9] The problem with the Commission has arisen as first the EEC, then the EC and now the European Union have increasingly approached the very core of national sovereignty of the member states. Nowhere is this clearer than in the case of the single currency project, but it also surfaces elsewhere.[10]

For instance, the Commission has wide-ranging powers to allow and forbid mergers among European companies, acting as investigator, prosecutor, judge and jury (with appeals possible only to the EU Court of Justice, which has a history of not going against the Commission on these issues). There are, on the one hand, the interests of EU citizens in favour of competition and of keeping monopolies or oligopolies at bay.

However, there are also general EU interests vis-à-vis say, a US or Japanese mega-corporation that might otherwise threaten European jobs. How can the Commission legitimately decide when it has no popular mandate to fall back on? Indeed, whatever it decides it will be criticised. Which leads us on to the question as to whether it should have the power to decide. But if it should not, then who should? (Bringing us back to the question of democracy versus efficiency.)[11]

An even trickier example is provided by the Commission's powers in relation to subsidies. Article 92 in the 1957 EEC Rome Treaty states that state aid 'which distorts or threatens to distort competition by favouring certain undertakings or the production of certain goods shall, in so far as it affects trade between member States, be incompatible with the common market'.

However, when the Commission in the mid 1990s came out, on the broader grounds of European competition policy, against one of the German (new) *Länder*, Saxony, which, democratically, had decided to subsidise the building of a local Volkswagen plant, critics posed the question as to what right it should have to go against the will of the people of that *Land*, with the German government as an embarrassed intermediary, torn between its double loyalties to the EU and to one of its *Länder*.[12]

When the Commission decides, 'one last time', in favour of allowing yet another French government subsidy to Air France, to whom should it have bowed? To a French democratic interest in protecting its national flight carrier, or to other EU airlines, which have long since been weaned off state support, such as British Airways, or which with the support of their governments are indignant that their plans for expansion to new EU markets are thwarted in this way and the playing field rendered 'unlevel'? Again, the Commission cannot take the 'right' stand, for it has no democratic legitimacy and is being reproached by all kinds of actors who believe that *they* do.

In the case of the 1996 'mad cow' disease crisis (which a few years later had become even more serious), the question seemed reminiscent of Watergate. When did the Commission know about the origin of the disease and how much did it know? To whom should it bow? To the lone German scientists who in 1993 claimed that transmission from cattle to humans was indeed possible and even probable, and that exports of British beef from animals born before a certain date should therefore be banned? Or to the voices of the majority of its scientific veterinary committee, who claimed the link was fictitious, and that even the official mention of a possible link would cause panic and consumer resistance among the general public (as indeed happened as a result of a subsequent UK report, with enormous economic suffering to EU farmers in its wake?

The Commission settled for the latter course (and even asked the German government to take the scientist in question to task and ask him to keep silent – an action which would cause it considerable embarrassment when the matter was eventually unearthed). Again, whatever the Commission had decided it would have been wrong, because it had no democratic mandate (other than arguably a very limited one from the European Parliament). Indeed, it had nothing to guide it in reaching its decision, except pressure from others and pressure from within the bureaucracy itself.

However, the extent to which the Commission may be held to account by the European Parliament bears further mention. Since the Maastricht and Amsterdam Treaties, the Commission's President and overall composition are subject to a vote of approval by the European Parliament. Moreover, from the very inception of the European Coal and Steel Community, the European Parliament has had the power to dismiss the Commission. Furthermore, the European Parliament, together with other EU bodies, can take the Commission to the EU Court of Justice if it believes it has acted wrongly.

Nonetheless, collective approval/dismissal (known as the 'censure motion') is a blunt instrument, with the likelihood of very serious consequences to which the European Parliament has never taken recourse (although several votes of no confidence have been held, the last time in March 1999 over alleged corruption and mismanagement). Furthermore, the Commission's accountability for its actions before the Council of Ministers is almost negligible. Generally speaking, the Commission is only accountable to anybody else for respecting procedure (and, after March 1999, integrity) in areas within its remit, and even then only to a limited extent. For the substance, contents and direction on what it is doing, there is no such accountability.

The Commission has traditionally been a vehicle that chooses its own direction and speed. In the days of the EEC–EC, direction and velocity were largely determined by the rather obvious obstacles to trade. 'Create a common market!' was the call of governments then, and the machine did so, taking away first the visible, then the invisible, trade barriers (even though that latter job to some extent remains to be finished). Today, however, the EU touches on issues at the heart of national sovereignty. The Commission is willing and eager to show the way. However, as it does – such as taking a country to task over the handling of its budget within the EMU's Stability and Growth Pact – the member states often get cold feet and start asking who gave the order and criticising both the destination and the road taken.

The Commission was created to move European integration forward. Suppose, however, that – for instance due to a changed world economy or a new political situation – the optimal degree of EU integration has already been reached, or indeed surpassed. (The former British Prime Minister, Margaret Thatcher, maintained as much when she claimed that the Treaty on European Union was 'one treaty too far'.) Or suppose that member states, in their heart of hearts, did not want more integration. The Commission would not know, for, driven by its very *raison d'être*, it continues to move forward. It is empowered to propose and develop policies and legislation, execute programmes, guard the legal framework, represent externally and negotiate on behalf of member states (such as in external trade), mediate and conciliate. If this was acceptable in the early days of the EEC–EC, there is no guarantee that it must in all circumstances be necessary, desirable or even acceptable today. There is a growing risk that the EU blindly – without realising it – pursues policies which are no longer wanted by the peoples of the Union and their national parliaments, and eventually even by a growing number of member state governments.

With the Commission at the heart of political Europe, decisions may be 'objectively' right (if that can ever be established), but never subjectively perceived as such by the component populations. Individual EU decisions may be brilliant, but seen in succession over time they are likely eventually to go wrong, for they cannot be corrected one by one in a democratic process, as shown by the increasingly Byzantine Common Agricultural Policy.

It may also be asked to what extent the Maastricht Treaty (the Treaty on European Union) was in fact shaped by the European Commission. Ironically, we could have a situation where a body suffering from a major 'democratic deficit' has helped to shape treaties of democratic countries. Official history will of course say it was the European Council, bringing together the heads of state or government, which did it all, and to a certain extent it probably did. (Most of the wide array of issues covered in the Maastricht Treaty were originally suggested by one or the other national capital). As for the European Council, it meets for the purpose stated in the various treaties, namely to move the Union towards greater integration. It feels obliged to make new proposals whenever it convenes – proposals that have been largely conceived and given shape by the Commission.

Furthermore, it is uncertain how many EU governments in the 1989–92 period, when Maastricht was elaborated at two intergovernmental conferences, really wanted a Common Foreign and Security Policy and a single currency as under the EMU. It is certain, however, that the role of the Commission was not insignificant. Maastricht very nearly wrecked the EU integration project, precisely because many of the peoples in the EU felt alienated by it, in so far as they managed to grasp its meaning. One is therefore justified in asking whether the Treaty on European Union, or the Amsterdam Treaty, would have been what they became if it had not been for the Commission's input, or indeed if they would have come into existence at all. This 'distance' from the peoples of the EU could also help to explain the alienation from the institution felt by many EU citizens and manifested in, for instance, the negative vote on the Nice Treaty in the Irish referendum in 2001.[13]

There is a major difference between having the EU Commission propose to an EU Council of Ministers, and a national ministry preparing government policy. A government wants to be re-elected and must therefore over time follow the will of the people. Even though a ministerial bureaucracy may have wishes of its own (think of the British television series *Yes, Minister*), these are limited by and bend to the needs of the relevant ministers, and the Prime Minister, to survive politically. Direction comes from above, and ultimately from the people.

In the EU, however, the majority of initiatives come from the Commission or are prepared by it on the basis of proposals from the member states. Here there is no pressure to do as any electorate may wish, for the Commission is deliberately isolated from democratic pressure in its role as the independent engine of the EU. Proposals which the Commission presents may be rejected by the Council of Ministers, when the majority of governments feel that they are not in the national interest.

However, Commission proposals have a way of coming back in revised form, in a 'war of attrition' of sorts, until a, sometimes only slight, majority of EU member governments are won over. For instance, in the case of an EU-wide ban on tobacco advertising, the Commission, over a twelve-year period starting in 1989, presented its proposals in favour of such a ban all of ten times to a hesitant Council of Ministers. Nine times the Council of Ministers – perhaps mindful of the considerable tax income from tobacco products at national level – rejected the draft, before the measure was finally passed in 1997.[14] The Commission felt empowered to make proposals to protect the health of EU citizens. However, whether the ban was actually wanted by national governments, parliaments or national populations in the member states is more than uncertain. The driving force was, rather, determined Commissioners and Commission staff (and to some extent the European Parliament).

A directive has direct application in the member states and supersedes national law. It reflects not necessarily what a majority of EU citizens want, but what the Commission wants, although possibly in a diluted or slightly altered shape, since it has to be adopted by a qualified majority of member state governments in the Council of Ministers.[15] The EU citizenry may blame their respective national governments for this, or they may blame Brussels. If they choose the former, the government in question normally throws up its arms and points to Brussels. However, it is difficult to pinpoint responsibility in Brussels. The Council of Ministers is still a secretive body, with virtually none of its meetings public, although it is a fundamental tenet of democracy that any law-making meeting of any legislative body must be public. The same holds for meetings of the Commission.

In 1996 the United Kingdom was forced through a verdict by the EU's European Court of Justice to abide by a 1993 directive on maximum working time and related matters. The UK had argued that this was a social issue and should therefore have required unanimity, when in fact it was approved by a majority in the Council of Ministers. The Court argued, however, that it was a measure intended to protect the health of workers. Hence, it only required a majority in the Council of Ministers. Whatever the merits of regulated working time, the issue at stake here is whether a national parliament, in this case that of the UK, should have the right to decide in an area of central concern to its citizens, or whether that right should be given to a supranational court not acting within a federal system.[16]

If you try to contact a Commissioner or an ordinary staff member, you may have to compete with some of the around 700 Euro-lobbies (and many others at industry, national or subnational level).[17] They, unlike yourself, know whom to contact, whether they advocate higher tariffs to protect the EU sugar beet industry or seek special favours for European cars, shipbuilding or explosives. (The lobby phenomenon has much less of a tradition in Europe than in the United States. There is a difference, however, between lobbying an administration official or a member of Congress (or their staff) and lobbying with the Commission; for the administration official, member of Congress or Senator have a popular mandate and go against the popular will only at their peril.)

The conclusion of the preceding reasoning is that everybody in the Union must start to reflect on whether the Commission – whose role as we have seen derives from the ECSC High Authority, though in diluted form – should have essentially the same functions today as forty years ago. The question is all the more important as the President of the Commission, Romano Prodi, declared that he wanted the Commission to become a European 'government'.[18] The founders of constitutions, whether in the United States of America in 1787 or in the Federal Republic of Germany in 1949, know that everything hinges on the principles of democracy and accountability pervading all branches of government. It is doubtful whether in Philadelphia in 1787 anyone would have even have dreamt of, let alone accepted, a Commission.

As we have seen, neither intensified intergovernmentalism nor supra-nationalism is good for democracy, if political unification does not proceed apace and is accompanied by an exclusive legislative authority by a directly elected parliament. The EU has the latter in the form of the European Parliament, but that body does not possess exclusive legislative authority. The obvious solution to this problem would seem to be to equip the European Parliament with such powers. However, and here we are back to our original question, are the peoples, national parliaments and national governments prepared to relinquish such authority to the European Parliament? This is far from certain.

New EU transparency rules

In the summer of 2000 the Council of Ministers pushed through a new secrecy directive banning public access to most EU correspondence and documents. This was deemed necessary to protect confidentiality on matters touching on the European Security and Defence Policy. However, the directive also inevitably came to include much of the rest of the EU. At the end of 2000 the European Parliament therefore launched a complaint with the European Court of Justice against the new secrecy directive, calling for case-by-case secrecy authorisations rather than the blanket one foreseen. Complicating the matter were other complaints against the European Parliament itself over secrecy rulings by its internal leading bodies vis-à-vis ordinary European Parliament members. The EU's fight for openness thus promises to be long and hard-fought.

The issue of access to EU documents was finally resolved in May 2001, when the European Parliament, the European Commission and the EU's Council of Ministers reached an agreement guaranteeing access to most such documents. The transparency code will give citizens access to most preparatory and final documents produced by EU institutions or sent to it by others. Each EU body will have to establish a register of all the documents it holds, including confidential ones.

However, critics are concerned over the limits imposed, such as excepting documents considered to 'prejudice the public interest', those containing 'individual opinions for internal use' or those which submitting countries do not want to see published. (The latter would not even be referred to in EU registers.) Areas of exception include defence, foreign policy, inner security, financial and economic policy and commercial interests. Requests are to be judged by specially trusted persons and not judges. Finally, the EU agreement supersedes national law in member states, signifying that, for instance, countries with extensive access rights are not at liberty to exercise them as regards EU documents.

The agreement did not fully meet the wishes of certain 'open' countries, such as Denmark, Finland and Sweden, while others called it a victory for transparency. It was perhaps the most forthcoming possible, given that the EU is now not only a political and economic, but also a security and defence institution.

Intergovernmentalism or supranationalism?

We shall return to the question as to where the EU is heading when we discuss the Convention on the Future of Europe set up in 2002. But it is worth examining the different institutional forces at play in deciding whether the trend is toward more intergovernmentalism, more supranationalism or more parliamentarianism. Some observers believe that the European Parliament – whose role has been continuously strengthened over the years – will come to enjoy appropriate powers. This is far from certain, however. National governments and parliaments are not keen on further expanded European Parliament powers, and will no doubt fight them at every stage, openly and by other means. National parliaments may not be able to do much, since they are not part of the EU machinery. National governments, however, form part of the EU's most powerful institution, the Council of Ministers. They are likely to try to make sure that the Council of Ministers remains the strongest.

Characteristically, Agenda 2000 – the Commission's vast reform project for agriculture and regional support – was agreed by the Council of Ministers, not by the European Parliament, even though it had to approve and amend the project subsequently. The European Parliament feels it has history on its side, fighting for democracy within the European Union on behalf of the people. However, given the sensitive issues ahead, the peoples of the EU member states are likely to place their trust more in the national governments when it comes to defending the national interest than in an only vaguely understood political process in the European Parliament. This tendency can be expected to grow stronger with a wider, more heterogeneous, membership. The low voter turn-out for the European Parliament elections is a sign of indifference and perhaps even distrust vis-à-vis the European Parliament and the EU as a whole.

Whatever the effects of inevitable EU enlargement on the institution's finances or on the uniformity of its policies, enlargement will mean a push towards intergovernmentalism. It will be country against country, bloc-of-countries against bloc-of-countries along a number of dimensions: 'new' versus 'old' countries, North versus South, small versus big, net contributors versus net beneficiaries, or even between one set of net beneficiaries and another if EU largesse does not suffice for them all.

The battleground is likely to be the Council of Ministers, in spite of claims by the European Parliament that it should be given that role. In the essentially intergovernmental EU it is the member states alone that decide on changes in EU treaties, and they are unlikely to give complete and exclusive legislative authority to the European Parliament, on the grounds that it is not a sufficiently fine instrument with which to adjudicate between interests and also in order to preserve their own powers as exercised via the Council of Ministers. The Commission will be squeezed between an European Parliament wishing to extend its powers and a Council of Ministers eager to preserve or even expand its own.

Supranationalism through EMU

If anything can be expected to come after the present EU intergovernmentalism, it is EU supranationalism through Economic and Monetary Union (EMU). On 1 January 1999 eleven of the fifteen EU countries introduced the single currency – the 'euro' – marking the final stage of a long process towards the EMU. They were Austria, Belgium, Ireland, Italy, Germany, France, Spain, Portugal, Luxembourg, the Netherlands and Finland. The United Kingdom, Denmark and Sweden chose not to join from the outset but possibly to do so later. Greece wanted to join but was not accepted. In early 2000 it announced its desire to join in 2001. The request was granted in June, 2000 and Greece became the twelfth EMU member on 1 January 2001.[19]

The run-up to the EMU in the months preceding its launch on 1 January 1999 was smooth, with interest rates converging down or up – depending on the national currency concerned – toward the target single rate of 3 per cent set by the European Central Bank. For countries struggling to come out of recession at the time, such as Germany and France, the absence of an interest rate cut (or a raise of the rate) meant renewed risk of a stifling of economic growth. For countries in a more expansionary phase, like Italy, Portugal or Ireland, the necessary lowering of the rate (in some cases by half) carried the danger of overheating their economies and stronger inflationary pressure. However, the 'locking' of the various exchange rates was achieved without great difficulties and the euro at its start stood at 1.18 to the dollar.[20]

The reasons for entering the EMU on the part of the twelve participating countries differed for each one of them. France saw joining as a way to regain the monetary sovereignty it had effectively lost to the Deutschmark, but also as a means to tie Germany closer to it and to enable France thereby to play a larger role in Europe and the world. Germany saw it as a way to assure its EU partners that it was genuinely seeking a federated Europe, in which it would be a loyal and constructive partner, not intent on seeking hegemony or striking out alone in Central and Eastern Europe. The Benelux countries had sought greater EU integration ever since 1957 and were always enthusiastic EMU proponents. Finland chose EMU membership essentially for political reasons, and in spite of the risk of 'asymmetric shocks' due to its peripheral location and its dependence on price-sensitive products such as forestry and pulp. For Spain, Italy and Portugal EMU membership was vital to joining mainstream economic Europe and shedding any notion of a less serious 'Club Med' mentality. They made major sacrifices to qualify, with Italy even introducing a special 'eurotax', which was stoically endured by a population anxious not to be left outside 'Euroland'.

The Economic and Monetary Union is likely to increase the pressure in the direction of a federal European Union, with a strong supranational character, not only among the participating countries (the 'ins'), but also vis-à-vis the non-participating EU members.[21] This in turn could mean a vastly expanded role for the Commission in the economic sphere, as it would work to supplement the European Central Bank. With one currency, national economic policies in Euroland have to be much more co-ordinated. Deviations larger than the minimal are inhibited by such things as EU fines or withdrawal of EU funds under the Stability and Growth Pact, by which the members wanted to ensure adherence to the 'convergence criteria' of budgetary discipline.[22] A much higher degree of Euroland economic and monetary co-ordination will have to be established in due course if the EMU is to work, as national politics will become increasingly irrelevant and incapable of achieving the co-ordination necessary to compensate for the varying impact of a single currency on different countries and regions.[23]

A major argument for the EMU is that it permits the single market to function better. Previously, a depreciation by one country meant a commensurate competitive advantage for its exporters vis-à-vis a EU country whose currency had not changed in value. With inflation (though not necessarily inflationary pressure) the same in different EMU countries under one currency, depreciation by some can no longer develop over time. Trade and investment are likely to grow more quickly in an atmosphere of currency certainty, leading to more efficient economies, more employment and greater prosperity. EU enlargement, it is argued, will enhance this effect further, just as the EU saw its economy revive in the wake of earlier increases in its membership.

Finally, competition is believed to increase as people are supposed to be better informed about price differences in different countries, say of cars, causing prices to fall and consumption to rise. Tourism is undoubtedly becoming easier as the euro is the valid currency in many countries of destination. Cross-border mergers and take-overs are already more frequent, although not to the degree that many would have wished to see as a sign of true European integration.

Capital has become easier and cheaper to come by, due to consolidation in the financial sector. There are even attempts at mergers among stock exchanges, even though differences in legislation and culture have so far made their realisation difficult. In sum, the euro forces Euroland firms to think in European terms when conducting business, something that North American companies had to start doing already in the nineteenth century.[24]

EMU supporters go further. Euroland citizens, they say, are coming closer, drawn together by the psychological impact of 'one currency – one destiny'. This facilitates the political unification sought through the EMU. Political unification will in turn permit Europe to play the role it might on the world stage – a rival to the US at times, an equal partner and ally at others. Finally, proponents say, the euro is more stable and better protected against world currency turmoil, now that it has a central bank able to draw on all the national central banks under its authority.[25]

Monetary union without political union?

If the above describes the thinking of euro-enthusiasts in a nutshell, how do those who are less convinced reason? For one thing, they doubt that the peoples of Euroland are sufficiently close to each other, temperamentally and politically, for economic federalism to be followed by friction-free political federalism. They do not believe that Eurolanders are united enough to be able to stick to one and the same economic and monetary policy and they fear international and domestic frictions such an inability may engender – tensions that were previously avoided by having each among them adapt the strength of their national currency to their particular economic situation.

Before EMU, depreciations often paved the way for economic recovery and 're-appreciation' of the currency. Through appreciation, foreign capital came in to supplement domestic capital, as did imports, thereby taking some of the heat off the economy and dampening inflationary pressure. Depreciation and appreciation of currencies, according to this way of seeing things, permit relatively smooth adaptations to an altered domestic or foreign economic environment. As neighbouring economies grow in this stop-and-go fashion, they are also able to stimulate their neighbours. Within an EMU such a corrective mechanism no longer exists.

Even though trade is stimulated due to the absence of currency fluctuations (since there is now only one currency), overall growth is hampered by interest rates being too high for some countries (leading to economic stagnation), too low for others (leading first to an overheated economy and then to excessive contraction) and at the right level for just a few. If it is too high for a major country, such as Germany or France, then that country will be unable to pull out its smaller neighbours from a recession, leading to prolonged weak growth for all.[26] Some critics therefore contend that the member countries of the EMU do not form an 'optimal currency area'.[27]

The main argument of the critics is that integration among sovereign peoples must be first political, then monetary. They would presumably have been less apprehensive if EU governments had stated their intention first to aim for a true EU government, creating, for example, a bicameral parliament with exclusive legislative powers over EU matters, before going for a single currency.

The order of political union before economic union was the one chosen in Philadelphia in May 1787, as representatives of thirteen American states came together to amend the articles of the Confederation loosely holding them together. By September, they found that they had drawn up a constitution uniting them politically. Only three years thereafter, in 1790, did the newly appointed Secretary of the Treasury, Alexander Hamilton, present a First Report on the Public Credit.

All obligations of the old Confederation, and the war debts of individual states, could be exchanged for bonds of the new national government. A national bank, quasi-public and patterned after the Bank of

England, was to issue notes – eventually dollars – based on the public debt. The Act creating the Bank of the United States was passed in 1791, but it would take some thirty years until all the currencies of the several states had ceased to be in circulation. Only in 1862 was a single currency formally adopted. Full monetary integration was not achieved until 1913 with the creation of the Federal Reserve.

American monetary integration was possible because of the threat of British invasion. The early prevalence of one language, English, was certainly helpful as well. Decades of 'national' identity, not centuries as in Europe, inspired the thirteen states. The expected expansion westwards, requiring resources larger than could be mustered by individual states alone, provided further impetus.

Differences between the EU and the United States

Monetary union survived in the United States due to the victory of the Union in the Civil War and the gradual economic integration between the states, facilitated by the elimination of the obstacles to interstate trade and investment, and a highly mobile workforce.

Close to a fifth of all Americans move in a typical year from depressed to more prosperous areas – whether from the east coast to California or from the 'rust-belt states' in the north to the 'sun-belt states' in the south. In total, 3 per cent of the national population, close to eight million people, move officially every year from one state to another. Between 1990 and 1994 Utah saw a 24 per cent increase in the number of jobs, or 200,000. Colorado added 300,000, a 20-per-cent increase over the same period. Between 1960 and 1990 the proportion of the US population living in California rose by 37 per cent, and between 1980 and 1992 the number of Californians grew by over 2 per cent per year. Conversely, during the 1993–94 recession, 850,000 people left the state. The proportion of the US population living in Florida almost doubled between 1960 and 1990, whereas the number of people living in New York fell by more than one quarter. This kind of labour force mobility helps explain why a single currency can function in the United States. People move without hesitation to where the jobs are.

By contrast, only 0.1 per cent of the total EU population moved from one country to another in 2000 and only 1.2 per cent changed region within a country.[28] It is difficult to imagine a mobility within Europe similar to that in the United States without considerable political and social upheaval, as most people out of work are not prepared to move abroad or would not be able to find work abroad due to a lack of knowledge of the language of the country or countries where jobs might be available. Although the European Union has taken important steps towards ending the formal barriers which existed for citizens of any of the member states to move to and live and work in another member state, significant informal barriers remain. Linguistic and cultural differences are major impediments to wide-scale cross-country migration, and the possibility of accumulated pension rights accruing from employment in different countries is extremely limited, especially for ordinary workers. With unemployment figures close to 10 per cent in many EU countries, these countries ability to receive large numbers of foreign job-seekers is restricted.

European mobility may of course increase over time. (It may also become less important for economic growth as the latter is driven increasingly by information and communications technologies, which reduce the importance of geographical distance.) More retired people from Northern Europe may seek out sunnier climes along the Mediterranean, much as their American counterparts move to Florida. As the multilingual workforce expands, more workers may find the attractions of higher pay and the excitement of living in a different culture alluring. However, this does not describe the Europe of today, where unemployment first and foremost hits those with less education. Europe cannot yet rely on a pan-European labour force mobility anywhere near that of the United States.[29]

Closely related to labour mobility is the degree of 'flexibility' of labour markets, a theme raised in nearly every speech by ECB officials as they exhort EMU governments to undertake 'structural reform' in order to assist the euro. Most euro-zone countries have a panoply of labour market regulations that tend to restrict economic growth. Costly social programmes are financed by taxes that curtail business incentive. Generous payments to the jobless diminish their incentive to take up work. The costs of lay-offs to employers discourage them from hiring in the first place. Labour market flexibility in the UK and the US compare favourably with that in Euroland on all these counts. Flexibility extends beyond the labour market. The basic culture in the United States, and to some extent the United Kingdom, observes the principle of government non-interference in business life and encourages the seizing of business opportunities and risk-taking more than is the case in most countries in the euro-zone. (This may not always lead to higher lasting growth, however, as the various corporate scandals in the US in 2002 illustrated.)

Another difference between the EU and the United States is the compensating effects of latter's considerable fiscal transfers via its uniform income tax. As California grew in the 1987–91 boom-years, it contributed nearly 17 per cent of additional federal tax revenue, raising its percentage contribution to federal tax receipts from 12 to 13.4 per cent. Conversely, during its economic crisis from 1991 to 1994, the state's share of increased federal tax revenue fell to just 8.1 per cent and its share of the national burden declined to 12.5 per cent. If California's tax share had stayed unchanged during the period in question, its 1994 federal tax payments would have been $11 billion higher than they actually became. This $11-billion decline is equivalent to roughly $350 per capita in tax relief. Thus, many of the stabilising properties of the progressive tax system in the United States manifest themselves in an automatic regional redistribution of the income tax burden through the high mobility of the workforce. In other words, states within the United States are assisted in overcoming recessions by contributing less to the federal budget, while states with a growing economy pay more. In addition, the federal government makes large transfers to individual states in the form of grants and aid programmes, further equalising conditions among them.

Europe, by contrast, has no such automatic fiscal transfer mechanism. Labour mobility is much lower. Furthermore, the budget of the European Community is much smaller (when compared with the combined GDP of EU member states) – about 1.2 per cent – than the US federal budget, which amounts to about 20 per cent of the country's GDP. It is true that EU expenditure does involve some transfer-oriented programmes, such as the Common Agricultural Policy and the various regional funds. But this is little by comparison, apart from the fact that the destination of this type of EU funding does not change readily along with recessions in individual regions. Overall, Europe lacks the kind of automatic stabilising properties which a unified fiscal mechanism affords the United States as an alternative to exchange rate variations. (This invites the argument that the EU should as soon as possible try to unify itself fiscally. However, as we have seen, formidable political obstacles stand in the way of any rapid development in this direction.)

The stabilising properties of a currency zone-wide fiscal process are thus not in place in Europe. Nor are they likely to be so in the near future, given the reluctance of EU member states to increase the institution's budget. Indeed, the EU 2003 budget of around €100 billion is practically the same in real terms as that in 1996, and the EU is agreed that this should remain the case for the years to come.[30]

Significant fiscal flexibility is difficult under EMU, unless a country has built up a solid budgetary position in the past, such as by having shown budget surpluses in years of strong growth. The Stability and Growth Pact foresees fines of up to half a percentage point of GDP on any EMU country that goes beyond a maximum 3-per-cent budget deficit in other than exceptional circumstances or for a brief period. (This is necessary for the value of the euro to be maintained. An example of what could happen was given in the spring of 1999 – a few months after the introduction of the euro – when Italy was given permission by the other EMU members to go slightly beyond its original budget deficit forecast. Even though the deficit was less than the maximum 3 per cent, the move caused the euro to fall sharply vis-à-vis the dollar.)

The concerns about inflation and solidarity among the Euroland countries as regards fiscal orthodoxy are understandale. Yet it is difficult to see the sinning country, already in economic difficulties, readily agree to pay a fine of the order foreseen, since it would a priori take away even more purchasing power from its citizens and risk channelling popular fury against 'Brussels' or Frankfurt (where the ECB is based).

Europe's low birth rates and rapidly ageing population also pose a danger to the stability of the euro. As fewer people in active ages have to support more, and longer-living, old-age pensioners (including a growing number of early retirees), public finances in Euroland countries will come under great strain, starting around 2010. The situation is aggravated by the fact that almost all the EMU countries rely almost exclusively on taxpayer-financed, 'pay-as-you-go' types of pension systems. Either taxes will have to rise to much higher levels, impeding growth, or government spending will have to be drastically cut, threatening social peace.

Furthermore, since the single currency has locked the economies of the EMU countries together, increased pensions payments in a country in a demographic crisis, such as for example Italy, will raise inflation also in a country with a younger population, such as Ireland. If, say, France spends its way into a deep deficit to assist an ageing population, Dutch homebuyers may end up paying higher mortgage interest, since big government budget deficits tend to raise interest rates by increasing competition for capital. Ireland and the Netherlands may protest, but there will be little they can do, since Italy and France are sovereign in their budgetary decisions – the EMU's Stability and Growth Pact notwithstanding. Governments in Europe, especially those resulting from coalitions or with weak majorities, are more likely than not to delay or dilute the necessary reforms. The cart of Euroland-wide single currency management may well find itself put before, not the horse but the horses, of national politics.

An 'exit risk' would likely be exacted by the financial markets, were ever any doubt to arise as regards the future of the EMU as such. As long as monetary union is not accompanied by political union, the risk of such doubt occurring cannot be ruled out. Two scenarios are possible. In the first, economic difficulties, especially high unemployment, lead to a political sea change in a major euro-country and therefore to popular pressure within it to leave the EMU.[31] In the second, though less likely scenario, a given country develops such high budget deficits in spite of the Stability and Growth Pact that others insist that it leave. In either event, there would be a massive flight of capital from the country in question. This would lead to downward pressure on the euro in all the participating countries and to general confusion in all areas of economic life, not least as assets or debts in the currency will have no clearly defined national domicile.[32]

It remains to be seen whether, as a result of EMU, the peoples of Euroland will start moving internationally to a greater extent. Perhaps the unstoppable rise of English as the world's, and Europe's, lingua franca even for the less educated will help reduce linguistic, and perhaps even cultural, barriers to migration.[33] Perhaps the single currency will eventually bring about a more federal Europe, with a more centralised fiscal policy. Perhaps such a larger fiscal role for the EU could then become more of a regional stabiliser to assist countries or regions in recession, even though it is unclear whether and how this could apply in those EU countries which do not participate in the EMU. It also remains to be seen how the peoples of the EU would react to such a development.

The EMU gamble

The EMU countries of the European Union showed considerable courage in going for the single currency in 1999. Monetary unification was sought before political unification – a feat which had never succeeded in the past (the most notable attempt being the ineffectual and eventually collapsed Latin Monetary Union among a few European countries from 1865 to 1925).[34] Furthermore, EMU countries were not very integrated economically, since the EMU 'convergence criteria' dealt exclusively with 'expressions' of economic performance (so-called 'nominal convergence'), and not with 'indications of true convergence', such as similar unemployment rates. Finally, EMU was started in the absence of two major instruments to manage it: high labour mobility, and a central fiscal authority with efficient means at its disposal.

Should the above-mentioned arguments have been sufficient cause for the EU not to attempt or to abandon the EMU project, at least at this stage in European history? The alternative would have been to go on living with a single market – malfunctioning in the absence of a single currency. Complaints would have continued over excessive exchange fees charged by banks and over exchange rate instability.

However, critics of EMU maintain that the status quo of using different currencies should have been kept, considering the present early state of European political integration and economic convergence. The Internal Market would still have functioned, they say, even with the handicap of occasional currency swings between EU members, and it would not have been divided between the twelve in Euroland and the three outside it. Countries could have depreciated their currency, but they would have had much less leeway to do so in an effort to gain competitive advantage. Depreciation would not have been undertaken principally for the purpose of gaining competitive advantage, but simply to help the national economy adapt to new circumstances. Furthermore, countries could first have concentrated on internal structural reform in their economies to create real convergence among them, and only then entered into a single currency with all the further economic and political convergence it would require.

One reason why countries today behave much more responsibly with their currencies – and hence why the EU might have been able to live also without an EMU – is that the confidence of international markets in an excessively and continuously depreciating country evaporates quickly, causing capital flight and reducing foreign investment. This factor is far more important today than in, say, the 1960s, when capital was much less internationally mobile. Another is that a country which is tempted to depreciate for reasons of competitive advantage is also likely to have a considerable government debt, much of it incurred in foreign currency and owed foreign lenders. Depreciations thus add to the public debt, providing a further disincentive to follow this path. In short, countries are much less prone to engage in currency depreciation for 'frivolous' or 'disloyal' reasons today than in the past.

Critics of the EMU are not necessarily defenders of large numbers of small currencies, especially within an intensely trading community such as the EU. They do, however, point to a number of advantages. First, the currency is managed – at least formally (and that is important) – by the people of the country, for even an independent central bank is accountable before it. Second, on a more practical level, a depreciating currency of a country with a weak economy can gain certain export advantages and will import less, permitting the economy to recover, the currency to appreciate, exports to be reduced and imports to rise. Conversely, a country with a strong economy, and an appreciating currency will, allowing for time lag, normally see its exports decrease and its imports rise, reducing the risk of overheating. The resulting downturn in the economy will restore the 'natural' value of the currency vis-à-vis others. Trade predictability will suffer – perhaps therefore trade itself. However, in a community of nations with low labour mobility and many different languages, this may be the lesser of two evils.

The debate between those in favour of a single currency for the EU and those against it is, of course, now water under the bridge as far as the twelve Euroland countries are concerned. However, the pros and cons still matter for those three EU countries – the United Kingdom, Denmark and Sweden – which are still outside it and for all the candidate countries preparing to join the EU and, hence eventually, the EMU.

The European Central Bank: independence versus accountability

The European Central Bank (or, more precisely, the European Central Bank and the European System of Central Banks) is meant to operate in complete independence. This had been at German insistence, reflecting that country's traumatic experience with inflation in the 1920s and the success of its post-World War II economic recovery, which to a large degree had been built on *Bundesbank* independence and a strong Deutschmark. Other countries, such as the United Kingdom and France, had had a somewhat different tradition implying a certain, but not total, independence of their central banks vis-à-vis the government and parliament. (Now, however, both countries, along with others, have given their central banks much greater independence, in part to satisfy EMU requirements.) The justification for central bank independence is that politicians may otherwise be tempted to have central banks ease money-supply conditions as a painless (but often ultimately self-defeating) way to overcome a recession, or to win an impending election.

A careful balance has, in fact, to be observed between central bank independence to prevent manipulation of the economy for political ends and the people's need to keep any institution set up to govern it accountable before the electorate (this latter being the touchstone of democracy). The challenge facing the countries participating in the EU single currency is therefore one of developing post-Maastricht rules for the European Central Bank which successfully balance accountability and independence. This, of course, is rendered more difficult at the present time, since the political structure of the EU is itself in rapid evolution.

Ultimately, responsibility and accountability to the public at large are the things that matter. Accountability to intermediary institutions that do not themselves possess the legitimacy given by public accountability will not be enough.

Accountability and independence should not be seen as polar opposites. In a democracy, any central bank or monetary policy institution which stresses only its independence and ignores its ultimate accountability to the body politic may soon find its independence at risk. The basis of central bank independence is the role it can play in correcting some imperfections in the normal democratic process. However, such independence is granted democratically, temporarily and continually by virtue of that process. There is currently a great deal of argument among policymakers in favour of central bank independence as thus defined, but such independence must ultimately be subordinated to the higher principle of accountability before the people.

How democratic, or accountable, is the European Central Bank (ECB)? Its President and the members of the Executive Board are appointed by the heads of state or government of the member states, after consultation of the European Parliament. The President of the ECB reports regularly on the system's operations, and the ECB issues an annual report. The ECB President also appears before the European Parliament to explain the policy followed. Transparency of ECB policy is further enhanced by the provision that the President of the EU's so-called ECOFIN Council (of European Union Ministers of Economy and Finance) and a member of the European Commission may attend meetings of the ECB's Governing Council, albeit without voting rights, just as the ECB President can attend ECOFIN meetings.

However, it is doubtful whether this amounts to sufficient democratic control. Governments, who are two steps away from the people (the parliament being one step away), scarcely possess sufficient democratic credibility in this arena, especially when they have to share their influence over the ECB with the governments of other EMU participants. The European Parliament – which is democratically elected but which does not have the same legislative function in the European Union as a national parliament – is not in a position to fill the gap.[35]

This can lead to problems. To the extent that the ECB will eventually be forced to follow strict monetary policies, these will easily form the object of national and populist anger at being governed not by one's national capital where there is direct democratic representation – say, Paris or Madrid – but by a distant Frankfurt where the ECB is based. No longer would the blame be laid at the national door, but at those of

Frankfurt, 'Brussels' or fellow EMU countries. To this should be added the risk of fines of the order of billions of euros imposed on countries found in violation of the Stability and Growth Pact. Even if it is not the European Central Bank that decides on such fines, it would risk being associated with them in the minds of ordinary people. 'Enough Brussels and Frankfurt!' could easily become a rallying cry for populist movements.

The euro from 1999 to 2003

As already indicated, the euro started out as a strong currency, standing at €1.18 to the dollar at its launch in January 1999. Already by April 1999 – four months into the EMU – difficulties started to emerge. Ireland, whose economy looked as if it might be overheating, would presumably have wished a rise in the ECB's 3-per-cent policy-setting interest rate then in force. Others, and especially Germany, wanted to avoid the risk of sinking into renewed recession and would have been in greater need of a rate cut. In the end, the ECB lowered the interest rate to 2.5 per cent in April 1999, hoping that it would help to revive in particular the German economy. The ECB warned, however, that no further lowering would be forthcoming within the foreseeable future, and that Euroland governments would now have to start in earnest with structural reform to stimulate growth.

The value of the euro sank from about €1.18 at the currency's launch to around parity with the greenback by mid-1999. Among other things, there were doubts about ECB independence in the wake of calls by several Euroland governments for lower rates, but also in view of (in comparison to the US) lower economic growth in the region and the approval by the EU–Eleven of a larger budget deficit for Italy than financial markets would have preferred. The conflict over Kosovo in the spring and summer of 1999 also hurt the euro, as the whole stability of Europe was called into question. Later in 1999 it recovered somewhat following the return to peace in Kosovo and more optimistic economic forecasts in such key countries as Germany and France.

However, by May the following year, 2000, the euro had sunk well below parity with the dollar, to around 90 cents. The decline reflected lacklustre performance of the Euroland economies and pessimistic forecasts; perceived interference by politicians in attempting to influence ECB policies; and the continued vigour of the US economy, leading to the continued popularity of dollars in the currency markets. The euro's depreciation helped exports but also raised inflation due to higher import prices. Markets seemed to demand far-reaching structural reform in Euroland and insist that policymakers speak with a single voice on monetary matters rather than in a cacophony of often conflicting statements. Markets also appeared to react to various political or social crises in EMU countries. It seemed exceedingly difficult to 'talk up' the euro and all too easy to 'talk it down'. The weakness of the euro stood in stark contrast to the ECB policy-setting interest rate, which by April 2000, had been raised successively to 3.75 per cent, with further increases held out.

The ECB now faced a dilemma. If it raised the interest rate to attract investors, it would risk stifling for example the growth of the German economy, the largest in Euroland. If it lowered it, the German engine might go into higher gear, but already over-extended economies might overheat and an already weakened euro slide even further. Exports might increase, but with the US as the world's only remaining 'importer of last resort' this would add to that country's already large trade deficit, with negative consequences for the world economy.

The EMU suffered a further setback when, in a September 2000 referendum in Denmark, 52 per cent of the population announced itself against the country's entry into the euro-zone. The Danish fears of losing monetary, or even national, independence were somewhat illusory, since the krone (unlike the Swedish krona or the British pound) closely followed (± 2 per cent) the value fluctuations of the euro (also reflecting Denmark's predominant trade links with Euroland). In mid-August 2000, the euro stood at around $0.90, signifying a reduction of close to 25 per cent from its initial $1.18. Exports from the EMU area were rising, especially to the US with its strong dollar, but also to EMU 'outs' (or 'pre-ins') such as the United Kingdom, whose manufacturing industry was complaining about lost exports to Euroland countries due to the relatively stronger pound.

The euro had also weakened against an array of currencies around the world not known for their strength. This was making Euroland imports more expensive, especially products denominated in dollars such as oil. Furthermore, in the absence of a country-specific interest rate weapon, various EMU members such as Ireland, Spain and Portugal were experiencing inflation rates of over 5 per cent due to economic overheating, while inflation in core countries like Germany and France was close to or above the 2 per cent inflation limit established by the European Central Bank as a trigger for interest rate hikes. The ECB interest rate had been raised repeatedly in the spring and summer of 2000 to reach 4.25 per cent. Further increases looked necessary to stem inflation and defend the currency's value, not least in the face of capital leaving especially for the US with its higher (6.5 per cent) federal funds rate and higher economic growth.

However, the export boom was contributing, at least temporarily, to rapid economic growth in the EMU area (of between 3 per cent and 4 per cent in 2000) and a tangible reduction in unemployment (to less than 10 per cent). Many people were attributing the good times to the EMU or had not started thinking about it, as they were still paying and being paid in the national currencies, now truly only existing on paper.

Additionally, internal Euroland trade had grown more intense in the two years of EMU existence, and a more integrated European financial market, including that of London, had begun to emerge, making the region less sensitive to external shocks. The EU's work to harmonise economic life in line with EMU requirements had also manifested itself in an agreement to combat the evasion of taxes on interest income (requiring member countries either to impose a withholding tax on foreigners or to share information with these foreigners' national tax authorities) and a common company code meant to facilitate mergers.

In the early spring of 2001 – with the euro sinking toward the $0.85 level – the European Central Bank withstood pressure from EU governments, international institutions and financial markets that it lower its policy-setting rate, in the meantime raised to 4.75 per cent, to prevent Euroland from sliding into recession. The ECB's argument was that inflation was too high and risked rising further if the rate was lowered. In May 2001, however, the ECB changed course and lowered the rate to 4.5 per cent, arguing that it had overrated actual inflation. Markets did not take to this kindly and the euro weakened further to $0.83 in July, but then firmed at around $0.90 during the autumn.[36]

The ECB's dilemma perfectly illustrated the previously mentioned difficulty of having one currency among politically independent countries with, in addition, such widely divergent, perhaps even diverging, economies. For some, such as Ireland, Spain, Portugal and Finland, the interest rate was too low and gave rise to inflation. For others, like Germany and Italy, it was too high, jeopardising growth. Inflation in the former group was so high as to pull Euroland-wide inflation up towards 3 per cent, past the ECB's self-imposed inflation limit of up 2 per cent (beyond which it had decided it could not lower the ECB central rate). The ECB's helplessness now risked producing 'stagflation', in that the Euroland economy might well stagnate even as it suffered inflation. Thus, in the spring of 2001, Germany had both a slackening economy and an inflation close to 3 per cent.[37]

Neither the 'bursting' of the 'new economy' bubble as from the spring of 2001, nor the terrorist attacks on the United States on 11 September the same year, could seriously dent the value of the dollar vis-à-vis the euro. The US economy continued to attract foreign funds (in spite of several US interest rate cuts to historically low levels that should in theory have made the dollar less attractive). Investors were attracted by the prospect of resumed high US growth after 11 September and were further encouraged when this happened.

However, throughout the period of a strong dollar against the euro, the Japanese yen and other currencies, lasting from early 2000 to the middle of 2002, the US had accumulated a huge current account deficit that made some kind of correction inevitable. It came in mid–2002, when the euro rose to above parity with the dollar, in reaction to a series of corporate scandals involving serious accounting irregularities, which the markets felt had betrayed them.

The euro's rise was in spite of indications that the requirement in the EMU's Stability and Growth Pact for a maximum 3 per cent budget deficit might be difficult for some countries to meet. These included Germany, France, Italy, Portugal and Greece, which all reported worsening prospective deficits for 2002 close to the 3-per-cent level. Much discussion in the EU's Council of Ministers in early 2002 was devoted to whether Germany and Portugal should be formally warned (in the end they were not, despite urgings by the European Commission, which started an 'excessive deficit procedure' against Portugal in the summer of 2002, after the country officially reported a 4.1-per-cent deficit for 2001). There was also concern that France's budget deficit might increase even further as a result of promises by the new right-of-centre government both to lower taxes and to increase expenditure.

The Stability and Growth Pact suffered a further setback when the President of its prime guardian the European Commission, Romani Prodi, called the Pact 'stupid'.[38] However, Prodi's remark had the effect of bringing on a debate about the value of the Pact in an economic environment much less propitious than that which had prevailed at the time of its conception in the 1990s. Even though the Pact was meant to be 'pro-cyclical' – that is, have governments reach budget surpluses in fat years to be used up in lean years – this did not happen, since governments have a tendency to want to be re-elected. The result was that in bad times, when deficit spending would be needed, the Pact would largely forbid it. Still, a number of adaptations to the Pact were possible. One would be to have the deficit limit apply only over an entire economic cycle (from the boom stage to the recession stage) of, say, four or five years, rather than each year. Another would be to define an acceptable size of a country's deficit when compared to its national debt (which would land, for instance, Italy in a much stickier situation than say, Ireland) and that borrowing should be allowed outside the deficit calculation for infrastructure investment.

In late 2002 the ECB lowered its policy-setting interest rate from 3.25 per cent to 2.75 per cent, the lowest in three years. The reduction took place even as inflation in the euro-zone stood at above the 2-per-cent limit, beyond which the ECB had said it would not lower interest rates. The action was largely in deference to Germany, whose economic situation had continued to deteriorate. The economy had barely grown in 2002, while the budget deficit had soared to 3.7 per cent, well above the Pact's 3-per-cent limit. A number of smaller European countries with stronger or indeed overheating economies had to bite the bullet, even though a lower rate would result in even higher inflationary pressure there. Their acceptance was also a consequence of their lesser influence in the ECB Executive Board when compared to the bigger countries, and because a further weakening of the German economy, the biggest in Euroland, would soon spell trouble also for them.

Shortly thereafter the European Commission started an 'excessive deficit procedure' also against Germany, which was now in a bind. Unemployment was bound to rise, leading to less tax income and greater unemployment expenditure. Government cutbacks to reduce the deficit would further dampen economic activity. Devaluation was not a possibility in a currency union. Deficit spending *à la* Keynes to kick-start the economy was impossible under the Stability and Growth Pact. No relief via exports could be expected, given the euro's firming against the dollar. Exports to other countries in the euro-zone might eventually accelerate due to the lower inflationary pressure in Germany (1.3 per cent in 2002) when compared to, say, Spain (4 per cent in 2002), but then Spanish inflationary pressure would in the end also seep into Germany, as happens in any currency union over time, thus reducing that advantage.[39]

Finally, the German reforms needed – deregulating the labour market, cutting the cost of health care, overseeing the pensions system, reducing payroll taxes and decentralising wage bargains – would take considerable time in a country which had made social solidarity a central part of its post-war reconstruction.

France's economy was still holding up reasonably well, with growth at around 1 per cent in 2002 and a budget deficit approaching but not yet exceeding 3 per cent. This, however, caused the European Commission to issue an 'early warning', especially after France made a cavalier announcement that its ability to reduce its deficit would depend on how fast its economy grew.

Italy showed similar figures, but its government debt of 110 per cent of GDP made its situation uncomfortable. The European Commission complained about a 'lack of information' about many economic aspects. With growth slowing ominously and deficits rising in the three dominant euro-zone economies – Germany, France and Italy – overall prospects were bleak, even as virtually all the other members of Euroland showed budgets in balance or in surplus.

The euro by early 2003 had risen further, reflecting, however, more the dollar's weakness than any inherent strength in the Euroland economy. The dollar suffered from fears for the US economy against the prospect of a looming invasion of Iraq, for which the US was the leading proponent; the large US current account deficit; and US economic growth which, though higher than that of Euroland, was slowing down considerably.

A pattern was developing in 2003, in which the European Commission and the European Central Bank – joined by 'behaving' countries such as Ireland and Finland with balanced or surplus budgets – would call on 'sinning' EMU governments to cut deficits and pursue 'structural reform', with the latter reporting difficulties and asking for postponement of the 2004 deadline when the budgets of all would have to be in, or close to balance (a deficit of not more than 0.5 per cent). The postponement was duly granted by the Commission in September 2002, when it extended the deadline to 2006, while calling on countries to reduce 'structural deficits' (that is, those not depending on countries' position in the business cycle). The Commission's retreat was all the more understandable as Euroland as a whole showed a 2-per-cent combined deficit in 2002, a situation which would have made a return to balanced national budgets by 2004 an impossible task.

As a result of these difficulties, the Commission suggested a bigger role for itself in determining EMU policies. Thus its 'recommendations' to Euroland governments should become 'proposals', which could be adopted through a simple, instead of a qualified, majority in the EU's Council of Ministers. Furthermore, the informal euro-group of EMU Finance Ministers should receive a more official status and its chairmanship should be prolonged from six months to two years. EMU member states, anxious to preserve their freedom of action, reacted coolly to these ideas. In sum, the Commission's proposals illustrated the difficulties, referred to earlier, of reconciling the requirements for highly co-ordinated management of a currency area with the present nation-based running of the central aspects of the EMU. Presumably, the greater the difficulties the euro may face in future, the greater the need (as apart, perhaps, from the wish) will be to entrust its management to the EU. [40]

However, another development is possible, under which the Commission, under pressure from countries with embarrassing budget deficits, will increasingly 'look the other way' in awareness of its powerlessness to 'force' sovereign countries back on to the straight and narrow. This would of course meet with protests from euro-zone countries showing fiscal rectitude, but they would be powerless to do much more than shout. Whether this would necessarily hurt the euro is not clear, since financial markets are more pragmatic than doctrinaire and may welcome an occasional vivifying shot of good old Keynesian deficit-spending in order to get an economy back on track.

EMU, the 'outs' and the others

Alongside the twelve EMU 'ins', three EU members have opted to stay outside the single currency for the time being. The United Kingdom under the Labour government under Tony Blair indicated its intention to hold a referendum on the issue during the 2001–6 legislature, provided a number of criteria were considered to have been met as to whether it was in the British interest to join.[41] Denmark opted not to join following a referendum in September 2001, in which a majority of voters rejected membership. The Swedish government, after sticking to a 'wait-and-see' attitude for several years, in 2002 announced that it would hold a referendum in September 2003 to settle the matter. In the event of a 'yes', Sweden could be expected to join the EMU in 2006.

The single currency debate necessarily concerned also the rest of Europe. European countries outside the EU were major trading partners of the European Union. About half the exports and imports of the Czech Republic, Hungary and Poland were to and from Austria, France, Germany and the Benelux countries. The economies of an increasing number of Central and Eastern European countries were by now highly integrated into those of the EU. Trade with the EU and the four EFTA countries (Iceland, Liechtenstein, Norway and Switzerland) was practically liberalised, and the few remaining restrictions on capital flows no longer constituted a serious constraint. The monetary and exchange rate policies within the EMU area would therefore have a direct impact on Central and Eastern European economies.

After EU candidates joined – ten being foreseen for membership in 2004 – they would be expected, in accordance with the Maastricht Treaty on European Union, also to join the Economic and Monetary Union – that is, have the euro replace their national currency. This would take place after a two-year participation in the so-called ERM II

(Exchange Rate Mechanism) of a maximum +/– 15-per-cent variation of their national currency vis-à-vis the euro.

This would not be an easy operation, however. Firstly, the euro might suffer if international money markets feared for the economic stability of an EMU candidate country, a situation that existing Euroland members would want to avoid. Secondly, since growth rates were often higher in candidate than EU countries (also because they grew from a lower basis level), they had the choice of either accepting the resulting appreciation of their currency vis-à-vis the euro and thereby enjoy lower inflation, or keeping a firm exchange rate to the euro but instead suffer higher inflation. The former course of action might make eventual entry into the EMU more difficult by 'locking' the national currency to the euro at too high a level at the moment of entry (thereby hurting exports). Thirdly, the ECB's decision-making bodies would have to be reformed to avoid paralysis under a widened EMU membership.[42] Finally, joining the EU would necessitate considerable public investment and pension reform, thereby making the Maastricht EMU criteria of a limited budget deficit more difficult to reach. [43]

With ten of the twelve EU candidate countries expected to join in 2004, it seemed realistic to foresee them joining the EMU at around 2008. Inflationary divergence – and resulting inner monetary tension – in the thus enlarged Euroland could be expected to be even greater than today.

Notes

1 From *Praefatio* 4 by Titus Livius, the Roman historian (59 BC–AD 17). The Latin text reads: '*Ab exiguis profecta initiis eo creverit, ut iam magnitudine laboret sua*'.

2 See Weiler, 1997.

3 The real power resides in the COREPER – subdivided into the COREPER II for ambassadors dealing with the more important matters and the COREPER I of their deputies, who take care of more technical subjects. They are assisted by some 250 working parties in different subject areas.

4 Meeting between representatives of the German *Länder* and Romano Prodi, President of the European Commission, as reported in the *Neue Zürcher Zeitung* on 26 May 2000.

5 For a more detailed discussion of the growing power of the European Parliament, see Neuhold (2000).

6 Some, such as Westlake (1998, p. 127) are more optimistic as regards the development towards democracy in the EU. He sees the European Parliament as asserting increasing control powers over the Commission and as sharing

more and more influence with the Council of Ministers through the gradual extension of its budgetary powers and the 'co-decision procedure' obtained in the Amsterdam Treaty in particular. All three institutions have had to become increasingly transparent in the process, helped by technological advances such as the internet. New members such as Sweden and Finland with their traditions of openness in public affairs are also, in his view, contributing to this trend. Indeed, he says, with more and more EU members, the Council of Ministers is increasingly becoming a kind of assembly, or senate, with meetings involving over 75 people more akin to a 'station concourse' (and correspondingly open). He sees a constant dialectic in the EU between 'effective government' and 'democratic government', with trade-offs having been traditionally in favour of the former but with the tide now turning. Indeed, he argues, the Commission always 'knew that its unaccountability was an aberration ... No bureaucracy, however enlightened, could act in the absence of political authority. The Commission sought out the democratic legitimacy of the Parliament, much as plants seek out the light; in the longer term, it knew that the Commission could not survive without it.'

7 Members of the European Parliament have no real home constituencies, as do national parliamentarians. The Council of Ministers, for its part, has, with its fifteen members, long ceased to be a forum for real debate, as opening statements alone during the customary one-day ministerial meetings may take up to three hours to read out. Most Council decisions are pre-prepared by powerful and unaccountable civil servants. Extensive veto or blocking powers by no more than a few countries (even after the December 2000 Nice Summit) cause many issues to be postponed, even as, at national level, decisions in the areas concerned are postponed on the grounds of 'waiting for the EU'. That the Council of Ministers has evolved in this way is not only due to Parkinson's Law (Parkinson, 1957), but also to the fact that it is not directly accountable to any electorate, with national governments being able to 'blame Brussels'.

8 This raises the question as to whether the EU should have a constitution or not, and whether it is indeed sufficiently united to be able to forge one – a subject to which we shall return in a later chapter. A constitution would have to address not only democracy in the Union government itself, but also the rights of member states vis-à-vis the Union. What rights should member states have as against perceived encroachments on their powers by the 'centre'? Should they have the same rights of 'nullification' as US states enjoy in regard to Washington? Should an EU majority – in the European Parliament or the Council of Ministers – be enough on matters vital to member states, or should an additional 'second majority' be required among the individual member states through parliamentary approval – or through referenda such as in Switzerland?

9 The philosophy behind the creation of the Commission is not, in fact, so dissimilar to that of the Gosplan in the Soviet Union at the time. A predominant

belief in the 1950s was in uniformisation. This notion is, however, ill-fitting in an era when the world economy is fuelled by decentralisation and diversification.

10 Featherstone (1994, p. 165) concludes that: '[Jean] Monnet's original conception of an elitist, technocratic High Authority to lead integration has been found wanting. The very form of today's EC Commission weakens its capacity to exert political leadership. It is too vulnerable to attack, as a result of its lack of accountability and democratic legitimacy ... In different senses, the Commission has been overtaken by the progress of integration: more intensified forms of integration highlight the Commission's lack of democratic legitimacy; all too often it is not up to the job of exerting political leadership.'

11 It could be argued that, for instance, the *Bundeskartellamt* is equally powerful within Germany. However, the *Bundeskartellamt* is under the control of a directly elected German Parliament with exclusive legislative powers over its statutes and operations.

12 In 1996 the Commission allowed Saxony to give a limited subsidy to Volkswagen. The conflict erupted when Saxony was felt to have given too big a subsidy. In its verdict of December 1999, the European Court of Justice's Court of First Instance supported the Commission's refusal to allow any additional subsidy to Volkswagen in Saxony. Since then, Germany and other EU countries have repeatedly insisted on their right to subsidise companies in difficulties, especially in suffering regions, and the Commission's statutory obligation to try to prevent them has been used by politicians for electoral 'Brussels-bashing' purposes. Often, the Commission has in the end permitted reduced subsidies rather than take the recalcitrant country to the European Court of Justice.

13 This is in no way meant to call into question the dedication or competence of those who work for the European Commission. Many of the achievements which Europe takes for granted today would not have come about, at least not so early, without the Commission. The work continues. The Commission is the driving force in many areas, among which can be mentioned the liberalisation of the energy sector leading to lower prices, foreseen by 2004 for businesses and by 2007 for consumers; the introduction of a single air traffic management for civil aviation, reducing delays; the creation of a single capital market, reducing borrowing costs; and anti-trust legislation to increase competition.

14 In October 2000 the European Court of Justice overturned the EU ban on advertisements for tobacco. The Commission had argued that the ban would facilitate trade. Not so, said the Court, maintaining that it rather hindered than helped the trade objective. Undeterred, the European Commission, which had proposed the ban, said it would think of new ways to reduce tobacco consumption (even as the EU gives €1 billion in yearly subsidies to its tobacco growers). In May 2001 it returned with another proposal for an

EU-wide ban on virtually all forms of tobacco advertising and sponsoring of events by tobacco companies. In December 2002 the EU adopted a directive meeting most of the Commission's demands, against the opposition of the United Kingdom and Germany. The ban would take effect in 2005.

15 The need for impartiality becomes acute in such an instance of Commission unaccountability. In March 2000, for instance, the Volvo truck division wanted to merge with the Scania truck division, but the request was turned down by the Commission, which argued that the merger would give the new company too dominant a position in Scandinavia. The Swedes complained, however, that earlier Renault–Iveco and Mercedes–Kässbohrer mergers had been approved, even though they meant a similar or even greater domination over parts of the EU market. In other words, what drives the Commission in the absence of any democratic accountability? *Quis custodiet ipsos custodes?* The answer came in 2002, when the European Court of First Instance (established in 1994 to relieve the European Court of Justice of some of its workload) issued two verdicts overturning merger vetoes pronounced by the Commission. The Court's complaints – that the Commission had based its decisions on insufficient analysis – caused a crisis within the Commission and calls for an overhaul of its working methods in this area.

16 The same can, of course, be said about the Council of Europe's European Court of Human Rights, with the exception that this body is meant to deal with alleged violations of fundamental rights and freedoms as enshrined in the European Convention on Human Rights and Fundamental Freedoms. Yet when it comes to its judgements on corporal punishment in schools or parental spanking of children, it, too, has aroused much controversy in, for example, the UK.

17 Greenwood (1998, p 587) refers to 700 'Euro groups', mostly based in Brussels, together with a variety of less formal collectives, 200 firms with their own Brussels-based public affairs capacities, and a cluster of around 25 public affairs consultancies operating from the Belgian capital. Such 'overcrowded lobbying' raises the issue not only of possible 'lobbying abuses' but also 'broader concerns in European public governance, including key concerns regarding the democratic deficit, the management structures and capacities of European institutions themselves, and standards of decision-making'.

18 Interview in *Le Figaro* of 17 June 1999. Prodi, asked whether his Commission would be 'a government or rather an administration at European level', answered: 'A government, of course'. He also said: 'The Commission will be a team inspired by the same philosophy, like a government cabinet. Not a Commission of left or right, but a European Commission'. Some observers will support such a stance. Toulemon (1998, p. 121), for one, argues: 'Nominated by the governments of the member states for a limited period, most frequently drawn from the political milieu, collectively responsible before the European Parliament which, since Maastricht, approves their nomination; members of the European Commission enjoy the same democratic

legitimacy as government ministers nominated by a head of state and responsible before a parliament ... The truth is that the Commission is constantly done down by those who do not wish to see Europe equipped with a true government, effective and legitimate.'

19 Greece was admitted to the EMU in spite of its not meeting some of the so-called 'convergence criteria'. Thus, its debt-to-GDP ratio in 2000 stood at 104 per cent, far above the required 60 per cent (although exceptions had been made also for other EMU members before it). Furthermore, inflation had been brought down to 2 per cent, but there were questions as to whether this could be sustained. Finally, the Greek economy was considered as still in need of structural reform, especially in the highly regulated markets for certain goods and services. However, joining the euro was seen in Greece as an important political commitment that would speed up the modernisation of the country's economy.

20 One of the reasons for success in reaching the start of the EMU was that there was never any fall-back position if preparations had run into serious trouble, such as if pressures on candidate currencies became unbearable. The same holds now that the euro exists. There was no clause in the Maastricht Treaty foreseeing any way out for countries, individually or collectively, from the euro. The reason for the absence of any 'retreat position' on the part of EU governments (such as postponement) was, of course, that this would have whetted the appetite of speculators from the start.

21 EU parlance speaks about the countries participating in the EMU as the 'ins', whereas those outside are referred to as the 'pre-ins' or the 'outs'.

22 The Stability and Growth Pact foresees fines of up to half a percentage point of GDP on any EMU country that goes beyond a maximum 3-per-cent budget deficit in other than exceptional circumstances (a systemic shock or a severe recession) or for a brief period. This is necessary for the value of the euro to be maintained. It also obliges participating countries to reach close to balanced budgets by 2004, a deadline which the Commission in 2002 said could be postponed until 2006, provided a standby reduction was reached in the meantime in that part of the budget which did not depend on conjunctural factors ('structural deficit'). The Commission speaks about a 'breathing budget', which would make the Stability and Growth Pact less of a straitjacket. The possibility cannot be excluded that EMU members will introduce a new and looser definition of 'government spending' if deficits continue to be embarrassing for some among them. One option would be to exclude public investment, on the understanding that it would both stimulate the economy *à la* Keynes and permit stronger economic growth in future via improved infrastructure.

23 In a sign of growing influence by Brussels, EU Finance Ministers in February 2000 agreed to let the Commission frame the circumstances in which a member state can change its mix of tax and spending policies. In particular, 'pro-cyclical' tax cuts that fuel inflation in an already overheating economy were ruled out.

24 However, in July 2001 the European Parliament rejected a legislative proposal that would have considerably facilitated cross-border company takeovers, including hostile offers, by making such bids conditional on agreement by the management of the targeted company. While this was seen by some as preserving a bulwark against American-style capitalism, to others it was considered contrary to the implications of the EU Internal Market and the single currency. At the same time the European Commission blocked a takeover bid by General Electric vis-à-vis Honeywell on the grounds that it would overly restrict competition, not by control over a given market but by the presumed dominance, through subsidiaries, of several markets. This did not go down well with the Americans, whose antitrust legislation (court-based rather than Commission-led) tends to be more strictly oriented towards consumer (as opposed to competitors') interests.

25 This indeed turned out to be the case even before monetary union in the latter half of 1998. The prospective 'Euroland' was scarcely affected by the Russian or the Brazil currency crises, and this held also for weaker currencies such as the Italian lira. It continued to be the case in the 1999–2002 period, in the face of major fluctuations in the value of the US dollar and Japanese yen.

26 To use an allegory, a 'one-size-fits-all' interest rate is like having twelve people wear same-size suits. For some their suit is too big and for others too small. All in these two groups will be hindered in their walking. Only for a few of the remaining twelve will the size be comfortable and the walking unhindered, but they risk being slowed down by the others, since all now have to walk in tandem.

27 Growth rates in the EMU area in the 1999–2002 period seem to bear this out. Average GDP growth was only slightly over 2 per cent, compared to about 3.5 per cent for the United States and around 2.5 per cent for the biggest non-EMU member state of the EU, the United Kingdom. (Source: *OECD Economic Outlook.*)

28 Source: European Commission.

29 The European Commission in 2002 recommended that EU member states increase labour mobility by, for instance, making it easier to collect pensions and unemployment benefits in countries other than one's own, by introducing an EU-wide health card that would speed up reimbursement for medical expenses and by creating a central information office for jobs across the EU.

30 The European Council in 2000 fixed the annual EU budget for the 2002–6 period at around €100 billion, or about 1.2 per cent of the EU GDP.

31 An example was the unexpected advance to the second round in the French presidential election in the spring of 2002 by Jean-Marie Le Pen, the leader of the extreme right *Front National* party. Le Pen said he wanted, if elected, to take France out of the EMU. In this case, however, the euro did not weaken noticeably, since the left-of-centre voters immediately shifted their allegiance from the defeated candidates in the first round (especially Lionel Jospin) to the Gaullist candidate Jacques Chirac, who was thereby assured a

large victory. There is no guarantee, however, that such a propitious outcome will always occur.

32 The European Central Bank (and the European System of Central Banks
which it heads) is much more decentralised than the US Federal Reserve. In
fact, it very much resembles the more decentralised Federal Reserve structure which was in place from 1913 to 1933 and which had to be abandoned
after the Depression in favour of a more centralised system. The ECB, unlike
the Fed, lacks four main competencies of a central bank – the latter being
still with the national central banks of EMU members. The four lacking
competencies are: a monopoly over the issuance of money; the right to set
refinancing interest rates on behalf of national central banks; the rejection of
insufficient securities for loans; and the ability instantly to supply the
totality of liquidity needed in a crisis situation. The ECB must therefore be
considered much more vulnerable than the Fed.

33 The EU of the fifteen member states has eleven official languages. There are
at present over a hundred different language combinations for translators
and interpreters. In the EU of twenty-five member states as from 2004 the
number will be over 300. Although German is the language most widely
spoken in the EU Fifteen (90 million people), its role in the EU is limited
when compared to English and French, with the former rapidly gaining
ground against the latter.

34 The Latin Monetary Union (LMU) entered into effect in 1866 and would in
due course include Belgium, France (the dominant member), Greece, Italy
and Switzerland. A 'bimetallic' treaty, it soon ran into severe difficulties
such as how to deal with the Austrian–Italian war in 1866 and the Franco–
German war of 1870–71 – let alone World War I, by which time it was
practically defunct. Vanthoor (1996, p. 37) sees the core problem of the LMU
as lying in the 'insufficient convergence of the policies conducted by the
Member states. As a result, the country abiding by the rules most stringently
was inevitably flooded by the speculative capital flowing from Member
states whose currencies felt the pressure of their expansionary spending
policies.' There were, apart from the LMU, also the lesser known – gold-
based and similarly inoperative – German–Austrian Monetary Union from
1857 to 1867 and the Scandinavian Monetary Union from 1872 to 1931.

35 The European Central Bank is not part of any government since no European government exists, nor is it truly answerable before the European
Parliament. Amtenbrink (1999), for one, deplores this lack of democratic
control and warns that: 'Where power is delegated by the legislative or the
executive branch to independent bodies which are not considered as part of
a government, the traditional mechanisms of democratic accountability run
the danger of failing to a large extent, as the latter may be out of reach of
such mechanisms as democratic elections, answerability to Parliament, or
even control by the executive government.'

36 The European Central Bank's mandate was, and is, exclusively to maintain

price stability, soon defined as not tolerating inflation exceeding 2 per cent. To measure current inflation and inflationary pressure in the short and medium term, two pillars were to be used: monetary growth in the eurozone, termed 'M3'(monetary targeting); and a more broadly based assessment of inflationary pressure (inflation targeting). The ECB had early on announced that it would primarily be guided by M3 in determining its policy-setting interest rates (as had been the policy of the German *Bundesbank* in the pre-euro days). However, when the ECB lowered its central interest rate in April 1999, M3 growth stood at 4.5 per cent, well above the 2-per-cent inflation limit. If anything, the ECB should have raised the interest rate, not reduced it, even though a lowering stood to reason given the recessionary tendency in Germany, the biggest euro-zone economy. The same contradiction between announced criteria and actual policy was manifested on several occasions in 2000 and 2001, leaving financial markets unimpressed and contributing to the euro's slide against the dollar. However, it also signified a shift in ECB policy toward 'inflation targeting', which may be considered a more flexible and pragmatic approach under the circumstances. See, for instance, *Economic Survey of Europe*, of the United Nations Economic Commission for Europe (2000 No.1, pp. 35–7).

37 Unlike the ECB, the US Federal Reserve has a three-pillar mandate: checking inflation, fighting unemployment and stimulating growth. Its freedom of action is correspondingly wider.

38 Prodi said: 'I know very well that the Stability Pact is stupid, like all decisions that are rigid'.

39 In 2002 real interest rates, i.e. allowing for inflation, were negative in countries like Spain and Portugal, signifying that keeping money in the bank there meant a loss for the depositor.

40 The European Commission in 2002 called on the EMU countries in particular to lower labour costs and integrate their markets for energy, communications and financial services. Tax reforms would have to be such as not to worsen budget deficits. Public health reforms should reduce expenditure. The Commission's recommendations were adopted at the 2002 EU summit in Seville, Spain, though in dilated form. Thus France made its compliance with the 2004 goal for a balanced budget conditional on sufficient economic growth (3 per cent), which, apart from being somewhat unrealistic, also opened up loopholes for others.

41 The five 'tests' to be made before the British government would decide to hold a referendum and recommend British entry into the EMU were (1) that the British economy was converging with that of the EMU area; (2) that it would remain capable of responding flexibly to outside shocks; (3) that the euro was proven to benefit investment; (4) that it was shown to assist financial services and especially the city of London; and (5) that it would promote employment.

42 Up until enlargement, the ECB's Governing Council would have eighteen

members: one from each national central bank in the European System of Central Banks plus the six members of the ECB Executive Board. After enlargement to twenty-five EU states and assuming EMU membership for all new members, the Governing Council would have twenty-eight members. If Denmark, Sweden and the United Kingdom were to join, the number would be thirty-one. Given the major difficulty of making such a numerous body function, the ECB in 2002 floated a proposal foreseeing a system of 'weighted voting', according to factors such as the size of a member country's economy, its contribution to ECB resources, and a sub-division into two – and with further enlargement eventually three – 'groups' of countries with a differing say in decisions and with a rotating membership.

43 Birth rates in the EU candidate countries in Central and Eastern Europe were already low in communist times, as women were strongly encouraged to join the workforce. They continued to be low after the transition process to a market economy began, since women now had to keep working in a more competitive economic climate. Meanwhile, the currencies of most of these countries, contrary to what was expected, appreciated considerably vis-à-vis the euro they were scheduled to join after EU accession, making EMU membership all the more difficult to achieve. The appreciation was being caused by substantial foreign investment and productivity gains, permitting exports to be maintained at strong levels in spite of the currency exchange disadvantage.

8
A new NATO

The Great role of conduct for us, in regard to foreign nations, is in extending our commercial relations to have with them as little political connection as possible. … Europe has a set of primary interests, which to us have none, or a very remote relation. Hence she must be engaged in frequent controversies, the causes of which are essentially foreign to our concerns … 'Tis our true policy to steer clear of permanent Alliances, with any portion of the foreign world. (George Washington)[1]

Summary

The disappearance of the Soviet Union and the end of its hold over Central and Eastern Europe posed the question of the future of NATO. What continued purpose could NATO serve? How far east could it enlarge without upsetting Russia? NATO's first enlargement in 1999 included the Czech Republic, Hungary and Poland, while various co-operative programmes with other countries in the region, including Russia and Ukraine, were expanded.

NATO's first ever armed conflict was with Yugoslavia in the spring of 1999 over the latter's Kosovo province and over Serbian mistreatment of ethnic Kosovo Albanians. After three months of aerial attacks, NATO stood victorious and a major international troop presence restored relative calm to the province.

The Kosovo War led to intensified discussion in Europe and the United States over the need for increased European defence spending and operational efficiency within the alliance and over the prospects of more 'out-of-area' peacekeeping or peacemaking operations, such as in the 'former Yugoslav Republic of Macedonia' in 2001. European efforts to achieve greater defence autonomy (see also Chapter 9) met with initial scepticism by the United States. The Europeans showed similar scepticism as regards preliminary US plans for a Strategic Missile Defence project aimed at developing the capacity for shooting down incoming missiles.

The terrorist attacks against the United States on 11 September 2001 and the converging interests of the United States and Russia by mid-2002 modified the situation. Both sides abrogated the 1972 Anti-Ballistic Missile Treaty, thus permitting the US anti-missile project to go forward. The two countries also concluded the Treaty of Moscow, signifying deep cuts in their strategic nuclear arsenals. Russia's relations with NATO became even closer with the creation of a NATO–Russia Council. At a summit in Prague in November 2002, NATO undertook its second enlargement in the post-Cold War era, as it invited Bulgaria, Estonia, Latvia, Lithuania, Romania, Slovakia and Slovenia to join in 2004.

However, questions regarding NATO's continued relevance arose anew, as the US showed an increasing propensity to act independently of the organisation, as the Europeans lagged behind in defence spending and technology and as differences in the willingness to use military might began to appear, such as in the Iraq crisis in 2003, which exposed deep rifts in the perception of outside threats and the action to be taken in their regard. NATO was not likely to disappear as it was still useful to both sides, but the communality of purpose was not the same as it had been during the Cold War.

NATO in the 1990s: where is the enemy?

When Mikhail Gorbachev began to apply his 'new thinking' to foreign policy in the late 1980s, Georgi Arbatov, his expert on North America, jokingly issued this threat to a NATO official: 'We will do something terrible to you – deprive you of your enemy'. This threat came true when the Warsaw Pact was dissolved in the summer of 1991 and the Soviet Union ceased to exist in November of that year.

A military alliance without an enemy has every difficulty of surviving. NATO would have to find a new enemy, or at least a mission equivalent thereof, and with it a new role. A first effort was made in 1991, with the announcement of a new Strategic Concept. The enemy found was 'insta-bility'; the method was inclusion or enlargement; and the role was a shift from major war-preparedness to, primarily, crisis management, peace-making, peacekeeping and other 'soft' uses of military might.

The successive decisions leading up to this new posture started with a number of questions. First, after the break-up of the Soviet Union and the dissolution of the Warsaw Pact, should there remain, on the land-scape of Europe, a military alliance, or should NATO dissolve? The official answer by the NATO countries to this first question was that an alliance was still needed, because their security might continue to come under threat. Such contingencies could arise from regional conflicts or instability due to ethnic and other tension inside one country or between countries; or they could be external, from the south or from the east, especially in an era of modern missile technology, weapons of mass destruction and terrorism.[2]

Second, should a new alliance take the place of NATO? NATO members, and in particular the United States, concluded that it would be easier and cheaper to build on something already existing rather than start from scratch. Furthermore, NATO had come to be seen as the symbol of North American commitment to the defence of Europe.[3] Finally, NATO had proved its ability over the years to assist in peaceful integration and democratic development of the continent – such as in helping the defeated powers of Italy and Germany to join it; in the European construction efforts since the 1950s; in spurring reconciliation between France and Germany; in keeping peace, however fragile, between Greece and Turkey; and in providing a unified military command, thereby creating transparency and trust among the member states and removing the incentive for military competition among West European powers.

A third question to be answered was whether a continued NATO should enlarge or not. In the end the 'yes' prevailed. Part of NATO's post-Cold War mission had become to promote an evolution in the countries of Central and Eastern Europe towards civil society, a market economy and peace with their neighbours. It was felt that NATO membership for the countries concerned would benefit this process. Conversely, a decision not to expand would risk being seen by these countries as a parallel to the decision of the United States not to join the League of Nations after World War I; as relegating them to a permanent 'buffer zone' between East and West; and as a punishment for having involuntarily been conscripted to the Warsaw Pact during the Cold War. Both internal and external instability might have followed. As the leaders of the sixteen NATO member states gathered in Madrid in July 1997, the question was therefore not whether, but how far, the alliance should enlarge.

Three new NATO members in 1999

At US (and British) insistence, invitations were initially limited to the Czech Republic, Hungary and Poland, with most European NATO members (and especially France and Italy) advocating early membership also for Romania and Slovenia (they were singled out in the final communiqué as being next in line for 'preferential consideration'). Negotiations with the Czech Republic, Hungary and Poland were finalised by the end of 1997 and NATO's third enlargement was celebrated at a summit in Washington in April 1999, the fiftieth anniversary of the Washington Treaty (at which time the alliance might statutorily have been dissolved).

The decision to undertake a 'mini-enlargement' of this kind capped a longstanding effort on the part of the three successful candidates – the Czech Republic, Hungary and Poland – for full economic and political integration into what could still, though somewhat archaically, be called 'the West': a Euro-Atlantic community of shared values and goals, while holding out the same prospect for their neighbours in the region. Neither the Council of Europe nor the OSCE had been able alone to satisfy this aim.

The Washington Summit also decided to build a European Security and Defence Identity within the alliance. The policy called for a much stronger European responsibility in handling future conflicts of the Kosovo type. New threats would be brought to NATO's attention, giving it a right of 'first refusal'. In cases where the alliance would not want to act as such, a European Union chain of command would be expected to take over responsibility, borrowing equipment from NATO (and especially the United States). Such material could include spy satellites, cargo planes and position-guided cruise missiles.

Russia had not expressed any wish to join NATO. Instead, a NATO–Russia Founding Act on Mutual Relations, Co-operation and Security (falling short of treaty value) had been signed in Paris in May 1997, establishing a Russian diplomatic representation at NATO headquarters in Brussels and concrete procedures for consultation and co-operation between NATO and Russia. They included a Permanent Joint Council meant to soothe Russian apprehension about the alliance's eastward enlargement and to step up co-operation on peacekeeping (such as in Bosnia and Kosovo), anti-terrorism and ways to curb the spread of weapons of mass destruction.[4]

In addition, Russia was invited to join numerous other non-NATO members – and all NATO countries – in a new, at the time, forty-three-member Euro-Atlantic Partnership Council (EAPC) with basically the same purpose.[5] A similar agreement – a Charter of a Distinctive Partnership (again no treaty value) – was concluded in Madrid in 1997 between NATO and Ukraine, providing for the two sides to develop a crisis mechanism to consult together whenever Ukraine perceived a 'direct threat to its territorial integrity, political independence or security'.[6]

The emphasis in these agreements was on contacts, co-operation, sharing and rules of conduct. They had in common that they wanted to include, not exclude – perhaps even to a fault in that it might become difficult for a continuously enlarged NATO to live up to its collective defence commitments.[7]

The war over Kosovo

In the night of the 23 March 1999, almost to the day fifty years after its creation, NATO fired its first shot in anger, as aircraft took off from bases around Europe and the US to bomb Yugoslavia. Thus ended fifty years in which the alliance had not had to act, and therefore had successfully realised its mission.

The main reason for the attack, named 'Allied Force', was the way Yugoslavia, under its President, Slobodan Milosevic, had been treating the ethnic Albanian majority in its southern-most province of Kosovo. Killings of civilians, executions of able-bodied men and 'ethnic cleansing' of entire towns and villages was leading to thousands of refugees leaving Kosovo for shelter in the neighbouring 'former Yugoslav Republic of Macedonia', Albania and Montenegro (the second state in the Yugoslav federation). Such atrocities were happening in many other places in the world. However, this was Europe, NATO's doorstep. NATO was driven into action after it had delivered a long series of threats and ultimatums which, when not met, called into question NATO's very credibility.

The conflict was to last much longer than anyone had expected, until June 1999 when Yugoslavia accepted the conditions for a ceasefire belatedly agreed among the members of the United Nations' Security Council.[8] On NATO's side the war was waged entirely from the air to avoid the delays, cost and potential casualties among troops and civilians associated with a land-based invasion of Kosovo (or even Yugoslavia) – a process during which NATO's fragile inner cohesion could easily have frayed.

This, however, inadvertently became an excuse for Serb militias and even regular Yugoslav troops to accelerate their 'ethnic cleansing', driving additional thousands of ethnic Kosovo Albanians into especially the 'former Yugoslav republic of Macedonia'. It also bolstered a feeling of martyrdom among the Yugoslavs and strengthened their patriotism, especially after NATO began bombing major bridges and other infrastructure in Serbia. The Serb leadership for its part underestimated NATO resolve in continuing with the air strikes and the ability of its members, including those least enthusiastic about the war, to stick to the battle plan. Serbian leaders also overestimated Russia's willingness, or ability, to support them, while in the end that country's role as mediator became essential to putting a stop to hostilities.

In the war's aftermath, as peace returned to Kosovo and along with it thousands of ethnic Albanian refugees, there was awe of NATO's military prowess, and especially that of the United States. However, there was also criticism, especially as the Kosovo Albanian side was becoming increasingly aggressive vis-à-vis the remaining Serbs and other ethnic groups. Furthermore, questions were asked whether the negotiations conducted with Yugoslavia in February 1999 to reach an agreement over Kosovo had been more than a series of ultimata that had been exceedingly difficult for the Yugoslav leadership to accept, such as the one demanding right of access of NATO troops to any part of Yugoslavia.[9]

Europe after Kosovo was in many ways different from what it had been before the conflict. In launching the war, NATO's nineteen members – all democracies – were aware that they were abandoning a basic principle in international law, forbidding an attack against a country that had not violated international borders (unless, since the establishment of the UN, mandated to do so by its Security Council). It was clear to all that the Federal Republic of Yugoslavia had not violated any international border, nor had it threatened to in this case (even though it had done so a few years earlier, in its wars against the then newly established Croatia and Bosnia-Herzegovina).

If the NATO action over Kosovo did not conform strictly to established international law, it nevertheless reflected the moral outrage felt by the international community at the forced expulsion of a whole people and the systematic murdering of thousands. Milosevic's actions flew in the face of the efforts of half a century of the United Nations, the Council of Europe, the European Union and NATO to reconcile nations, peoples, and promote human rights and tolerance.[10] NATO's action was in line with a more recent trend in history in the direction of greater international intervention on behalf of humanitarian values, as witnessed for instance in the creation of an International Criminal Tribunal for the former Yugoslavia in The Hague a few years earlier.[11]

This new component in international law had been in gestation over the previous decade and had found expression in various OSCE and Council of Europe summits, even though it has not been enshrined formally as has, for example, the sanctity of borders. The world is still grappling with the terms by which the international community may intrude on national sovereignty to redress genocide or other atrocious crimes perpetrated by governments against their own populations.[12]

NATO and Russia in the 1990s: how far should enlargement go?

Many people in the early 1990s were opposed to any NATO enlargement, along the lines of 'If it ain't broke, don't fix it'. Among them was
the ageing George Kennan, the great scholar of Russian affairs, who in
1946 had first warned about Soviet intentions vis-à-vis the West. Kennan
maintained that enlargement could 'inflame nationalistic, anti-Western
and militaristic tendencies in Russian opinion'. To such commentators,
1989 marked a break in European history, in that it ended a comparatively stable balance-of-power era. NATO and the Warsaw Pact had
stood against each other during the Cold War, ensuring an uneasy and
at times tense balance. 'Armed transparency' had been achieved thanks
to new technologies of verification, leading to arms-control measures,
détente and eventually the peaceful collapse of one side. Since 1989, it
was argued, there had not been any balance, but rather economic and
political co-operation and integration. Why, then, now enlarge NATO
and thereby risk unbalancing and remilitarising a relationship between
Russia and the West, which since 1989 had been relatively stable?

Russia, critics maintained, was likely to view such an expansion as an
extension of US hegemony in Europe – with NATO as the instrument of
US predominance not only in Western Europe but also in its Central and
Eastern parts. It would, it was argued, weaken the 'Atlanticists' in the
Russian political establishment and give new wind to militaristic and
nationalist circles – in the process jeopardising Russia's ratification of
the US–Russia START II Treaty reducing nuclear missiles and the
beginning of negotiations for the even further-reaching START III. Why,
those against NATO enlargement continued, humiliate Russia when it
was on its knees – its army in tatters, facing a resurgent China to its south-
east and a score of Islamic and potentially hostile central Asian countries
to its south?

Those in favour of enlargement, however, argued that Russia was not
in a position to halt the enlargement process to any significant degree,
due to its economic and military weakness. When it became stronger on
all these fronts again, as inevitably it would in time, it might well find
that there was nothing to fear from neighbouring NATO countries,
whose foreign policy ambitions could perhaps better be held in check by
NATO membership and the common desire for European peace and a
stable and prosperous Russia. Russian relations with NATO and the
West in general would, they felt, to a large extent depend on whether the
country could be successfully integrated economically with the rest of
Europe and the world. Economic integration with the West, coupled

with co-operation with NATO, could provide stability on Russia's western flank and prevent a remilitarisation of its economy.[13]

Slovenia, Romania and possibly Bulgaria seemed likely new entrants in the early years of the new century. Slovenia was in many ways the most likely candidate in such a 'second wave', as it could easily finance its membership and had never been a member of the Warsaw Pact. In addition, it would give NATO a presence (beyond Greece and Turkey) in South-Eastern Europe and thus help stabilise that volatile region.[14]

The Baltic States – Estonia, Latvia and Lithuania – fervently aspired to NATO membership. The question remained whether NATO members would risk taking a step that in Moscow might be seen as a provocation, if not a threat. The Charter of Partnership signed between the United States and the three Baltic presidents in Washington in 1998 was not a treaty. But it put on record the 'real, profound and enduring interest' of the US in the independence and security of the three countries and a US commitment to support their aspirations to join NATO.

Soon the opinion in NATO capitals swung in favour of wider and earlier enlargement. Sensing this, nine Central and East European countries – Lithuania, Latvia, Estonia, Bulgaria, Romania, Slovenia, Slovakia, Albania and the 'former Yugoslav Republic of Macedonia' – in May 2000 pledged to work together for a 'big bang' solution to early NATO membership involving them all. [15]

A year later, in Warsaw in June 2001, President George W. Bush in a speech boldly stated:

> All of Europe's democracies from the Baltic to the Black Sea, all that lie between, should have the same chance for security and freedom – and the same chance to join the institutions of Europe – as Europe's old democracies ... I believe in NATO membership for all of Europe's democracies that seek it and are ready to share the responsibilities that NATO brings ... As we plan to enlarge NATO, no nation should be used as a pawn in the agendas of others. We will not trade away the fate of free European peoples. No more Munichs. No more Yaltas.[16]

This statement was an indication that the US, too, was now prepared for a radical NATO enlargement. The US Congress would find it difficult to refuse to go along, given the large 'ethnic vote' in the US with roots in the different candidate countries involved.

A NATO transformed: the 2002 US–Russia Treaty of Moscow and the NATO–Russia Council

In May 2001 US President George W. Bush announced his administration's determination to build a Ballistic Missile Defence (BMD), a broad array of defences to protect against missiles launched by so called 'rogue states' or 'states of concern'.[17] The project, which had been contemplated also by the preceding Clinton administration, was received with caution in European NATO capitals, suspicion in Moscow and hostility in Beijing.

One complication was that, if installed, the BMD would violate the 1972 Anti-Ballistic Missile (ABM) Treaty between the United States and the Soviet Union, which forbade anything more than minimal missile defences for either side.[18] West European concerns were that the BMD would be seen by the rest of the world, and especially by Russia and China, as confrontational and menacing rather than co-operative and that it would have destabilising consequences for the international nuclear arms balance.

However, criticism was subdued for several reasons. Firstly, it could prove politically costly to protest too strongly against the right of the American people to defend itself, especially as it seemed to stand so solidly behind the project. Secondly, it was difficult to argue against a defensive as opposed to an offensive system, not least since the Europeans, including the Russians, might some day benefit from it in defending against rogue attacks – Western Europe, say, from the Middle East, or Russia from its south and south-east. Thirdly, the European NATO allies and Russia could benefit from being included in a system that neither would be able to afford on their own. Finally, NATO–Europe might also in exchange receive a more positive US attitude to the European security and defence policy and the latter's Rapid Reaction Force.[19]

By June 2002 both the Ballistic Missile Defence issue and that of the ABM Treaty appeared to have been solved. President Bush abrogated the ABM Treaty, arguing that the terrorist attacks against the United States on 11 September 2001 had clearly demonstrated that the Cold War was over and that BMD was urgently needed. Russia followed suit the following day and at the same time announced that it no longer felt bound by the START II Agreement that had outlawed multiple-warhead missiles and other especially destabilising weapons in the two countries' strategic arsenals.[20]

Both sides' abandonment of the ABM Treaty and Russia's leaving START II would have sent shock waves through the world only a few years earlier. As it happened, however, they were preceded by a series of agreements that rendered them relatively benign. In May 2002 Presidents

Bush and Putin signed the Treaty of Moscow, which committed the US and Russia to reducing their nuclear arsenals from about 6,000 warheads each to no more than 2,200 by 2012.[21] Talks would also start on the difficult issues of better transparency and verification as regards nuclear warheads, whether in use or scrapped.

A few days later, a NATO summit in Rome established a NATO–Russia Council, which in essence brought Russia inside the alliance by giving it an 'equal partnership' role on issues such as counter-terrorism, peacekeeping interventions and the spread of nuclear weapons, though not on core military issues such as those relating to collective defence or out-of-area peacemaking operations.[22]

The NATO–Russia Council held several advantages to all sides. It reduced Russian apprehensions about any future NATO enlargements and indeed stimulated co-operation between Russia and the European Union, as well as with future NATO members it had once dominated. It ensured Russian support for NATO's and the West's fight against terrorism and helped diffuse the criticism in Russia that the country had received little in return for its support of the West in that struggle since the terrorist attacks against the United States on 11 September 2001. It also bound NATO closer to Russia in the protection of its interests vis-à-vis its southern neighbours in central Asia.[23] Furthermore, the NATO-Russia Council aligned NATO to a new European reality, which transcended the former Cold War divide between East and West, as symbolised by the forthcoming enlargement of the European Union. The United States (and Canada) could thereby retain a formal role in fostering security in that more integrated Europe.

On the other hand, the agreement by the same token diluted NATO's role in the eyes of those NATO candidate countries which had viewed NATO membership as a bulwark against any future Russian attempt to dominate them. There was also the general European apprehension that, as during the Cold War, Moscow and Washington would now settle the big issues among them, indeed worsening a situation where Washington seemed only to be using NATO when it pleased it, such as in building a coalition (as it happened, outside NATO) for the war in Afghanistan following 11 September.

The 2002 NATO summit in Prague: seven new members

The NATO summit in Prague in November 2002 brought the answer to the growing sentiment in favour of NATO enlargement. At the summit, the organisation agreed to undertake its second enlargement in the post-

Cold War era by permitting seven new countries to join in 2004, thereby bringing the membership to twenty-six. The seven new members were Bulgaria, Estonia, Latvia, Lithuania, Romania, Slovakia and Slovenia.

The speeches at the summit referred to the final closure of the legacy bequeathed by the 1939 Hitler–Stalin Pact, Yalta and Potsdam. Luxembourg Prime Minister Juncker exclaimed: 'Our grandfathers and fathers could not have imagined what has become reality today!', while departing Czech President Vaclav Havel, himself a former political prisoner under the communist regime, described the event as the end of European power politics and of the imposition of the stronger's will on the weaker. There was something truly remarkable in the fact that not only several countries in the former Warsaw Pact had joined, but also those Baltic states which only a decade before had formed part of the Soviet Union – and this with barely an eyebrow raised in Moscow.[24]

The Prague Summit also resolved to adapt the alliance to the new security needs that had arisen as a result of terrorism and the spread of weapons of mass destruction. It was decided to establish a 20,000-strong NATO Response Force (NRF), which would be fully operational by 2006 and consist of highly mobile elite forces capable of intervening also in faraway places. The Response Force was politically anchored in a so-called Prague Capabilities Commitment, by which the member states vowed to remedy shortcomings in areas such as air transport, munitions and protection against atomic, biological and chemical weapons.

To certain less Atlanticist EU members, such as France, the NATO Response Force might not have been an entirely welcome development, since it would have to draw on limited resources in competition with the EU's own emerging Rapid Reaction Force. They may have seen US pressure for the NATO force as a deliberate means to make the EU force toothless. If so, the new NATO members could be expected to come to the support of the US, as they were on the whole more Atlanticist than some West European EU members.

Using Central European forces for the NATO Response Force would also be convenient, considering the clear US wish to see NATO's future as lying primarily to its east and south-east, that is, in central Asia and east of Turkey. This also helped to explain US pressure for early Turkish membership in the EU. Both NATO and the EU would then be in a position to project their influence on to the Caspian Sea region and even to its east. (Georgia and Azerbaijan had both announced an interest in joining NATO.) The aim would be to be in a better position to fight terrorism, open new oil and gas fields in the Caspian Sea region and secure the transport of these resources to Europe and the world.

For the European Union, the question became one of deciding on how far it wished to follow the US on this course and, if it chose not to, whether it could muster the political will to part ways with NATO. Given the imminent enlargement of both NATO and the EU to include more Atlanticist countries in the east and south-east – to which should be added traditional Atlanticist members such as the United Kingdom and the Netherlands – the likelihood of that happening was limited.

NATO's future mission and relevance

Even before the Prague Summit, questions had arisen as to NATO's future mission, and indeed relevance.[25] It was clear that NATO would be needed in the fight against terrorism and out-of-area interventions such as in the Balkans. Furthermore, as the European Union's efforts to mount a Rapid Reaction Force independent of NATO showed signs of fatigue, the Europeans (and especially the countries of Central and Eastern Europe) seemed to acknowledge that they would not be able to defend the continent without NATO.

Aside from its new tasks, NATO will inevitably change its character simply by being enlarged. Peacemaking or peacekeeping inside or among member states and out-of-area operations, for instance to rescue civilians in countries south or east of the Mediterranean, are likely to become NATO's operational mainstay, rather than the massive mobilisation of forces for defence of NATO territory that so dominated past thinking. Furthermore, NATO intervention – or NATO-approved intervention by the US or one or more European NATO members – undertaken without the sanction of the UN Security Council may become more frequent, as the Kosovo conflict demonstrated.

NATO is developing a 'southern strategy' for NATO to supplement its historical 'northern' one in Central Europe. It is based, not on territory, but on common interests, to the extent these can be found. It includes countering terrorist states that brandish weapons of mass destruction, preventing conflict in the Balkans, undertaking rescue operations of civilians in faraway places, and maintaining access to Gulf oil.

The 'southern strategy', while potentially embraced by all, would probably see ad hoc 'coalitions of the willing', with membership depending on the particular threat posed. Thus Mediterranean NATO countries may co-operate in rescue operations in North Africa. The strategy would have to gain the support both of NATO's northern European members, naturally more concerned about the 'northern strategy', and its Southern European members, more worried about NATO's southern and south-eastern vicinity.

Already, additional emphases are coming to the fore, reflecting the fear on both sides of the Atlantic of a menacing triad of 'rogue states', weapons of mass destruction (WMD) used without or with little warning, and terrorists. In brief, unless prevented from doing so, 'rogue states' such as North Korea would be in a position to produce WMDs and sell them to terrorists, who could transport them to, say, New York harbour, Washington DC or central London. This would be the ultimate nightmare from the defence point of view, since deterrence would have failed and retaliation would be made difficult or impossible for want of an identifiable aggressor country.

The resulting change in US defence doctrine consists in adding 'prevention' or even 'pre-emptive prevention' to 'deterrence', since 'deterrence' – in a departure from what was the case during the US–Soviet stand-off during the Cold War – cannot be counted on to work against a suicidal rogue-state ruler, and even less against terrorists.[26]

Related to the above is a growing concern over a breakdown of countries as such and the resulting greater ease for terrorists to operate in them, such as has occurred or is still the case in countries like Somalia, Afghanistan and the Sudan. State breakdowns would force the established powers to engage in additional preventive action and thus further erode the tenet of border inviolability in classical international law. The preservation of states and their ability to control terrorism within their borders can therefore be expected increasingly to form part of the security policy of the established powers.

A new National Security Strategy of the United States, presented in 2002, makes this clear. Quoting from a speech by President Bush in 2001, it states that:

> We must be prepared to stop the rogue states and their terrorist clients before they are able to threaten or use weapons of mass destruction against the United States and our allies and friends. Our response must take full advantage of strengthened alliances and the establishment of new partnerships with former adversaries, innovation in the use of military forces, modern technologies, including the development of an effective missile defence system and increased emphasis on intelligence collection and analysis.[27]

If NATO's European members truly desire to maintain the organisation's relevance for, and support from, its strongest member, the US, they will have to contribute to this strategy plan also for the protection of Europe itself, since the effective threat against Europe from terrorists and weapons of mass destruction is as great or perhaps even greater than that against the United States.[28]

The US attitude to NATO: still the priority?

Another question became how the Americans felt about the organisation and how well it fitted in with their own perceptions of the world and interests. NATO had enjoyed a revival of sorts in the 1990s and early 2000s in Bosnia, Kosovo and the 'former Yugoslav Republic of Macedonia'. The overriding question was whether another one could be expected in the future without a fundamental scrutiny of what the organisation should stand for.

The United States had waged its war in Afghanistan outside the NATO framework, merely calling on one or the other NATO ally to perform ad hoc tasks, whether in the United States to protect the skies against new acts of air terrorism or in assisting in clean-up operations in Afghanistan. It could even be expected that in many and perhaps most cases, the United States would take recourse to 'coalitions of the NATO-willing', as in Iraq in 2003, in order to avoid the 'warfare-by-committee', Kosovo-style intervention. NATO as such would then be used for political support, and as a 'toolbox' for identifying the 'willing' and the 'able' – and especially those both willing and able – and for post-military peace-keeping. Waging war alone would also present fewer problems related to the widening technological gap between the US and its allies, a factor that had made joint operations increasingly difficult.

Beyond such considerations, there were the different views of the world held by either side. The Europeans had reason to believe that they had moved their continent to a rules-based unity and harmony via decades of negotiation and co-operation and the renouncement of force. Surely the world could be brought to the same happy state via international treaties such as the International Criminal Court, which would bring miscreants such as any new Pol Pot or Milosevic to justice.

If that was Europe's new *mission civilisatrice*, the US by contrast saw the world as a much more anarchic place, where strength and power still mattered, where recourse still occasionally had to be taken to unilateral action, such as in Afghanistan against Al Qaida, or against the 'axis of evil' – to use President George W. Bush's expression – of Iraq, Iran and North Korea. To the Americans, the Europeans were able to persist in their high-minded approach only because the US persisted in its own more Darwinian approach. As one writer put it, 'Europe's Kantian order [of "perpetual peace"] depends on the United States using power according to the old Hobbesian rules' of unreliable international principles and potential evildoers that would have to be overcome.[29]

These philosophical differences would not necessarily destroy NATO.

Indeed, in a world that might still function according to the dictum of the nineteenth-century Prussian soldier Clausewitz that 'war is nothing but the continuation of politics by other means', they might complement each other. However, they could set the stage for quarrels over both the purpose and means of contemplated actions and thus cause alienation to grow and cohesion to weaken, as became manifest in the Iraq crisis in 2003.

On that occasion, NATO found itself seriously divided as it became clear that – due in particular to the threat of a French (but also Russian and Chinese) veto – no UN Security Council Resolution would be passed that authorised the use of military force against Saddam Hussein's Iraq over its alleged non-compliance with previous Security Council calls for the destruction of its presumed weapons of mass destruction.[30]

On the one side stood NATO members France, supported especially by Germany (a non-veto member of the UN Security Council at this time) and Belgium, who argued that NATO should not send even defensive military equipment to protect its NATO partner Turkey against any attack by Iraq. In the opposite camp were countries like the United States, the United Kingdom, Spain, Italy and several of the newer NATO members in Central and Eastern Europe. They felt that military action was now called for and in line with NATO obligations.[31]

In the ensuing invasion of Iraq, NATO was not involved, leaving the alliance deeply split and rendering its role uncertain in any future conflict where perceptions of outside threats and the action needed to counter them might differ.

Notes

1 From his Farewell Address, 1796. The United States followed George Washington's precept of not entering into alliances up until 1947, when it concluded the Rio Treaty on the Defense of the Western Hemisphere with a number of Latin American countries, followed, in 1949, by the Washington Treaty creating NATO. US participation in the two world wars was not based on any formal alliances.

2 The NATO enlargement in 1999 was ratified by the US Senate by a large majority, in spite of concern about its cost. The US State Department in 1997 put the total cost (for all the members) of the first enlargement at between $27 and $35 billion over 12 years, while other studies pointed to added expenditure of between $42 billion and $100 billion. However, a NATO study of early 1998 (considered 'definitive'), placed the extra expenditure at less than $2 billion. The enlargement project provided for a minimum of communication and 'interoperability' between new NATO members and current ones. It was meant to enable NATO to respond well in time should

Russian capabilities or intentions ever change. The project also foresaw that the defence of new members be based on reinforcement in crises, rather than on the permanent stationing of combat forces in those countries.

3 Article 5 in the 1949 North Atlantic Treaty states that: 'The Parties agree that an armed attack against one or more of them in Europe or North America shall be considered an attack against them all'. Article 1 says that: 'The parties undertake … to settle any international dispute in which they may be involved by peaceful means in such a way that international peace and security and justice are not endangered, and to refrain in their international relations from the threat or use of force in any manner inconsistent with the purposes of the United Nations'. Article 7 recognises the 'primary responsibility of the Security Council for the maintenance of international peace and stability'. (The intervention in Iraq in 1991 had been undertaken under the authority of the UN. Similarly, in Bosnia, in 1995, NATO action had been authorised by the UN Security Council. In the Kosovo case, UN Security Council intervention was secured only *ex post facto*, in fact leading to the end of the hostilities following Milosevic's acceptance of the terms of Security Council Resolution 1244.) Finally, concerning enlargement, Article 10 states that: 'The Parties may, by unanimous agreement, invite any other European state in a position to further the principles of this Treaty and to contribute to the security of the North Atlantic area to accede to this Treaty'. (The previous enlargements had been Greece and Turkey in 1952, the Federal Republic of Germany in 1955 and Spain in 1982.)

4 Russia withdrew from co-operation with NATO in March 1999 in reaction to the Kosovo conflict. Co-operation was gradually restored after the end of the conflict.

5 The EAPC included the previously mentioned Partnership for Peace (created in 1994) and replaced the Council for North Atlantic Co-operation (established in 1991). By 2002 the EAPC had grown to comprise forty-six countries (nineteen NATO members and twenty-seven others). Moreover, the Dialogue on the Mediterranean, started in 1994, was to be enhanced. Finally, the 1997 Madrid Summit decided on a reform of NATO's military structure aiming at greater operational flexibility, fewer headquarters and greater openness to working with outside partners in preparing joint operations.

6 The NATO–Ukraine Charter included regular political consultations on security-related issues, defence reform in Ukraine and Ukrainian participation in NATO-led peace support operations in Bosnia and Kosovo. It followed on substantial Ukrainian steps in the defence field, such as the country's destruction of nuclear weapons on its soil following the collapse of the Soviet Union; its accession to the Non-Proliferation Treaty as a non-nuclear state; and its agreement with Russia over the sharing of the Soviet-era Black Sea Fleet. Ukraine army units have participated in numerous exercises with NATO forces since 1994 and contribute troops to the KFOR mission in Kosovo. It provided vital air transport during the military intervention in Afghanistan in 2002.

7 The Madrid Summit Agreement also linked up with the 1990 Conventional

Forces in Europe (CFE) Treaty also known as the Conventional Arms Control Treaty). The latter entered into force in 1992 and has so far been ratified by over thirty countries. The CFE meant a historically unprecedented reduction in conventional forces in Europe. A revised agreement did away with the previous NATO–Warsaw Pact balancing act and instead sought to define 'national' and 'territorial' and 'zonal' 'ceilings', especially in Central Europe. However, the relevance of the CFE to today's Europe was increasingly called into question, for instance in regard to Russia, especially after the creation, in May 2002, of the NATO–Russia Council. Russia's military strength and readiness in the conventional field never came close to the threat limits established in the CFE, other than during fighting in Chechnya.

8 NATO's conditions included a Serbian military withdrawal from Kosovo; the return of all refugees; a well-armed international military presence to protect them; and a Kosovo autonomy within Serbian sovereignty.

9 The Rambouillet Agreement of February 1995 – signed by the ethnic Albanian side but not by the Federal Republic of Yugoslavia – foresaw that Kosovo would remain a Serbian province, but with extensive autonomy for its Albanian majority, to be supervised by NATO peacekeeping forces. After the conflict it became a dead letter for many ethnic Albanians, who could not conceive of having their province form part of Yugoslavia after the atrocities committed against them.

10 Guéhenno (1998–9, p. 10) speaks of the 'ascendance of a humanitarian view of foreign policy', in which 'upholding moral standards could become a strategic goal'. However, he also sees, for example, the Dayton Agreements of 1995 as revealing

the limited depth of the West's commitment to such standards. Although moved to act by moral pressure as much as by traditional strategic considerations, the solution found at Dayton was of a traditional nature. Rather than deploy sufficient forces to uphold international standards of behaviour, the US and its European allies created a balance of forces on the ground between the Muslim–Croat federation and the Serbs. The horrors of the Muslim–Croat war were conveniently forgotten and the Serbs contained, but Bosnia's *de facto* division through ethnic cleansing was accepted, and no side could claim the moral high ground. The war was, at least temporarily, ended; it is, however, unclear whether peace was made.

11 The move toward effective universal jurisdiction took a major step forward with the coming into existence of an International Criminal Court (ICC) in April 2002. The ICC has the right to go after what it perceives as war criminals anywhere in the world, even in countries not party to it. Supporters argue that this is vitally needed to apprehend the likes of Milosevic (who is now before the International Criminal Tribunal for the former Yugoslavia in The Hague). Opponents, however, see in the ICC a court lacking meaningful political oversight and potentially dominated by unscrupulous regimes. They consider the international political arena as, essentially, not appropriate for legal action. The United States, under President George W. Bush in 2002 nulli-

fied the Clinton administration's signature of the ICC Treaty and announced that it would not send it for ratification to the Senate. It even threatened to withdraw from UN peacekeeping operations such as in Bosnia, unless the UN Security Council guaranteed that no US soldier would be brought before the ICC over alleged war crimes. A compromise was eventually reached for a suspension of the threatened action. A dispute with the EU over the issue was at least temporarily resolved in 2002, as the latter permitted the US to conclude deals with individual EU (and candidate) states ensuring immunity from ICC prosecution for US soldiers and government officials. EU countries strongly supportive of the ICC considered the compromise a defeat in the quest for a common EU foreign and security policy.

12 Shawcross (2000) points to what he sees as a considerable inconsistency on the part of the world community – as represented by the UN and its Security Council – in crisis or conflict intervention since the end of the Cold War. Why Cambodia, Bosnia, Kosovo and East Timor, and not Rwanda, the Congo or Chechnya? The determinants, he concludes in resignation, are practical politics and money, and not moral outrage. He also argues that the intervention of peacekeepers can sometimes prolong conflicts, such as when they prevented either the government or the UNITA rebels from winning the civil war in Angola in the early 1990s.

13 Russia had considerable problems in reducing the size of its military. Entire branches of service were foreseen to disappear, and along with them the careers of thousands of officers, with unknown consequences for social stability and employment. Furthermore, scores of cities in the Urals, the Caucasus and elsewhere, built purely for military purposes during the Soviet era, would have to convert to civilian production or simply be closed down for lack of a civilian purpose. The cost of all this was uncertain, but without economic development the process would be even more difficult.

14 Ukraine – a resource-rich country, bigger than France – was considered of great importance to European stability. Located between Russia and South-Eastern Europe, it served as a counterweight to the former at regional level. Western Europe and NATO would have a natural interest in seeing a strong and stable Ukraine, while NATO membership was not for the near future. By contrast, the undemocratic government of Belarus and its international isolation was considered to preclude any early membership in NATO.

15 The selection of the countries with which NATO would start membership negotiations was to follow criteria established under a Membership Action Plan (MAP), covering not only military but also economic, political and legal aspects and building on the 1994 Partnership for Peace programme. In the end, however, the decision on membership would be taken as much on political grounds as on the basis of technical criteria.

16 Address by President George W. Bush to faculty and students of Warsaw University, Warsaw, Poland, 15 June 2001 (www.whitehouse.gov/news/releases/2001/06/20010615-1).

17 The Ballistic Missile Defence is to consist of five sub-systems: (1) a satellite-borne early warning system; (2) an additional earthbound early warning system, permitting more precise predictions of missile direction and the identification of decoys; (3) an equally land-based 'X-band' radar system for the same purposes; (4) launch of destroying missiles and destruction of targets; and (5) success evaluation and, in the event of failure, launch of additional destroying missiles. Construction of a first site in Alaska would start in 2004 and lead, in the first instance, to the readying of around twenty destroying missiles by 2006. The installation is meant to counter long-range ballistic missiles and will be supplemented gradually by systems installed on warships to shoot down short and medium-range enemy missiles.

18 The 1972 ABM Treaty stipulated that the United States and the Soviet Union could have only two missile defence sites of not more than one hundred rockets; one around the capital and one around an attack missile centre. The treaty, once ratified by both countries, underwent several mutually agreed modifications. Building on the Mutual Assured Destruction (MAD) doctrine, it was an important building block for the subsequent Strategic Arms Limitation Talks (SALT), especially SALT I, and for the later START II agreements. The United States in 2001 had 7,000 strategic nuclear weapons, a number meant to fall to around 3,000 under START II. In 1997, Washington and Moscow agreed in principle that a forthcoming treaty should lower the number of missiles for each side to around 2,000. This goal came closer with the signing, in 2002, of the Treaty of Moscow, signifying cuts to this level.

It could be argued, in the case of 'MAD', that it has kept world peace for over fifty years. However, its weakness is that it assumes rational behaviour by all sides concerned. However, what if there is a leader of a 'rogue' nation, recently equipped with nuclear weapons, who is not rational but irrational, perhaps suicidal, somewhat like Hitler or Milosevic? Even in the Cuban missile crisis of 1962, the US and the Soviet Union behaved rationally only in the end, and then almost by chance. A Ballistic Missile Defence could lift the threshold for the application of the MAD doctrine, by permitting a country which is being attacked to shoot down a missile and thus avoid instantaneous massive retaliation, at least until after all the facts of the incident have been established.

19 Some experts on nuclear deterrence, such as Allison and Zelikov (1999, pp. 397–401) argue that the risk of a nuclear exchange originating in Russia is not yet over. They in particular point to (1) 'Russia's deteriorating command and control systems, both technical and human, that increase risks of unauthorised or accidental launch of nuclear weapons'; (2) 'the decline of Russia's conventional military capabilities [which] has increased reliance on nuclear weapons [in a crisis]'; and [3] 'loose nukes', that is, Russian nuclear weapons that are stolen, sold to terrorists or rogue states.

20 However, in 2003 Russia proposed to the United States the conclusion of a

new Ballistic Missile Defence Treaty, by which Russia would benefit from the US BMD system. If this becomes reality, NATO's European partners would be hard pressed to join, too.

21 The Treaty of Moscow leaves either country free to rebuild its forces as from one year after the treaty's expiration if it is not extended or amended.

22 The NATO–Russia Council effectively replaced the NATO–Russia Permanent Joint Council, which had been largely ineffectual, not least during the period when Russia–NATO relations cooled during the Kosovo conflict.

23 Russian efforts to exercise greater influence over its southern flank became manifest in the spring of 2002, when it announced the creation of a Collective Security Treaty Organisation also including the Community of Independent States partners Armenia, Belarus, Kazhakstan and Tajikistan.

24 The enlargement, to be formally declared at a NATO summit in May 2004, was expected to pave the way for various other countries such as Albania, the 'former Yugoslav Republic of Macedonia' and Croatia, provided they made further progress on democratic consolidation and defence readiness.

25 As NATO undergoes enlargement in coming years, the relevance of its forty-six-member-state Euro-Atlantic Partnership Council (EAPC) and its Partnership for Peace (PfP), which also includes certain countries in South-East Europe and Central Asia, is being called into question. While the EAPC may well disappear, the PfP may remain as a means for projecting NATO power into Afghanistan and other countries in the region.

26 Reflecting the international community's growing fear over the proliferation of weapons of mass destruction, over ninety countries – including the United States and Russia – in 2002 signed the International Code of Conduct against Ballistic Missile Proliferation. The Code is not, however, of a binding nature; nor does it foresee any control mechanism, sanctions or ban on exports of such weapons or their components. Among the non-signatories are India, Pakistan, China, North Korea, Syria and Israel.

27 Speech by President George W. Bush, West Point, New York, 1 June 2002; quoted in *The National Security Strategy of the United States of America*, September 2002 (The White House). The National Security Strategy raises many other objectives, such as that to 'build a balance of power [in the world] that favours freedom … [and] bring the hope of democracy, development, free markets and free trade to every corner of the world'.

28 Naumann (2002, p 195) recommends a strategy for conflict prevention and peace maintenance as having two elements: '*Conflict pre-emption* seeks to resolve conflicts by political means and prevent new causes of conflict from arising through assistance. Thereby the soil in which terror and violence thrive will be taken away. *Conflict prevention* seeks to make attacks purposeless through the greatest possible protection of states and societies, and to show potential aggressors through intervention far away from their own regions that they run the risk of losing their capacity for attack as well as that of being apprehended. It is the idea of the carrot and the stick, of helping and

punishing … The time may have come to develop a comprehensive political strategy, in which the military element plays an irreplaceable – but not the only and often not even the dominant – role.' (Translated from the German original.)

29 Kagan (2002, p. 1).

30 UN Security Council Resolution 1441 of 8 November 2002 threatened Iraq with 'serious consequences' in the event of any further 'material breach' of Security Council Resolution 678 of April 1991 (adopted in the wake of the 1991 allied military intervention in Iraq and as a condition for an armistice) and more than a dozen UN Resolutions adopted in the intervening years. The United States, the United Kingdom, Australia and other countries considered that the words in Resolution 678 authorising the use of 'all necessary means' in the event of Iraqi non-compliance with an earlier Resolution 660 of 1990 (following Iraq's occupation of Kuwait) should apply also in 2002, whereas the countries opposed to military intervention argued that 'serious consequences' did not authorise such action in the absence of another UN Security Council Resolution including words such as 'all necessary means'.

31 Article 4 of the North Atlantic Treaty states: 'The Parties will consult together whenever, in the opinion of any of them, the territorial integrity, political independence or security of any of the Parties is threatened'.

9
A new European Union

A state without the means of some change is without the means of its own conservation. (Edmund Burke)[1]

Summary

A series of EU summits – Amsterdam in 1997, Berlin and Helsinki in 1999 and Nice in 2000 – focused on the need for inner reform of the institution against the prospect of future enlargement and new competences. The general tendency was for increased intergovernmentalism, that is, more power in the hands of the EU's Council of Ministers and greater influence for the European Parliament.

The Helsinki Summit decided to accept candidacies of thirteen countries (including Turkey) and to start negotiations with twelve (all but Turkey) on an equal basis, with 2004 as a possible date for joining by the first in line. It was also decided to establish, by 2003, a 60,000-strong Rapid Reaction Force capable of performing peacemaking or peacekeeping operations autonomously of NATO.

The Nice Summit confirmed and codified the trend towards intergovernmental dominance in the EU, especially by the larger member states. This may have been one reason why the Nice Treaty was rejected by the Irish in a referendum in June 2001, an outcome that jeopardised the treaty's planned entry into force in preparation of enlargement.

Various leading politicians in EU member states in 2000 and 2001 offered their visions of the necessary future structure of the institution – ranging from the federal to the (continued) intergovernmental to the interparliamentary to the (continued) bureaucratic. With EU funds scarce, efficiency suffering, democracy found lacking, the physical introduction of the euro imminent and major enlargement around the corner, the debate had come none too soon.

An EU Convention on the Future of Europe was consequently convened in 2002 with a mandate to make proposals to governments for a new EU constitution in 2003. This would be necessary also to prepare for the 'big bang' enlargement decided at a summit in Copenhagen in December 2002, where it was agreed to invite ten candidate countries to join in 2004: Cyprus, the Czech Republic, Estonia, Hungary, Latvia, Lithuania, Malta, Poland, Slovakia and Slovenia. Negotiations would continue with Bulgaria and Romania, with a possible date of accession set for 2007. It was also decided that an attempt would be made in 2004 to set a date for the start of membership negotiations with Turkey. Thorny questions remained, however, such as how to reform the Common Agricultural Policy and EU finances overall in order to accommodate the many new and less wealthy member states.

The Amsterdam Summit, June 1997

The European Union is characterised, strangely enough, by both inertia and capacity for change. Some policies – such as those on agriculture, fisheries and regional support – bitterly resist renewal, while others – such as on enlargement, monetary unification and security – show remarkable adaptability in the face of new impulses. It is worth following how EU thinking has evolved over the 1997–2003 period, as manifested in the decisions taken at six summits: Amsterdam in 1997, Berlin and Helsinki in 1999, Nice in 2000, Laeken (Brussels) in 2001 and Copenhagen in 2002 .

In Amsterdam, in June 1997, EU leaders crowned the efforts of an Intergovernmental Conference (IGC) started fifteen months earlier, by adopting the Amsterdam Treaty. The treaty foresaw EU membership negotiations to start in 1998 with six 'first wave' applicant countries: Cyprus, the Czech Republic, Estonia, Hungary, Poland and Slovenia. Five other countries would later be invited to start negotiations for a 'second wave' enlargement: Bulgaria, Latvia, Lithuania, Romania and Slovakia. 'First wave' accessions were considered likely around 2004 at the earliest.

In the Amsterdam Treaty environment protection was given a higher profile (at Scandinavian insistence), in that individual member states would be able to introduce stricter standards than those valid for the rest of the EU. Majority voting in the Council of Ministers was extended (at the cost of the unanimity rule).[2] And the position of the European Parliament was strengthened, as was the say of national parliaments.[3]

However, other tasks remained largely unresolved. One was EU institutional reform, seen as a prerequisite for enlargement, since with the present machinery the institution would risk paralysis with more than, say, twenty members. Here it was decided to continue negotiations nearer to the time of actual enlargement, presumably in the hope that urgency would help concentrate minds. (It was subsequently agreed that an overhaul would be undertaken as from twenty member states, i.e. between the 'first' and the 'second' wave.) All that could be agreed on in Amsterdam was a strengthening of the position of the Commission's President and to have the number of Commissioners remain at a maximum of twenty.[4] Furthermore, Amsterdam saw a battle between the smaller and the bigger EU member states, in particular as regards the 'one-country-one-vote' principle in the Council of Ministers. The bigger had hoped for a weighted voting system based on population, but the smaller put up successful resistance.

The Common Foreign and Security Policy vaguely set out in the Maastricht Treaty was left nearly in the same embryonic stage in which it had found itself previously. The Amsterdam Treaty also saw procedural simplifications in the complicated decision-making process, the creation of a joint planning body, and a raising of the status of the Secretary General of the EU Council of Ministers.

One innovation of the Amsterdam Treaty was the introduction of 'flexibility' in the future construction of the Union; that is, the possibility for a qualified majority of countries (71 per cent of the weighted votes) to engage in deeper co-operation in various fields without being stopped by the others. Flexibility, it was felt, would become more and more necessary as the EU was enlarged to include more and more heterogeneous countries from the political, economic and cultural point of view. It would therefore become increasingly difficult to 'deepen' the Union in ways that could be supported and implemented by each and every one. The 'EU-isation' of policies on asylum, immigration and visas, as well as the Schengen Agreement on uncontrolled internal EU borders, was seen as already illustrating this, as they contained many exceptions for different countries. The challenge for the EU would be to ensure that flexibility did not lead to uninhibited 'Europe à la carte' policies by its member states and to any further weakening of its cohesion.[5]

The relatively meagre results of Amsterdam reflected the resistance waged by intergovernmentalism against integrationism. That is, the member states, through their governments (and to some extent parliaments) fought for the powers of the Council of Ministers to be defended against the increased powers of the Commission. In this sense Amsterdam meant a development of the EU towards a more classical international set-up such as the Strasbourg-based Council of Europe.[6]

The Berlin Summit, March 1999

The emphasis in Amsterdam in 1997 had been on the principle of EU enlargement and the inner reforms necessitated by it. In Berlin in March 1999 it shifted to budgetary reform to finance the EU's various programmes during the 2000–6 period, and to the question of who should pay how much. An Agenda 2000 for an overhaul of the EU's financial structure, the CAP and regional support was agreed, though in a much toned-down form compared to what the Commission had originally proposed.

Germany had not been able to reduce significantly its role as the biggest net contributor to the EU budget (about €9.3 billion more in contribution than in receipts in 2000, or 60 per cent of EU transfers from richer to poorer members), but as host it had a strong interest in avoiding a breakdown in the negotiations. Other major net payers – the Netherlands, Sweden, Austria – were not much relieved either, nor were net receivers much disturbed. Spain, in the last night of talks, managed to squeeze out an extra €3 billion from the EU's structural and regional funds, which in total would amount to over €200 billion for the six-year period. (In a reform of how the funds should be distributed, the summit decided that more should go to the very poorest regions in the EU, rather than to all except the richest, as had previously been the case.)

The United Kingdom was able to keep most of the special rebate it had obtained in the Thatcher years (due to the particular situation of its agriculture). France obtained most of what it wanted, in particular smaller reductions than foreseen for its own and other countries' farmers. Yearly CAP expenditure was to be kept at around €40 billion, less than half of the equally 'frozen' total EU expenditure of about €90 billion (representing a maximum of 1.27 per cent of EU GDP). In all, the Berlin Summit was a grab for money from all sides, a struggle to keep privileges, however outmoded, or of redressing perceived injustices.

The agreements reached in Berlin, like those in Amsterdam in 1997, appeared meagre, especially when measured against the original proposals in the Commission's Agenda 2000. Consumers and tax-payers could have gained more if CAP prices had been more free-market-oriented. More could have been done with less EU money if the structural policy had been more specifically directed at the poorest regions. Greater understanding could have been shown with regard to the big net payers' positions.

However, a basis was thought to have been laid for sounder EU finances in the future, in that the CAP and overall expenditure was stabilised up to the year 2006. EU enlargement seemed more feasible from the financial point of view. The summit also showed a realisation that 'bribe money' would not be available to the same extent as in the past in order to smooth over disagreements between member states. The net payers promised to be less generous in future and the net receivers were warned they might have to adapt to a 'leaner and meaner' EU.

The Helsinki Summit, December 1999

At the December 1999 EU summit in Helsinki it was decided to bring the number of EU candidate countries from the six agreed at Amsterdam (Cyprus, the Czech Republic, Estonia, Hungary, Slovenia and Poland) to thirteen. Negotiations would start in 2000 with Bulgaria, Latvia, Lithuania, Malta, Romania and Slovakia. In addition, and more controversially, Turkey was accepted as a candidate, although no date for the start of negotiations for membership was fixed.[7]

The talks with all the twelve candidates (i.e. minus Turkey) would take place concurrently, along the lines of the so-called 'regatta model': all were to depart from the same starting line as far as their actual or expected adherence to each and every one of thirty-one 'chapters' in the *acquis communautaire*. The progress of each country would be judged according to the same criteria. (To the various economic requirements should be added the so-called 'Copenhagen criteria' agreed within the EU earlier, calling on EU candidates to maintain democracy, the rule of law, respect of human rights and the protection of minorities.) It was hoped that, in this way, improvements reached by especially the original six candidates would not delay their accession, while new candidates would have a chance to accelerate their reform process and catch up with the rest.

Some Balkan countries were excluded from candidate status, such as Bosnia-Herzegovina, Croatia, the 'former Yugoslav Republic of Macedonia' and, for obvious political reasons at the time, the Federal Republic of Yugoslavia. At least the first three could, however, be said to have been covered by the Stability Pact for South-Eastern Europe,[8] while awaiting the day when their economic (and political) maturity might be such as to qualify them for candidate status.

Meanwhile, the EU was to reform itself in order to be ready in its turn to receive new members. An Intergovernmental Conference (IGC) would be set up in 2000 and given until 2002 to finish its work (i.e. one or two years before the first expected enlargement). The main task was to make sure that a much larger EU could work efficiently and reach decisions.

Among the issues discussed were the size and composition of the Commission; the number of votes per country in the Council of Ministers and a possible wider use of qualified majority voting in that body; and prospects for a further enlarged role of the European Parliament.[9]

Turkey's inclusion among the candidate countries in the eleventh hour of the Helsinki Summit gave rise to considerable debate among commentators. Some were asking where the EU was heading in preparing to accept a predominantly Muslim country or where indeed Europe's political, cultural and geographic borders could now be said to lie. Others, however, pointed to Turkey's major, and growing, geopolitical importance and the need to bind it more closely to Europe.

European co-operation in the political, security and defence fields took a major step forward, at least on paper, when the Helsinki Summit also agreed to create, by 2003, a 60,000-strong, air and navy supported Rapid Reaction Force (RRF) ready to go into action within sixty days.[10] The Rapid Reaction Force, meant to form part of the EU's European Security and Defence Policy (ESDP), was to be used only in extreme cases of conflicts in Europe or its vicinity. Emphasis would be laid on the so-called 'Petersberg tasks' of peacekeeping or peacemaking. These also included conflict identification and prevention, including emergency assistance, police training, the building of a civil society and even trade policies for economic stability. The tasks of the Western European Union, which up to then had served as the main expression of European security defence policies, would for all practical purposes be taken over by the EU.[11]

The UK, France and Germany would together provide around 40,000 troops, with all the other EU members making up the remaining 20,000 – all from within a pool of 200,000 men for rotation purposes. Troops from EU countries that were members of NATO would be 'double-hatted', that is available for either EU or NATO duties as the situation might require. (One can therefore not talk about any 'European army' in its own right, only about the use of national armed forces, whether from NATO or non-NATO EU countries.) They would be used for more limited roles of crisis management when NATO as a whole was not involved.)

It was also agreed that EU military activity would come under its Council of Ministers, with no role for either the Commission or the European Parliament. As if to underline this fact, the policy was to be managed by about a hundred military staff at EU headquarters in Brussels, under the EU's High Representative for Security and Foreign Policy, who was also the Secretary General of the Council of Ministers.[12]

The Helsinki decision to create a Rapid Reaction Force built on the British-French St Malo Declaration of 1998 and had to be seen against the background of the relatively undistinguished military performance by the European members of NATO during the Kosovo conflict. For France, the new project represented a means to assert increased European independence and power. For a United Kingdom outside the Economic and Monetary Union, it provided a chance to continue to play a leading role in European affairs. With Germany, perhaps surprisingly, so enthusiastically behind the new initiative, it became a fait accompli for many of the smaller, more hesitant and sometimes neutral EU member states.

The US (and Canadian) reaction to the European Security and Defence Policy was ambivalent, reflecting the age-old US uncertainty as to whether its security, and that of Europe, was better assured by exerting a dominating influence over it or by withdrawing from it. US worries included: a possible 'decoupling' of North American and European security; discrimination against the US, or against non-EU NATO members Iceland, Norway and Turkey and these countries' exposure to new risks, especially since they might have to come to the rescue of EU members also belonging to NATO, under the latter's collective defensive obligation; a lacking European will to increase defence capabilities to the level necessary for separate action; and duplication of effort, as the new EU structures would work parallel to already existing NATO ones set up to cater for European-led operations (after a Defense Capability Initiative was adopted at NATO's fifty-year anniversary summit in Washington in 1999 to improve the strength of European military forces).

Further transatlantic worries concerned the risk of reduced 'interoperability' between NATO and EU defences; possible clashes resulting from further NATO and EU enlargement (now with defence commitments) such as in the case of the Baltic States; possible confusion in future crises, such as over who should intervene – NATO or the EU (or both); and the risk that the EU might 'rush in where angels fear to tread' in order to prove its untested worth.

Complicating the situation was the fact that France, although a NATO member, was not part of NATO's integrated military structure. Could EU military planning take place apart from NATO when the EU would for a long time need NATO resources? Would the US (and the Canadians) remonstrate by not sharing intelligence or by reducing their commitment to NATO.

Above all, would the EU be able to afford the establishment of a European Security and Defence Policy, given not only the growing gap between US military technology and that within the EU, but also shrinking defence budgets in most EU countries?[13] It was estimated that the already under-financed military forces of the UK, France and Germany would have to increase by half in the next ten years to meet the ESDP commitments – a politically delicate task before electorates that could see no real security threat on the horizon.[14]

On the other hand, the project was seen as having the potential to encourage transnational mergers in the European defence establishment, permitting it to recuperate some of the US lead in weapons technology. Furthermore, stronger economic growth could permit defence budgets to start growing again, especially since defence spending could create new employment.[15] The bigger countries – especially the UK, France and Germany - seemed to feel that a single security policy was a natural next step after the Internal Market and the single currency. Such a policy would be particularly needed if the United States should ever wish to 'decouple' itself from Europe. At the same time it could provoke such a 'decoupling'. This was, in brief, the Europeans' dilemma.

It remained to be seen how great an impact on NATO the European Security and Defence Policy would have and whether the Rapid Reaction Force would actually be deployed independently of NATO. A number of factors made this less likely. First, it would be difficult and slow for the EU to reach agreement on actually deploying the RRF, since the member states – three of which (Austria, Ireland and Sweden) considered themselves unable to join military alliances – were all democracies, eager, under popular pressure, to avoid foreign policy initiatives, especially if these had a military component. EU members would likely interpret threats differently. Only when all agreed on a threat scenario and the necessary measures to combat it would it be possible to deploy troops (a hope punctured by the Iraq crisis in 2003).

Second, major EU players such as France, Germany and the UK had different interests in creating the ESDP, a circumstance that was seen as likely to hamper its effectiveness. France wanted it eventually to lead to full security independence from the US and NATO. Germany wanted greater EU integration, a development that would require greater defence autonomy. However, Germany also wanted a lasting US–NATO presence to prevent any emerging national rivalries within the EU. Finally, the UK needed to be shown to be involved in Europe at a time when it was outside the Economic and Monetary Union.

EU foreign policy in the early 2000s often lacked coherence, as it often criticised and sought to be distinct from US positions without presenting clear alternatives. The latter were all the more difficult to identify as the various EU countries, each with its own foreign policy establishment and objectives, stood far apart on many issues. One example was a sudden EU diplomatic opening to North Korea in 2001, unaccompanied, however, by any tangible initiative to solve that country's conflict with South Korea. This was followed by a near-absent EU policy on North Korea as the showdown over that country's nuclear armament came to a head in 2003.

A second example was the serious split over Iraq in 2003 between those – such as the UK, Spain and Italy – who stood by the US in seeking Saddam Hussein's ouster, if necessary through an invasion; and those countries, led by France, Germany and Belgium, who advised against any invasion until a UN Security Council authorising it could be secured. As the US–British led invasion took place, the EU's attempts to forge a common European Security and Defence Policy suffered a serious blow, since nobody could guarantee that perceptions of outside threats and the action required to counter them would be any less diverse than they had been over Iraq.

However, EU successes in the foreign policy field were also scored, such as in the 'former Yugoslav Republic of Macedonia' in 2001, where a peace agreement was reached between Slavs and ethnic Albanians, thanks to concerted EU (and US) action, and where the EU took over peacekeeping duties in 2003.

The Nice Summit, December 2000

During three days (and nights) in December 2000, European Union leaders laboured to make the Union better fit to receive up to twelve (thirteen if Turkey was included) new members.[16] The internal reform would have to include especially the decision-making Council of Ministers but also the Commission. The general drift was towards even more intergovernmentalism, that is, the joint rule by national governments in the Council of Ministers, fortifying the thesis made by some observers that the EU, far from heralding the end of the nation-state, in fact had come to its rescue and had perhaps been invented by EU member states to preserve it.[17]

In the end, in a confusing night session on the third day of negotiations, when nobody quite knew how the arithmetic would work (indeed it had to be fine-tuned in the weeks to follow), the 'big four' (France, Germany, the UK and Italy) received 29 votes each, Spain 27, the Netherlands 13, Greece, Belgium and Portugal 12 each, Sweden and Austria 10 each, Denmark, Finland and Ireland 7 each and Luxembourg 4. It was agreed that 88 votes out of the total 227 would be enough to block decisions in a majority-decision domain of activity.[28]

Nice also signified a drift within the Council of Ministers towards greater dominance by the bigger countries – France, Germany, the UK, Italy and Spain – vis-à-vis the smaller ones, based on size of population. (This was natural enough, considering the drift toward intergovernmentalism. With more power for the Council of Ministers, greater care had to be taken to ensure that this power reflected demographic realities.)

A further sign of big-country domination was the request to limit the right of veto to fewer areas in favour of majority decisions. (Veto right is above all a means of defence for the smaller countries to resist decisions going against them.) In the end, the new areas where majority decisions would replace the unanimity rule were fewer than had been anticipated, as different countries, not least the big ones, exercised their veto rights to prevent change: the British against any extension to fiscal and social matters, the French and the Finns on culture, the Germans on immigration and asylum, the Danes on labour market issues and so on. In the end, majority voting was extended to thirty-five new areas, including regional funding and services (but not cultural services such as television and film).

Nice also agreed that, as from 2005, the Commission would keep its current size of twenty Commissioners regardless of any further EU enlargement. The five countries with currently two Commissioners (France, Germany, the UK, Italy and Spain) would content themselves with only one, leaving five seats to any new members. By the time the EU had reached twenty-seven member states, the number of Commissioners was to be reduced from twenty to a lower, still undecided, number. The concession by the big countries could be better understood when seen against the background of the reduced power of the Commission. Why bother about representation in a body that presumably would have less influence? Furthermore, since Commissioners were at any rate supposed to be neutral and work for the EU – not for their countries of origin – and were normally forced by inside and outside pressures to do so anyway, the fact of giving up a seat might not amount to much.

One achievement in Nice was to prepare the ground for 'flexible integration' in various fields, such as social policies or taxation, among a stipulated minimum of eight member states, along the lines of the Economic and Monetary Union. Even though this potentially prepared the ground for 'several EUs within the EU', it also reflected the need for a more heterogeneous membership to integrate at different speeds. It remained to be seen which countries would then team up on what subjects, in order to proceed in advance of the others. Finally, Nice produced a Charter of Fundamental Rights, which did not have treaty value but which some people hoped would form part of a future EU constitution.

Even though the immediate reactions from member states – especially the smaller – after Nice were sceptical or disappointed (also at perceived French bullying during the negotiations), it remained to be seen how the agreement would work in practice. Would power move even more in the direction of the member governments as widely foreseen, and away from the Commission and the European Parliament (whose powers had, after all, been increased in the Amsterdam Treaty)? Would the Commission and the Parliament 'gang up' against the Council of Ministers to compensate for loss of influence, and how effective would such an alliance be? Would the (moderately) increased number of areas where majority voting was to replace the unanimity rule make the EU less prone to decision-making paralysis and instead make it more effective? Would the EU's new 'flexibility' clause, which permitted groups of countries to go further than others, be a source of division and confusion, or would it resolve the old 'deepening-versus-widening' dilemma of the institution? Would the EU be perceived by EU citizens as being closer to them, as 'national' interests were defended by 'their' government in the Council of Ministers? Or would it be perceived as being further away from them as the role of the European Parliament – the 'voice of the people' – was less prominent and as the Council of Ministers decided by a majority vote in more areas?

There was genuine concern about the EU's 'distance from the people' as the institution embarked on matters more and more central to the everyday life of citizens, such as the management of the euro and the migratory pressure to be expected from the next stages of enlargement. Nor was there any agreement upon the 'finality' of the EU, nor the road there. The risk was one of growing resistance – and a resulting rise of populist, nationalist parties – against continued EU integration as it reached nationally 'vital' areas. Alternatively, there could be a growing feeling of 'togetherness', as various acts of bringing the European Union together took place, as had indeed been the case over much of the Union's history.

In a first setback to the Nice Treaty, Irish voters in a referendum in June 2001 rejected it by a margin of 54 per cent to 46 per cent (with only about a third participating in the vote). Together with the Danish referendum 'no' in 2000 to the euro, the Irish referendum was a renewed reminder to the EU that something was amiss in the unification process.

Irish voters had above all been uneasy that Nice was relegating smaller powers in the EU to a secondary position, through loss of voting power in the Council of Ministers and the increased use of majority decisions in that body. Furthermore, the Irish objected to what they saw as their country's forced abandonment of its neutrality through the new military responsibilities of the EU. The Irish vote pointed to a growing estrangement on the part of EU citizens vis-à-vis the EU, which was seen as increasingly opaque and secretive and distant from EU burghers and their concerns. By contrast, the vote did not seem to reflect any popular sentiment against EU enlargement, even though that was highlighted in the international reaction within the EU, where many argued that enlargement and the Nice Treaty in general would have to go ahead regardless.

The other EU countries refused any renegotiation of Nice with the Irish (as had been done with the Danes on Maastricht) and still expected ratification by all the Fifteen (i.e. including Ireland) to permit the treaty's entry into force in 2003. However, the treaty's requirement that it be ratified by all countries, coupled with the uncertain prospect of a 'yes' in another Irish referendum to be held in October 2002, would have forced the EU into unchartered legal territory, had it gone ahead as if nothing had happened.

It was fortunate for the EU, therefore, that a second referendum in October 2002 approved the Nice Treaty by a comfortable margin, permitting it to enter into force in February 2003. Some critics wondered what referenda on EU treaties were worth, if negative results were not tolerated and new ones had to be held until approval was won. Others asked why referenda were admitted at all and recommended that ratification through the national parliaments should suffice in all member states.

New visions for the European Union

In the spring and summer of 2000 the debate on the future of Europe and especially the EU was given new impetus with a speech by German Prime Minister Joschka Fischer.[19] Fischer, in May 2000, called for an EU federation with a constitution, a directly-elected President, the Commission as a form of government, and a bicameral parliament – with a Senate representing the member states and the European Parliament representing the EU population as a whole. The locomotive behind such a development should be a 'core Europe', a 'centre of gravity' – of Germany and France and any other willing country. It was time, he said, at a later press conference, to finish with the 'Monnet method' of opaque and technocratic decision making behind closed doors that had started with the Schuman Plan in 1950 (as devised by Jean Monnet) and the 1958 European Coal and Steel Community and had ended with the Maastricht Treaty.[20]

The French reply was courteous but reserved. President Jacques Chirac, a few days later, approved of the 'core Europe' idea and the need for stronger French–German integration, but never once used the word 'federal'. Instead he emphasised the enduring importance of the nation-states, whose 'natural convergence', he maintained, constituted Europe's real strength.[21] The French Minister of the Interior, Jean-Pierre Chevène-ment, went so far as angrily to react against a 'Germany still dreaming of the Holy Roman Empire of the German Nation', adding that it had 'not yet recovered from the derailment caused to its history by national socialism'.[22]

The reactions from Italy and Spain were subdued, and that of the United Kingdom as reserved as could be expected from a Blair govern-ment wary of even submitting the EMU issue to a referendum. The small nations seemed to be against the Fischer proposal, mainly because they feared the increased dominance in the EU that it presaged for the big EU countries.

Responding to Fischer's call for an EU federation of nation-states and Chirac's urge for a limited number of countries to pursue closer inte-gration if they so wished, British Prime Minister Tony Blair in a speech in Warsaw in October 2000 said that EU enlargement should be the priority, lest Europe again be split in two halves, and that national governments should play the leading role in the running of the EU as the 'basis of democratic legitimacy'. He also called for a second chamber of the European Parliament comprised of members of national parliaments, to ensure that the Union would stick to common EU matters and not interfere in national policy areas.

Blair also suggested an EU 'troika presidency' to shorten the time between national EU presidencies for member states (intervals of seven years with fifteen members and thirteen years with twenty-five). Blair did not wish to see an EU constitution established, but rather an 'EU Charter of Competencies' of a non-legislative nature, clearly spelling out EU and national prerogatives. He also proposed a second EU legislature, supplementing the European Parliament and consisting of members of national parliaments. Its task would be to supervise the respect of the 'Competencies Charter'. (The role of the European Commission would be correspondingly reduced.)

The former French President Valéry Giscard d'Estaing and the former German Chancellor Helmut Schmidt made their contribution to the debate by announcing a preference for an EU restricted to the present Fifteen plus Hungary, Poland and the Czech Republic. The other candi-dates should, they said, belong to a new, separate organisation to be established for economic and trade co-operation, with only a minimum of political integration.

In April 2001, the President of Germany, Johannes Rau, outlined his vision of the future EU before the European Parliament in Strasbourg. His main concern was the preservation of Europe's diversity and he therefore proposed a federation of EU member states based on a federal constitution (similar to Blair's ideas). The constitution would have three parts: the Charter of Fundamental Rights declared at the Nice Summit in December 2000; a definition of EU and member-state rights; and a structure for the federation consisting of a two-chamber parliament where the EU Council of Ministers (not the national parliaments as in Blair's proposal) would form a second chamber supplementing the European Parliament.

Furthermore, to remedy the European Commission's 'democratic deficit', Rau proposed that the Commission's President should be elected directly by the EU population or by the two chambers of parliament. However, the European Commission would keep the right to propose EU legislation, since in his view the limits of intergovernmental initiatives had been reached.

Following the Fischer and Rau proposals, and as if to underline Germany's leading role in the new EU, German Chancellor Gerhard Schröder in April 2001 presented his ideas for the European Union's future. The European Commission would be the EU's government. The European Parliament would gain critical new powers by having 'complete budget authority', while the present power broker, the Council of Ministers, would become the EU's second chamber of parliament, supplementing the European Parliament, and thereby filling the EU's 'democratic deficit', which Schröder saw as lying in the Council's secretive deliberations. By contrast, competence over issues like the EU regional and structural policy would be returned to the nation-states.

In May 2001, Romano Prodi, President of the European Commission, predictably called for much more power in the hands of the Commission, which should be turned into a 'European government' for economic policy, foreign policy and defence (with the EU's High Representative for Security and Foreign Policy joining it as a member). It would serve as the political counterweight to the European Central Bank for management of the euro. It would also administer a 'European tax', replacing the present budgetary system of the EU. In other words, an EU run by a bureaucratic body without any direct democratic accountability.

Also in May 2001, French Prime Minister Lionel Jospin added his 'vision', which was very reminiscent of that of Prodi. Its emphasis was on the need for continued intergovernmental rule over the EU through the Council of Ministers; more harmonised social and labour legislation; universal access to supplementary schooling in another EU country; an 'economic government' to supervise the European Central Bank; more subsidies for European culture; a transnational, multilingual European television network; more European agencies such as an EU police force and a European prosecutor; a harmonised European corporate tax level; and more restrictions on tax advantages in different EU countries and on competition in international trade.

Jospin also called for the election of the President of the European Commission by the European Parliament (and not, as at present, by member states with the approval of the European Parliament) and for the right of the Council of Ministers (on the advice of the Commission or of member states) to dissolve the European Parliament.

In sum, the 'visions' ranged from the federal-parliamentary (Fischer, Rau and Schröder) to the intergovernmental (Chirac and Blair) to the bureaucratic-intergovernmental (Prodi and Jospin). The discussion was refreshing, since it showed how open the EU's future still was. It was not too dissimilar from what took place when the American constitution was drawn up in Philadelphia in 1787, with the difference that in the EU's case years went by, not weeks. The big question was, however, whether the EU intergovernmental conference convened for 2004 to review EU institutional reform would have a constitutional mandate (as the Germans, Dutch and others preferred) or not (as was the British wish in particular).

Would Europe be able to manage these challenges? The writer Michael Prowse saw the '21st century as belonging to Europe – to that unique and underrated political organisation called the European Union'. The twenty-first century would be Europe's, he argued,

> because it will offer the world the most satisfying overall combination of individual liberty, economic opportunity and social inclusion. It will offer the individual more freedom than intolerant Asia. And the value of this freedom will be enhanced by a sense of community and a commitment to social welfare that is largely missing in atomistic America. That will make Europe an unbeatable bargain.[23]

A contrasting view was put forward by Lord Howell of Guildford, at the time the chief Tory spokesman for foreign affairs in the House of Lords. Howell argued that what Europe needed might in fact be less integration, not more. He wrote:

> The merging of nation states, like corporations, and the building of bigger and bigger blocks and institutions to preside over them can sometimes mean

advance. But it can also mean heavy centralisation and stagnation. In the modern milieu of webs and electronic networks, ideas of block-building and centralisation can seem particularly inappropriate ... and it may prove easier to bind people and societies together by *not* pushing them together.

Howell went on to call on the builders of modern Europe to muster the

courage to show that there are different models for European advance, and that closer integration is not necessarily the best one ... There may not even be a clearly definable goal for modern Europe. It may turn out to be more of a continuous process of bargaining and adjustment, managed by a reformed and a sharply downsized Commission.[24]

Not all of Howell's compatriots would have agreed. The British political thinker Larry Siedentop, for example, urgently wanted the EU to adopt a federal constitution, not so that it would become more centralised but, to the contrary, so that clear limits could be set against any encroachment by Brussels into the proper domains of member states or regions. Only in this way could real meaning be given to the Maastricht concept of 'subsidiarity'.

Siedentop saw three current national approaches to EU integration. The 'French' approach – born out of France's traditional centralism under a *grande école*, still essentially Jacobinic, elite – would try to do the same with the EU, thereby making it centralist, bureaucratic and secretive. The second was the 'British' approach, which was to avoid excessive centralisation on an ad hoc basis, but without any grand strategy or theory for doing so. This method, Siedentop feared, was bound to fail in the face of the centralist onslaught brought about by the 'French' approach.

The third approach, and the one favoured by him, was the 'German', building on the positive German experience with a federal constitution established after World War II and largely inspired by that of the United States. By overly fearing the 'F-word' (federalism), Siedentop concluded, those against excessive Brussels power were in fact undermining their own cause. Only a constitution setting out the strict limits of central power could lastingly protect the prerogatives of member states and democracy itself.[25]

The 2002 Convention on the Future of Europe

The EU summit in Nice in 2000 had concentrated on ways to enable the institution's decision-making machinery, above all within the intergovernmental Council of Ministers, to cope with the arrival of up to twelve new members from the mid–2000s onwards. This was clearly not sufficient to prepare the EU as a whole – that is, its other institutions and its policies – for such a development. The 'vision' debate on the EU's future (described earlier) therefore started shortly after Nice and led to the establishment, at the EU summit in Laeken (Brussels) in December 2001, of an EU Convention on the Future of Europe.

The convention, presided by former French President Valéry Giscard d'Estaing, started its work in February 2002. It brought together around a hundred delegates and representatives of national governments of EU member states and candidate countries, the European Parliament, national parliaments and the European Commission around a mandate of proposing necessary changes to EU treaties (or a new treaty), to ensure that the institution could function democratically, efficiently and close to EU citizens in decades to come.[26] The proposals of the convention would be ready by 2003, for ultimate adoption (after likely modification at an intergovernmental conference) at an EU summit. The new treaty would be in place, it was hoped, in time for the next EU enlargement in 2004.

Valéry Giscard d'Estaing in his speech opening the convention in February 2002 said that it should ask itself what the Europeans in an enlarged EU wanted Europe to be, now that the continent had overcome its divisions and found peace. The world as a whole, he continued, needed a strong, united and peaceful Europe that stood by its international commitments and promoted tolerance and democracy. The convention should shape its recommendations according to all these expectations, in defining the EU's institutional architecture, competences, inner functioning and democratic legitimacy. Above all, he concluded, it would have to arrive at a consensus on a single document and not let itself break up into factions.

Pat Cox, the Irish President of the European Parliament, in his speech on the same occasion emphasised the need to make the EU more democratic and more parliamentary, while Romano Prodi, the President of the European Commission, spoke of the development of the EU as a harmoniously functioning model of a supranational democracy and one where no member state should dominate any other, presumably via a strong role for the Commission.

During the convention's first few months of work, proposals flowed in from many quarters.[27] There were certain similarities (but also important differences) between Brussels in February 2002 and Philadelphia in 1787 or Bonn in 1948, to mention just a few conventions entrusted with shaping a new constitution for a state or group of states.[28] The actors –

governments, national parliaments, the European Parliament, the Commission and others – were all present and eager to present their ideas and defend their interests. The quality of the end result would determine whether all those absent but who mattered most – the ordinary citizens of the enlarged EU – would start feeling that the EU was with them and in their hearts, rather than above and apart from them.

By early 2003 the convention still held together well and had made steady progress in reaching its aim of presenting a joint text to the new member states within the timeframe foreseen. Thus there was now a broad consensus to draw up a constitutional treaty, a framework for which was presented at the end of 2002. EU legislation would come under a single legal entity (signifying a departure from the 1992 Maastricht Treaty on European Union) and would be drastically simplified, as would EU procedures.

A first part of the future constitution would deal with fundamental rights, EU powers and institutions, democratic government, finances and representation vis-à-vis the outside world. The framework described the EU as 'a Union of European states which, while retaining their national identities, closely co-ordinate their policies at the European level and administer certain common competences on a federal basis'. Subsidiarity would be assured by 'the principle that any competence not conferred on the Union as a constitution, rests with the member states', thus limiting the scope for institutions such as the Commission to gain undue power. A 'Congress of the Peoples of Europe' was foreseen in order to give a voice to national parliaments and to preserve subsidiarity. Countries would if they so wished be able to leave the EU, whose final name would be decided in due course.

A second part of the framework dealt with various EU policies, without seeking large modification to them, such as the free movement of goods and people, economic policy, competition and internal security. A third and final part took up legal issues, such as the continuity in relation to the European Community and the repeal of earlier treaties.

As the convention attempted to go from framework to constitution proper, several countries – notable among them France and Germany – sent their Foreign Ministers to represent them. Among the first proposals they had to consider was one from the Commission, in which it asked to be given the central right of initiative in all fields relating to legislation and an almost exclusive executive authority. The Commission President should be elected by the European Parliament and confirmed by the European Council (of heads of state and government). As a counterpart, the Commission would be politically accountable before these two bodies. The European Parliament would be given the same legislative powers as the Council of Ministers, while the veto power within the latter would be abandoned in favour of majority decisions. A single 'Foreign Secretary' would be responsible for external relations, rather than divided between a High Representative of the member states and a European Commissioner, as at present.

In early 2003, France's President Chirac and Germany's Chancellor Schröder proposed a dual EU presidency: an EU President would be appointed by the Council of Ministers to serve as the public face of the EU and as its political driving force, also on foreign policy. A European Commission President would be elected by the European Parliament. The EU's 'Foreign Secretary' would work under the EU President but be based in the Commission. The French–German compromise proposal was considered as having a chance of being accepted by many other member states, since the differing French and German views – France's being more intergovernmental and that of Germany seeking a stronger influence for the EP and the Commission – rather well reflected the major strands of opinion in the EU as a whole.

However, the most difficult choices still remained to be made. What should be the final purpose, 'identity' and popular legitimacy of the EU – questions all the more pressing given the already achieved high degree of integration? Should the EU be given more capacity for action in the international arena, such as in ensuring the success of the euro in world markets? Or was this not necessary, to the extent that member states felt they could safeguard such interests better individually or in (shifting) coalitions, such as dealing with Iraq in 2003?

Should the EU be a confederation along the Swiss model, a 'Europe of states'? Or should it be a federal state, a 'United States of Europe'? Or should it be a combination of the two – more federal internally via increased powers for the Commission, and more confederal in its international relations, via the intergovernmental Council of Ministers? Or should the 'community model' be sought along the lines of the present set-up, with the Commission as the engine behind final decisions to be taken by the Council of Ministers and approved by the European Parliament? What should be the balance of power between the EU institutions and to whom should they be accountable? Presumably, final answers to these questions would essentially have to be given at the truly political level, that is, at the post-convention stage of deliberations.

The EU's policing of its inner democracy: the 'Haider affair'

In February 2000, the Austrian People's Party (*Österreichische Volks-Partei – ÖVP*) formed a government coalition with the Austrian Freedom Party (*Freiheitliche Partei Österreichs – FPÖ*) led by Jörg Haider, a far-right populist who had made statements, later withdrawn, praising aspects of Hitler's rule.[29] The government had come about as coalition negotiations between the ÖVP and its earlier partner, the Austrian Social-Democratic Party (*Sozialdemokratische Partei Österreichs – SPÖ*) had broken down. The other fourteen governments of the EU reacted by downgrading relations with Austria, provoking a bitter debate about the meaning of national sovereignty and about whether the quest for morality as the basis for an emerging new international order should take precedence over the democratic expression of a people's will.

With the FPÖ obtaining virtually as many votes as the ÖVP in the national elections of October 1999, and well ahead of the SPÖ, the coalition seemed natural enough, if it had not been for Haider's extreme remarks and his party's perceived xenophobia or even antisemitism.[30] The French and Belgian governments were in the forefront of a weekend move, which by the following Monday had virtually isolated Austria diplomatically from the rest of the EU and which would continue, it was declared, for as long as the coalition remained. The French and Belgian fervour was due not only to the personal convictions of the leaders of these countries, but also the particular inroads into the political arena made by the extreme far-right *Front National* in France and the *Vlamse Bloc* in Belgium.

However, the rather hurried decision among the Fourteen also drew fire from some quarters. Why, it was asked, had it been rushed through over a weekend, without much consultation of especially some smaller EU member state governments or any consultation of national parliaments or the European Parliament?[31] Why was it made even before the new government had even been formed, let alone taken any actions that might have represented 'serious and persistent' breaches of the principles of liberty, democracy and respect for human rights, in the words of a recent EU treaty revision? Where was the respect for an EU 'subsidiarity', in this case the right of each country to decide on its own government? Would the EU have done the same to a big or central country as it had done to Austria?

The proponents of the action argued, however, that incursions by the extreme Right had to be nipped in the bud, especially in view of forthcoming EU enlargement to the new democracies in Central and Eastern

Europe. If Europe had shown similar resolve in 1933, they said, the Third Reich and World War II might have been avoided. Finally, if political Europe was to have any meaning, the political situation in any one country would have to be the concern of all, especially if it went against basic EU principles.

In the summer of 2000 a delegation of 'three wise men' was dispatched to Austria to judge the country's policies as well as the evolution of the FPÖ.[32] Finding a way out had become more and more of a necessity for the Fourteen, as the sanctions were proving ineffectual and unpopular in the EU. An Austrian referendum on the sanctions was to be held in October, 2000, and it was feared that the boycott would influence a Danish referendum on the euro the preceding month in the direction of a rejection.

In the autumn of 2000, the sanctions of the Fourteen against Austria were lifted following a report by the 'three wise men'. The report said that, although the FPÖ had often used ambiguous and xenophobic language and had 'trivialised' Nazism, it had not used such language after it had joined government. The latter, the report went on, had respected 'European values' and its record on minorities, refugees and immigrants was no worse than in any other EU country. Under such circumstances, the 'three wise men' concluded, it would be counterproductive to continue the sanctions. These were subsequently lifted.

Whatever view one took, the EU would now have to follow a rather interventionist course if it was to be faithful to the Austrian precedent. Nor was it clear how such a course would work out in different EU countries with strong xenophobic or far-Right parties. The road from European union to European disunion and paralysis could be shorter than one cared to think .[33]

Turkey and the EU

Turkey first applied for EU membership in 1963 and soon was given association status and preferential trade links. However, it was told that membership would have to wait, until even that hope was thrown out at an EU summit in Luxembourg in 1997. The arguments raised by the EU included the as yet unresolved Kurdish question and Turkey's human rights record, which was perceived as inadequate. Turkey was urged not to try to hinder the accession of Cyprus to the EU and to improve its relations with Greece. In order to patch up relations, Turkey was invited to participate in a special Europe Conference in London in 1998, an invitation subsequently spurned by Ankara. (The conference brought together the Fifteen and the eleven 'first and second wave' states, but left few traces.)

When Turkey was finally included among the seven ''second wave' candidate countries in 1999, it was in part in recognition of the country's support as a NATO member during the Cold War and its key strategic position in between three restless regions: the Balkans, the Caucasus and the Middle East. A Turkey in the EU would radically increase the institutions's influence in these regions, while a Turkey outside it would correspondingly diminish it. Turkey was a major, and rapidly developing economy, with its sixty-six million people and one of the fastest growing and youngest populations in Europe. As an EU member, however, Turkey would of course also be part of the Internal Market, implying free movement of, among other things, labour. With unemployment high in many EU countries and xenophobia not far below the surface, the effects of likely large-scale immigration by Turkish workers was an issue of considerable concern to some EU members. Finally, Greece's opposition to Turkey's entry went deep, because of memories of past Ottoman domination, the conflict over Cyprus and strife over borders in the possibly oil-rich Aegean Sea. By the early 2000s, however, relations between Ankara and Athens had improved considerably.[34]

Turkey, for its part, was not without options. With a customs union in place with the EU since 1996, its immediate economic interests (minus the EU financial assistance that would come with membership) had largely been secured. The country was unlikely to stop playing its other cards even as an EU candidate, especially if membership negotiations were to drag on. These included closer relations with the United States, Russia, Israel and culturally and linguistically related countries in central Asia, not least in view of the oil and gas riches in and around the Caspian Sea. To the extent that these cards were played skilfully, the EU might well find that delaying Turkish entry could carry with it a cost, in that it was shut out of deals between Turkey and its new partners. Amidst all this there was, in Turkey, a strong and, some argued, growing Islamic fundamentalism. While this was not likely radically to alter the overall orientations of the country (which were largely geostrategically determined), it could still add to political instability.

By the time of the December 2000 EU summit in Nice, Turkish relations with the EU had cooled considerably.[35] It was clear from a critical report by the Commission of November 2000 that the EU candidate in question was far from actual membership negotiations due to the Kurdish, human rights and Cyprus issues. Ankara responded with anger, by downgrading contacts with Brussels. It also blocked the approval by NATO (of which it was a member) for the EU's wholesale use of NATO resources for the purposes of its Rapid Reaction Force.

Turkey began a major reform process in 2001, one purpose of which was to prepare it for EU membership. Constitutional and legislative changes were made ensuring gender equality, liberalising party and trade union legislation and consolidating civilian control over its National Security Council. In 2002 the death penalty was abolished, the Kurdish language permitted on radio, television and in education, and religious rights protected.

The reforms were enough to extract from the 2002 EU summit in Copenhagen a promise that a decision would be taken by the end of 2004 on the principle and date of the start of membership negotiations with Turkey, provided that the reform process was continued and implemented and progress reached on the issue of the still-divided Cyprus. Behind the EU's commitment lay strong US pressure and Turkey's agreement to lift its veto, referred to above, against letting the EU's Rapid Reaction Force use NATO resources – an issue that had hampered the Force's realisation since the 1999 Helsinki Summit.

The inner logic of EU enlargement: ten new members in 2004 and more in line

For the European Union, enlargement is central to its very essence and *raison d'être*. Previous chapters have related how the United Kingdom, Denmark and Ireland joined in 1973, followed by Greece in 1981, Portugal and Spain in 1986, and Austria, Finland and Sweden in 1995.

It had been clear already in the early 1990s that the newly liberated countries in Central and Eastern Europe would eventually join, the only question being when this would be possible given the European Union's rather exacting *acquis communautaire* and the still low economic output of the countries in question. As they strengthened their democratic institutions, they were able to join the Strasbourg-based Council of Europe in growing numbers, but one of their main ambitions, apart from joining NATO, was EU membership.

It was also obvious that the EU, in order to be able to include many new members, would have to reform its inner functioning, both as regards institutions and financing. The former were essentially the same as, and construed for, an EU of six or perhaps at most a dozen or so members, as had been the case between 1986 and 1994. The finances would have to be reviewed as the candidate countries were comparatively poor and had large farming populations.

The EU summit in Amsterdam in 1997 had agreed to the principle of enlargement with the number of 'first wave' new members – considered to have reached furthest in economic and political development – soon crystallising at six: Cyprus, the Czech Republic, Estonia, Hungary, Poland and Slovenia.

The 1999 Helsinki Summit – in a departure from the earlier 'small bang' enlargement plans to a 'big bang' variant – widened the circle of recognised candidate countries from six to thirteen by including Bulgaria, Latvia, Lithuania, Malta, Romania, Slovakia and Turkey, even though negotiations would start with Turkey only at a later, unspecified date. The Nice Summit in 2000 concentrated on readying the EU from the institutional and decision-making points of view for such a further enlargement.

The EU would have to enlarge in its capacity as the main unifying force in Europe, even as nobody could predict where the EU's 'final' borders to the east and south-east might some day lie. Unlike earlier such unifying forces – a France under Napoleon or a Germany under Hitler – this was not an empire in the making, but an institution in which countries joining would do so voluntarily and be part of the management. Some sovereignty – unknown how much – would have to be abandoned, but it would presumably be the same for all members, new and old.

A power vacuum that had arisen with the disappearance of the Soviet Union and its area of influence in Central and Eastern Europe needed to be filled. NATO, a pure defence and security organisation, would not suffice. There was therefore a logic which pushed the EU toward enlargement far into the east, up to the borders of Russia (and a Ukraine not yet deemed fit for candidacy), a country that would have to be brought into as a close a partnership as possible with the EU. The US was also supportive of the effort, as it saw the EU as a stabilising force largely serving its own security concerns and presence in this part of the world, as underpinned by NATO enlargement.

The candidate countries, especially those that had been under Soviet sway, were on the one hand keen to preserve as much as possible of their newly won national sovereignty and freedom of action – achievements they might have partly to give up along with EU membership. On the other hand, there was the political and security protection offered by the EU and the prospect of important EU financial support for these countries' agricultural sectors and poorer regions. The EU still had the aura of Europe's 'rich men's club' and membership in it was seen as a sign of economic and political success, of having 'made it' into established Europe. Meanwhile, during the candidacy process, the goal of membership would give these countries' foreign policy and economic reform efforts stability and direction. Less clear to the candidates was perhaps the fact that membership would not mean any automatic acquisition of prosperity but would rather imply a continued commitment to the, increasingly, stringent *acquis communautaire* as regards, for instance, the opening of markets and the reduction of domestic subsidies.

In 2000, the European Commission, which negotiated with the twelve candidates on behalf of the EU, announced that it hoped to conclude the talks, focused on thirty-one 'chapters' of the *acquis communautaire* by the end of 2002, so that a formal target date for entry could be fixed for 2004, ahead of the elections for a new European Parliament foreseen for that year. By mid–2002 this forecast was confirmed by the Commission, even though the number of likely new members in the 'first wave' had now shrunk from twelve to ten following a decision at the 2001 EU summit in Brussels.[36]

The prospective membership of Lithuania and Poland presented the EU with a major problem in its relations with Russia. The Kaliningrad region – a part of the former East Prussia (Königsberg and surroundings) sandwiched between Lithuania and Poland, ceded to the Soviet Union after World War II and now forming part of Russia – had become geographically separated from the rest of that country as a result of Lithuanian independence. With Lithuanian and Polish membership of the EU – and hence participation in the Schengen Agreement foreseeing the free movement of people and goods across borders – the one million inhabitants of Kaliningrad would not be able to move freely between the region and the rest of Russia. Instead, as non-EU citizens, they would need a visa. This, Russia argued, would mean an unacceptable infringement of their human rights. Russia asked for 'corridors' through Lithuania and Poland, something which, however, neither of these two countries nor the EU felt they could accept. A solution was becoming urgent, both for EU–national relations and for the people of Kaliningrad who, isolated from Russia and the outside world in general, were sinking into greater and greater poverty.

There were tensions among the EU member states as to the extent and timetable of enlargement. The UK was in favour of wide and speedy enlargement, believing that the resulting larger heterogeneity would weaken any feared 'deepening' of EU integration. The Nordic EU countries – Denmark, Finland and Sweden – were eager to include the Baltic states (Estonia, Latvia and Lithuania) as well as Poland – as was a Germany keen on stability to its east. All EU members agreed on the need eventually to include also Bulgaria and Romania to promote stability in South-Eastern Europe.

However, some EU members feared that too wide and speedy an enlargement would hasten the arrival of the day when an increasingly financially strained EU would have to cut its regional and agricultural funds to the older members. Countries like France, Portugal, Spain, Greece and Ireland therefore emphasised the necessity for the candidates to meet all parts of the *acquis communautaire* before accession – a requirement that would tend to slow down the process – and also wanted to make support levels lower for new members than for the current ones. The candidates, by contrast, insisted on a number of temporary exemptions from the *acquis* and on uniform financial-support models to avoid becoming 'second class' EU members. Meanwhile, net contributors to the EU, and in particular the biggest net payer Germany, insisted on not having to pay (much) more into the EU budget following enlargement.

The EU's long-awaited 'big bang' enlargement came at its summit in Copenhagen in December 2002, when it decided to admit ten new members by May 2004: Cyprus, the Czech Republic, Estonia, Hungary, Latvia, Lithuania, Malta, Poland, Slovakia and Slovenia. The EU's population would increase by 70 million to over 450 million. Following the agreement to the enlargement by the European Parliament in 2003, the accession treaty would have to be ratified by all the fifteen current member states (and perhaps submitted to referenda in a few among them). The EU would also monitor the implementation of the commitments given by the future members, including reforms promised in the administrative and judicial domains.

Meanwhile, negotiations would continue with Bulgaria and Romania, with a possible date of accession set for 2007. Finally, as has been mentioned, an attempt would be made in 2004 to set a date for the start of membership negotiations with Turkey.

Negotiations with the ten candidate countries were difficult up until the Copenhagen Summit. They focused on the level of agricultural and regional support to be given to the new members and on whether compensation to their farmers would be the same as that paid to their colleagues in the 'old' member states. The added costs to the EU for the 2004–6 period were budgeted at around €40 billion.

The Copenhagen Summit was truly historic, as had been the NATO Prague Summit a month earlier, where it had been decided to invite seven new members to join the defence alliance. The Copenhagen Summit came only nine years after the EU summit of 1993 in the same city, where the so-called 'Copenhagen accession criteria' – now met – had been agreed, and twenty-one years to the day after communist Poland had proclaimed martial law in 1981. As in Prague, the speeches referred to the 'reunification of Europe that had been divided at Yalta' in 1945. Even the issue of the Kaliningrad region was resolved in parallel negotiations among the EU, Russia and Lithuania.[37]

The EU's enlargement was unlikely to stop at the ten invited in 2002 or those foreseen for the years thereafter. At least some of the countries in the Balkans would be next in line, as witnessed by the many association and assistance agreements concluded with the countries of the former Yugoslavia in particular. Since the Kosovo conflict, the EU had been paying much greater attention to the region. The Stability Pact, jointly administered by the EU and the World Bank, was not only about giving money, but also about enhancing trade and investment within the region – a difficult task given its recent and not so recent history of conflict. The EU, like the rest of the international community, expected, however, that borders would not be changed, as they would be if Kosovo or Montenegro were to leave what remained of the Federal Republic of Yugoslavia (which in 2002 decided to change its name to Serbia and Montenegro). The fear was that, if this happened, many other borders in the region would be called into question.

Finally, non-EU countries in Western Europe had begun to rethink their position, as the inconveniences of remaining outside the EU began to be felt. The EU's European Economic Area (EEA) Agreement concluded with Iceland, Liechtenstein and Norway in 1994 gave the latter free access to the EU's Internal Market in most areas (though not fisheries) but little say in decisions. The situation could only worsen in an EU which in 2004 would go from fifteen to twenty-five, especially as the EEA countries would have to pay much more into the EU's 'Cohesion Fund' used to assist the less wealthy new members. The EEA countries would also face new trade barriers with the new EU members, with which they had, paradoxically enough, already concluded bilateral free trade agreements via EFTA. Iceland treasured its exclusive control over its fishing waters, but other economic areas suffered from being outside the EU. Norway also had important fisheries interests to defend and would be a major net payer once inside the EU due to its oil wealth. Still, even there doubts about the advantages of remaining outside began to arise. Popular referenda on membership in those countries could not be excluded in some future.

Switzerland's relations with the EU had been defined in a so-called 'Bilateral I' agreement of 2002, but difficulties had emerged in the negotiations for a future 'Bilateral II' treaty, especially over customs issues and the taxation of income from interest to be paid by EU citizens on capital held in Swiss banks. A Swiss referendum on EU membership was not, however, on the cards for a variety of reasons. These included opposition against membership by a seemingly solid majority of the Swiss and difficulties in reconciling Swiss direct democracy with the EU's method of functioning.

Reform of the Common Agricultural Policy and the aid to regions

One area in great need of reform was the EU's Common Agricultural Policy (CAP). Ever since the crucial decision was taken by the EEC in the late 1950s to engage in price support (a guaranteed price for each unit of various commodities) rather than income support (a guaranteed income regardless of production), the EU had had to compensate for one administrative shortcoming in the system by adding another. Big farmers were favoured, deliberately at first so as to rationalise farming by creating larger units and forcing smaller farmers off the land into other occupations. This worked as long as production was not in excess, i.e. up until the mid–1960s. However, as from the early 1970s, when excess production of dairy products and beef in particular rose to worrying levels, the EU had to resort to dumping on the world markets (much to the irritation of North Americans, Australians and others), and pay for it through export subsidies. (The CAP and other agriculture-related expenditure still today accounts for about half of an EU budget, which has in the meantime become much bigger.[38])

The early 1990s saw various limited EU efforts to reform the CAP: cuts in price support beyond certain production levels; 'set-aside' programmes, i.e. payments to farmers for letting land lie fallow; reforestation and support for environment protection initiatives; and a cutback on export subsidies under international pressure (notably US). [39]

In 1997 the Commission, as part of its more general Agenda 2000 for revamping various EU policies, proposed further cuts in price support for main crops in order to return EU agriculture slowly to the free market and to lower prices for consumers. It further suggested greater reliance on supporting farmers' incomes, signifying a return to an idea discarded in the 1950s. The new aim would be to help smaller farmers stay on the land and thereby counter the flight to the cities where jobs were now scarcer, and to encourage local food varieties and higher food quality.

Reform of the CAP was all the more urgent in view of the forthcoming EU enlargement to the countries of Central and Eastern Europe with their large and comparatively poor farming populations. At the same time the EU would have great difficulties assuming any major extra outlays as a result of enlargement, especially since the new countries would all be net beneficiaries from the EU budget. With uniform and unchanged CAP payments throughout an enlarged EU financially almost impossible – and with reduced overall CAP payments politically difficult vis-à-vis farmers in the present EU member states – a non-uniform CAP giving less to the farmers of the new entrants might be the only way out.

The 1999 Berlin Summit, as described earlier in this chapter, showed that resistance against changes to CAP payments was fierce, not only from EU members that stood to gain the most, but also from strong and well-organised farming interests. Another idea – the 'renationalisation' of the CAP (i.e. its abandonment) – was floated by Germany in the lead-up to the Berlin Summit, but it was abandoned after heavy French resistance. Given the difficulties of reforming the CAP in any meaningful way, the enlarged EU was likely to face both a costly system and considerable excess production, especially in the meat and dairy sectors.

A new Commission proposal in 2002 suggested an even greater 'decoupling' of agricultural payments from farm production. A set sum would be paid to each farm, the size depending on past production and the farmer's contribution to environment protection, landscape improvement such as forestation, animal welfare and village renewal. This would lead to less production of commodities in excess, such as dairy products and beef, and hence to fewer export subsidies, considered to be in violation of World Trade Organisation rules. The new proposals would, however, keep intact many other features of the traditional CAP, such as price guarantees and levies on imported food. Meanwhile, farm aid to new member countries would be phased in as from enlargement, starting with a quarter of the EU level in 2004 and reaching it in 2013. The Commission's proposal led to fierce reactions on the part of several EU governments with important CAP payments to defend, especially France.

In 2002 France managed to rally Germany – normally a country in favour of CAP reform but now politically weakened over the Iraq crisis in particular – and eventually also the EU around a proposal to delay any strict limit on CAP spending and further reform until 2007, rather than the earlier 2004 date sought by the European Commission through countries like the United Kingdom and Sweden.[40]

The European Commission, eager to achieve reform, fought back, however, pointing out that an unreformed CAP of massive export subsidies and import restrictions might scuttle the ongoing World Trade Organisation's round of negotiations – the Doha Development Agenda – where other essential EU interests, such as in the services sector, were at stake. Agriculture was now moving to the very centre of international politics, with developing countries and major agricultural producers such as Australia, New Zealand and Canada pressing the EU, and increasingly also the US, to give up subsidies and let more imports in, or risk a collapse in trade negotiations and a brake on world economic development. The Commission, representing EU member states in the trade talks, faced a formidable balancing act.

It was similarly difficult to reform the EU's regional assistance programmes. At the beginning of the EU's history, regional aid was devoted to the assistance of the truly poorest regions of the then Six, such as the Italian *Mezzogiorno* or the eastern parts of the Federal Republic of Germany that had lost their links with the east due to the Iron Curtain. However, it was increasingly being used to compensate other regions or even countries which felt they gave much more to the EEC–EC than they received in return (this was the case with the British rebate). For every new enlargement, starting with Greece, regional support was used for such compensatory purposes by the existing member states, who saw their own receipts threatened if they had to be shared with newcomers, unless of course the overall EU budget was increased and they could receive extra funds. For the Twelve-to-Fifteen enlargement, a new Cohesion Fund was introduced, principally benefiting Greece, Ireland, Spain and Portugal. The Berlin Summit of 1999 meant both a restriction on the growth of regional outlays and a concentration on the poorest regions.

The EU's regional support amounting to some €30 billion per year (over 30 per cent of the EU budget) would face particular strain. Whereas in the EU of twelve member states one-sixth of the population lived in so called 'cohesion countries' (a per capita income of less than 90 per cent of the EU average – Greece, Portugal and Spain), that proportion would rise to one-third in an EU of twenty-seven member states. Similarly, in an EU of twenty-seven member states, the poorest 10 per cent of the population would have a per capita income of only about one-third of the EU average, as opposed to close to two-thirds of that level in the EU of fifteen states. Not only would this mean that more regional funds would have to be made available, but the 'cohesion countries' of the EU of twelve member states might receive less.

The fraud problem

CAP and regional aid are among the EU programmes most afflicted with fraud and payment 'irregularities', which are estimated to amount to close to €7 billion per year, or around 8 per cent of the EU budget. The EU's Court of Auditors in Luxembourg – an institution with great expertise and a strong will to remedy the situation but with a limited remit, in that it can only report but not initiate prosecution – regularly points to wrongly waived customs duties, export funds paid 'in error', and subsidies to farmers for non-existent or already subsidised set-aside land, for dreamt-up herds of cattle, olive groves and other products, or for surpluses of already rotten fruit. The absence of border controls through the Internal Market, coupled with VAT payments only at the point of delivery of goods (instead of at the point of departure), is reported to give rise to massive fraud involving organised crime, lorry drivers, transport companies and customs agents.

Even where there is no outright fraud, the Court has found many examples of inefficient use of funds due to poor planning, co-ordination or evaluation of projects. For example, regional support is often invested in ways that run counter to environmental objectives. Aid to non-EU countries is often inefficient because of a lack of ability of recipient countries to absorb it.

Even though the magnitude of fraud is thought to have come down following stricter procedures (many of them called for by the Court of Auditors) and even the use of informers, it still eats like a cancer at the whole EU edifice, affecting the morale of EU tax payers while building up the bank balances of profiteers. It is, however, difficult to see how it can be radically reduced, since normally the controlling and disbursing authorities are national (over three-quarters of all EU spending is administered by the member states), but the funds come from the EU as a whole. There is no obvious reason why a member state should devote all the effort it takes to check on the use of money which is mainly paid by fellow EU countries. It cannot be excluded that national controllers are even tempted to turn a blind eye to the problem. At issue is the unnecessary centralisation of payments, and the unaccountability of the central authority, the European Commission, before a popularly elected assembly that has greater powers than those at present enjoyed by the European Parliament.[41]

The risk of excessive uniformity

One problem for the EU is the rigidity of its legislative framework – the 80,000-page-thick *acquis communautaire*. A national parliament, acting under popular pressure or not, can with relative ease cancel or modify a law which has outlived its usefulness. However, to modify or cancel a directive is much more difficult and lengthy, requiring that several EU governments view things the same way and present a corresponding

proposal for change to the Council of Ministers; that the latter author-
ises the Commission to study the proposal and possibly prepare a new
draft directive for submission back to it; that the new text meets with the
approval of the required majority of governments on the Council of
Ministers (or them all, as the case may be); and, finally, that the new
directive is transposed into national law by all the countries.

Meanwhile, the world goes on at ever more tantalising speed, which
would require more rapid, not slower, adaptation of the legislation. The
EU seems to be caught in a time warp, stuck in an approach to life more
in line with the assumed exigencies of central planning, uniformity and
secretiveness of the 1950s than with decentralisation, flexibility, public
openness and the diversity associated with present times. Europe derived
its strength and dynamism over history from the inability of one power
to dominate all the others, thus preventing it from falling into the decline
of an Ottoman or Ming Empire. The price Europe (and the world) had
to pay were wars, of which the last two nearly destroyed it. The question
for Europe today is whether it can find a system with which it can preserve its dynamism by enabling its various regions to experiment with
different social and economic models, and at the same time to maintain
peace. (This is all the more important as the stagnation that is likely to
follow from excessive uniformity may itself engender conflict.)

One example of the above has been in the social field, where the Social
Protocol to the Maastricht Treaty was integrated into the EU *acquis
communautaire*, following signature and ratification by the last remaining EU member to do so, the United Kingdom, in 1997.[42] The UK made
it clear that it would continue to follow its own, more flexible – many
would say less social and less employee-friendly – social policies regardless. But the end result of further EU legislation in this field flowing into
the breach opened by the Social Protocol may well be the inability of any
and all to adapt the EU to new circumstances.[43]

The Common Agricultural Policy has already been mentioned. Here,
uniform principles collide with extremely diversified farming situations,
leaving as a result over many decades a myriad of ad hoc exceptions that
render the overall CAP regime largely impenetrable to the outsider and
hence the more difficult to change.

Subsidies, also in principle barred in the EU (although still frequent in
many sectors), are a special case. From a single market point of view, it
is of course desirable to equip a non-democratic European Commission
with powers to prohibit a country, say, France from subsidising Air
France or Crédit Lyonnais, or a German *Land* from supporting a local
Volkswagen plant. However, if the French or the German people

happen to want this to happen, they are in principle prevented from doing so by the EU, acting through the Commission. In a different type of EU, countries would have been free to subsidise whatever they wanted (as the individual states in the US can do), on the understanding that they would eventually pay the price in the form of slower growth due to higher taxes and less efficient companies (as a result of being subsidised).

Another example comes from the economic and trade arena. Germany, a nation particularly fond of bananas, traditionally imported them from whatever country offered the lowest price, whether or not it was linked to the EU through the so-called Lomé Agreement giving preferential trade status to a large number of so-called ACP (African, Pacific and Caribbean) countries. However, a judgement by the European Court of Justice in Luxembourg ruled that this was a violation of Lomé, in spite of Germany's protests that in buying from a country such as Costa Rica it only respected GATT–WTO principles. The economic interests of the Germans (who consume more bananas per person per year than any other EU member) and of other EU citizens were sacrificed on the altar of the economic interests of other EU and ACP nations and the uniformity of consumption, through a decision of a supranational court essentially deliberating behind closed doors.[44]

To some, the banana case and others similar to it highlighted the risk posed by excessive EU constraints to more open world trade and to the welfare of EU consumers. To them, an EFTA arrangement in place of the EU's customs union would never have created the problem in the first place, as there would have been no common external tariff on bananas or other products. Others maintained, however, that the EU must show solidarity to its own producers and to those in the ACP area, whether it be through trade preferences, regional support, the CAP or development assistance through the Lomé Convention, which from 1990 to the year 2000 disbursed some 24 billion ECU to the ACP region.

The EU's fishing policy – 'Blue Europe' – shows the risks caused by excessive uniformity vis-à-vis the resource itself. 'Blue Europe' is based on the noble EU principle that in a single market one must essentially share everything, in this case the fish stocks, whether they are inside or outside the traditional fishing zones of individual EU countries. However, in the 1980s it was discovered that free and equal access for all – Spanish fishermen in British waters, British in Spanish and so on – depleted stocks, since everybody suspected everybody else of catching more than they should and therefore did likewise. Before, each country managed its fish resources (sometimes giving quotas to foreign fishermen) and had an interest in ensuring the long-term stability of stocks.

Now, however, nobody knew who was in charge, unless it was a European Commission trying to act as an honest but largely ineffectual broker who found it easier to say 'yes' than 'no' to the various demands for more fishing rights coming from all sides.

Only a complicated system of EU quotas, inspectors, zones and fishing licences has managed to keep fish stocks at just above the extinction level – with recriminations over 'quota-hopping' by neighbours and occasional shoot-outs between coastguard vessels of different nations. Again, less emphasis on the 'communal' aspects of the European community idea and greater recognition of the specific characteristics of nature, and of nations, might have led to more (and cheaper) fish on the tables of EU consumers and less aggravation among fishermen and governments.[45]

Unemployment: too high for comfort

National economies in the EU – and elsewhere in Europe – have to grow by between 2.5 per cent and 3 per cent a year in order to keep unemployment from rising. Any growth rate below that range will tend to increase unemployment, while any rate above it will tend to reduce it. This is so because the implementation of the EU's Internal Market, and the continuing opening of markets under the World Trade Organisation process, will increase competition in many sectors of the economy and cause many firms to go out of business, 'downsize' their workforce or 'outsource' their production to countries with lower labour costs. As a result, many people will lose their jobs. Those with few qualifications – women, school leavers (especially those with interrupted studies), elderly people and even the not so elderly – are particularly exposed. Only with sufficient growth will new companies be created and established firms grow sufficiently to create new jobs to replace those that have disappeared. It has therefore become essential for EU member countries to show sufficient economic growth. Several Commission White Papers on the subject have seen the light of day and many EU summits have been devoted to it, leading to 'job pacts' and 'processes' meant to lead to lower unemployment.[46]

While economic growth came relatively easily in the 1950–70 period, with rates of 5 per cent or more, it became more difficult to reach them ever since the first oil crisis of 1973–74. Long-term unemployment – that is people being out of a job for several years – shot up in the 1980s despite resumed growth and has stayed high ever since. Job creation also began to lag behind the growth of the workforce (a result of the 'baby boom' of the 1940s and 1950s), causing overall unemployment to grow. The entrepreneurial spirit for whatever reason seemed to prosper less in the EU than, say, in the United States, where new jobs absorbed virtually all of an even more rapidly growing workforce.[47]

Unemployment in the EU in the 1990s remained high, at around 9 per cent. The early 2000s saw a reduction to around 7.5 per cent, assisted by economic integration and increased intra-EU trade resulting from the euro's introduction in 1999. However, as European Union growth in 2002 slowed to less than 1 per cent, with uncertain prospects for 2003, unemployment looked set to rise, especially in key countries like Germany and France.

Many problems remained. Labour markets were recognised as being too 'rigid', meaning that companies could not shed workers as fast or as cheaply as they would wish. Aware of this, they hesitated to hire when the going was good. High extra-salary costs further discouraged hiring. The start-up of companies was a complicated, lengthy and costly process in some countries. Taxes on companies were often so considerable as to deprive them of sufficient capital to grow and hence employ.[48] Taxes on individuals in many countries were too high to leave them with enough money to spend on goods and services, and hence permit companies to profit and grow.

Many of the jobless, meanwhile, remained outside the labour market so long that they lost the skills, motivation and self-confidence they would have needed to re-enter it. This raised the 'structural' unemployment rate, that is, the rate below which even an economy in full expansion cannot readily recruit from the pool of the unemployed, swelled by a growing number of people sent into 'early retirement'. Many jobless would not even make more money if they worked, or the difference might be marginal, and so would not take jobs offered to them. In the EU of the early 2000s, the structural rate of unemployment, below which the economy would not be able to recruit workers without igniting inflation, lay at around 8 per cent of the workforce, as opposed to 4 or 5 per cent in the United States.

The unemployment picture in the EU was, however, far from uniform. In Ireland it had come down from about 15 per cent in the early 1990s to around 4 per cent in the early 2000s, as the country profited mightily from the 'new economy' and the ICT (information and communications technologies) revolution. Spain, another 'tiger' in the new euro-zone context, had managed to reduce its unemployment from 16 per cent in the mid-1990s to around 11 per cent in 2002. The UK's unemployment in 2002 remained at about 5 per cent, even though with large differences between regions. The situation in 2003 was more serious in big Euro-land countries like France, Germany and Italy, with rates close to or in the double-figure range. The labour markets of these countries seemed particularly impervious to the increased 'flexibility' sought by, for instance, the European Commission and the OECD.

Longer-term prospects for the EU were not altogether bleak, however. Labour market reforms in the direction of greater flexibility were proceeding in many countries, setting an example to others. EU enlargement would increase trade and investment in the region and help to reduce the comparatively high unemployment rate in the new member countries. Finally, many more people in the EU would reach retirement age as from about 2010 and there would be fewer younger people to take their place, leading to an automatic lowering of unemployment (but also to many other problems discussed in Chapter 10).

Notes

1 In *Reflections on the Revolution in France*, 1790.
2 The new Labour government that came to power in May 1997 under Tony Blair made this concession, which its Tory predecessor under John Major had refused. For example, the provisions for an EMU in the 1992 Treaty on European Union required British acquiescence (in exchange for a British opt-out clause), whereas a future similar project could well be taken without the consent even of a large EU country.
3 These increased powers of the European Parliament included: individual approval of a new President of the Commission; the possibility of estab-lishing common rules, or at least principles, for the election of European Parliament members in the different countries; a greater say in sanctions against a member state in the event of serious human rights violations; and the right, within certain limits, to determine the status of rights of its members.
4 Presumably, the reformers took their cue from the British historian C. North-cote Parkinson, who in his *Parkinson's Law* (1957, p 49) postulated that no committee can succeed with more than twenty members since, at that point: 'It is finished. It is hopeless. It is dead.' On a more serious note, the number of Commissioners is highly arbitrary. The fact of having so many Com-missioners often leads to confusion and paralysis, especially where economic and political relations overlap, as they increasingly do. Thus, for example, the Commissioner in charge of EU enlargement risks clashing with the colleagues responsible for external trade, transport, agriculture, develop-ment co-operation and possibly others.
5 In October 1999 an EU summit in the Finnish city of Tampere agreed to speed up work aimed at the creation of an area of common EU law in such fields as asylum, migration and the fight against terrorism, financial crime,

organised crime, drugs, the trade in human beings and child labour.

6 Some observers, such as Shaw (1998, pp. 63–86), saw the Amsterdam Treaty as just as Byzantine as the Maastricht Treaty, and as an inconclusive way of restoring the EU's legitimacy following the latter's ratification hurdles: 'Amsterdam – following Maastricht – was the culmination of a growing legitimacy crisis in which all aspects of integration – processes, procedures, institutions, leadership, goals and *raison d'être* – were thrown into serious question for the first time in 40 years ... But real simplification requires something more than these forms of tinkering at the margins'.

7 The Cyprus issue presented many complications for relations between the EU and Turkey. The EU had made it a virtual condition for membership that the island overcome its division, since 1974, into a Greek-speaking part in the south (internationally recognised) and a Turkish-speaking part in the north (recognised only by Turkey and a handful of other countries). This might, however, be used by Turkey to stall a negotiated settlement and thereby unduly influence Cypriot membership. The EU tried to counteract this by making Turkish rapprochement to the EU conditional on progress on Cyprus.

8 The Stability Pact for South-Eastern Europe was established in 1999 at the initiative of the European Union. Its aim is to 'foster peace, democracy, respect for human rights and economic prosperity in order to achieve stability in the whole region'. It is led by a Special Co-ordinator and operates via different Working Tables dealing with democratisation and human rights, economic reconstruction and security. Its membership includes the EU member states, other west European countries, the non-European Group of Eight (G-8) countries (Canada, Japan and the United States) and several international organisations.

9 The 'Internal Reform IGC' was to base its work, among other things, on a report presented by the so-called 'Dehaene Committee' in autumn 1999. The report proposed extended majority voting as a way to avoid gridlock. Furthermore, it suggested that future treaties be divided into two parts: one containing fundamental principles to be ratified by all member countries; and another dealing with more detailed policies that could be changed through majority vote. This would facilitate any modifications necessitated by new circumstances.

In parallel to the above reforms, Commission President Prodi presented, in March 2000, a far-reaching administrative and structural reform of the European Commission. The competence of Commission staff would count for more than nationality (i.e. staff quotas for the different member states) in terms of recruitment and promotion. Greater staff flexibility was to be encouraged. The cabinets of Commissioners were to be made more 'international', i.e. less dominated by one nationality (that of the Commissioner in question) and would be made more transparent (thereby reducing the chances of the mismanagement of EU funds). An independent auditing unit was to scrutinise financial management. External agencies were to take over certain executive tasks. A charter was to be created to help protect whistle-blowers, along with a revised code of conduct to guide Commission staff in their work. The EU should come closer to citizens through delegation of tasks and decentralisation. The Commission should limit itself to core political tasks that would move integration forward, especially in the shaping and implementation of legislation. Even some of these, such as anti-cartel activities, should be pursued in greater contact with national authorities.

10 The army corps was to consist of up to fifteen brigades and would be supported by around five hundred aircraft and fifteen naval vessels. It was not yet clear to what extent the force would draw materieal from the existing Eurocorps in Strasbourg (with Belgium, France, Germany, Luxembourg and Spain as members). The hope of fielding a fully fledged Rapid Reaction Force by 2003 turned out to be unrealistic, however, owing to major lacunae in the military capabilities needed. EU sources spoke of 2012 as a more realistic timeframe for full ESDP operability.

11 The Western European Union (WEU), originating in the pre-NATO days of 1947–48, became the expression of the West Europeans' ambivalence as regards their own defence needs. Should it be within NATO or separate from it? However, even during the WEU's 'somnolent' years in the 1970s and the 1980s, it reflected, at various times, the 'European pillar of NATO' and the beginnings of a 'European defence identity', which would find its first expression in the communiqués issued at NATO's fiftieth anniversary. The WEU could be said to have prepared the ground for possible future Kosovo-type interventions under exclusive European management. See, for example, Deighton and Runacle (1998).

The Western European Union handed over its operative security functions to the EU at the end of 2000. However, the EU would not take over the WEU's collective security guarantee, in deference to the non-WEU members Austria, Finland, Ireland and Sweden. In this sense, the WEU would continue to exist.

12 A Policy and Security Committee was to exercise the political control and strategic direction of military operations in a crisis, taking its instructions from the EU's Council of Ministers meeting at the level of Foreign Ministers. It was to be assisted by a Military Committee consisting of Chiefs of Staff of EU member states and a Military Staff coming under the Council of Ministers and consisting of representatives of all branches of the armed forces. It would assume the conduct of military operations.

With the virtual disappearance of the WEU, European defence policies had become a purely intergovernmental affair, with the European Parliament having a right only to be informed, not consulted. National parliaments of the EU Fifteen, however, did not have the right to be informed, even though they alone had the formal right to engage their nation in war. The EU's 'democratic deficit' in the security and defence area could therefore be said to have been aggravated by the WEU's shrinking role. It was not clear how the situation could be remedied, especially under the EU's new secrecy rules.

13 Germany's defence allocations, which from 1970 to unification in 1990 stood at between 17 and 20 per cent of the federal budget, in 1999 amounted to only 8.7 per cent. Between 1990 and 2000, the *Bundeswehr* budget was reduced by over 20 per cent in real terms. The budget for 2000 was down a further DM1.7 billion from 1999, to DM45.3 billion. No reversal of the trend was likely unless spurred on by the new European Security and Defence Policy. Germany's defence reform effort was rendered more difficult by its continued reliance on obligatory conscription (now abandoned by both France and the United Kingdom) (Rühle, 2000).

    To illustrate the difference between US and EU military capabilities, the US – with 276 million people and a GDP of about $9.2 trillion – in 2000 had a military budget of $283 billion and a total troop strength of 1.37 million soldiers. The fifteen EU member states – with 376 million people and a GDP of $8 trillion – had combined military outlays of only $165 billion (58.4 per cent of those of the US) but a troop strength of 1.8 million soldiers. EU military capability, however, was considered to be less than 20 per cent of that of the US. (Source: International Institute for Strategic Studies: 'Military Balance 2000/2001'.)

14 Rearmament need estimates by Professor R. Seidelmann of Göttingen University, Germany, given at a Cicero Foundation Seminar on the European Security and Defence Policy, Paris, December 2000.

15 Increased military spending may not be harmful to economic growth under all circumstances, as the post-World War II period in Western Europe demonstrated. This is a complicated issue involving such factors as whether and how militarisation affects trade and investment, labour supply, the state of technological development, and spin-off effects from the military to the civilian sector. For instance, the longer-term effects of the Kosovo conflict on the region's economies or on those in Europe as a whole (especially those of NATO members) are not yet clear.

16 The thirteen candidates were Bulgaria, Cyprus, the Czech Republic, Estonia, Hungary, Latvia, Lithuania, Malta, Poland, Slovakia, Slovenia, Romania and Turkey.

17 This is the central thesis contained for instance in Milward's book *The European Rescue of the Nation-State* (2000, p 3), where he sums up his argument in these words: 'The European Community has been [the nation-state's] buttress, an indispensable part of the nation-state's post-war construction. Without it, the nation-state could not have offered to its citizens the same measure of security and prosperity which it has provided and which has justified its survival. After 1945, the European nation-state rescued itself from collapse, created a new political consensus as the basis of its legitimacy, and through changes in its response to its citizens which meant a sweeping extension of its functions and ambitions, reasserted itself as the fundamental

unit of political organisation. The European Community only evolved as an aspect of that national reassertion and without it the reassertion might well have proved impossible. To supersede the nation-state would be to destroy the Community. To put a final limit to the process of integration would be to weaken the nation-state, to limit its scope and to curb its power.'

Furthermore, it is significant that the EU's High Representative for Security and Foreign Policy is also Secretary General of the Council of Ministers, which represents the governments of member states. Finally, the Union's new Rapid Reaction Force likewise serves under the Council of Ministers, rather than the Commission.

18 The pre-Nice 'weighting' of votes in the Council of Ministers had been ten for the 'Big Four' against two for the smallest country, Luxembourg. Nice thus meant a reduction in the weight of the smallest country to the biggest from 1–5 to 1–7.25. It was not clear, however, that Nice would produce an EU better capable of overcoming its earlier difficulties in taking decisions. This was so because the new weighting still permitted any of the bigger countries to block decisions by alliances with just a few smaller ones, and because the 'unanimity areas' were not greatly reduced in number (since any country could veto the transformation of their own favourite veto area into a 'non-veto' area). There is even an 'olive oil' veto minority of 68 foreseen for Spain (27), Italy (29) and Greece (12) to defend the particular interests of these three countries. After enlargement to twenty-two countries, the total number of votes would go from the present 237 to 345, with 27 for a bigger new member state like Poland and 3 to a small country like Malta.

19 Speech at the Humbolt University in Berlin, 12 May 2000.

20 Press conference by Joschka Fischer, Minister of Foreign Affairs of Germany, Berlin, 13 May 2000.

21 Speech before the Western European Union in Paris, 30 May 2000.

22 'Streitgespräch Fischer contra Chevènement', *Die Zeit*, No. 26, 2000.

23 Prowse, Michael, 'An Unbeatable Bargain in the Making', *The Times*, 13–14 May 2000.

24 Lord Howell of Guildford, 'Maybe what europe needs is less integration', *International Herald Tribune*, 11 July 2000.

25 Siedentop (2000).

26 The convention was led by a twelve-member praesidium. The Chairman, Valéry Giscard d'Estaing, was assisted by two Vice-Chairmen, former Italian Prime Minister Giulio Amato and former Belgian Prime Minister Jean-Luc Dehaene.

27 In February 2002 the British government proposed that a 'statement of principle' be prepared specifying the division of powers between the EU and national capitals, following which national parliaments or the European Court of Justice should be empowered to enforce the principle of 'subsidiarity'. The heads of government of the member states should also be able to elect their own chairman, a de facto 'EU president' (a proposal reiterated

in 2002 in joint British–French and French–German contributions). Majority voting in the Council of Ministers should be extended. The size of the Commission should be limited and Commissioners should be answerable to the European Parliament. The latter should work more closely with national parliaments and be given greater influence over law enforcement.

In May 2002 the European Commission's President Romano Prodi submitted a proposal to the convention resuming many points he had made already in 2001. The proposal sought a two-speed EU, by which euro-zone countries would be able to make decisions on their own, possibly including legislation. Finally, he suggested that the European Commission be divided into two levels, with Commissioners responsible for more central EU areas forming the inner core. It was clear that the Commission by this time saw itself as the main proponent of true, supranational integration and also as the champion of smaller EU member states, whose interests risked being ignored in a more intergovernmental EU, where bigger countries could combine on important issues to establish qualified majorities in the Council of Ministers.

Finally, the European Parliament in May 2002 presented a report to the convention proposing that the EU be given a federal constitution with a clear separation of powers among the institutions as well as between the EU and the member states. Important policy areas, such as the functioning of the Internal Market, should be the sole domain of the EU, while the say over agricultural and fisheries policies should be shared with member states. The European Parliament and the Council of Ministers should be truly equal in the legislative field.

28 In Philadelphia in 1787 the task was to take over the government of a new country, the United States of America, from its former colonial master, Great Britain, and to shape it according to the people's will. In Bonn in 1948 it was about establishing a form of government that could take over from a military occupation that encouraged the undertaking, and to transform the unitary state that had existed under the Third Reich into a federal system. In Brussels in 2002 it was essentially to move democratic powers that already existed at national level to a higher level, that of the EU. Similarities with 1787 included the issue of federation, where, for example, the Federalist Papers inspired by Hamilton and Madison showed a strong federalist inclination. The issue could not, however, be pressed, due above all to the divisive question of slavery. Not until seventy years later, after the Civil War, could federalism take real hold, in the sense that Washington was given authority over the states in certain domains. Even today, however, the issue of 'states' rights' crop up occasionally (in their non-racial segregation context) in the decisions of the US Supreme Court. EU 'subsidiarity' might solve the dilemma more quickly and painlessly than was the case in the US.

29 Haider had, among other things, praised Hitler's labour policies, called Nazi concentration camps 'punishment camps' and had seemed to want to exonerate Austrian former members of the Waffen-SS of any war crimes.

30 Austria did not go through the same *Vergangenheitsbewältigung*, or 'reconciliation with its past', as Germany had done after the Hitler era and World War II, when Austria had been part of the Third Reich. The country had been fortunate in obtaining the 1955 State Treaty, which restored its pre-1938 borders, freed it from Soviet occupation and granted it neutrality. The controversial Wehrmacht past in the Balkans of Kurt Waldheim, Secretary General of the United Nations between 1972 and 1981 and Austrian President from 1986 to 1992, had brought major embarrassment to the country but had not led to any truly cleansing public debate about its share in the war guilt.

31 The decision by the fourteen EU countries to 'isolate' Austria cannot be considered an act by the EU itself, since such action would have to be taken by all the fifteen jointly. However, it was the EU presidency, Portugal, that announced the decision on behalf of the fourteen. Furthermore, the European Commission followed up with a warning to Austria, invoking the possibility of sanctions mentioned in Article 7 of the Treaty on European Union. These actions lent the decision an EU character that could be considered as going against the spirit and perhaps even the letter of EU legislation. At a minimum, the decision violated – was indeed meant to preach against – the *comitas gentium* (international courtesy).

32 The 'three wise men' were Marti Ahtisaari, former President of Finland; Marcellino Oreja, former Foreign Minister of Spain, former Secretary General of the Council of Europe and former European Commissioner; and Jochem Frowein, a German lawyer and Director of the German Max Planck Institute.

33 There was no similar action by the EU against Italy after its parliamentary elections in the spring of 2001, even though its government included representatives of a far-Right party.

34 Improved Greek–Turkish relations were vital to both countries, and to Europe. They could lead to an agreement to end the division of Cyprus, a mutually accepted delineation of territorial waters and air space in the Aegean, an earlier Turkish entry into the EU and greater Turkish alignment with EU policies in the region.

35 With the weighted voting system in the EU's Council of Ministers decided at the EU's 2000 Nice Summit, Turkey, with its close to 70 million people, would have a say equal to that of any of the biggest EU countries. Since many of its regions are poor in comparison with the EU average, a considerable reorientation of EU agricultural and regional would be the likely result.

36 Already at this time the EU gave major assistance to the candidate countries. In 2001 alone over €1 billion were awarded under the so-called Phare Programme.

37 A Facilitated Travel Document (a multi-entry and exit permit) would be available to Russian citizens for travel between the 'exclave' and Russia proper across Lithuanian territory, in future perhaps via a fast rail network. The EU would also assist Kaliningrad economically.

38 The Common Agricultural Policy also today ensures farmers the right to sell

much of what they produce at guaranteed prices to governmental purchasing agencies. Import levies, whose level varies according to world prices, protect against foreign competition, while subsidies enable exporters to sell at prices at or below those in world markets. Following various CAP reforms, the market regulating payments as a proportion of total CAP expenditures have been reduced considerably, with direct payments to farmers (independent of production) taking their place. Around 10 per cent of total CAP expenditure is devoted to countryside development in its widest sense.

39 The subsidised exports of EU surpluses to developing countries, now reduced, undercut local production in these countries and drove millions to slums in the cities. This contributed to a new imbalance between countryside and city in the world's poorer countries, rendering the countryside less and less able to compete with food imports from Europe and elsewhere, and turning cities into a source of cheap labour for industries that increasingly began to compete with those in developed countries. The loss of industrial employment in, for example, Western Europe through migration of multinational companies' production units to poorer countries may therefore in part be traced back to subsidised European food exports. Big EU farmers have been the big winners under the CAP, while the small farmers (whose numbers went up as poorer and more agriculturally oriented countries joined) also had to be supported, at least enough to be able to make a living. (This they increasingly have had to learn how to do, as there are fewer jobs to be had in the rest of the economy.)

40 In October 2002 the EU agreed to increase direct payment to farmers in ten new member states gradually from 2004, so that they would reach the overall EU level by 2013 ('phasing-in'). Total EU CAP expenditure would stay at the 2006 level during the 2007–13 period, at around €45 billion per year, with annual increases of 1 per cent permitted.

41 Kapteyn (1996, pp. 96–7) summed up the agricultural fraud problem as follows: 'Seen from a national state perspective, one would expect [the payment of subsidies and the decision to pay] to be more or less managed by a single authority, but this was not how the Community agricultural policy worked. Member states provided the Community with its 'own resources' … The subsidies were paid from these resources. The actual decision to pay, however, together with the procedure for checking the legitimacy of claims, became the province of national states; by comparison, the authority of the Community's control instrument, the Commission, was slight. It was given the task of comparing national decisions with procedural law and transferring money from Brussels to a member state on this basis … In the absence of a central authority, the member states' agricultural production and the subsidies on this production spiralled upward, while their national monitoring procedures spiralled downward.'

42 The European Social Charter of the Council of Europe (an organisation separate from the European Union), adopted in 1961 and revised in 1996,

provided the first impetus to a 'social dimension' to the Internal Market. EU summits from 1988 to 1990 prepared the ground further. The European Commission drew up its own version of a 'social charter' in time for the December 1990 summit, but because the UK did not agree, the text could not become EU legislation but only a set of political intentions. The *Maastricht Treaty* left the situation unchanged for the same reason, and the agreement was simply appended to it as a 'Protocol and Agreement on Social Policy' (commonly known as the 'Social Protocol'), with a UK derogation attached to it. It was only with the 1997 agreement by the new Labour government in the UK that incorporation into EU legislation could take place. Finally, many social rights were included in the Charter of Fundamental Rights declared at the 2000 EU summit in Nice, even though the charter did not have treaty value.

43 Indeed, any authority has a natural tendency to want to do something rather than nothing, as it would otherwise call its existence into question. And that something will normally be to control something else, rather than to leave it uncontrolled.

44 The banana dispute soon took on an international dimension. It pitted the United States (acting largely on behalf of the US food multinationals Chiquita and Dole Foods) and a number of central American banana-producing countries against the EU (including the European Fyffes company) and many former European colonies covered by the EU's preferential agreement with the over seventy so-called ACP (African, Caribbean and Pacific) countries. The latter, perhaps because of the preferential access they enjoyed to EU markets for their bananas, sold at a higher price than the non-ACP countries, which offered so-called 'dollar bananas' at lower prices but found themselves largely shut out of the EU area. The Commission argued that the EU had special obligations born out of history towards ACP countries, and that the higher prices meant better salaries for plantation workers.

However, the countries shut out, as well as the US, complained that this was contrary to WTO rules, and that the ACP countries concerned had developed an unsound and excessive concentration on bananas as opposed to other types of food production. A World Bank study estimated that EU consumers paid up towards €3.5 billion a year more than they would otherwise have done, and that only a little over €100 million actually benefited the ACP countries themselves. The WTO's verdicts at different stages of appeal, including the final one in early 1999, went against the EU.

Only in 2001 could the seven-year-old banana conflict be resolved. The EU agreed to abandon, by 2006, essential parts of its protection of imports from ACP countries and let more bananas in from non-ACP countries, especially from Latin America. The US for its part would lift its counter-measure tariffs on a series of EU exports.

45 The EU could learn from the Icelanders. Here, one country is in charge. Flexible limits – about 25 per cent of the fishable stock per year – are

established jointly by scientists, government and industry. The limits are raised or lowered based on constant sampling of stocks, coupled with brief periods of total bans during spawning periods or to allow young stock to mature in spawning zones. Stocks are growing steadily, adding to the country's wealth.

In 2002 the European Commission put forward a controversial proposal to restore seriously depleted fish stocks by radically cutting the size of the fishing fleet, establishing multi-year instead of annual fish quotas, tightening control over catches and protecting young fish. The proposal met with heavy opposition from especially Spain (the main beneficiary of the existing system) and also from France, Italy, Greece and Portugal. A compromise agreement reached in December 2002 was generally considered insufficient to protect threatened fish stocks.

46 The Commission in 1993 published a White Paper on growth, competitiveness and employment, calling for the halving of unemployment by the year 2000. In 1994 it presented a White Paper on European social policy, with new jobs and investment as its main themes. Employment considerations were prominent in the recurrent discussions about trans-European networks. An EU summit in Essen in Germany in 1994 agreed on a European strategy against unemployment, recommending, among other things, lower extra-salary costs for employers, greater flexibility in labour markets, and unemployment and other social benefits that would not discourage people from seeking employment. The Commission in 1996 presented an update of the White Paper called 'Confidence Pact for Employment in Europe'. The Amsterdam Treaty of 1997 contained an article providing for yearly reports on the unemployment situation in the EU, with guidelines – even for individual countries – to be decided for the upcoming period by a qualified majority in the Council of Ministers. Following a commitment made in Cardiff, Wales, in 1997, an EU summit in Luxembourg in November 1997 was entirely devoted to the unemployment problem. It decided to co-ordinate the struggle against joblessness by issuing common guidelines. However, no quantitative targets were given, and little in the way of new funds. The Cardiff and Luxembourg 'processes' flowed into the 'Cologne process' in June 1999 and led to a 'Jobs Pact', which was relatively short on specifics. In March 2000 a special summit on unemployment in Lisbon – rapidly termed the 'dot.com summit' – committed the EU to a major structural reform effort, including in telecommunications and financial services. By 2003, the Commission complained that little had been done to realise the Lisbon commitments and that the aim of having two-thirds of the EU workforce in employment by 2005 was at risk.

47 However, about 1.5 million American men were in jail in 2001, and about eight million more were on parole, together representing nearly 10 per cent of the male workforce. If one were to include these numbers, adjusted for parolees with jobs, US unemployment would rise considerably).

48 What is logical from the 'micro' viewpoint of the individual company, namely the reduction in the number of employees to bring down costs, may clash with the logic of society as a whole. To the extent that those shed from the workforce cannot find new employment, society will have to pay them unemployment benefits. These must be financed by higher taxes on companies, people (income taxes) or sales taxes (for consumers). Companies may then find that they have to lower their prices even further to find buyers, dismiss even more workers, etc. This could lead to a vicious circle of deeper and deeper recessions and the emergence of a world economy of 'glut' – long prophesied by especially Marxist thinkers – where there would be too many things and not enough people with the money to buy them. Eventually, however, increased profits by 'downsized' companies may well be such as to permit overall economic growth, and hence employment, to resume. Some maintain this is what happened in the United States and is happening in many European countries today.

10

Where is Europe heading?

Stability … has commonly resulted not from a quest for peace but from a
generally accepted legitimacy … It means no more than an international
agreement about the nature of workable arrangements and about the permissible
aims and methods of foreign policy. It implies the acceptance of the framework
of the international order by all major powers, at least to the extent that no state
is so dissatisfied that … it expresses its dissatisfaction in a revolutionary foreign
policy. A legitimate order does not make conflicts impossible, but it limits their
scope. (Henry Kissinger)[1]

Summary

As the EU and NATO enlarge, prospects for overall economic growth
and peace are good, even if tensions both within and without the
enlarged circle of EU and NATO member states could cloud the picture,
as over Iraq in 2003. Prospects for peace and prosperity improved in
South-Eastern Europe under a Stability Pact for the region, involving
major international assistance.

Continuing EU and NATO enlargement will mean an eastward shift
of Europe's 'centre of gravity', with a major role for Germany. That
country is, however, embedded in an EU and a NATO that, through
their inclusive and non-aggressive character, do not permit the 'alliance–
counter-alliance' structure of the Europe of the past. An intricate 'European security architecture' – provided by the two institutions mentioned
plus others – may be confusing and overlapping, but may also preserve
peace and co-operation via their multiple activities. Co-operation
intensified following the terrorist attacks against the United States on 11
September 2001, leading to a broad anti-terrorism coalition spanning
the Atlantic and beyond and causing Russia to become even more
involved in that architecture.

This does not mean, however, that country relations have ceased to be
of significance, only that they will remain sub-themes as European co-

operation progresses. Thus there may be fatigue but no break in the French–German marriage, especially as the two try to ensure leading roles for themselves in an enlarged European Union via joint initiatives. The United States and Germany have differences, such as over the Iraq issue in 2003, but share the conviction that a continued US presence in Europe is needed. The United Kingdom, torn between Europe and itself (and the US), continues to have an interest in seeing no single power dominating the continent. France wishes to play a leading role in an EU more independent of the US, but is also aware of the consequences that any US disengagement from Europe would have. Russia, strengthening politically as its economy recovers from the legacy of the Soviet era, wishes to play a significant role in Europe and especially its eastern part. However, it also has important interests in East Asia as well as in the Caucasus and Caspian Sea regions, with the latter's oil and gas riches forming an important consideration not just for Russia, but for other powers in the region and beyond.

Economic co-operation will intensify further under the pressure of EU integration (including the single currency) and ongoing globalisation, and Europe will be obliged to tackle, in international as well as European fora, such worldwide threats as terrorism, transnational crime, climate change, water shortages, deforestation, missile threats from 'rogue states' (also via terrorists), economic instability and democratic malfunctioning.

Europe is rapidly ageing. This places great strain on its finances, especially for old-age pensions, and is likely lead to a less dynamic and innovative society. Immigration from parts of Europe and other world regions with higher birth rates will become necessary if the economic and other consequences are to be mitigated, testing the tolerance of 'natives' vis-à-vis 'foreigners'.

Other forces of Europe's future include possibly reawakening nationalism in protest against state borders that are perceived as unreflective of ethnic realities (such as in the recent wars in the Balkans), pitting the 'European–universalist' mission of the European Union against the desire for 'apartness' and ethnic distinctness. Even religious conflict could revive, especially between immigrants and 'natives'. Overall, however, Europe is experiencing a unique period of peace and integration, in which it will have to choose in which political context its future should be shaped. The choice is essentially between some type of federation and something less, such as simply being good and close neighbours. While a federative system via the EU looks more likely at present, only the Europeans can in the end provide the answer.

11 September 2001 and its aftermath

On the morning of 11 September 2001, four US commercial jetliners were hijacked by nineteen men belonging to the Al Qaeda terrorist network led by a Saudi Arabian millionaire-turned-terrorist by the name of Osama bin Laden. Two of the planes rammed the two towers of the World Trade Center in downtown New York, one was flown into a wing of the Pentagon in Washington, and one (perhaps heading for the White House) crashed into the ground after the hijackers were over-whelmed by passengers. Nearly three thousand people – passengers and crew, those present in or around the buildings and firefighters – perished.

Political and economic life came to a standstill as people around the world went into a state of shock. A general economic crisis looked inevitable, since a large part of a major financial centre, Wall Street, had been destroyed or had to be evacuated. Share values plunged. Travel to and from the United States was halted for days. Trade in goods and services contracted. Terrorism had managed to strike at a nerve centre of the world's most powerful nation.

However, the United States and the rest of the world recovered with astounding speed. The US Federal Reserve lowered its policy-setting interest rates massively to revive the national economy. The European Central Bank, the Bank of England, the Bank of Japan and other central banks around the world followed. By early 2002, economic recovery was well under way, even though the various sequels, apart from those of a psychological nature, would continue to beset the world for a long time to come, in the form of, for example, slowed-down trade due to terrorist checking procedures against terrorism and higher insurance for buildings, airlines and other assets.

The day after the attacks, 12 September 2001, NATO – for the first time in its history and at the request of the United States – invoked Article 5 of the 1949 Washington Treaty calling for collective defence in the event of attack from outside.

As it turned out, the United States, having assured itself of NATO support, chose to wage its war against the Taliban regime in Afghan-istan, which was offering shelter to bin Laden and his followers, outside the NATO military command. The allies were instead asked to provide assistance in selected areas, such as in the surveillance of the US airspace against more hijacked planes, in naval surveillance in the Indian Ocean and elsewhere, and in various peacemaking and peacekeeping opera-tions in Afghanistan. Co-operation also intensified in the tracing of terrorist funding and the apprehension of suspected terrorists. The UN-sponsored Bonn Accord on Afghanistan in late 2001 established a post-Taliban government in that country, demonstrating the strength of the international coalition.[2]

However, transatlantic tensions began to appear soon after 11 September. Some Europeans had feared that the war to unseat the Taliban regime, started in October 2001, would take a long time or even fail and that, to avoid large-scale civilian suffering, a negotiated solution should be sought at all cost. When, after a few weeks, the Taliban regime fell along with Al Qaeda's fortified hideouts in the mountains bordering Pakistan, European critics raised their legal and human rights concerns over the fate of prisoners of war suspected of belonging to the Taliban or Al Qaeda. Would they, and any terrorist suspects arrested in Europe, face the death penalty if extradited to the United States? Would they be treated in conformity with the 1949 Geneva Convention on the treatment of prisoners of war (a status not granted them by the US administration)? A picture of blindfolded and chained prisoners who had been transferred to the US naval base of Guantanamo in Cuba raised these fears further and drew a storm of protest.

Transatlantic frictions rose further with President Bush's State of the Union message to Congress in January 2002, in which he threatened to overthrow the governments of an 'axis of evil' group of countries – Iran, Iraq and North Korea – through military or other means. The Europeans' preferred method of solving international conflicts through diplomatic and political means was exposed as standing in stark contrast to the US preference for early and resolute action against 'rogue nations' possibly in the possession of weapons of mass destruction and their means of delivery.

Underneath these developments a geopolitical sea change was under-way. Firstly, NATO had demonstrated its usefulness, in that Article 5 had been instantly activated, permitting a large transatlantic political and security coalition to be formed. (Paradoxically, it had been invoked not on behalf of European members, as had seemed the most likely during the Cold War, but following an attack on the United States.) New life had been blown into the organisation, at least for a time.

Secondly, 'September 11' caused Russia to move much closer to NATO and the US – culminating in 2002 with its relatively collected acceptance of the US abrogation of the 1972 ABM Treaty; the conclusion the same year of the Treaty of Moscow with the US reducing strategic nuclear missiles; and the creation of a NATO–Russia Council, also in 2002, by which Russia moved much closer to NATO. Russia in return expected help from the US and NATO in countering terrorist attacks and Muslim fundamentalism on its southern borders, and less foreign criticism of its military campaign to quell a rebel insurgency in Chechnya.[3]

Thirdly, China, which faced a Muslim insurgency in some of its western provinces, became a de facto partner in the anti-terror coalition. India also moved closer to the West, as did many other countries that feared for the stability of the international order. Terrorists, who had been able to find shelter and sometimes even support in some Muslim and other countries, now found they were no longer welcome.

Fourthly, the developed countries began to fear that there was a link between underdevelopment in poor countries and terrorism. Thus the World Trade Organisation's Doha Development Agenda launched in Qatar in 2001, the UN Conference 'Financing for Development' in Monterrey, Mexico in 2002 and the Africa Action Plan announced at the G–8 meeting in Canada that same year saw much greater openness to the concerns of developing countries than had been the case prior to 11 September. Furthermore, the international community intensified its efforts to find solutions to the Kashmir and Middle-East conflicts, in recognition of the importance of these regions as recruiting grounds for terrorists.

It was uncertain for how long the wide international coalition formed after 11 September would last. Coalitions are built around a specific purpose, often to avert a perceived common threat. When that threat is believed to have subsided, such as through a successful co-operation to fight it, the coalition may weaken too. Terrorists want to strike, but when they do, they harden the coalition, making it more difficult for them to strike again. Meanwhile, other issues that tend to divide the coalition will not go away, and may indeed grow bigger as they are not given sufficient attention due to the coalition's overriding cause. A successful strategy of those most eager to maintain the coalition must then be to keep the common cause alive, while also working to resolve other issues dividing the coalition partners.

The strain on the anti-terrorist coalition was shown in the Iraq crisis of 2003, when the United States, the United Kingdom and a number of other European countries saw the desired toppling of Saddam Hussein as necessary and as forming part and parcel of the fight against terrorism, while others, such as France and Germany, felt that military action was if at all possible to be avoided as it would prevent the world from concentrating on terrorism and indeed provoke new terrorist attacks.

The terrorism phenomenon

Terrorism may be defined as violence with a political purpose. It is aimed at provoking fear and uncertainty among the general public, sympathy among terrorism's own followers and a change in conduct on the part of the state (or international) authority attacked.

Terrorists justify their actions on religious, ideological, moral, ethnic-political, cultural or other grounds. Targets have in recent years increasingly been chosen for their symbolic value. The 11 September attacks are a case in point. In the eyes of the attackers and their supporters, the World Trade Center in New York stood for global capitalism as represented by Wall Street. The Pentagon symbolised US military might. The White House or the Capitol in Washington DC – where the plane that was forced down by passengers and crashed in Pennsylvania probably was headed – stood for US political power.

In future, terrorism is likely to be not only 'conventional', that is, to use guns or explosives, but also to use weapons of mass destruction involving radioactive, biological and chemical materials. 'Cyber-terrorism' may also be used, in the form of attacks with or against computer networks. Terrorism will try to use the mass media for greater impact, counting on the latter's interest in attracting the larger audiences that big news will yield.[4]

The international community for its part is first of all concentrated on crushing the Al Qaeda network, militarily and through better intelligence, especially by apprehending potential terrorists and cutting off their financial sources. The fight against other terrorist networks is also being pursued, including in Europe, such as against ETA in Spain and '17 November' in Greece. Co-operation between police, judicial and other authorities is being intensified, across Europe and worldwide. Countries in the Middle East, Africa and Asia that may have tolerated or even supported terrorists are being pressured by political and other means to mend their ways. Meanwhile, development assistance is targeted to counter the destabilising effects of globalisation and the impression in parts of the Muslim world that globalisation is destroying its culture and religion.

The war between terrorism and the established order will be very long and have a lasting effect on Europe, not least because it is one where there is never certainty that, say, the foiling of a plot or the arrest of a presumed terrorist marks the final defeat of a given terrorist network. Countries will draw together as their governments learn to co-operate more closely with each other to counter the common threat. New controlling technologies will arise, leading citizens to feel more under surveillance, even as they may accept it as the lesser evil. Human rights, especially the right to privacy, may be more narrowly interpreted in legislation and courts. Public appearances by political leaders as well as public gatherings in general will be less frequent and more cumbersome due to added security. Higher insurance premiums and new security systems for individuals, companies and official buildings will lay an extra burden on the overall economy but also give rise to new economic activities.

Europe's intricate security architecture

It cannot be argued that either the EU or NATO is directed against anyone. Rather, both the EU and NATO have as their long-term aim to include almost everybody that can fit geographically in their mandate (and have friendly relations with the rest). None of the 'outs' can form alliances with any of the 'ins', nor can any 'ins' form an alliance between them against one or more other 'ins'. This is in stark contrast with the European past, when stability could only be bought (temporarily) by alliances and counter-alliances. It is difficult to say for how long this fortunate situation will last. Much will depend on how far the economic inter-twining of the different countries and regions can proceed, making ruptures superfluous or more costly in terms of economic opportunities lost.

Another historical novelty is evolving: that of an, albeit confused, pan-European security architecture in the widest meaning of the term. It is confusing in the sense that there are many presumptive architects – or architectural companies – with considerable shareholder overlap. They include the EU, NATO, the Organisation for Security and Co-operation in Europe (OSCE), the Council of Europe, the OECD, the United Nations Economic Commission for Europe (and what remains of the Western European Union).

Sometimes these 'interlocking' institutions have rather given the impression of being 'interblocking'. However, even if no coherent European architecture may be in sight, an incoherent one exists and it is probably better than none; for the institutions make sure that a series of processes are constantly under way in parallel fashion – some failing, some moving forward, some ad hoc and specific, some more general and systematic. It is precisely their multitude and the ideas and projects they propose which from day to day creates a slightly new Europe.

Rather than a 'survival of the fittest', or even the domination by one institution or the other, there is a constant adaptation of them all to changing relations between countries or groups of countries. The overlaps that doubtless exist ideally serve to strengthen the architectural structure, somewhat like crossing beams in a ceiling. Whether the actions of one institution have a perfect logical consistency with those of all the others therefore becomes less important than the continuation and deepening of existing co-operation. The process – or processes – are often messy, but the end result may be more positive than if they were all entrusted to one central organisation upon whose success or failure European peace would stand and fall, such as was the case with the League of Nations in the period between World War I and World War II.[5]

The fields of action of the different institutions are well known: transatlantic security co-ordination through NATO, increasingly also involving Russia and Central Asia; political, economic and increasingly also security integration through the EU; pan-European co-operation in the political, human rights, democracy and rule-of-law fields through the Council of Europe; transatlantic and pan-European technical co-operation through the United Nations Economic Commission for Europe; virtually worldwide economic co-operation through the World Trade Organisation and the OECD; and the reaching out to countries in the southern Mediterranean through NATO and the European Union's so-called 'Barcelona process'.

To these European, Euro-Atlantic or worldwide institutions should be added the many 'sub-regional' co-operation forums that have sprung up alongside more long-established institutions: the Benelux co-operation (actually dating back to before World War II), the Nordic Council or EFTA. Such sub-regional organisations involve areas such as the Baltic Sea, the Barents Sea, the Black Sea and Central Europe, to mention just a few.[6]

This 'division of labour' among institutions – which themselves have arisen out of specific historical circumstances and have simply been added to one another as a new perceived need arose – is not very logical. The important thing to consider is, however, how well it manages to keep Europe at peace and working in at least relative unison. Here the jury is still out, as shall be seen below when the various 'new–old' forces in Europe will be discussed. However, the record so far is an indication that the architecture cannot be all that bad, examples being Europe's mastering of the challenges of the Cold War and its peaceful ending; the essentially non-violent dissolution of the Soviet Union; the introduction of democracy and a market economy in Central and Eastern Europe; the eventual, at least temporary taming of the conflicts in the Balkans; and the growing co-operation, indeed integration, in the economic, political and security fields across the Continent. As regards the future, much will depend on how the institutions in question manage to reform themselves and how they co-operate and co-ordinate with each other to create a 'synergy' among them.

NATO and the OSCE are of great importance in the overall security equation, even though the plans to have the OSCE assume the top position in the hierarchy of the institutions was never a realistic one. The OSCE monitors elections in troubled countries, oversees the respect of sanctions, engages in 'quiet diplomacy' over budding conflicts and minority rights, and runs disarmament talks, notably the follow-up to the Conventional Forces in Europe (CFE) Treaty. However, it also has weaknesses, such as an often paralysing near-unanimity requirement.

NATO's continuing importance for European stability has already been discussed. NATO and the OSCE serve to underline the largely Atlantic character of the European security architecture. The commitment of the United States to the security of Europe is still holding and can be said to have grown stronger after the creation of the NATO–Russia Council in 2002 and the ten-country NATO enlargement foreseen for 2004. Enlargement itself may strengthen transatlantic security ties, since the new NATO members in Central and Eastern Europe are more positive to continued US commitment to Europe than are some of the old, as shown in the crisis over Iraq in 2003. NATO's Partnership for Peace and Euro-Atlantic Partnership Council will lose some of their relevance as NATO enlarges, but can still serve as useful fora for the widest possible participation by countries in peacekeeping operations or 'coalitions of the willing'.

Finally, the EU has resolved, at least for the foreseeable future, one main source of geostrategic instability in Europe, that of what to do about too powerful a Germany. Out of that dilemma, which Germany itself could not do much about, had emerged the alliance–counter-alliance system which, although it provided some stability at times, also gave rise to both world wars. Only through the embedding of Germany first in the NATO security structure and then in the EU economic, political and security structure (plus those structures provided by others such as the Council of Europe and the OSCE), has it been possible to overcome the otherwise latent opposition between France and Germany, with the former's tendency to try to contain the latter with an alliance with Russia, leaving the countries of Central Europe as hapless pawns in between. Thus, provided Russia continues its already considerable integration with western Europe, the *Zwischeneuropa* (the Europe in between Germany and Russia) may definitely be relegated to the past, much to the benefit of countries from the Baltics down to Hungary and Romania. This, then, is another great achievement of the EU.

The above does not, however, mean that Europe's institutional arrangements are in any way perfect. One concern is how to give a proper role within the European concert to Russia, and also to Turkey, which is threatened by political marginalisation in Europe quite out of measure to its strategic importance. Nor is the structure invulnerable to any future economic or political rivalry between the EU and the United States, or to the unpredictable forces of nationalism.[7]

An eastward shift of gravity; international relations in the new Europe

As NATO and the EU enlarged eastwards, the first obvious result would be that Europe's 'centre' would move eastwards, too. Central and Eastern Europe in particular could not but help develop economically now that the region again enjoyed free trade and investment relations with especially Germany and all of Western Europe in general. Along with that development would come an enlargement of Europe's post-World War II 'arch of wealth' – south-east England, Benelux, north-east France, south-west Germany, Switzerland and northern Italy – to include Berlin, Budapest, Warsaw, Prague, Vienna and other economic centres in the region.

The late French President Mitterrand presumably foresaw the eastward shift in 1989, when he tried to prevent or at least considerably delay German unification and exacted the country's participation in the Maastricht Treaty and especially the EMU as a price for 'allowing' unification to take place. Thus in December 1989 he issued a joint declaration with President Gorbachev stating that border changes were premature and expressing support for an 'East German identity'. In the view of the historian Andrew Moravcsik, he also 'sought to establish a pan-European confederation, a policy that had the added advantage of possibly forestalling entry of East European countries into the EC, an event [he] is said to have hoped to delay for decades' After these efforts failed,

> Mitterrand's sole goal became to secure a monetary quid pro quo [with Germany] for France, backed by whatever concessions on political union were required … It is commonly asserted that the French government viewed Franco-German cooperation as a means to offset growing German power and, therefore, as a substitute for possible alliances with the UK or the Soviet Union.[8]

However, it was not certain that any effort by France to tie Germany closer to its western flank, and especially France, would work, for German interests were increasingly towards the east, aptly symbolised by the change of the nation's capital from Bonn to Berlin, and the

moving there of its government and parliament in 1999. In a new
Ostpolitik following that pursued during the Cold War, Germany had,
since the end of that era, pushed for expansion both of NATO and the
EU. With the 2004 enlargements of these two institutions, Germany
would for the first time in its history be treaty-bound to virtually all of
the countries in Central and Eastern Europe in the political, security and
economic fields. It hoped thereby to extend stability to the Balkans, the
Baltic States and other parts of the former Soviet Union. Good relations
with Russia were a top priority. German business interests were also
changing. Germany had become the biggest trade investment partner for
Poland, the Czech Republic and Hungary.

Max Jakobson, the Finnish diplomat and scholar, saw EU enlargement as essential in order to have German security enhance European
security. He considered what he called the 'German–French axis' as
obsolete and

> valid only as long as Germany was a western European country – an economic
> giant but a political dwarf. Following unification, however, Germany is no longer
> a western European country: it is a European power, again at the heart of the
> continent … Germany has an obvious strategic and economic interest in the
> furtherance of political stability and material progress in central and eastern
> Europe and in the Baltics, including Russia.

Jakobson therefore considered it essential that Germany's present *Drang
nach Osten* (eastward influence) be achieved through EU enlargement
and with Germany firmly within it.[9]

The half-a-century-old Franco–German marriage in the 1990s and
early 2000s showed renewed signs of fatigue. French leverage over
Germany had been reduced with the end of four-power status in Berlin
(where France had been a participant) and German unification in 1990,
which had made Germany the most populous country in the EU.[10]

This was natural since Germany was looking increasingly east and
France found it more and more difficult to count on generous German
funds for the EU and on German acceptance of French leadership of the
marriage, or of the EU. In 2003, the fortieth anniversary of the 1963
Elysée Friendship Treaty between the two countries gave them an
opportunity to declare that all in the marriage was indeed well and that
they would continue to provide EU leadership together.

A common stance against the US–British invasion of Iraq that same
year added to the impression of unity, as did a freshly announced joint
ambition, resulting from that stance, to pursue (with Belgium and
Luxembourg and possibly others) a defence integration on their own
that would leave other EU members, such as the UK, outside.

The celebrations could not, however, conceal numerous underlying differences, such as over the future running of the EU (with France opting for more intergovernmentalism and Germany for a stronger role for the European Commission and the European Parliament) and over EU security policy (where France wanted greater independence vis-à-vis the US). Seen against the background of the multilayered European security architecture, however, the ups and downs in the long-standing Franco–German relations might not matter overly, especially since they have so far served the strategic interests of both countries in Europe and beyond and will remain central to Europe in the future.[11]

Bilateral French–German military co-operation outside NATO was meant to be given a major push through the so-called Nuremberg Declaration of 1996. However, the results were mainly multilateral within the EU context, such as in the Strasbourg-based Eurocorps and the Rapid Reaction Force meant to come into being in 2003.[12] Budgetary difficulties in both countries have prevented more ambitious projects – especially since their participation in the peacekeeping forces in South-Eastern Europe and elsewhere absorbed a good deal of the resources that might otherwise have been available. Finally, co-operation on new weapons was hesitant, with Bonn often seeming closer to London or Washington than to Paris, not least because France's defence industries were still largely in state hands and thus less attractive partners to foreign companies.

New strains in French–German relations became apparent at the 2000 EU summit in Nice. France under President Chirac and Prime Minister Jospin insisted on the same voting power in the European Union's Council of Ministers as Germany, in spite of the latter's 30 per cent larger population. President Chirac insisted that this had been agreed for all time to come by de Gaulle and the German Chancellor at the time, Konrad Adenauer.

The insistence reflected the unwillingness of the French establishment to recognise not only that France could no longer claim to lead Germany, and hence Europe, via the European Union, but that now Germany was assuming the role of *primus inter pares* (first among equals). Paris could do little about Germany's gradually assuming the leading role in the European Union and working in favour of a federal EU structure in which Germany's larger population would give it a correspondingly strong role. Against France's insistence on its singularity and hence its vocation to lead Europe – in Europe and in the world – stood Germany's subtle assumption of this role, even as it tried to avoid worrying its neighbours, and especially France, by not overplaying its hand.

It was far from certain that the sentiments of the French 'establishment' in favour of French *grandeur* were shared by a rapidly 'Europeanising' French population and business community. Even a few intellectuals were beginning to have doubts. Claude Fouquet in his book *Délires et défaites* wrote: 'It is hard to abandon the historic dreams that continue to caress us because we love this imagined France. However, we have to give it up, firstly because truth demands it, but especially because it blocks our understanding of the modern world, and therefore our adaptation to it.'[13]

The US–German relationship also underwent strain, as Germany in 2003 ruled out participation in any US-led military action in Saddam Hussein's Iraq. To this came a concern in Germany (and perhaps in Europe in general) about how the United States exercised its position as the world's only superpower without heeding the advice of others. For all the friction, however, Germany's foreign policy in the early 2000s could be expected to emphasise close alignment with US policies, including on missile defence, even as Germany built up the European Security and Defence Policy with its EU partners. This was so because Germany realised more than most the importance of a US security presence in Europe to prevent European rivalries.

However, over the longer term, shifts in the strategic agendas of the two countries could have an impact. Firstly, Germany occupied much less of a place in US domestic policies than, say, during the medium-range missile crisis of the 1980s, not to mention the various Berlin crises from 1948 to 1961. With the ethnicity of Americans becoming less pre-dominantly European and more Asian in character, and with the principally Asia-trading US West Coast growing more important, the priorities of the new political class in the United States were shifting accordingly.

The US wanted Germany to assume its responsibilities more fully as Europe's major power, a role which the Germans were hesitant to fulfil for fear of raising apprehensions among their neighbours (and also due to financial difficulties). Furthermore, Germany's foreign policy could not be readily expressed, since it was largely tied down by the EU. To the extent it tried to pursue a foreign and security policy through the EU, the end result was often minimal. It could hardly be otherwise after initiatives had gone through the decision-making machinery of fifteen sovereign states plus the Commission. Meanwhile, any German foreign policy action taken independently of the EU risked causing an uproar among the other EU member states, and possibly others as well.

History therefore weighed heavily on Germany's shoulders. To the extent it tried to strengthen its own political voice in the European choir, it had to be done in ways acceptable to the others (and France in particular) and would have to be seen as being necessary for stability rather than heralding a return to a dreaded past. At the same time Germany wanted to assume a political influence commensurate with its still considerable economic might. Only within a politically strong and united Europe would this be possible.

One way for France to counter what it might consider excessive German (and US) influence was to cultivate relations with Russia. This had held both during World War I and World War II. Even though France joined NATO after the latter, there was also de Gaulle's decision to leave NATO's integrated command and his vision of a Europe extending from the Atlantic to the Urals.

After the fall of the Berlin Wall, France's overtures to Moscow repeatedly raised eyebrows in Washington, such as over joint oil exploration in Iran despite a US embargo, or a lifting of sanctions against Saddam Hussein's Iraq. Furthermore, France's refusal (together with Germany) to authorise force via the UN Security Council in deposing Saddam Hussein in 2003 led to major friction with especially the US and British governments (though not necessarily with all the citizens of these countries, especially the UK where public opinion was highly divided on the issue, at least until the start of the invasion).

On the other hand, France did join the war against Iraq over Kuwait in 1991 and that against Yugoslavia over Kosovo in 1999. It played a major role in the NATO peacekeeping force in Bosnia. And it supported NATO enlargement despite initial Russian reservations. The picture of France as a maverick in transatlantic co-operation is therefore not wholly justified. What seems to matter most to Paris is to remind Washington that the US is not the only major power in the world, but that France also counts for something. France fundamentally needs the United States in Europe vis-à-vis Germany, Russia and the Balkans more than it wants it out. French–US relations are therefore likely to continue in their hot–cold mode.

The UK's relationship with France has traditionally been ambiguous. Britain was Napoleon's main adversary and ultimate vanquisher. Its alliances with France in the two world wars had resulted mainly from a desire to check German ambitions rather than from any natural sense of common destiny, and in the aftermath of World War I the UK feared French hegemony in Europe before its concerns focused on Hitler. When the UK tried to join the EEC in the 1960s it was rebuffed by de Gaulle. Margaret Thatcher was vilified in France for her insisting on more EU funds in the 1970s and 1980s and for her opposition to the Maastricht

Treaty. To the French, the term 'Anglo-Saxon' – which has no clear meaning to the British or others – conjures up the notion of various British–American designs to take over the world economically, culturally and linguistically.

The UK has traditionally feared any single power gaining hegemony over continental Europe, whether a France under Napoleon, a Germany under Wilhelm II or Hitler or a Russia under Stalin. However, as France was removed from the European chessboard, as happened during both world wars, the UK came to its rescue (followed by the Americans) to avoid European domination by another power.[14]

The UK's relationship with Germany is similarly complicated. Twice in the twentieth century the UK came to the aid of France and Russia to contain German ambitions. However, after both world wars the UK was anxious to rebuild Germany into a power capable of filling a political vacuum in Central Europe, and of containing French and Russian ambitions for excessive dominance. This ambivalence reflects the UK's geographical position, outside the Continent and yet inexorably linked up with it.

With a modern Germany that since 1945 has shown no inclination to try to dominate Europe, the UK has had few problems and indeed an increasingly close relationship with the country. For the UK, this has been important in order to avoid having a Berlin–Paris link overshadow the EU and it helps to explain British efforts to participate in EU defence initiatives such as the Rapid Reaction Force, especially as Britain is not a member of the euro-zone. For Germany, close links with the UK have been important in order to avoid becoming too dominated by France in the EU. It is balance-of-power politics on a miniature scale, with the EU and the transatlantic relationship serving as obvious limits to anything more significant. This outcome has produced a broadly functioning *ménage à trois*, with Spain and Italy joining in as occasional mediators.[15]

A seemingly rock-solid 'special relationship' holds firm between the UK and the US. It is born out of a shared language and the origin of the United States as British colonies, and strengthened in two world wars. However, there is more, such as the desire of both to maintain a political equilibrium in Europe – as manifested in the world wars, during the Cold War, in the Balkans, and possibly even in today's Europe of the EU.

There could also be something else. A certain common approach to trade, investment and generally to doing business; a belief in a certain style of democracy born out of the 'township democracy' tradition in pre-industrial England and the American colonies; a duty to challenge (at least some) tyrants; and a certain pragmatism and an aversion to grand theory, in which a measure of the American 'universal mission' clashes only marginally with the 'little Englander' tendency in British politics (the latter being a cousin to American isolationism).

Italy and Spain continue to play important roles in European history. Spain in the 1970s brought down dictatorship in part to be able to 'join Europe'. Both countries made major and successful efforts to join the EMU. Northern Spain's and northern Italy's economic integration with Europe's economic heartland are complete. The two countries also serve as important links with other continents, such as Latin America. However, their geographical position on Europe's southern periphery gives them fewer options in the European *ménage* than, say, France, Germany and the UK enjoy. (This is a predicament shared by the countries in Europe's far north.) Italy and Spain find themselves in a position of weakness, since, unable to seek 'allies' in European affairs to their south, they have to turn north (or towards the US, as in the 2003 Iraq conflict).

Finally, with EU and NATO enlargement in 2004, the new members in Europe's east and south will play larger roles in the European concert. This holds especially for Poland, which not only has a population close to that of Spain but also holds a key strategic position between Germany and Russia.

Russia's natural place in the European arena is that of a major player, given its size, population and strategic position between Western and Central Europe on the one hand, and Southern and Eastern Asia on the other. From that viewpoint, the present situation of a still economically weak Russia is in a way unnatural and potentially destabilising. The West has been trying hard to involve it as closely as possible in various forums such as NATO, the Council of Europe and the EU. The semi-inclusion of Russia in NATO via the 2002 NATO–Russia Council bears witness to the success of this policy.

Russia is trying to regain influence not only in Central and Eastern Europe but also in Central Asia – with major consequences for Europe. Russia has enormous reserves of natural resources, including oil and gas. If these are developed efficiently – and this clearly is Russia's aim – the country could have major leverage over European affairs, especially as the supply of North Sea oil will start to decline in a few years' time.[16]

Russia's smaller neighbours to the south and west, such as the Baltic countries or Ukraine, may on the one hand welcome Russia's relative weakness, since it increases their freedom of action in relation to the EU and NATO. However, they also have an interest in an economically stronger Russia with which they can trade, which is stable politically, and which is co-operating closely with international institutions.

Europe, too, has an abiding interest in an economically healthy and politically stable Russia, since there would otherwise be no stabilising force projected to that country's south and south-east. A Russia closely involved in European affairs would also help maintain a North American political and security interest in Europe – a presence important for long-term peace and stability in Europe and for preventing European powers reviving old rivalries.

US–European relations

Europe will no doubt in due course assume main responsibility for its security and project its influence more independently towards regions where it has strategic interests. The European Security and Defence Policy and its envisaged Rapid Reaction Force, whatever their present difficulties, illustrate this trend. However, the experience of two world wars – followed by Western Europe's peaceful integration under the NATO umbrella and the West's ultimate, equally peaceful victory over Soviet communism – explains why many Europeans want North America to continue its contribution to European security and defence and the EU's own ambivalence in seeking a security and defence role of its own. The growing US military dominance in the world is likely to accentuate this tendency.

Political and security co-operation is strongly linked with economic relations. The United States and the European Union are the world's two leading economic powers and their economic relations in trade and investment are without parallel in the rest of the world. As the EU enlarges, it provides a goal and destination for many countries in Central and Eastern Europe and stimulates many domestic reforms necessary for membership – a process which is also in the US interest, not least since EU enlargement serves as a politically stabilising counterpart to NATO's own enlargement.

The euro in particular has created EU capital markets of a size, depth and liquidity that did not exist before. Decades of major capital flows in both directions have made the US and the EU increasingly intertwined. About five million Americans work for EU-based companies, and almost as many EU citizens work for US-owned firms. This fact of life helps to cool tempers and assists in the search for compromises to defuse conflicts, and it is likely to prevent any excessive drifting apart also in the political and security arena.

There is opposition to the US in Europe, as in the world – such as over Iraq in 2003 – but it is scattered and far from shared by all social strata.

It has, since the fall of the Soviet Union, failed to give rise to formal counter-alliances among countries – in the world in general and more particularly in Europe. Counter-alliances are rendered the more difficult since the US, through its might, provides 'public goods' to the world by keeping world trade and international financing functioning (through its strong role in the WTO and the International Monetary Fund), sea lanes open and global security intact by clamping down on countries intent on upsetting this world order. If it were possible to sum up the goals the United States has set itself for the world, it might be to maintain peace via arms control; prevent the spread of weapons of mass destruction; and promote democracy and free markets.

European elites tend to be sceptical of the US, either because they do not believe it is honest in pursuing these goals or because they do not share the American definition of democracy or its belief in the virtues of globalisation. Another grievance is the maintenance of the death penalty in many US states (and at federal level). Critics see the US as the main engine behind inhuman globalisation and 'MacDonaldisation' around the world. Still, with so many, especially young, people in Europe and the world attracted by American movies, culture, universities, food, clothing and technology, any united anti-Americanism has difficulties taking root.[17]

There is widespread denunciation among European political and cultural elites of US 'unilateralism', that is, the country's refusal to adhere to treaties such as the Kyoto Protocol on global warming and the treaty establishing an International Criminal Court to punish alleged war criminals. Generally, many Europeans feel estranged by the US's forward stance in the fight against terrorism and 'rogue states', which they see as additional signs of US hubris.[18]

In 2003 European division on the Iraq crisis not only led to diplomatic complications with the US but also, at least temporarily, frustrated any ambition to forge a common EU foreign and security policy. Following the declaration by France and Germany against early military action against Saddam Hussein, leaders of eight countries – including the UK, Italy, Spain and several Central and East European countries – published a message extolling transatlantic relations and the historical US contribution to the old continent and calling for a resolute attitude vis-à-vis Iraq. The declaration and the ensuing European row reflected both the divided views held by Europeans as regards the US and the dissatisfaction felt by many EU and other European countries, with a perceived French–German attempt to dominate the European agenda.

Many sceptical Europeans and others are waiting for the US to undergo decline like any other dominant power. This may happen, but the US has a formidable strength in its 200-year old constitution. As Watergate proved, the constitution does not tolerate any attempt at usurpation. Power is strictly divided between the President, the legislative and the judiciary. Such a system tends to involve the citizenry more than do parliamentary systems such as in Europe, Japan and elsewhere. It is a bulwark against excessive power gathered in one quarter, against overly hasty decisions and against any overreach in international endeavours. Where such overreach takes place, such as in Vietnam, it is likely to be corrected in time due to domestic opposition.[19]

The US scholar Robert D. Kaplan in his book *Warrior Politics*, devoted to the United States' future as a world hegemon, concludes that 'the very weakness and flexibility of such a non-traditional American-led empire will constitute its strength. The power of this new imperium will derive from it never having to be declared, saving it from the self-delusive, ceremonial trappings of the United Nations.' Referring to the Chinese fourth-century war historian Sun-Tzu, Kaplan argues that the 'strongest strategic position is "formless"; it is a position that adversaries cannot attack because it exists everywhere and nowhere ... Triumphalism has no role in [US] foreign policy: our ideals will have to grow less rigid and more varied if they are to meet the needs of the far corners of the earth.'[20] It can only be hoped that such 'less rigid and more varied ideals' will also encourage the United States to listen enough to its European and other partners.

The future of the Balkans

The future of the Balkans is still uncertain. The building of a civil and democratic society in Kosovo remains a difficult task, especially after the Kosovo Albanians split into at least two political factions bitterly opposing each other, and as the Serbian minority – dwindling as a result of harassment by some in the Kosovo Albanian majority – was either unwilling or unable to participate politically in the province's life. Organised crime is becoming a problem.

Municipal elections in Kosovo in 2000 resulted in overwhelming support for the more moderate Kosovo Albanians around its leader Ibrahim Rugova and the rejection of his more radical opponent. Both parties, however, were determined in their quest for ultimate Kosovo independence from Yugoslavia, something that neither Serbia and Montenegro nor the international community were a priori willing to grant, especially if Yugoslav democracy was strengthened. Indeed, the latter could come under strain if Kosovo headed for independence.[21]

In 2001 new risks arose in the Balkans. Minority Albanians in the 'former Yugoslav Republic of Macedonia', aided by militant brethren in Kosovo and Albania, started a guerrilla war against the Slav-dominated government, which called on the international community for help in quelling the rebellion. (A peace agreement in 2001 granting more rights to the ethnic Albanians and involving a NATO intervention to collect rebel arms forced a growing dialogue between the two sides.) Nearby, Kosovo Albanians attacked Serbian police forces across the Kosovo–Serbia border, where many ethnic Albanians lived. Ethnic Albanians attacked minority Serbs in Kosovo, prompting the international NATO-led KFOR (Kosovo Force) to come to the latters' rescue. Croats in Bosnia-Herzegovina requested to leave the country and establish closer ties with Croatia. Serbs in the Serbian part of Bosnia-Herzegovina sought closer ties with Serbia. Montenegro contemplated leaving Yugo-slavia to form an independent country.

The reconstruction of Bosnia-Herzegovina met with similar difficulties, as the three ethnic groups of the country – Croats, Bosnians and Serbs – experienced difficulties in agreeing on common policies. Economic stagnation followed. However, by 2003 refugees were returning in greater numbers and destroyed mosques and churches were reconstructed with international assistance.

The year 2000 saw welcome changes in Yugoslavia as Voyislav Kostunica, a soft-spoken academic, unseated Milosevic to become Presi-dent of Yugoslavia in September, and as the opposition also won the Serbian parliamentary elections against Milosevic's forces. Yugoslavia could now be welcomed back into Europe and the international community as a whole, including their financial institutions. Milosevic's transfer to The Hague in 2001 to face charges before the International Criminal Tribunal for the Former Yugoslavia led to an even stronger international acceptance of the country.

The rebuilding and economic revival of South-Eastern Europe would cost large amounts of money, which would have to be supplied by already financially strained Western countries.[22] Newly democratic Yugoslavia – under the new name of 'Serbia and Montenegro' – also had a long way to go before it had been rebuilt from after the war over Kosovo.[23] The economic development of countries like Bulgaria, Romania, Bosnia-Herzegovina, Croatia, Albania, Ukraine, the 'former Yugoslav Republic of Macedonia' and even Greece very much depended on the continued recovery of Yugoslavia, given its central location in the region. The Stability Pact gave a major operational responsibility to the EU (in particular the European Commission) and the World Bank, with many other institutions assigned supplementary roles.

For South-Eastern Europe these changes also meant that – with no 'black hole', Serbia, any longer in its middle – the region's reconstruction could start in earnest. The Stability Pact still had problems co-ordinating among its many participants. However, with many projects nearing implementation and the recipient countries concentrating on building closer links with 'Europe' – if not as convincingly among themselves – the pact was enough to offset whatever problems and uncertainties remained, such as Kosovo Albanians' harassment of Kosovo Serbs, Bosnia's stagnant economy or Serbia and Montenegro's lingering difficulties in shaking off the Milosevic heritage. The international community's (at least temporary) determination to continue to deploy troops in Kosovo and Bosnia illustrated Europe's and NATO's resolve not to let the Balkans explode yet another time, with possible ripple effects on the rest of the Continent.

All these developments placed before the international community a series of dilemmas. Should it try to keep together – at great cost in the form of troops and aid money – what apparently did not want to stay together? Should the international community restrict itself simply to monitoring the 'controlled' dissolution of countries and the establishment of new ones? If Croatian areas in Herzegovina were to join Croatia and the *Republika Srpska* were to unite with Serbia, what would become of predominantly Muslim Bosnia? If the 'former Yugoslav Republic of Macedonia' were split into an Albanian part (possibly joining Kosovo or Albania) and a rump Slav part, would Skopje, the capital, be divided into two parts – an Albanian and a Slav – as well? What would become of the Muslims in southern Serbia and the many minority Serbs in whatever new country came into being?

The international community fears any changes of borders, since they could open up a Pandora's box of new demands. For Kosovo, it sought to preserve the 'substantial autonomy' already achieved, without letting it proceed to independence. The same held for Montenegro, in a change from the days of Milosevic's rule in Belgrade, when the West cautiously encouraged Montenegran independence. The international community would also try to maintain Bosnia and Herzegovina and the 'former Yugoslav Republic of Macedonia' as intact countries. It was likely to maintain a military and civilian presence in the region for a long time to come, in spite of the high costs and simply because withdrawal could be even more costly in the form of wars and many refugees. Efforts would be made to strengthen regional co-operation and economic development, for instance through the Stability Pact, the integration of minorities and the promotion of democracy and decentralisation. EU and NATO membership would be held out as baits.

The Balkans could thus end up with a number of virtual 'international protectorates', for as long as the international community was willing to supply the necessary troops and funds: Bosnia, Kosovo, 'the former Yugoslav Republic of Macedonia' and, possibly, Montenegro (should 'Serbia and Montenegro' fall apart).[24] Alternatively, if the fullest aims of the Stability Pact were realised, then the countries concerned might come to see the advantages of living together in peace and greater prosperity within existing borders. However, the risk was real of further pronounced nationalism in the Balkans, jeopardising what had been achieved. For instance, when visitors enter Bosnia-Herzegovina from Croatia, they are met, not by that country's flag, but by that of Croatia. Throughout Herzegovina, the Croat-dominated part of the country, Croatian flags are everywhere. This illustrates the difficulties of the international community in forging a national consensus in the region in conformity with internationally recognised borders.[25]

The Caucasus and the Caspian Sea region; Europe and the rise of China

Europe has a major stake in political stability in the Caucasus and Central Asia, not least considering the oil wealth of the Caspian Sea region. The area is believed to contain up to 200 billion barrels of oil, worth as much as $4 trillion at current prices, plus comparable resources of natural gas. Azerbaijan, Georgia, Kazakhstan, Turkmenistan, Turkey, Iran and, of course, Russia are closely involved in this gamble – in their capacity as either sitting on the riches, acting as potential hosts to pipelines over their territory or being major powers with a strategic interest in the region.[26]

The struggle over Chechnya in the mid 1990s and Russia's assertion of its power in the province in the early 2000s is better understood when one considers the oil riches under Chechnya itself and the fact that vital pipelines to the west were likely to go across it. Peace there, and in the region as a whole, would depend on whether all parties concerned could find an agreement which accommodated them. Efforts were under way to establish an overall Caucasus security system. Washington was actively involved (a fact underlined by the strong presence of US oil companies in the region), as were major West European countries.[27]

Azerbaijan, Pakistan, Turkey and Uzbekistan tended to work closely with US companies. Armenia, Iran and Kazakhstan had strong links with Russian firms. China was still lying low but could be expected to become more active as it developed further economically. Russia had the advantage of having most of the existing pipelines cross its own territory or former Soviet territory.

The biggest present and future producers – Azerbaijan and Kazakhstan – realised that European and US investment was needed for the major investments necessary. Investors, for their part, need peace and stability in the region through government involvement. A new pipeline from Azerbaijan via Georgia to Turkey and the Mediterranean (the port of Ceyhan) would be finished by 2005 and others were envisaged across Iran to the Persian Gulf, via Georgia to the Black Sea, from Turkmenistan via Afghanistan and Pakistan to China, and from Kazakhstan to China.

The countries and companies involved often have conflicting interests over access, ownership and transport of the oil and gas. However, they share an interest in overall peace so that those resources can flow. There is every reason to expect the Caspian–Caucasus oil and gas game to figure prominently in world affairs in coming years. Europe, as a main potential beneficiary of Caspian oil and gas, therefore has a strong interest in good relations between Russia and China and in the Caspian region in general.[28]

China is a rising power in East Asia and the world. While it still has some way to go before it can be considered an economic superpower, its natural strategic and political interest lies in re-establishing its historical primacy in Northern Asia. This can only be achieved if the Japanese–American alliance is weakened and America's presence in the region reduced. Both Russia and the United States would be against this: Russia because of concern for the security of its eastern regions; and the United States because it would see it as upsetting a balance of power, which in reality is a strong US economic and military predominance. Japan's position is ambiguous. On the one hand it would like to reduce the US dominance in the region in order to enhance its own. On the other it realises that this would facilitate China's (and Russia's) rise. China, similarly, needs the United States to keep in check any political and military ambitions of Japan.

The persistent force of nationalism

In eastern Serbia there are four small regions – Kula, Tran, Tsaribrod and Bosilegrad – which were ceded by Bulgaria in the 1919 Treaty of Neuilly. At the stroke of a pen, villages were cut in two and families separated. For decades, no contact was possible. Then the borders were open for one day in a year. Still, the division is intact.

The Bulgarian poet, Stoyan Chilingirov wrote:

> Those of you who wish to learn what injustice means and what is a wound to the living body of a people: come here all of you! Come here twice if you are Bulgarians and want to see how a Solomonic farce became a true condemnation at Neuilly. Come and see how an international frontier turns the garden of a person into two state territories. How, on the one side of an invisible frontier the daughter sighs, while on the other a mother turned grey by pain is crying. How on this side the son is waiting for his father, and how on the other the father does not even have the right to see his son.[29]

The Neuilly Treaty – by which Bulgaria also lost western Thrace and with it its access to the Mediterranean – was preceded by those of Saint-Germain, Trianon and Sèvres, all parts of the Paris Peace Conference which convened in 1919 to draw up separate treaties for each state on the side of the vanquished powers in World War I. To mention only a few of the territorial consequences, Slovenian and Dalmatian lands went from Austria to the new Kingdom of the Serbs, Croats and Slovenes (later Yugoslavia). Hungary lost Transylvania and part of the Banat to Romania. Hungary also ceded Croatia, Slavonia and the rest of the Banat to the new South Slav State.

After 1919 nearly a quarter of Eastern Europe's total population of 110 million inhabitants found themselves as minorities under alien rule. If these accords settled, in a comparatively enduring way, many of the territorial questions that had long distracted Balkan politics, they also laid landmines for an indeterminate future. Subsequent agreements negotiated under duress, such as after World War II, led to a situation where virtually all the countries of Europe, especially in its central and eastern parts, became either 'amputees' or possessors of lands with foreign minorities who had lived there for centuries if not millennia. Albanians in Kosovo and what is today 'the former Yugoslav Republic of Macedonia'; German-speaking Tyrolians in Italy; Lithuanians in Poland; Poles in the Ukraine; Greeks in Albania; Hungarians in Romania; and Germans in Poland. This *pêle-mêle* list is not even half complete. Only a few fortunate countries, such as the Nordic ones, seemed to have borders on the whole reflecting ethnic, linguistic and cultural bonds, although that was of course different in centuries past.[30]

The international community redrew borders – which were far from reflecting ethnic realities – in part as rewards for victors (along the theory that wealth equalled territory) and punishment for losers and their allies. In part it was also done to create greater stability, on the assumption that the victors would remain stronger in the future, especially with more territory. However, arbitrariness and ignorance also accompanied negotiations. Maps were rolled out and staff ordered to work out the details – perhaps leaving Stoyan Chilingirov's village divided rather than intact as a result of a glass too many at lunch for the pen to hold steady.

The world's hope that 'national self-determination' would satisfy the minorities and be respected by the majorities – or that borders would become so 'porous' as to unite ethnic groups across countries in all but nationhood – has been realised occasionally but remains frustrated as a rule. Even internationally 'midwifed' exchanges of populations, such as between Greece, Turkey and Bulgaria in the late 1920s, have come back to haunt an era later when, for example, thousands of Turks rebelled in the 1980s after they were threatened with a forcible adoption of Bulgarian family names to replace their Turkish ones. Even where deportation of whole peoples were undertaken – such as the Tatars and the Volga Germans under Stalin – the dead seem to govern the living, to use the words of the French author Auguste Comte. If Soviet domination in Central and Eastern Europe managed temporarily to suppress nationalism in the name of communism, ethnic tensions were never far below the surface. Once communism disappeared, the migration of minorities and ethnic disputes resurfaced as contentious issues.

The international community basically pursued the same policy in the early 2000s as after the two world wars, with Bosnia-Herzegovina and Kosovo as good examples. The notion of a state was upheld, with a majority of Croatians, Serbs and Bosnians still maintaining considerable suspicion among them. The big question remains whether humans can be changed by circumstances or not; whether the three groups can learn to live together as a result of internationally induced first efforts at co-operation; or whether old hatreds will surface, once the foreign troops and mediators are gone.

In Kosovo, two kinds of nationalism collided: that of memory, where Serbia considered Kosovo its national birthplace because of a valiant, though lost, battle against the Ottoman Turks in 1389; and that of ethnicity, where the province's overwhelming Albanian majority wanted independence if not reunion with neighbouring Albania. The world was horrified by the Serbian treatment of the Albanians in the late 1990s. At the same time, however, the international community was fearful of calling into question established international borders. Kosovo was confirmed as forming part of Yugoslavia after both world wars – against 'ethnic logic' even at that time – as well as in 1992 when the newly truncated Yugoslavia saw the light of day. An independent Kosovo or one united with Albania could, it was feared, give rise to similar claims by Albanians in the multi-ethnic 'former Yugoslav Republic of Macedonia' – who had already started a 'war of liberation' in 2001 – and by minorities elsewhere. Thus, a painful status quo was preferred to a new arrangement that, it was felt, could lead to even greater chaos.

What, then, is 'nationalism'? To William Pfaff, the American columnist and author, it is

> the most powerful political force in the twentieth century and it is likely to prove the most powerful of the twenty-first as well. Nationalism is a profound, if often maligned, expression of human identities, a negative force but also a positive one. It is an expression of love as well as of hate. It is a fundamental element in modern political life and international relations. It demands to be better understood.[31]

Nationalism is not an ideology, he says, because it has no universality (unlike the universal and rational messages of the French and American Revolutions). It is a feeling that neither depends on nor observes the rules of logic. It is not an idea but a prejudice – like racism or, to put it more positively, like a preference for one's own group. It is an expression of love of the particular – one's family, town, region or country – at the expense of larger, or abstract realities such as Europe or the world (even though a 'country', too, is a highly abstract notion). Carlton J. Hayes, the American scholar, said:

> Nationality is the product of remembered or imagined factors from a people's past which together produce the conviction of being a separate and a distinct part of mankind ... Nationalism is an emphasis upon this distinctness at the expense of the similarities of mankind as a whole, and for that reason easily becomes an aggressive attempt to impose the difference as a superiority.[32]

What, then, is a 'nation', the very object of nationalism? If it is language, why did the former Yugoslavia, which largely shared one, fall apart? However, language seems to hold France together. What keeps the United States intact, where there is not even an official language (only one used in official texts)? If history were logical, Yugoslavia would embrace under one flag, while the United States would be a mosaic of quarrelling tribes.

Nationalism is not a very old phenomenon. It arose in nineteenth-century Europe, largely from German resistance against French armies under Napoleon and from universal philosophies born under the French Revolution. As both French and German socialists, who in theory adhered to a universalistic creed, went into the trenches to fight for the *patrie* and the *Vaterland*, nationalism triumphed over universalism. The Soviet Union, while declaring itself built on the universal principles of

Marx, in reality built on Russian nationalism, which in the end ran aground on the nationalisms it had tried to subjugate. Nazism was an internationalist ideology only in so far as it was based on racial characterisation and myth – that of the Nordic peoples over allegedly lesser races, peoples and their nations. Yet it, too, was defeated by the joined forces of the nationalisms (and internationalism) it had tried to eradicate.

Today, the comparatively lofty, pan-European aspirations of the European Union confront the loyalties and remaining national prejudices of many citizens of its member states. Against the message of nationalism stands that of the French and American Revolutions – and, one could argue, the Council of Europe with its European Convention on Human Rights and Fundamental Freedoms. This message is rational and universal. It holds that all people everywhere are equally endowed with natural rights, regardless of creed or blood, and that no nation is superior to any other. The origins of universalism can be traced to the notion of international law first developed by Grotius in the seventeenth century, later inspiring various peace treaties. The 1815 Congress of Vienna tried to bring order to European affairs after the Napoleonic Wars through an international system of dynasties. The Congress of Berlin in 1878 attempted to do the same after the upheavals of 1848. Both events in the end represented efforts to create a universal political order (Europe was considered the world at the time), which would be able to cope with the phenomenon of nationalism. (Nationalism had, in the nineteenth century, taken the place of the cultural internationalism of earlier eras shared by the elites of Europe.)

The conflict between universalism and nationalism – between a feeling of 'sameness' and 'common destiny' as against 'differentness' and 'separate destiny' – is presumably eternal. They to some extent correspond to the 'id' and the 'super-ego' within a human. Our intellect insists that all human beings are equal, and that in order to uphold that equality we need impartial, universal systems of justice and morality. Our hearts, urged on by more basic instincts, argue that our loyalties begin and end at home, with father, mother, 'fatherland' and 'motherland'. Human beings are capable of complex abstract thought at the same time as showing behaviour like that of a social animal, fiercely loyal to its group. The author and philosopher Arthur Koestler once said that when a patient lies down on a psychiatrist's couch, a horse and crocodile lie down beside him. Fans battling each other during a football match display a kind of nationalism – one's own club being the 'nation' – while the referee is expected to, and in the best of cases does, represent universalism or, say, the UN. The British television commentator in a match between England and, say, Germany is supposed to be both celebrating English goals yet commenting fairly on the performance of the two teams rather than disparaging the foreigners.

Anyone doubting the force of nationalism would presumably have changed their mind in watching the 1998 World Cup in football, with a Brazil in mourning after the defeat in the final against France. Up to a million people filled the Champs Elysées the day after to salute their players. Yet anyone who would equate this with condescension for opponents – traditionally the reverse side of nationalism – would probably be wrong. Television showed the role of chance in the game, the unlucky bounces, the dubious penalties or offsides awarded or not awarded. It also displayed the agony, real or faked, of felled players, showing all to be real or false sinners or sufferers as the case may be, but above all as humans in struggle, jubilation, grief and comradeship, who were exhibiting fair play and even friendship across teams. An example was when the Korean and Turkish teams ran hand in hand around the football field with each other's national flags after having fought it out in the match for third place in the 2002 World Cup. In other words, they acted as humans.[33]

In the media-focused world of today it may therefore become difficult for any national leader, should they have wanted it, to depict members of another nation as monsters or brutes, unlike in the old days when countries marched to war. If anger among at least some countries can be limited to a dispute over the rightfulness of a red card, and if nationalism can be given a proper outlet through a goal scored, then football (and sport in general) will have done world peace a service.

Since longing for the particular and the longing for the general are both part and parcel of the human make-up, we cannot choose between or blend them into something that meets all our needs. History becomes a moral battleground between those fighting for universal principles, unification and harmonisation of various kinds, and those struggling for separation, or independence on ethnic or other grounds – in brief, for the right to particularity. The French Revolution, and even more the history of Marxism under Lenin and Stalin, show what can happen to the rational, enlightened, universalistic approach to history when it proceeds to the 'liquidation' of classes and nations for the 'higher' purpose of human brotherhood and the perfect world. Hitler's nationalism, with its near obliteration of the Jews of Europe and the killing of at least twenty million Soviet citizens and huge numbers of other nationalities, was on a similar scale of evil.

G.K. Chesterton in his novel *The Napoleon of Notting Hill*, published in 1904, looks eighty years into the future, into a drab, bored world where democracy has ceased to function and general political apathy is 'an assumed condition'. In London, an ordinary man is chosen to be monarch, King Auberon. The King is whimsical and given to pranks, one of them being to revive the local patriotism in the different London boroughs. But one Adam Wayne, the Provost of Notting Hill, takes him at his word. Dressed in a red robe and armed with a sword, his fanatical stand to defend the honour of Notting Hill against other boroughs soon has the city plunged into savage street warfare. Chesterton's message with *The Napoleon of Notting Hill* is that people must have values worth dying for if life is to be worth living, however derisory those values may appear. The thousands of young Britons who leave their education or jobs to travel with, and fight for, their favourite football team would presumably agree with Chesterton if they read him.

Still, the life of Britons, and of Europeans, today is on the whole immeasurably less drab than in Chesterton's day of smokestack industrialism. The ghost of the Notting Hill Napoleon still manifests itself in various ways, however. One of the most illustrative is what one might call the 'Hell's Angels syndrome'. The motorcycle gang Hell's Angels (originally formed in California in the late 1940s) has spread to Europe, where it now fights the Bandidos (created in Texas in the 1960s). In otherwise peaceful Denmark, for example, this absurd warfare in the 1990s claimed several dead and wounded. Each gang has flags and other 'national' ensigns. Gangs with equally fancy names are more or less affiliated with either. Drugs, beatings and large amounts of money are involved, as are the quest for the 'freedom of the road', group identification and opposition to others on the flimsiest of grounds. In Sweden, too, these and other motorcycle gangs have been responsible for several murders and the intimidation of witnesses and judges in trials.[34] Chesterton presumably smiles, or rather weeps, in recognition in his heaven, while the rest of us are left to reflect on human nature and folly.

Rarely were the front lines between nationalism, as here defined, and internationalism clearer than in the city of Strasbourg in 1997. The *Front National*, the extreme-Right party in France, held its national congress in the city. On the one hand there were the speeches in the Congress Centre, with their explicitly anti-immigrant and implicitly racist, protectionist and 'France-first' messages. On the other there were the mass demonstrations, with participants from all over France and beyond outside the building, defending the *valeurs républicaines*, human rights, democracy and other universal principles. The city administration had placed murals with 'Liberty, Fraternity, Equality' in several languages around the city.

It is to be feared that the battle in Europe between these two philosophies will be a dominant theme in European politics in the years to come. The Flemish *Vlaams Blok* in Belgium, the Northern League in Italy and many similar parties in Central and Eastern Europe have substantial followings. The aims of these parties differ. Some, such as the *Vlaams Blok* and the Northern League mainly seek greater autonomy (or even eventual independence) for Flanders and northern Italy, respectively. Others want the redrawing of national borders to include kin minorities now outside them.

Regional autonomy or independence movements exist in many countries in Europe. They are also nationalistic – not for the existing nation-state but for a desired region-state – whether they concern the Basque country in Spain, Corsica in France or the north of Italy. In part they represent a changing economic situation, in part history. In the era of industrialisation and imperialism the resources of the whole nation – a united Germany, Italy or United Kingdom – were needed to defend borders in Europe and expand beyond the Continent, such as in Africa. Today imperialism is gone and big countries often mean richer regions having to pay more for poorer ones.

The Flemish – who since the Industrial Revolution have seen themselves as a working class subjugated and exploited by a ruling class of Walloons – now have the upper hand economically and increasingly want to see Flanders gain greater autonomy within Belgium, with some even seeking independence. Language plays a role here and elsewhere, as does history. Belgium is a relatively young country, formed uneasily after the Napoleonic Wars as a common home for the Flemish-speaking Flems and the French-speaking Walloons. However, language plays no dividing role in Italy. Indeed, the Italian tongue was the major rationale for Garibaldi's successful unification of Italy in the nineteenth century. Germany is younger as a nation than Belgium, yet there is no secession movement in Germany, only quarrels between 'Wessies' and 'Ossies' after unification.

Whatever the situation, in several European Union countries the nation-state is threatened both from below by regionalism and from above by EU supranationalism.[35] Perhaps this helps explain why some member states want to push for greater powers for the EU Council of Ministers (representing national governments) while trying to hold down both the Commission (supranationalism) and the European Parliament (where constituencies, as opposed to nations are represented).[36]

Why have the UK and Germany been largely spared strong nationalist movements? In the UK's case, it may be the feeling that successive governments 'stood up' to Brussels. Or it may be that the country's imperialist past and victory in two world wars make its people feel proud of their country as it is. Or it may be British pragmatism, perhaps impervious to grand theories of national superiority. Or is it the friendly and civil social intercourse that is said to so inspire British society and that impresses many foreign tourists? Is it that the sizeable minorities from all around the world have been more successfully absorbed there than in, say, France (even though recent riots by immigrants in several towns in northern England would belie such a belief)?

In Germany's case the extreme Right parties have never after Wolrld War II gained more than a few percentage points in national elections. But twice in this period they rose considerably in the polls. The first was in the 1960s during the *grosse Koalition* (grand coalition) between the Social Democratic Party and the Christian Democrats (CDU and CSU). Presumably extremism flourishes when there is no major opposition to a government majority. The second instance was in the early 1990s, when hundreds of thousands of people from all over the world sought political asylum in Germany, under cover of the constitution – adopted in 1949 in the wake of the Nazi experience – that guaranteed persons persecuted on political grounds the right of asylum. Under much domestic and international criticism, the Christian Democrat–Liberal government under Helmut Kohl pushed through a corresponding change in the constitution, restricting political asylum considerably. As a result the extreme-Rightist vote receded to near-insignificance (even though it has maintained some ground in the former East Germany, where it has taken the form of a protest vote against alleged 'Wessie' neglect of the new *Länder*).

Given the seeming perenniality of nationalism, there can be few more urgent tasks than to find a European modus vivendi that keeps nationalist urges within bonds while permitting the universalist forces to keep Europeans talking to and dealing with each other. Was de Gaulle's *Europe des patries* the right middle road? Has continued EU integration through successive treaties from Maastricht to Laeken now gone so far as to break that unspoken, perhaps unconscious, agreement between the countries or even peoples of the European Union not to push integration beyond a certain point, as public scepticism and negative referenda in Denmark and Ireland would tend to suggest? However, can the European bicycle of integration remain upright unless it moves forward? Should it be equipped with a 'kick stand'? But is it any fun peddling a bicycle that is not moving? Would a 'standstill' imposed on integration not rapidly turn into its opposite, disintegration?

Christianity and Islam

Anyone who travelled across devastated Europe in 1648 must have thought any reconciliation between Catholics and Protestants impossible. Yet an evolution in thinking, combined with material progress, has rendered such conflict generally unthinkable nowadays, other than in Northern Ireland (where it is more social than religious in character). It has even made most people in Europe (except in places like Northern Ireland and parts of the Balkans) unaware of, or indifferent to, the religion of their neighbours. However, intra-Christian reconciliation has also been helped by the external challenges of secularism and other religions, in particular the spread of Islam in Europe and elsewhere. After all, why would Christians fight amongst themselves over doctrine when Christianity itself may be under threat?

There are probably many reasons for the growing indifference to religion in general and the Christian faith in particular in many countries in Western Europe, including in bastions such as Ireland. There is less fear of war affecting the Continent, even though terrorism and its potential use of weapons of mass destruction have many people fearful again; joblessness perhaps, but no starvation. Nature is better understood and utilised by science, though far from mastered, as demonstrated by the threat of global warming and increasing reports of drug-resistant bacteria and viruses.

This does not prevent the possibility, of course, that Catholicism and Protestantism may still compete for European souls, nor that there may still be philosophical differences between Catholic Southern Europe and predominantly Protestant Northern Europe. Some in the Protestant countries see the EU as principally of Catholic-socialist inspiration and therefore suspect its motives – a contention belied by the fact that a predominantly Protestant country such as Germany has been a driving integrationist force within it. It is difficult, however, to imagine a more 'a-religious' undertaking than the EU, religion being an area upon which it has never spoken a word (although a future EU constitution may make some oblique reference to it) and which is fully outside its remit.[37]

Only in regard to Turkey, an EU candidate with a predominantly Muslim population, have some EU politicians – prominent among them the President of the EU Convention on the Future of Europe, Valéry Giscard d'Estaing – ventured that it ought not to qualify for membership

as the EU consists of only 'Christian nations'. They thereby overlook the
fact of a growing Muslim population in heartland Europe. British Asians,
both Muslim and Hindu, are playing an increasing role in defining the
identity of the United Kingdom. And something similar is happening in
Germany, France and Italy, where many young people are excited by
Muslim, Turkish and Arab culture, whose synthesis with European and
North American youth culture is particularly visible in the rap and hip-
hop scene.[38]

Yet there is a void, a yearning – conscious or subconscious – for a
higher Being inside many people. It is as fundamental as the quest for the
competing psychological phenomena of separatism or universalism discussed above under 'nationalism'. This is where sects like the Solar Temple
find their niches (or, in officially atheist China, the *Falun Gong* sect).

It is also where one expression of religion, Islamic fundamentalism,
may have found fertile ground, especially among Muslim immigrants in
and around the large cities of Western Europe. Unable or unwilling, as
the case may be, to integrate into the host societies, often jobless, linked
up by satellite dishes to the television programmes of their countries of
origin, some are choosing to adopt their idea of fundamental Islam.
Islamic fundamentalism seemingly shows a way out, by rejecting a
Western culture that they feel is rejecting them, and by holding out the
prospect of a future where God, Allah, is not relegated to a corner of
society, or the mind, but takes control of it. Islamic fundamentalism
must also be seen as a reaction against the failure of 'Arab socialism' in
the post-World War II period in countries like Algeria, Iraq, Libya, Syria
and Egypt to bring greater material wealth to their populations, and the
regimes becoming increasingly oppressive as a result.

There is a basic difference between Islam and Christianity (and indeed
earlier heathen beliefs in Europe). Christianity – starting with Jesus'
advice to render unto Caesar the things that are Caesar's and to God the
things that are God's, and continuing with Thomas Aquinas – believes
that there are two sources of knowledge: divine revelation and human
reasoning. While the former is privileged, the latter is permitted and even
encouraged. This allowed philosophy, the humanities and eventually the
sciences to advance, including those dealing with government, economics and social affairs.

The British political philosopher Larry Siedentop sees Christianity as
enjoying certain distinct advantages when it comes to competing for
humanity's souls. Christianity, he argues, is the only religion which
allows a truly 'one-on-one' relationship between God and the individual, in what he terms its 'deep individualism' coupled with its

'universalism' and its call for 'moral equality' and 'equal liberty' between all humans. Christianity, he says, appeals to each person's inner, outside his or her family, clan or society. He sees this message of Christianity as having, historically, eventually upended feudalism in medieval Europe and as directly underlying the American constitution. While it has also contributed to today's, in his view, excessive individualism, consumerism and 'economism' in politics – phenomena that he deplores, the appeal of Christianity should not, he concludes, be underestimated.[39]

In the fundamentalist version of Islam, the purpose of the state and government is to enable the individual Muslim to lead a good Muslim life and to return society, and the whole of the Islamic world, to the golden age of Mohammed. This has, over more recent centuries, led to a stifling of independent thought, science and open societal discourse, marking a departure from the early Middle Ages, when Arab scholars from Spain and elsewhere played a major role in developing philosophy and in transmitting the teachings of the ancient Greek and Roman philosophers. The now prevailing doctrine casts a shadow over the Muslim world. Fundamentalist regimes such as those in Saudi Arabia and to some extent Iran try to reconcile an orthodox reading of the Koran with the exigencies of a society that depends on economic and social development for its survival. Democracy faces a difficult task when religion claims to be not only God but also Caesar (a fact with which the Christian world of the Inquisition was not unfamiliar, of course).

Many Western experts on Islamic fundamentalism argue that, despite its undeniable efforts to recruit among immigrants in Western Europe, it is basically defensive and, in addition, influences only a small fraction of what is in fact a very diversified and splintered European Muslim population. They see it as trying to avoid a 'Westernisation' of the masses in the Islamic world that arrives via a satellite-transmitted, mass-market, commercial, Hollywood-type of culture.[40] Other observers see the aggressiveness of Islamic fundamentalism as a revenge for long-standing domination of the Arab world by Western powers, or as a reaction against secular nationalism, such as in Egypt.[41]

How much of a threat is Islamic fundamentalism to Europe? On the one hand it may win over some people, such as amongst the jobless young. The greater its following, the more it risks being perceived by 'ordinary' French, Germans, etc. as a menace, and the greater the rush to parties like the *Front National*. On the other hand, Islamic fundamentalism would presumably find the going rather tough in trying to win over anything more than a minority in Western Europe, even among more receptive immigrants. Its very intolerance against deviations would likely prevent it from becoming a mass, unified movement, just as conflicts among (and within) Arab countries, say between Shiites and Sunnites, permit outside powers to divide if not rule, as between Iran and Iraq since the early 1980s. Moreover, it is difficult to see how any larger number of Western women could embrace the fundamentalist variant of a religion that casts them down from hard-earned improving legal and social equality with men to ideological subjugation. The threat to Europe from Islamic fundamentalism may well lie less in its spread than in the popular and political reaction by those who feel threatened by it.

Demography: ageing in Europe, pressure from without

Another challenge to the 'natives' of Europe comes from migratory pressure, both from other European countries and from outside the Continent. Just as a television advertisement showing an attractive woman slipping into a sports car on the Champs Elysées may, according to some, 'subvert' an Islamic mind, female or male, so it may also attract it to escape the pressure of poverty or oppression.

Western Europe has become a major destination for migrants from many of the world's poorest countries seeking refugee status or political asylum. They come from both developing countries and from poor countries in Europe itself. Some southern European countries such as Greece, Italy and Spain, which for centuries had net emigration to the New World and to Northern Europe, now experience major net immigration. For example, hundreds of people risk their lives every month in hazardous voyages across the Strait of Sicily to southern Italian islands from nearby Tunisia, or from Morocco across the Strait of Gibraltar to Spain – often paying small fortunes to traffickers. Countries in Central, Eastern and South-Eastern Europe, meanwhile, send migrants, mainly to Western Europe. They also receive them, either from neighbouring countries following the freer migration climate after the fall of communism, or from outside Europe. The Central, Eastern and South-Eastern parts of Europe also serve as transits for migrants wanting to go further west.

The reasons for migration also include racial and religious intolerance, wars, including civil wars, and deteriorating economic and political conditions. During the first few decades after World War II migration was only a trickle, largely explained by labour shortages in the 1960s in a country like Germany. Today it has become a tide, which receiving countries that may face high unemployment and extreme-Right parties on the rise are doing their best to halt. The means are several: stricter criteria for granting refugee or asylum status; speedier processing of pending requests; visa requirements vis-à-vis more countries; greater policy co-ordination among European countries on migration and asylum; and greater efforts to integrate foreign populations into national life. All these measures have led to a sizeable reduction in legal migration into Western Europe. However, illegal migration is considerable, with statistics by definition uncertain. It is subjecting those who engage in it to nightmarish underground lives in a new, unfamiliar setting – often leading to crime, drug peddling and prostitution. It has also led to even more xenophobia in receiving countries, as people attribute such activities to foreigners as a group.

Economic development may well determine the outcome. If unemployment can be reduced in Western Europe through more rapid economic growth, then the perceived threat from foreigners may be reduced. As the countries in Central and Eastern Europe reach higher economic growth, migratory pressure to the West may lessen. If a growing number of developing countries in the South can continue to evolve, then this will reduce migration to the North. The more developed countries in Asia, Latin America and the Arab world already receive large numbers of immigrant workers from poorer countries nearby or further away (although the living and working conditions of the people concerned are likely to be even worse than if they had gone to a European country). To the extent that Europe wants to reduce immigration from distant lands, it therefore has a strong interest in global economic development.

If Europeans instinctively tend to fear massive immigration, demographic facts may well in the not too distant future make them change their stance. Falling birth rates are bringing about major changes in the age structure of the populations in most countries. The 'baby boomers' of the 1940s and 1950s are still working, thus helping to support the relatively smaller number of retired people. However, already by the 2010s, the baby boomers will have reached retirement age, the active population will fall and the number of the very elderly – the over-eighties – will rise sharply as people live longer. The age structure in many countries will change from the classical pyramid – more younger people at the base and fewer older ones at the top – to more of a cylinder. If in 1960 the old-age dependency ratio – that is, the proportion of those retired to those of working age – was about 15 per cent, today it is about 20 per cent. By 2030 it is expected to be around 35 per cent. By 2050, two active people will have to support each pensioner, while today the burden can be shared among four.

This would pose less of an economic problem if it had not been for the fact that most European countries – such as France and Germany – have relied on a 'pay-as-you-go' system for the payment of pensions. Present-day workers pay for present-day pensioners. (The opposite system, practised by a few, such as the United Kingdom, consists in having future pensioners pay funds, mainly private, which are not touched by others than themselves, and this only when they reach retirement.) 'Pay-as-you-go' works well as long as the pyramid shape holds, but less so with a cylinder-shaped population age structure.[42] Pensions may have to be reduced or taxes increased, or both, with unknown political consequences. The young may refuse to pay and the old may all turn into ardent defenders of their pension rights. Early retirement – now an oft-used method to hold down unemployment – would most probably have to be curtailed, while retirement age may have to go up. Financial markets will be affected, as more savings will be called upon to finance more and more time spent in retirement due to increased longevity. Public health costs will rise, since older people have more health problems than young people.[43]

However, one should be careful as regards the economic consequences. The same forces which are now causing 'downsizing' and unemployment – computerisation and automation (increasingly by robots) – could well in future permit a smaller proportion of the population to support both the elderly and themselves. To the extent they do not, immigration could provide a way out and may in the process become more politically palatable, especially if the immigrants can take up qualified jobs that will add to the national income. In other words, people's fear of what is foreign may come to be weighed against that of an empty wallet.

The European Union's 'four freedoms' – for people, goods, services and capital – had in principle come true through the realisation of the Internal Market (the '1992 project') in the 1990s. The Economic and Monetary Union, started in 1999 with the introduction of the single currency, at least partly completed the process as far as capital was concerned, while the Schengen Agreement did the same for people and goods.[44]

However, the weakness of Schengen was that, once illegal immigrants – whose numbers had risen considerably by the 1990s and the early 2000s – were inside the Schengen area, it was difficult to prevent them from moving to any other Schengen country. In the 1990s, various efforts to arrive at a harmonised legislation on immigration and asylum at EU level had failed. There was only the general commitment in the 1997 Amsterdam Treaty to introduce it by 2004.[45]

At the EU's 1999 summit in Tampere, Finland, only a general plan to reach harmonisation was agreed. Another three years were to pass until the EU's summit in Seville in 2002 stated the ambition to reach political agreement on all aspects regarding immigration and asylum by 2004. This would include co-operation among police and border-control authorities and exchange of information, and would also involve non-EU sending and transit countries.[46] The EU's sudden activity was in part explained by the success of the extreme-Right *Front National* candidate, Jean-Marie Le Pen in the first round of the French presidential election in the spring of 2002 and by the rise of an anti-immigration party in the parliamentary elections in the Netherlands shortly before. (Individual EU countries such as the United Kingdom and Italy toughened their immigration and asylum legislation at around this time, making harmonised EU legislation more difficult to achieve.)

The EU's ability successfully to integrate immigrants from its periphery as true EU citizens will be one of its main challenges in the years to come, not least because the EU will need a new supply of labour to compensate for its low birth rates. However, can the EU absorb the numbers required without in the meantime giving added fuel to extremist, anti-foreigner parties? The alternative could be to try to encourage higher birth rates through taxation policies and the like. In many countries two bread-winners are necessary for a typical family to make ends meet. Even so, many women feel they want to make a career or at least to do 'something useful' and so delay the first child until they are in their thirties. This leads to longer 'inter-generation gaps' and hence to reduced birth rates, as also do fewer children per couple.

Globalisation

Today, more people, and more world regions, are part of the world economy than ever before – the type of economy where money counts (as opposed to a barter economy) and where the different parts are related to each other through trade in products, services and through investment. The process is often referred to as globalisation – an economic and social process essentially driven by technology, especially in the information and communications sector. Globalisation benefits especially from falling costs of transport and communications, the volumes of data that can be transmitted across the globe and the liberalising economic policies pursued by governments both at national level and internationally. The WTO is the main instrument for promoting globalisation in the way it can best prosper, namely as a single, coherent system based on increasingly open trade and worldwide rules.

However, it would be wrong to consider the WTO as such as an independent, Machiavellian actor in this process, as many of those opposed to globalisation do. The WTO is simply a secretariat, trying to make its nearly worldwide membership agree on proposals made by any country or group of countries. As such, it depends entirely on the will of its members, especially the two dominant economic powers, the EU and the United States.

Trade liberalisation and investment can be pursued, delayed or halted, depending on political choice. The nature of that choice depends on the costs and benefits associated with free trade, in particular relating to employment and living standards. If these are seen as not being lastingly advanced through freer trade at worldwide level, the reaction will be a new emphasis on regional trade groupings, such as the EU or NAFTA. Already such a trend is noticeable. Protective tariffs may be introduced against outside countries or trade groupings, on the argument that these engage in dumping with the aid of state subsidies. Other reasons invoked may be that they do not sufficiently safeguard minimum social and environmental standards, workers' rights, democracy and human rights.

The world community's weighing of the costs and benefits of the WTO's system is illustrated both by the failure of its 1999 summit in Seattle and by the, in the end, successful – but painful and ambiguously worded – agreement on a Doha Development Agenda reached in Qatar in 2001. Paradoxically enough, developing countries are today the WTO's main supporters, as they try to gain better access for their textiles, agricultural commodities and raw materials to the markets of the world's richer countries. The latter for their part need the WTO for their sales of many advanced products and services, and for the protection of intellectual property rights as they relate, for instance, to computer software and music. It is only the awareness of the cost of protectionism and of any breakdown in the world's trading system that keeps both groups, so far, prepared to accept the cost of further market openings, thereby permitting globalisation to continue.

Modern information and communications technologies open up daunting vistas to humankind. It is expected that internet access via mobile phones and computers will rise from 2.5 per cent in 2002 to 30 per cent by 2010.[47] Business is profiting from this development. There is hardly any barrier any longer between buyers and sellers. The former can, at the push of a button, find the particular product or service they are looking for at the best possible price. Competition among sellers will increase, reducing inflationary pressure. Large sums are being saved through the large-scale avoidance of middlemen. Instant information can be had through increasingly refined software relating to inventory, sales projections and so forth.

Globalisation has doubtless increased overall global wealth. Many countries in Central and Eastern Europe, Asia, Latin America and Africa have shown impressive growth rates over decades thanks to it, permitting large parts of their populations to lead better lives. However, it is also leaving many people and countries behind. It uproots millions, forcing them to move from countryside to city in search of a precarious existence, after the local agriculture cannot compete against imports, often subsidised, from abroad. It smashes traditions without replacing them with any new. Alongside the nouveaux riches of a rising entrepreneurial class is a sub-prolitariat living in shanty towns around increasingly unmanageable mega-cities in Africa, South America and Eurasia. The poor in Bombay are directly affected by decisions taken in Wall Street or the City of London.[48]

It is on these sides of globalisation that its many detractors focus their criticism. They see it as leading to unaccountable corporate control over the world economy, the loss of workers' rights in the global marketplace, and austerity-oriented policies of the World Bank and the International Monetary Fund in their lending to developing countries, leading to increased poverty, environmental degradation and the destruction of local cultures.

The violent protests against globalisation in Seattle in 1999, Prague in 2000, Göteborg and Genoa in 2001 may in the main have been the work of professional rioters, but many thousands of peaceful protesters joined in the demonstrations on behalf of hundreds of non-governmental organisations with widely different agendas. Apprehension is spreading to many policy-makers, especially in developing countries and so-called 'emerging economies', for even countries that have followed globalisation's precepts face economic difficulties.

If, however, globalisation were reversed – through, say, new trade barriers, a breakdown in the multilateral trading system, restrictions in the flow of capital and nationalisations of industry – then the economic consequences could easily be catastrophic in the form of a worldwide depression that would also hit Europe hard. In a manner of speaking, globalisation has put the train of the world economy on a new track with an unknown destination. Pulling the brakes could easily derail it. Jumping off could kill you and, if not, will leave you in the middle of nowhere.[49]

It is too early to know the worldwide political, cultural and social effects of globalisation. Sceptics foresee that it will exacerbate conflict between civilisations as opposed to states.[50] Others believe it will instead erode differences between civilisations, making them more likely to understand each other and so less likely to turn to conflict. An author such as Thomas Friedman in *The Lexus and the Olive Tree* argues that the struggle is between traditional societies of all sorts (symbolised by the olive tree) and technological innovations that lead to globalisation (symbolised by the luxury Lexus car). Governments risk losing control over their nations' destinies as they cannot opt out of globalisation since it driven by technology. If such technology is the 'hardware' of globalisation, it can only be used successfully if coupled with globalisation's 'software', i.e. a well-educated workforce and the legal systems, transparency and honesty that come with a functioning democracy.[51]

The role and future of the multinational enterprise

Multinational enterprises (MNEs) are the main vehicles by which globalisation takes place. They have existed for a long time, as has indeed globalisation itself. What is new is the way they combine with information and communications technologies to change the world economy. Their antecedents were the trading companies. In earlier times these were a driving force behind European colonialism. Their aim was to collect raw materials or specially sought-after products such as gold, silver, tea, porcelain or silk and take them back to the home country. There these products could be sold at a profit, which was all the larger as the companies could use slave labour or poorly paid workers in the colonies and often enjoyed (crown-protected) monopolies at home.

During industrialisation, when the wealth of the home country was increasingly seen as dependent on a steady supply of cheap raw materials, such enterprises became the main expression of imperialism. As in colonial times, however, sales in the colonies were secondary to those in the mother country. The break with the old came in the late nineteenth and early twentieth centuries, when a few companies – for example, Nobel of Sweden in Germany, Bayer of Germany in the United States, and Singer of the United States in Scotland – began to establish themselves abroad for the purpose of building up markets. Foreign subsidiaries were sought in order to overcome punitive tariff barriers, which were so high as to render exports unprofitable. Often the companies gained market advantages with patented products or processes. The United Kingdom was the dominant foreign investor up until the end of World War I. After that the United States took the leading role – its companies having grown wealthy and more visionary as a result of a long experience with continent-wide operations.

Multinational enterprises could not really take off in the period between the two world wars, as they had been able to do in the pre-

World War I era, when the world was in many respects as 'globalised' as it is today.[52] Operations in different countries were rarely co-ordinated. Tariffs were high. It was difficult to move capital across frontiers due to exchange controls. Communication was slow. Cartels in oil, steel and other sectors were not only tolerated but even encouraged by European powers. They were seen as stabilising markets, even at an international level. National economies had to be kept 'pure' – i.e. as free of foreign capital as possible – and exports of capital were generally looked at with suspicion, at least by the continental European powers. The aim was to export as much, and import as little, as possible in true mercantilist tradition. Trade agreements were mainly bilateral between countries, and modified with each new ministerial meeting between the countries. The result was a jungle of rules, in which few companies could expand their foreign trade and investment. There followed the inflation of the 1920s, the depression and deflation of the 1930s, the currency instability after the abandonment of the pound's gold footing in the wake of World War I, and the rise of totalitarian regimes in Italy, Germany and elsewhere.

World War II changed all that. After the war, US companies could start expansion in Western Europe – first the United Kingdom and then on the Continent. They were even encouraged to do so by various provisions in the Marshall Plan (in particular that non-repatriated profits would remain untaxed). Numerous factors contributed to this development: lower labour costs in Europe than in the US; the need for reconstruction; the rise in personal income in Western Europe permitting companies to expand and new consumer markets to develop; greater knowledge on the part of decision-makers about how economies work; the rise of management studies, first in the US and then in Europe; a steady increase in the supply of better educated people, filling higher positions in companies; multilateral and ever-more open trade regimes under the General Agreement on Tariffs and Trade; greater currency certainty under the Bretton Woods system – with the dollar, linked to gold, as the world's anchor currency; strong defence needs due to the Cold War, fuelling the rise of an 'industrial–military complex'; and new and quicker means of communication and transport.

For the first time MNEs could co-ordinate the activities of subsidiaries in different countries. Knowledge became the primary engine behind the growth of companies and national economies – as opposed to earlier eras when access to physical labour, raw materials or the ability to mass-produce manufactures had been decisive. Knowledge – first how to produce things, but increasingly how to co-ordinate the knowledge and efforts of others – became the most important factor behind growth.

Paradoxically enough, the technological progress in communications technology that served MNEs so well in the 1945–90 period has now gone so far as to jeopardise the very existence of the traditional, major MNE conglomerate. Before, the 'proprietary knowledge' of MNEs could be kept inside the company walls with relative ease. New knowledge could be added through expansion and the hiring of talent. Today, however, communications are so easy, cheap and instantaneous that this method is less successful. The internet makes it so much easier to 'steal' and share knowledge that the organisational cost of MNE expansion – co-ordinating actions and making sure that information is not leaked to competitors – may in many cases become too high to justify the benefits of size alone. Those MNEs that tried to remain big *and* centralised – such as IBM in the 1980s and early 1990s – faced major problems. Those that decentralised almost to the point of being MNEs only in name – such as today's reformed IBM – have sometimes fared better, even though the question then arises why the different operations should come under one company.[53]

In future, MNEs are likely to have to go down this path, with the possible exception of 'vertically integrated' industries such as oil companies (well–pipeline–port–truck–petrol station). Decentralisation will also become necessary in order to adapt products and services to more local conditions. Boeings or Airbuses may only have one appearance worldwide. However, more and more consumer goods, even cars, may have to be different depending on the region. 'Just-in-time' production (to minimise stocks) will be supplemented by computer-guided 'just-in-quantity' production lines. More and more MNEs will loosen links with subsidiaries, or shed them, and instead work with temporary partners for each project. Knowledge will be sought on an equally ad hoc basis, with outside consultants anywhere in the world being hired for individual undertakings.

Europe in the world of the future

The five above-mentioned forces – nationalism, terrorism, religion, demography and globalisation – are of course not the only ones likely to have an effect on the evolution of Europe over the coming years and decades. Many others could have been raised, such as AIDS and global warming, but they belong in a different book.

While it is difficult to predict particular developments in the coming decade, it is less so to foresee general world trends to which Europeans will have to adapt. The world in 2015 is expected to have a population of some 7.2 billion people, up from slightly over six billion in 2002. More than 95 per cent of the increase will be in the developing countries (although birth rates are going down there, too), whereas Europe's population will decrease.

The risk of war among developed countries is low. Most conflicts are likely to be small-scale internal upheavals due to religious, ethnic, economic or political discord. However, terrorism could provoke more important international conflicts, such as between India and Pakistan, or between the US (or a US-led coalition) against a country of the 'axis of evil' type, or even against a terrorist group not based in any one country. They are likely to become more lethal with the arrival of weapons of mass destruction (nuclear, biological and chemical), longer-range missile delivery systems and other technologies.

Transnational criminal organisations are expected to grow and become increasingly skilful at exploiting the global spread of sophisticated information, financial and transportation networks. They will try to corrupt leaders of unstable, economically vulnerable or failing countries, infiltrate banks and businesses in difficulties and co-operate with insurgent political movements to control sizeable geographical areas. They will earn their money from trafficking in human beings, narcotics, racketeering, the smuggling of toxic materials, hazardous wastes, illicit arms, military technologies and contraband.

There is likely to be dynamic economic growth, especially in the so-called emerging markets, such as China and India. Globalisation will lead to more international trade and hence interdependency among countries. This could contribute to greater overall international stability. However, some countries may not be able to join fully in this development, including those in sub-Saharan Africa, the Middle East, Latin America, Central Asia, the Caucasus and even in South-Eastern Europe. Income gaps in countries are expected to widen and large regions will be left behind.

Environmental problems will persist and sometimes worsen. With increasing land use, the already significant degradation of arable land will continue. Water will become even more of a scarcity in large parts of the world. More tropical forests will be cut down and greenhouse gas emissions will increase substantially, potentially worsening any 'global warming'.

In such a world, Europe will have to help others, as well as itself. It will have to invest in technology, in public education and in broader participation in government to include increasingly influential actors, such as non-governmental organisations. Europe will also have to be on its guard against both primitive and precision-guided weapons threatening from other world regions, by developing counteracting technology of the missile-defence type, as well as intelligence, military and diplomatic capabilities. Other threats are weapons of mass destruction planted by terrorists in European cities or against nuclear plants. Europe will also have to co-operate more closely with others on a global scale, to counter the many economic, financial, environmental, criminal, security and other threats mentioned.

Europe's choice of its future

The European Union is, at present, the most important vehicle for European unification. It forms an essential framework for continued peace and development in Europe. It provides direction for economic and political reform in the many countries in Central, Eastern and South-Eastern Europe which prepare or hope to join it. If unification succeeds – say, in the form of a functioning EU federation – it will be a remarkable feat, for it would be in the absence, or at least fading presence, of the many elements that brought about West European integration in the first few decades after the World War II.

If, however, the peoples of the EU were to say 'no' to federation before or after it has come about – as expressed through the rise of 'Euro-phobic' parties in member states or major political divisions as regards further integration – then Europeans will have to think of an alternative, which, for want of a better name, could be called 'good-neighbourliness'. They would be close to one another, but not formally unite in a federation. They would trade, invest and move freely about as far as each country would want and permit. Time could be expected to take care of the rest – with the present degree of international contact and means of communication signifying that the process would be unlikely to lead to anything but further rapprochement. Countries would follow different courses as they saw fit, for others to emulate or avoid. With an outside threat perceived, joint defence would come into play, via NATO or with Europe acting on its own.

There are two problems with such a more timid outcome. As one observer puts it:

> Of course, most of those ... who would resist deeper supranational integration of the federal type, and are content with intergovernmental co-operation, would not welcome disintegration. But a shallow Europe, held together only by concertation among diplomats, would be unable to avoid sporadic disunity that might deteriorate eventually into renewed conflict. In such circumstances, national sovereignty preciously preserved would be practically useless.[54]

The second difficulty with a status quo solution to the question of further European integration has to do with its lack of adventure, of mission, of direction, of vision. People need goals, and simply keeping the same level of inter-country integration, being content with what has been achieved, is for many not sufficiently inspirational. If the sails do not billow, the rudder cannot steer. Hence the quest for integration as the way to find a new driving force, a new purpose, especially in a world of fiercer and fiercer competition and new threats.

Whatever choice Europeans make, there is nothing deterministic about it, as Europe's own history since World War II has taught us. Europe's most noble task will be to believe in its own capacity for change, while preserving democracy, human rights and the rule of law. Democracy is slow, but precisely because of this, it has time to adjust its course. A snail has more time to adjust than a speeding hare. Moreover, wherever democracy goes, it knows it has the people with it – even those who are in the minority – and that is half the success of any national or federal venture. Democracy – a healthy, uncorrupted democracy where debate is free, a multitude of opinions can come to the fore and corruption and crime are nipped in the bud – is also the best way to prevent the rise of usurpers and tyrants.

There are probably Hitlers, Stalins and Milosevices all around us. However, they – unknown to us and probably also to themselves – will remain only potential tyrants and unable to start their wars and oppression as long as democracy remains strong. They will not be able to impose their obsessions or complexes on the rest of us. And their butchers – the Dzierzynskis, the Berias, the Himmlers and the Fouchés – will be unable to take up their gruesome profession. There may be fewer spectacular pages in history books this way but, more importantly, there will be fewer people suffering. As Montesquieu put it: 'Happy the people whose annals are blank in the history books'.[55]

Europe's annals have been anything but blank. We must then seek comfort in a more recent thinker, the Spanish philosopher José Ortega y Gasset. In his book *Toward a Philosophy of History* – published in 1941, the darkest year of World War II – he said: 'Man's real treasure is the treasure of his mistakes, piled up stone by stone since thousands of years'.[56] Europe has suffered enough. It must surely by now have learnt enough.

Notes

1 Kissinger (1973, p. 1).
2 The Bonn Accord on Afghanistan was remarkable for the number of countries contributing to it or approving of its results. They included, in addition to the NATO countries, Russia, Iran, Pakistan and India.
3 The conflict in the Chechen Republic (Russian Federation) – erupting in 1994 and halted via a fragile peace agreement between 1996 and 1999 – had not been resolved, in spite of the fact that Russian troops had gained control over most of the territory and Moscow exercised direct administration since 2001. Some 200,000 refugees had fled to neighbouring republics and about 5,000 Russian soldiers and an unknown number of Chechen insurgents had died since 1999 alone. Chechen terrorists seized a theatre in downtown Moscow in 2002 and took some 800 people hostage. In the ensuing attempt to liberate the hostages, 129 of them died along with the terrorists. A bomb attack by Chechen terrorists against the central administration building in Grozny shortly afterwards claimed over fifty lives. A referendum in Chechnya on a constitution for Chechen autonomy within the Russian Federation was held in 2003, with an overwhelming majority voting in favour. It was not certain, however, that the result would translate into an end to the hostilities.
4 See, for example Hirschmann (2001, pp. 7–15).
5 The League of Nations – established in 1919 and dissolved in 1946 following the creation of the United Nations and the League's failure to prevent World War II – nevertheless represented a noble idea and the beginnings of an international order, the main lines of which were to be followed after 1945 by the United Nations, NATO, the European Union, the Council of Europe and others. As MacMillan (2000, p. 85) writes: 'The League did represent something very important: both a recognition of the changes that had already taken place in national relations [as a result of World War I] and a bet placed on the future ... Of course power still counted, of course governments looked out for their countries, but what that meant had changed ... Now war was a cost to all players, as the Great War proved. National interests were furthered better by peace, which allowed trade and industry to flourish. And the nation itself was something different, no longer embodied by the monarch or a small elite but increasingly constituted by the people themselves.' If the United States had joined the League – as did its successors after World War II – that conflict might never have occurred.
6 Von Loringhoven (1998, pp. 13–19) sees 'sub-regional' co-operation in Europe as important in at least three respects: it accompanies and facilitates EU and NATO enlargement; it provides 'soft security' by promoting co-operation in practical fields; and it furthers democratisation by involving local and non-governmental actors. He considers the strengthening of sub-regional co-operation particularly important in Central and Eastern Europe and the Balkans.
7 There are numerous examples of economic rivalry between the EU as such and the US that could spill over into the political domain. They include trade

issues within the World Trade Organisation and EU insistence that the US negotiate with it as representing all EU members, rather than deal with them individually, in areas such as air connections and the inspection of ship cargoes to the US to check for the presence of weapons of mass destruction. Given the extent of transatlantic economic relations, these differences are not likely, however, to lead to major political friction. Conversely, political friction, such as over the Iraq conflict in 2003, could well affect economic relations via consumer boycotts and investment that avoided certain countries considered to be in the 'opposite camp'. Again, however, any such action is also likely to hurt employment in the home economy due to the pronounced intertwinement among developed economies.

8 Moravcsik (1998, pp. 407–8).

9 Jakobson (1994, p. 314). Translation from the German original.

10 There are major official efforts to have larger numbers of Germans learn French and more French learn German, but they are frustrated by the growing role of English. There is perhaps also a general difficulty for a Latin and a German culture fully to understand each other, in spite of there being a mutual attraction between the two, as reflected for instance in the number of tourists in both directions. Furthermore, France's perceived 'universal civilising mission', born out of the French Revolution, contrasts with Germany's greater emphasis on its own national identity and cohesion and on finding its proper place in Europe. Another irritant has been France's relative comfort with a certain protectionism, as opposed to Germany's more free-trading instincts.

11 Pedersen (1998, pp. 196–204) goes so far as to call the France–Germany tandem 'Europe's co-operative hegemon', with France granting Germany indirect primacy in the economic-monetary sphere and Germany letting France lead in the security and defence areas: 'The most important reason for the survival of Franco-German collaboration in the post-Cold War era is … Germany's offering France a share in its evolving regional hegemony *and* the opportunities for regional hegemonic rule which such a continental leadership offers both countries'.

12 The Eurocorps, headquartered in Strasbourg, was established in 1992 following the establishment, in 1988, of a Franco-German Joint Security and Defence Council on the initiative of German Chancellor Helmut Kohl and French President François Mitterrand. Belgium, Luxembourg and Spain soon joined France and Germany as members. Eurocorps is integrated into the NATO military command structure and is composed of 65,000 troops stationed on the territory of the member countries for rapid dispatch in the event of a crisis. It has 800 tanks, 1,700 armoured vehicles and 500 artillery at its disposal.

13 Fouquet (2000, pp. 9–10), translation from the French original. One is reminded of the lament of the early twentieth-century French statesmen Georges Clemenceau, who said that: 'There are always twenty million Germans too many' ('*Il y a toujours vingt millions d'Allemands de trop*').

14 The sophisticated love–hate relationship between the UK and France has given rise to a considerable literature. The two nations seem at the same time

to admire and disparage their cultural differences, while having more in common at a more fundamental level. Any aspiring Briton must know at least some French. Yet the British feel a little superior to the French, as if the perceived relative disorder of French political and civic life, the alleged carelessness of French drivers or French 'amour' were national characteristics and a cause for amusement. The French, by contrast, do not look down on the British. They often secretly admire them for taking the contrary viewpoint in, say, the EU, even as they may criticise them for not toeing the line.

15 German–British relations have also been helped by the fact that the Germans have more readily accepted the domination of the English language in Europe and the world. German is of course much closer linguistically to its Germanic neighbour English than is Latin-based French. English words – whether or not they exist in English, such as the German word for a mobile phone (Handy) – invade the German language, and the Germans (except the linguistic purists) readily take to them. No doubt German, because it is a Germanic language like English, will be able better to incorporate the onslaught of English than, say French or Italian. Since Germany, unlike France, does not have any universal ambitions for its language, it is not likely, either, to have the same fierce opposition to English as France. Something more than language is afoot, however. On many issues the Germans and the British seem to understand each other better than they do the French, who may at times seem to them a little overbearing and as having ulterior designs for France, as opposed to the EU as a whole. There may be a cultural-linguistic reason for this, a Latin–Germanic divide, so to speak. However, perhaps also a more decentralised view of things in federal Germany and 'devolutionised' the UK than in comparatively centralised France can explain this.

16 Russia has concluded an agreement with Turkey to lay a pipeline under the Black Sea to deliver close to twenty billion cubic meters of gas annually, covering more than half of Turkey's needs and enhancing Moscow's influence in the country. Russia is also pressing Azerbaijan to have the latter's oil go through Russian pipelines and ports. Russia's military campaign in Chechnya must also be seen within an energy context, since a granting of Chechen independence would mean losing an important oil supply and transit area. Furthermore, Kazakhstan and Turkmenistan – which together have oil and gas reserves equivalent to those of Saudi Arabia – are receiving assistance from Moscow to fight Islamic fundamentalism and could easily draw closer to Russia and thereby increase the latter's energy leverage over Europe.

17 There is no US government encouragement, let alone financial support, for MacDonald's, say, to set up a (franchise) store on the Champs-Elysées, or for Disneyworld to build an amusement park in Japan. The only argument could be that the US supports free trade and investment through the WTO and other fora, and that this facilitates US multinationals to invest abroad. However, it is difficult to fight against that when all countries – including

developing nations playing host to multinationals – seem to support such WTO principles.

18 The rest of the world often does not realise that US difficulties in following international initiatives derive from the country's division of powers, especially between the administration and the Congress. Thus, even if the US administration had wished, say, to abolish the death penalty, it could only do so at federal, not state, level. The Kyoto Protocol on climate change would have met insuperable opposition on Capitol Hill, as would efforts in the early 2000s to have the US Senate ratify the convention for the establishment of an International Criminal Court. In a parliamentary democracy of the European type, by contrast, a government by definition has a (more or less secure) majority also in parliament, including for the ratification of treaties.

19 May (1992, pp. 106–7) sees at least two strands in US foreign and security policy: Jefferson's call for an 'empire of liberty', by which Americans 'thought of their nation as destined to be a great empire, but not on the European or Roman model. The United States would not acquire and rule colonies', but rather provide an example through its own political system and thereby enhance its own security. The spread of the 'American system' constituted the second strand of thought, by which the United States would build relations with other countries through the 'natural affinity of republics and the natural unity of states'. Both strands have informed US foreign policy, also in regard to Europe, up until the present day.

20 Kaplan (2002, p. 148).

21 The UN Security Council's Resolution 1244 of 1999 reaffirmed the sovereignty of the Federal Republic of Yugoslavia over Kosovo but indirectly left the region's future open and entrusted its management to a UN Interim Administration.

22 A study by UNICEF (United Nations Children's Fund), the OSCE and the United Nations High Commisssioner for Human Rights published in 2002, drew a particularly sombre picture of the human trafficking situation in the region. Entitled *Trafficking in Human Beings in South-Eastern Europe*, the study said that an estimated 80 per cent of the victims of human trafficking in Albania are under the age of eighteen. The price for a prostitute in Romania was reported to be between €50 and €200 and in Kosovo between €700 and €2,500. The study called for clear human rights standards to assist the victims and equally clear legislation against human trafficking in national law.

23 The disappearance of Yugoslavia – a state founded after World War I that saw its various parts secede during the 1990s, leaving in the end only Serbia and Montenegro – marked the end of the effort to unite the 'South Slav' nationalities under a single roof. The 'Serbia and Montenegro' declared in 2003 came about mainly as a result of European Union pressure. It did not have a capital city, only an administrative centre, Belgrade; nor did it have a common central bank or currency, as Serbia used the dinar and Montenegro the euro. After three years, either side would be entitled to hold a referendum on whether it wanted to gain independence.

24 In 2002 NATO decided to reduce, by mid–2003, its forces in Bosnia and
   Herzegovina from 19,000 to 12,000 troops and in Kosovo from 38,000 to
   33,000 troops. The EU took over responsibility from the UN for training
   and supervising Bosnian police forces in 2003 and could be expected soon
   also to take over peacekeeping duties from NATO. In the same year NATO
   handed over to the EU the peacekeeping in the 'former Yugoslav Republic of
   Macedonia', in a first manifestation of the EU's emerging European Security
   and Defence Policy.

25 Richard Holbrooke, the chief US negotiator for peace in Bosnia in the 1990s,
   in his foreword to Margaret MacMillan's *Paris 1919: Six Months that
   Changed the World*, wrote: 'As our American negotiating team shuttled
   around the Balkans in the fall of 1995 trying to end the war in Bosnia, the
   Versailles Treaty was not far from my mind. Reading excerpts from Harold
   Nicolson's *Peacemaking 1919*, we joked that our goal was to undo Woodrow
   Wilson's legacy. When we forced the leaders of Bosnia, Croatia and the
   Federal Republic of Yugoslavia to come together in Dayton, Ohio, in Novem-
   ber 1995 and negotiate the end of the war, we were, in effect, burying
   another part of Versailles' (MacMillan, p. x).

26 Oil (proven and possible) reserve estimates for the Caspian Sea region range
   from 30 billion to 200 billion barrels. Industry analysts often use a middle
   range figure of 90 billion barrels, similar to the estimated reserves of China
   and Mexico (Forsythe, 1996).

27 Separatist movements gained new strength in the Caucasus region in the early
   1990s following the breakup of the Soviet Union. In the south Caucasus,
   intense fighting broke out between Azerbaijan and Armenians in Nagorno
   Karabach, a region of Azerbaijan predominantly populated by ethnic Armenians, before a ceasefire could be established in 1994 with international
   assistance. Fighting also broke out in Georgia when two regions, Abkhasia
   and South Ossetia, sought independence. Ceasefires were reached here also.
   Common to all these conflicts is that they have not as yet found a political
   solution. Tens of thousands of people were killed and hundreds of thousands
   were displaced and still remain so.

28 The possible effects of a Chinese–Russian rapprochement are complex and
   multiple. It may increase pressure on North Korea to negotiate an end to the
   Korean War and permit nuclear inspection. It could also increase Chinese pressure
   on Taiwan, push Japan closer to the United States and Russia and assist
   Japanese investment in Siberia by promoting a more stable political environment.

29 From 'The county of Tron', in *Selected Articles* by Bulgarian author Stoyan
   Chilingirov (available only in Bulgarian).

30 By way of example, over two million Hungarian speakers live outside Hungary's
   borders – in the Czech Republic, Slovakia, Romania (Transylvania), Ukraine,
   Serbia and Montenegro, not to speak of North America and Australia. Over
   thirty-two million Russians live outside Russia's borders in fourteen countries formerly belonging to the Soviet Union. (Source: 'Britannica world data',
   Encyclopaedia Britannica 1999 Year Book.)

31 Pfaff (1993, p. 13).

32 As related in Pfaff (1993, pp. 53–4).

33 The 2002 Football World Cup had many political overtones. Korea reaching the semi-finals was reported to have impressed the North Koreans, perhaps bringing reunification between the two countries closer. Many Americans were concerned that the unexpectedly strong performance of the US team would expose the US as trying to dominate the world in yet another domain. It was remarkable to see how the world came together during the month-long tournament, with teams from all corners of the globe meeting each other in friendly competition and permitting billions of people to see that any differences between humans are insignificant when compared with their similarities. However, football can also lead to different feelings. One only has to think of the frequent hooligans' riots after games and the 1969 Hondura–El Salvador 'Futbàl War', which was provoked by a controversial match between the two countries.

34 In a first ever joint publication on 30 November 1999, four major Swedish dailies (*Dagens Nyheter, Aftonbladet, Svenska Dagbladet* and *Expressen*) argued that there was close co-operation between neo-Nazi groups and motorcycle gangs; that every third prosecutor had been forced to abandon cases after intimidation and threats; and that nine out of ten policemen said that the threat to the rule of law was increasing, with many admitting that they dared not apprehend certain suspected criminals out of fear of retaliation.

35 De Winter (1998, p. 221) maintains that: '[First,] European integration weakens the national state "from above", as many competences pass to "Brussels". Second, following the setting up of the Internal Market, the European Union developed a large number of programmes at the regional level. At the same time, in several countries, the unitary state was weakened "from below" through the process of federalisation (Belgium, and Italy in the future?), the granting of autonomy to specific communities (Spain) and devolution (France). Hence, in relative terms, the regional level gained in importance as a policy level vis-à-vis the unitary state … Independist parties hope that the decline of decision-making relevance of the state will facilitate its demise.'

36 The EU actively supports transfrontier co-operation among its member states, where about 10 per cent live in border regions and roughly half a million cross borders daily to go to work. The so-called 'Interreg' programme within the EU's Agenda 2000 foresees spending close to €5 billion on cross-border co-operation between 2000 and 2006, some of it with EU candidate countries in Central and Eastern Europe.

37 One difference may be, for instance, in the approach to EU agreements, where Protestant nations are reported to hesitate for a long time before signing but then to do their best to live up to them afterwards. By contrast, Catholic nations are said to sign more readily but then be more easy-going about implementation. The Swedish journalist von Sydow reports speculation among EU civil servants in Brussels, to the effect that Catholics are supposed to like legal frameworks, including constitutions, when Protestants

prefer informal negotiations; that Catholics have an aversion to free markets where Protestants like them and see them as the EU's *raison d'être;* that Catholics are centralists and have an aversion to decentralisation, whereas Protestants are worried about a resurgence of a 'Roman Empire' and prefer the nation state (von Sydow, 1999, pp. 15–22).

38 It is also often forgotten that Muslims carried the torch of Greek and Roman learning during Europe's Dark Ages, eventually helping to bring Europe out of a period of obscurantism and furthering its coming together.

39 Siedentop (2000, Ch. 10).

40 One is indeed left to wonder what goes on in the mind of a woman in, say, Saudi Arabia who sees how an actor like Michelle Pfeiffer lectures and seduces a glamorous Robert Redford in between plane trips and television shows as in the film *Up Close and Personal* – while the woman in question herself cannot venture outside unless veiled and cannot in any way help shape the society in which she lives except in the home and among the family, where her influence may be considerable. Similarly, the film *Titanic,* which may have been seen by most of mankind, has a young woman in luxury class abandon her arranged husband in favour of a charming young third-class passenger who, aside from his Hollywood idol looks, has nothing to offer but his love. How will that film, and others like it, affect world history by modifying perceptions or cultural patterns? Presumably, many people in the more strict Muslim countries will become slightly schizophrenic as they try to reconcile their strict, absolute principles with the values, or lack thereof, beamed to them by all dominant Western media.

41 Tibi (1997, pp. 31–46) believes that today's Islam is engaged in a desperate battle to fight the cultural dimension of (Western) modernity, while readily accepting the scientific-technological part. He sees the trauma of trying to 'de-Westernise' modernity through such 'partial modernisation' – i.e. 'dividing the indivisible' – as underlying much of present Islamic fundamentalism.

42 Privately placed payments for future pensions will, however, depend on the performance of the funds in which they have been invested, a not entirely reassuring prospect in view of the numerous corporate scandals in recent times and the fall in stock prices they provoked.

43 The European Union's population is projected to fall from its present 375 million to 330 million by 2050. Italy, for example, is expected to lose 28 per cent of its population by that time, while in Spain 43 per cent of its population is forecast to be older than sixty, up from 22 per cent today. (Source: United Nations Population Division.) The working-age population in the EU is foreseen to decline by at least 2.15 million people between 2005 and 2015, but only 1.25 million new working-age citizens will be available to take their place. Fewer people means that unemployment will come down, but also that wage-led inflation may go up. The euro – assuming it by that time encompasses many more countries – could be expected to increase labour mobility in an even more integrated EU. Coomans (1998, pp. 5–28),

with whom these figures originate, in this situation expects massive labour movements to more expansive regions, also from Central and Eastern Europe, which he sees as a major workforce pool in tomorrow's Europe. Even so, birth rates there are also low.

44 The European Commission in 2002 reported mixed progress on the implementation of the EU's Internal Market provisions. Sweden, Finland, Denmark, the Netherlands and the United Kingdom had an 'implementation deficit' of less than 1.5 per cent, while for France, Greece and Portugal it was in excess of 3 per cent. For some countries the deficit was indeed growing due to new directives being adopted.

45 The Amsterdam Treaty committed the EU to a harmonised EU legislation on immigration and asylum by 2004 via the 'qualifying majority' decision-making procedure in the Council of Ministers. However, Germany, at the EU summit in Nice in December 2000, refused to yield its veto right in the area of asylum and immigration, arguing that its inner social cohesion was at stake if it was not left to manage its own immigration policies. Germany in 2000 had 5.5 million immigrants, with some 300,000 arriving each year. The country received 320,000 refugees during the war in Bosnia and Herzegovina and 200,000 following the Kosovo conflict, even though many have since returned to their regions of origin.

46 In 2002 the EU agreed on a directive (the so-called 'Dublin II' Agreement, following an earlier Dublin Convention on First Asylum), stating that a country where an asylum-seeker first entered the EU would remain responsible for examining his or her request, even if that person subsequently moved to another EU member state. A new centralised data system, Eurodac, would use fingerprints to trace the person's movements within the EU.

47 Estimate by Manuel Castells, Professor of Sociology at the University of California and author of the trilogy *The Information Age: Economy, Society and Culture*, as reported in Kaplan (2002, p. 5).

48 Coffee is an example. Coffee consumption increases steadily around the world. When at first prices paid to the coffee farmers in developing countries rose in response to heightened demand, producers in many countries which had not traditionally grown the crop began doing so, causing global production to rise and prices to fall to lower and lower levels. As the preference for better coffee quality rose in richer countries (a wealth effect sometimes referred to as the 'cappuccino effect'), millions of smaller coffee producers were unable to adapt and had to abandon production. With few outlets for other crops remaining, due not least to subsidies for agricultural exports from rich countries, their future looked bleak. Neither the general public nor prospering roasting companies seemed to pay much attention to this example of globalisation's downside aspects.

49 There is also the related risk of generalised deflation. If inflation – considered the main threat during much of the post-World War II era – is 'too much money chasing too few goods', deflation can be said to be 'too many

goods chasing too little money'. It is a process in which the prices of products (and services) tumble along with corporate profits, when there is suddenly not enough demand to absorb the amounts produced. Price deflation became a fact in several OECD countries in the early 2000s, most notably in Japan. In factories around the world robots are working twenty-four hours a day (some of them producing new robots). This may pose a problem for the future of manual labour, first in industrial production and then in lower-level services, where robots already clean cars and rooms. (However, other services where tasks are more complex or demand a relationship with the customer may flourish, such as in restaurants, personal care and gardening.) If companies begin to undercut each other severely in order to sell, inter-national tensions and protectionism could rise as certain countries would be faced with rising trade deficits. Eroded corporate profit margins could trigger new lay-offs in order to reduce costs, while higher unemployment could impact on consumer spending, not only among those affected spending less, but also those who fear they may be next in line. Such a 'glut world economy' would be difficult to overcome.

50 Huntington (1993, p. 25), one of the main proponents of this theory, sees the 'clash of civilisations' that he expects will shape the world as being especially between the 'Western, Confucian, Japanese, Islamic, Hindu, Slavic-Orthodox, Latin American, and possibly African'. Since Europe encompasses at least two of these, its role in such a 'clash' would seem uncertain. Park (1997, p. 124), citing various scholars, argues that 'modern economic globalisation is entirely consistent with nationalism', especially since 'nationalism originally was able to spread only because a degree of globalisation already existed. The communications revolution also contributes to nationalism, since it leads to the growing perception of political and economic inequali-ties between ethnic groups ... There is also a global "demonstration effect", in which the example of one successful ethnic nationalism stimulates the claims of another.'

51 Friedman (2000).

52 See, for instance, Wolf (2001, pp. 178–90). Wolf observes that the portion of world production traded on global markets is not much higher today than it was in the years leading up to World War I. International mobility of labour was clearly higher at the time. For instance, the United States increased its population in the 1890s by 9 per cent due to immigration. International capital flows were also considerable in the nineteenth and early twentieth century. In the case of the UK, it averaged 4.6 per cent of GDP between 1870 and 1913, a level unparalleled in any country in today's world.

53 See e.g. Buckley and Casson (1991, pp. 102–13).

54 Duff (1997, p. 3).

55 Attributed to Montesquieu by Thomas Carlyle in his *History of Frederick the Great*, 1858–65.

56 As related in Kaplan (2002, p. xvii).

Appendix: seminal events since 1945

1944

Bretton Woods Conference establishes International Bank for Reconstruction and Development (later World Bank) and the International Monetary Fund

1945

Yalta Conference of post-World War II world order

End of World War II in Europe; occupation of Germany by the four victorious powers (the United Kingdom, France, the Soviet Union and the United States)

Potsdam Conference on the future of Germany

The US explodes nuclear bombs over Hiroshima and Nagasaki; End of World War II in Asia

Founding of the United Nations (UN)

1947

Announcement of the Marshall Plan to assist European recovery

The Soviet Union declines participation in Marshall Plan (and obliges countries in its 'sphere of influence' in Central and Eastern Europe to do the same)

Cominform (Communist Information Bureau) formed under Soviet auspices to promote communism internationally

1948

The General Agreement on Tariffs and Trade (GATT) enters into force

Communist *coup d'état* in Czechoslovakia

Brussels Treaty (on West European defence) signed

Congress of Europe held (in The Hague)

Currency reform in the US, British and French occupation zones in Germany (and Berlin)

Soviet blockade of the western sectors of Berlin (lifted in May 1949)

1949

Comecon (Council for Mutual Economic Assistance) established under Soviet leadership to promote economic integration in Central and East European countries under its influence

North Atlantic Treaty (Washington Treaty) on collective defence signed
Council of Europe founded
Founding of the Federal Republic of Germany (West Germany) following the
    end of military occupation of the US, British and French zones.
Founding of the German Democratic Republic (East Germany)
Establishment of the North Atlantic Treaty Organisation (NATO)
The Soviet Union detonates atom bomb, ending US nuclear monopoly
Chinese civil war ends in victory for communist side
Belgium, the Netherlands and Luxembourg form Benelux Economic Union

1950
Schuman Plan for European co-operation on coal and steel presented
Korean war starts

1951
European Coal and Steel Community (ECSC) founded (Belgium, France, the
    Federal Republic of Germany, Italy, Luxembourg and the Netherlands)

1952
European Defence Community signed (project abandoned in 1954)

1953
Stalin dies (leading to reduced East–West tension)
The Soviet Union proposes German unification (rejected by Western powers)
Worker uprising in East Berlin (suppressed by the Soviet Union and the East
    German regime)
Korean war ends (leading to further reduction in East–West tension)

1954
French National Assembly turns down proposed European Defence Community
French garrison at Dien Bien Phu falls, eventually leading to French withdrawal
    from Indo-China

1955
Austrian State Treaty enters into force (re-establishes sovereignty and foresees
    neutrality and the withdrawal of foreign troops)
Western European Union (WEU) established
Federal Republic of Germany gains sovereignty; joins NATO
Warsaw Pact founded
Messina Conference on a future European Economic Community (EEC) held
    (Belgium, France, the Federal Republic of Germany, Italy, Luxembourg, the
    Netherlands and the UK; British withdrawal from the negotiations in
    November 1955)
Soviet–West German relations formalised

1956

Khrushchev criticises Stalin at Twentieth Congress of the Soviet Community Party ('de-Stalinisation' and reduced tension with the West follow)

Worker unrest in Poland

Hungarian revolt against communist regime and Soviet domination (suppressed by the Soviet Union, acting via Warsaw Pact forces, in November)

Suez crisis

1957

European Economic Community and Euratom Treaties ('Rome Treaties') signed

Sputnik satellite launched by the Soviet Union

1958

European Economic Community and Euratom Treaties enter into force

European Industrial Free Trade Area (to include the EEC) proposed by the UK (rejected by France)

1960

European Free Trade Association (EFTA) enters into force (Austria, Denmark, Norway, Sweden, Switzerland and the UK)

Organisation of Petroleum Exporting Countries (OPEC) established

1961

Berlin crisis

Berlin Wall is built

The UK applies to join the EEC (rejected by France)

1962

Cuban missile crisis

1963

France and Germany sign Friendship Treaty

Nuclear Test Ban Treaty concluded between the US and the Soviet Union (forbidding atmospheric, outer space and underwater testing)

1964

Strategic Arms Limitation Treaty (SALT I) signed between the Soviet Union and the US (limiting strategic nuclear weapons)

1965

The US bombs North Vietnam; begins major military escalation in South Vietnam

1968

'1968' youth rebellion in France and elsewhere

Prague Spring, marking a Czechoslovak effort at political and economic reform (suppressed by the Soviet Union, acting via Warsaw Pact forces, in August)

1969
West German *Ostpolitik* begins, to improve relations with the Soviet Union and the countries of Central and Eastern Europe
The UK, Denmark and Ireland open accession negotiations with the EEC

1970
EEC Werner Committee presents plan for economic and monetary union by 1980 (project abandoned in 1974)
Renewed Polish unrest against communist regime

1971
The US severs the connection between the dollar and gold

1972
Norway popular referendum rejects EEC membership
SALT I between the Soviet Union and the US ratified, including Anti-Ballistic Missile (ABM) Treaty
Federal Republic of Germany (West Germany) and German Democratic Republic (East Germany) establish formal relations

1973
The UK, Denmark and Ireland join the EEC
Paris Agreement marks beginning of US military withdrawal from Vietnam
OPEC raises oil prices, contributing to (first) oil crisis

1975
North Vietnamese troops conquer Saigon (leads to a united Vietnam in 1976)
Helsinki Final Act signed; Conference on Security and Co-operation in Europe (CSCE) established (Organisation for Security and Co-operation in Europe (OSCE) as from 1995)

1979
European Monetary System (EMS) formed within the EEC
SALT II signed (never entered into force)
Second oil crisis
The Soviet Union invades Afghanistan (withdrawal in 1989)

1980
Solidarnosc ('Solidarity') self-governing trade union founded in Poland

1981
Greece joins the EEC

Polish government under General Jaruzelski imposes martial law; suppresses popular unrest

1985
Mikhail Gorbachev appointed Secretary General of the Community Party of the Soviet Union; initiates reform
Height of NATO–Warsaw Pact 'medium-range missile crisis' (leading to negotiations and an agreement, in 1987, to dismantle such weapons in Europe)

1986
Portugal and Spain join the EEC
GATT negotiations for a Uruguay Round start (completed in 1994 and leading, in 1995, to the creation of the World Trade Organisation (WTO)

1987
Single European Act of the European Community (EC) enters into force (initiates quest to complete the EC Internal Market by 1993 ('1992 project') and launches the EC's European Political Co-operation project for a common foreign policy)

1989
Berlin Wall falls

1990
Conventional Forces in Europe (CFE) Treaty concluded, leading to considerable reduction in such forces on all sides
German unification

1991
Kuwait is liberated from Iraqi occupation by US-led international coalition
Warsaw Pact dissolved
Estonia, Latvia and Lithuania declare independence
Break-up of Yugoslavia begins; declarations of independence by Croatia, Slovenia and Macedonia (subsequently named the 'former Yugoslav Republic of Macedonia') and by Bosnia (in 1992); fighting erupts between Yugoslav and Slovenian forces and between Yugoslav and Croatian forces
The Soviet Union is dissolved

1992
EU Treaty on European Union ('Maastricht Treaty') signed (includes a timetable for reaching Economic and Monetary Union (EMU) by 1999 at the latest and a commitment to the shaping of a Common Foreign Security Policy (CFSP)
European Bank for Reconstruction and Development established
Serb Republic of Bosnia and Herzegovina announces wish to join Yugoslavia
Fighting erupts in Bosnia and Herzegovina

Danish popular referendum rejects the Maastricht Treaty, preventing its entry into force

France in a popular referendum narrowly approves the Maastricht Treaty

1993

The European Union's Internal Market ('1992 project') enters into force

EU Schengen Agreement (free circulation of people) enters into force

Danish popular referendum approves (amended) Maastricht Treaty

Exchange Rate Mechanism of the European Monetary System collapses

UN-mandated economic embargo against Yugoslavia

1994

Partnership for Peace (PfP) programme launched by NATO, with wide European participation

'Euroagreements' between the EU and several countries in Central and Eastern Europe concluded

European Economic Area Agreement enters into force, closely associating five EFTA countries (Austria, Iceland, Liechtenstein, Norway and Sweden) with the EU Internal Market

Conflict erupts in Chechnya (Russian Federation) between Chechen rebels and Russian forces (peace agreement reached in 1996)

1995

Austria, Finland and Sweden join the EU

Organisation for Security and Co-operation in Europe (OSCE) created (succeeding the CSCE)

Fighting continues in Croatia (Krajina) and in the western part of Bosnia and Herzegovina

Dayton Agreement brings an end to hostilities in Bosnia and Herzegovina; establishes NATO contingent in Bosnia

1996

Russia joins the Council of Europe

1997

NATO–Russia Founding Act on Mutual Relations, Co-operation and Security signed

EU Amsterdam Treaty signed (prepares for envisaged 'small bang' (six countries) EU enlargement)

Stability and Growth Pact concluded to strengthen the EU's EMU

NATO Euro-Atlantic Partnership Council established

1999

The EU's EMU enters into force (non-physical introduction of the euro)

Czech Republic, Hungary and Poland join NATO

EU Berlin Summit agrees on (limited) reform of various policies (Agenda 2000)

European Commission resigns, setting off an institutional crisis in the EU

NATO attacks Yugoslavia over Kosovo (peace settlement reached in June)

Defence Capability Initiative to bolster European defence capabilities agreed at NATO Washington Summit

Stability Pact for South-Eastern Europe launched

Renewed fighting erupts in Chechnya (Russian Federation) between Chechen rebels and Russian forces

EU Helsinki Summit agrees on the principle of 'big bang' (thirteen candidate countries) enlargement and on the formation of a Rapid Reaction Force by 2003 as part of the European Security and Defence Policy

2000

EU diplomatic isolation of Austria over the 'Haider affair' (ends in October 2000)

EU Nice Summit modifies the EU's decision-making process to prepare for enlargement; arranges for 'flexible integration'

2001

Plan to build a Ballistic Missile Defence announced by the US

Irish popular referendum rejects EU Nice Treaty, preventing its entry into force

The US announces readiness for 'big bang' NATO enlargement

Terrorist attacks on the US ('September 11')

NATO activates its Article 5 on collective defence against the perpetrators of September 11

US-led coalition attacks Afghanistan; deposes Taliban regime

UN-sponsored Bonn Accord paves the way for new Afghan government

World Trade Organisation concludes the Doha Development Agenda on new trade negotiations

2002

Issuing of euro notes and coins, as part of the EMU

President Bush assails 'axis of evil' countries

EU Convention on the Future of Europe starts its work and presents elements for a future EU constitution

The US and Russia abrogate the 1972 Anti-Ballistic Missile Treaty

Treaty of Moscow on further cuts in nuclear missiles signed between the US and Russia

NATO–Russia Council created, giving Russia an 'equal partnership' role in certain (non-core) NATO areas

EU Nice Treaty approved in second Irish popular referendum, permitting its entry into force

NATO Prague Summit invites seven countries in Central and Eastern Europe to join in 2004, bringing membership to twenty-six

EU Copenhagen Summit invites ten countries in Central, Eastern and Southern Europe to join in 2004, bringing membership to twenty-five

2003

International crisis worsens over presumed weapons of mass destruction in Saddam Hussein's Iraq, leading to invasion by US, British and Australian forces (supported by those of other nations)

Looming international crisis over North Korea's nuclear programme

References

Allison, G. and Zelikow, P., 1999, *Essence of Decision – Explaining the Cuban Missile Crisis*, Longman, New York.

Alting von Geusau, F. A. M., 1992, *Beyond Containment and Division –Western Co-operation from a Post-Totalitarian Perspective*, Martinus Nijhoff Publishers, Dordrecht.

Amtenbrink, F., 1999, 'The European Central Bank – democratically elected or unconstrained?', *Nederlands Juristenblad*, No. 2.

Ash, G., 1993, *Im Namen Europas: Deutschland und die geteilte Kontinent*, Carl Hanser Verlag, Munich.

Baun, M. J., 1996, *An Imperfect Union – The Maastricht Treaty and the New Politics of European Integration*, Westview Press, Boulder, Colorado.

Bideleux, R., 1996, 'The Comecon experiment', in R. Bideleux and R. Taylor (eds), *European Integration and Disintegration*, Routledge, London and New York.

Bohlen, C. E., 1973, *Witness to History. 1929-1969*, Norton, New York.

Brown, A., 2000, 'Mikhail Gorbachev: systemic transformer', in M. Westlake (ed.), *Leaders in Transition*, Macmillan, London.

Brugmans, H., 1965, *L'idée européenne 1918–1965*, De Tempel, Tempelhof, Bruges.

Buckley, P. J. and Casson, M., 1991, *The Future of the Multinational Enterprise*, Macmillan, London.

Busschaert, J., 1998, *Significance of a Regional Integration Project: The Case of Benelux*, Institut d'études européennes, IEE-Documents, No. 8.

Coomans, G., 1998, 'L'emploi en Europe en 2005', *Futuribles*, No. 234, September.

Craft, S., Redmond, J., Wyn Rees, G., and Webber, M., 1999, *The Enlargement of Europe*, Manchester University Press, Manchester.

Csernatony, G. von, 1973, *Le Plan Marshall et le redressement économique de l'Allemagne*, Imprimerie Vandoise, Lausanne.

Deighton, A. and Runacle, E., 1998, 'The Western European Union 1948–1998: From the Brussels Treaty to the Treaty of Amsterdam', *Studia Diplomatica*, Vol. 51, Nos 1 and 2.

Denman, M. J., 1996, *The Origins and Development of the European Union 1945–1995*, Routledge, London and New York.

Drucker, P. F., 1993, *Post-Capitalist Society*, Harper Collins, London.

Duff, A., 1997, *Reforming the European Union*, Federal Trust, London.

Ellwood, D. W., 1992, *Rebuilding Europe: Western Europe, America and Postwar Reconstruction*, Longman, London and New York.

Engstrom, H. (ed.), 2000, *Socialist Songbook*, http://engstrom.best.vwh.net/songbook/preface.html

Erhard, L., 1963, *The Economics of Success*, Thames and Hudson, London.

Featherstone, K., 1994, 'Jean Monnet and the 'democratic deficit' in the European Union', *Journal of Common Market Studies*, Vol. 32, No. 2.

Forsythe, R., 1996, *The Politics of Oil in the Caucasus and Central Asia*, Adolphi Paper 300, Oxford University Press, Oxford.

Fouquet, C., 2000, *Délires et défaites – une histoire intellectuelle de l'exception française*, Albin Michel, Paris.

Fowkes, B., 1997, *The Disintegration of the Soviet Union*, St. Martin's Press, New York.

Friedman, Thomas, L., 2000, *The Lexus and the Olive Tree*, Farrar, Straus and Giroux, New York.

Fukuyama, F., 1993, *The End of History and the Last Man*, Penguin Books, London.

Gillingham, J., 1991, *Coal, Steel and the Rebirth of Europe: The Germans and the French From Ruhr Conflict to European Community*, Cambridge University Press, Cambridge.

Gimbel, J., 1968, *The American Occupation of Germany: Politics and the Military*, Stanford University Press, Stanford, California.

Gladwyn, H. M. G. J., 1969 *de Gaulle's Europe or Why the General Says No*, Secker and Warburg, London.

Greenwood, J., 1998, 'Regulating lobbying in the European Union', *Parliamentary Affairs – A Journal of Comparative Politics*, Vol. 51, No. 4, October.

Grosser, A., 1980, *The Western Alliance*, Continuum, New York.

Guéhenno, J. M., 1998-99, 'The impact of globalisation on strategy', *Survival*, International Institute for Strategic Studies, Vol. 40, No. 4, Winter.

Hirchmann, K., 2001, 'Terrorismus in neuen Dimensionen', *Aus Politik und Zeitgeschichte*, Bonn (B51/2001).

Huntington, S., 1993, 'The clash of civilisations', *Foreign Affairs*, Vol. 72, No. 3.

Hurlburt, H., 1995, 'Russia, the OSCE and European security architecture', *Helsinki Monitor*, Vol. 6, No. 2.

Jakobson, M., 1994, 'Frieden und Stabilität – eine Fata Morgana', *Europa-Archiv: Zeitschrift für internationale Politik*, Vol. 49.

Jones, J. M., 1955, *The Fifteen Weeks: February 21–June 5, 1947*, Viking Press, New York.

Kagan, R., 2002, 'Power and weakness', *Policy Review*, June/July.

Kaplan, R. D., 2002, *Warrior Politics: Why Leadership Demands a Pagan Ethos*, Random House, New York.

Kapteyn, P., 1996, *The Stateless Market – the European Dilemma of Integration and Civilisation*, Routledge, London.

Keersbergen, K. van and Verbeek, B., 1994, 'The policy of subsidiarity in the European Union', *Journal of Common Market Studies*, Vol. 32, No. 2.

Kennan, G. F., 1972, *Memoirs, 1950-1963*, *Vol. II*, Little, Brown, Boston and Toronto.

Kennedy, P., 1987, *The Rise and Fall of the Great Powers*, Random House, New York.

Keynes, J. M., 1920, *Economic Consequences of Peace*, Macmillan Press, London.

Kissinger, H., 1973, *A World Restored*, Gollancz, London.

Kissinger, H., 1994, *Diplomacy*, Simon and Schuster, London.

Knischewski, G., 1996, 'Post-war national identity in Germany', in B. Jenkins and S. A. Sofos (eds), *Nation and Identity in Contemporary Europe*, Routledge, London and New York.

Leffler, M. P., 1992, *A Preponderance of Power: National Security, the Truman Administration and the Cold War*, Stanford University Press, Stanford, California.

Loringhoven, F. von, 1998, 'Regionale Zusammenarbeit: Brücken im Zusammenwachsenden Europa', *Aussenpolitik (German Foreign Affairs Review)*, Vol. 49, No. 3.

Luif, P., 1995, *On the Road to Brussels – The Political Dimension of Austria's Finland's and Sweden's accession to the European Union*, The Austrian Institute for International Affairs, Vienna.

MacMillan, M., 2002, *Paris 1919: Six Months that Changed the World*, Random House, New York.

Malmborg, M. af, 1994, *Den ståndaktiga nationalstaten – Sverige och den västeuropeiska integrationen 1945-1959 (Sweden and West European Integration, 1945–1959)*, Lund University Press, Lund, Sweden.

Mastny, V., 1998, *The Soviet Non-Invasion of Poland in 1980-1981 and the End of the Cold War*, Working Paper 23, Cold War International History Project, Woodrow Wilson International Centre for Scholars, Washington DC.

May, E. R., 1992, 'National security in American history', in G. Allison and F. Treverton (eds), *Rethinking America's Security – Beyond Cold War to New World Order*, W. W. Norton and Co., New York and London.

McCullough, D., 1992, *Truman*, Simon and Schuster, New York.

Milward, A.S., 2000, *The European Rescue of the Nation-State*, Routledge, London and New York.

Moravcsik, A., 1998, *'The Choice for Europe: Social Purpose and State Power From Messina to Maastricht*, Cornell University Press, New York.

Naumann, K., 2002, *Frieden – der noch nicht erfüllte Auftrag*, Mittler, Hamburg.

Neuhold, C., 2000, 'Into the New Millennium: The Evolution of the European Parliament from Consultative Assembly to Co-legislator', *Eiposcope*, No. 1.

Nicoll, W. and Salmon, T. C., 1990, *Understanding the European Community*, Philip Allan, New York.

Oxford English Dictionary, 1933, Oxford University Press, Oxford.

Park, A., 1997, 'Theories of post-communist nationalism', in D. Carlton and P. Ingram (eds), *The Search for Stability in Russia and the Former Soviet Bloc*, Ashgate, Aldershot.

Parkinson, C. N., 1957, *Parkinson's Law*, Penguin Books, London.

Pedersen, T., 1998, *Germany, France and the Integration of Europe*, Pinter, London and New York.

Pfaff, W., 1993, *The Wrath of Nations*, Touchstone, New York.

Ross, G. (ed.), 1984, *The Foreign Office and the Kremlin. British Documents on Anglo-Soviet Relations 1941–1945*, Cambridge University Press, Cambridge.

Rühle, H., 2000, 'Und ewig schrumpft die Bundeswehr – der 'Partner in leadership' als NATO-Schlusslicht', *Neue Zürcher Zeitung*, 7 January.

Sassoon, D., 1997, *Looking Left: European Socialism After the Cold War*, I.B. Tauris Publishers (in association with the Gramski Foundation, Rome), London and New York.

Servan Schreiber, J. J., 1968, *The American Challenge*, Hamish Hamilton, London.

Shaw, J., 1998, 'The Treaty of Amsterdam: challenges of flexibility and legitimacy', *European Law Journal*, Vol. 4, No. 1, March.

Shawcross, W., 2000, *Deliver Us From Evil: Peacekeepers, Warlords and a World of Endless Conflict*, Simon and Schuster, London.

Shonfield, A., 1973, *Europe: Journey to an Unknown Destination*, Allen Lane, London.

Siedentop, L., 2000, *Democracy in Europe*, Penguin Books, London.

Swann, D., 1995, *The Economics of the Common Market*, Penguin Books, London.

Sydow, E. von, 1999, *När Luther kom till Bryssel*, Bokförlaget Arena, Smedjebacken, Sweden.

Talbott, S., 1979, *Endgame: The Inside Story of SALT II*, Harper & Row, New York and London.

Tibi, B., 1997, *Il fondamentalismo religioso*, Bollati Boringhieri, Turin.

Toulemon, R., 1998, 'For a democratic Europe', in M. Westlake (ed.), *The European Union Beyond Amsterdam*, Routledge, London and New York.

United Nations Economic Commission for Europe, 2000, *Economic Survey of Europe*, No. 1.

Urwin, D. W., 1991, *The Community of Europe*, Longman, London and New York.

Vanthoor, W. F. V., 1996, *European Monetary Union Since 1848 – A Political and Historical Analysis*, Edward Elgar, Cheltenham.

Weiler, J., 1997, 'Legitimacy and democracy of union governance', in G. Edwards and A. Pijpers (eds), *The Politics of European Treaty Reform: The 1996 Intergovernmental Conference and Beyond*, Pinter, London and Washington.

Westlake, M., 1998, 'Maastricht, Edinburgh, Amsterdam: the 'end of the beginning', in V. Deckmyn and I. Thomson (eds), *Openness and Transparency in the European Union*, The European Institute of Public Administration, Maastricht, The Netherlands.

Westlake, M. (ed.), 2000, *Leaders in Transition*, Macmillan, London.

Winter, L. de, in L. de Winter and H. Türsan (eds), 1998, *Regionalist Parties in Western Europe*, Routledge, London and New York.

Wolf, M., 2001, 'Will the nation-state survive globalisation?', *Foreign Affairs*, Vol. 80, No. 1.

Index

Note: 'n.' after a page reference indicates the number of a note on that page; references to CAP, ECSC, EEC and EMU are listed separately from EU.